Getting StartED with CSS

David Powers

friendsof

an Apress company

GETTING STARTED WITH CSS

Copyright © 2009 by David Powers

ISBN-13 (pbk): 978-1-4302-2543-0

ISBN-13 (electronic): 978-1-4302-2544-7

Printed and bound in the United States of America 9 8 7 6 5 4 3 2 1

Distributed to the book trade worldwide by Springer-Verlag New York, Inc., 233 Spring Street, 6th Floor, New York, NY 10013. Phone 1-800-SPRINGER, fax 201-348-4505, e-mail orders-ny@springer-sbm.com, or visit www.springeronline.com.

For information on translations, please e-mail info@apress.com, or visit www.apress.com.

Apress and friends of ED books may be purchased in bulk for academic, corporate, or promotional use. eBook versions and licenses are also available for most titles. For more information, reference our Special Bulk Sales–eBook Licensing web page at http://www.apress.com/info/bulksales.

The source code for this book is freely available to readers at www.friendsofed.com in the Downloads section.

Credits

President and Publisher:
Paul Manning

Lead Editor:
Ben Renow-Clarke

Technical Reviewer:
Peter Elst

Editorial Board:
Clay Andres, Steve Anglin, Mark Beckner, Ewan Buckingham, Tony Campbell, Gary Cornell, Jonathan Gennick, Michelle Lowman, Matthew Moodie, Jeffrey Pepper, Frank Pohlmann, Ben Renow-Clarke, Dominic Shakeshaft, Matt Wade, Tom Welsh

Coordinating Editor:
Kelly Moritz

Copy Editor:
Heather Lang

Compositors:
MacPS, LLC

Indexers:
BIM Indexing and e-Services

Artist:
April Milne

Interior Designer:
Anna Ishchenko

Contents at a Glance

Contents

xiii

About the Author

David Powers is an Adobe Community Expert for Dreamweaver and author of a series of highly successful books on web design and development, including *The Definitive Guide to Dreamweaver CS4 with CSS, Ajax, and PHP* (friends of ED, ISBN: 978-1-4302-1610-0) and *PHP Solutions: Dynamic Web Design Made Easy* (friends of ED, ISBN: 978-1-5905-9731-1). He also served as the technical reviewer on *Cascading Style Sheets: SeparatingContent from Presentation, Second Edition* by Owen Briggs, Steven Champeon et al (friends of ED), and *Head First HTML with CSS & XHTML* by Elisabeth Freeman and Eric Freeman (O'Reilly).

As a professional writer, he has been involved in electronic media for more than 30 years, first with BBC radio and television and more recently with the Internet. What started as a mild interest in computing was transformed almost overnight into a passion, when David was posted to Japan in 1987 as BBC correspondent in Tokyo. With no corporate IT department just down the hallway, he was forced to learn how to fix everything himself. When not tinkering with the innards of his computer, he was reporting for BBC TV and radio on the rise and collapse of the Japanese bubble economy.

David has also translated several plays from Japanese. To relax, he enjoys nothing better than visiting his favorite sushi restaurant.

About the Technical Reviewer

Peter Elst is a freelance web 2.0 consultant and Founding Partner of Project Cocoon — a collaborative project of web designers and developers based in South India. As a respected member of the online Flash platform community, Peter has spoken at various international industry events and published his work in leading journals.

www.peterelst.com

Acknowledgments

Many people have helped and inspired me in my quest to learn CSS. The person who first opened my eyes to its possibilities was Al Sparber of Project Seven (www.projectseven.com). He still amazes me with his in-depth knowledge of the subject and the thoroughness of his cross-browser testing. Others who have helped me directly or indirectly include Eric Meyer, Owen Briggs, Stephanie Sullivan, Thierry Koblentz, and a secretive group that goes by the name of "No Nephews" (you know who you are). My thanks go to them all.

I would also like to thank everyone at Apress/friends of ED who contributed to bringing this book to fruition. Particular thanks go to my editor, Ben Renow-Clarke, and technical reviewer, Peter Elst. Both made valuable suggestions that greatly improved this book.

Introduction

Most people who build websites fall into one of two categories: geeks (like me) who take great pleasure in working with code, and artistic types who think in terms of overall design. Of course, that's a sweeping generalization. To be successful in modern web design, you need an element of both. But most people will be stronger in one field than the other.

If your main strength lies in visualizing an overall design and you find code a bit of a turn-off, learning how to style websites with Cascading Style Sheets (CSS) might seem a daunting task. But it needn't be. . . . Think of CSS as the *language of design*. The code in a style sheet is simply telling the browser how you want your pages to look. It defines the fonts, colors, and layout of the various elements on the page. You might find yourself despairing at how long it takes to put together a style sheet to reflect your visual design. Take heart; even if you're an expert, it's not something you can dash off in a few minutes. Attention to detail is important—and, as always, it shows in the results. Moreover, once you have created the style sheet, the visual design is automatically applied to every new page that you build. That's the magic of CSS.

Code warriors face a different challenge. The amount of code involved in CSS is quite small. There are fewer than 100 properties to learn, and most of them are intuitively named. It doesn't take a genius to work out that the `border-top` property defines the top border of an element. The syntax is also very simple. As a result, an experienced developer might expect to have the whole thing licked in a couple of days. You won't.

Regardless of your background, learning CSS takes time. It's not because CSS is hard—far from it. What takes time is understanding the infinite number of ways CSS properties can be combined with each other, providing a stunning degree of control over the look and layout of web pages. The other challenge—although it's becoming less significant by the day—comes from the way different browsers interpret CSS. Older browsers, particularly Internet Explorer 6 and 7, don't understand all CSS properties or have bugs. However, all other browsers in widespread use (including Internet Explorer 8) have excellent support for CSS. As long as you build your style sheets to work in a modern browser, you can usually fix any problems in older browsers at the end of the design process.

Although you won't become a CSS master overnight, you can achieve impressive results quite quickly. I have organized the chapters in this book in a logical sequence to lead you from simple beginnings to progressively complex concepts. Even if you already have some experience of CSS, I recommend that you read the chapters in the order they are presented. Each chapter contains a mixture of reference material and hands-on exercises that build on what you have learned previously. The appendix at the end of this book also serves as a quick reference to all the properties in the current version of CSS (CSS2.1), as well as CSS selectors used in all mainstream browsers.

Take things gradually. You'll get there in the end, and you'll discover the time invested eventually repaid in websites that not only look good, but are much easier to maintain.

Who this book is for

This book is aimed at anyone involved in building websites using HTML (or XHTML). It assumes no prior knowledge of CSS, but I do expect you to understand the basics of HTML and web page construction. After the first couple of chapters, the book moves at a fairly rapid pace, so this book should also appeal to readers who have dabbled with CSS, but still haven't quite "got it." If you already know some CSS, I strongly urge you *not* to skip the early chapters, because I try to steer you away from overreliance on CSS classes and other bad habits.

Although I show you a lot of cool tricks on the way, throughout this book I concentrate on teaching you how CSS works. Cool tricks are fine, but if you don't understand why something works a particular way, you'll find it difficult to adapt the CSS to achieve the particular effect that *you* want. As far as possible, I steer away from hacks. The primary emphasis is always on how CSS should work in a standards-compliant browser. But until Internet Explorer 6 and 7 finally disappear, you need to know how to deal with the problems they cause. So, I include workarounds for all the major problems with those browsers.

Using the files for this book

The files for all the exercises and examples in this book can be downloaded from the friends of ED website at http://friendsofed.com/download.html?isbn=9781430225430. The files are organized into a separate folder for each chapter, and all the internal links are document-relative. To ensure that the internal links continue to work, I suggest that you create a new folder called workfiles at the same level as the individual chapter folders, as shown in the following screenshot:

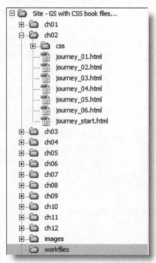

Copy each file as you need it into the workfiles folder. You should also create a css subfolder inside workfiles, and build or copy the style sheets there. This will maintain the correct relationship between the files and the images in all the pages.

Chapter 1

What Is CSS, and Why Should I Learn It?

In the beginning, the Web was simple. Figure 1-1 shows what the first-ever public web page looked like. As you can see, it consisted of plain, unadorned text. Headings were in large, bold type; links were blue and underlined—and that was it.

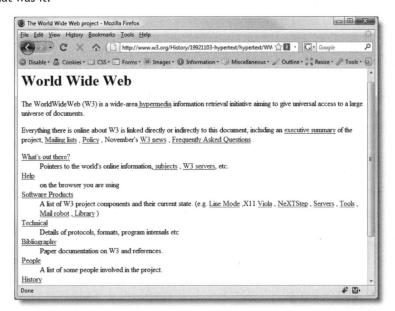

Figure 1-1. The first-ever web page contained just text and links.

LinkED

The original, which was created toward the end of 1990, no longer exists, but you can see a copy at www.w3.org/History/19921103-hypertext/hypertext/WWW/TheProject.html.

The lack of images and any attempt at styling the page seem odd to us now, but the Web's origins lie in the scientific community, not with artists or graphic designers. The inventor of the World Wide Web (WWW), Tim Berners-Lee, was working at the European Organization for Nuclear Research (CERN) in Switzerland and was frustrated by the need to log onto different computers to get information. So he devised a way of sharing information among computers. Putting aside the technical details of how information is transferred from one computer to another, the principle behind the Web is very simple. Documents are marked up to indicate what's a heading, paragraph, list, and so on; and links (or hyperlinks, to give them their correct name) tell the web browser where to find related documents. The tags used to mark up the text evolved into what we now know as HyperText Markup Language (HTML).

It didn't take long before people other than scientists realized the potential of the Web and began to demand the ability to include images. Once images began to brighten up web pages, designers wanted not only a way to make text look more interesting but also to lay out the contents of a page in more attractive ways than just headings and paragraphs. In addition to new tags being added to HTML, designers began to use their imagination to invent new uses for existing tags. Most notably, the <table> tag, which was intended to display scientific data in tabular form, was adapted to provide a grid structure for page layout.

The rapid growth of the Web was exciting, but it was also chaotic. HTML was being stretched beyond its limits. Tags such as <h4> were no longer being used for low-level subheadings, but to display small, bold text. The <blockquote> tag, often nested several levels deep, became a way to indent objects, rather than to highlight a quotation from another source. Document structure was thrown to the wind, making it difficult and expensive to maintain web pages or adapt them for other uses, such as printed materials.

The answer was to restore HTML to its original purpose—marking up the structure of the document—and create a new markup language devoted to styling the look of a web page. That new markup language was called Cascading Style Sheets (CSS), and that's what this book is about.

ExplainED

CSS stands for Cascading Style Sheets, but most web designers say "CSS is . . ." rather than "CSS are. . ." This is because they're referring to CSS as a technology and not to individual style sheets.

In this chapter, you'll learn about the following:

- The advantages of CSS and why now is a good time to start learning
- How to write style rules and apply them to your web pages
- How to avoid common beginner mistakes
- Choosing the tools to help you work with CSS

A short history of CSS

Many designers think of CSS as the "new" way to style web pages, so it comes as quite a surprise to discover that CSS has been with us for years. The original specification (see Figure 1-2) was published by the World Wide Web Consortium (W3C) at the end of 1996.

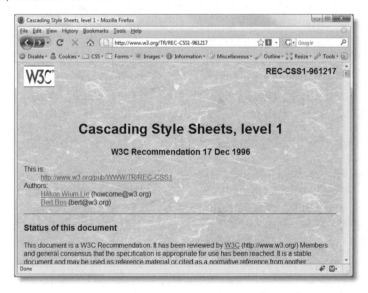

Figure 1-2. The original CSS specification used a very basic set of rules to style the page.

ExplainED

The W3C (www.w3.org) is the body responsible for drawing up agreed standards for the Web. Its members include all the big software and technology companies, as well as government and research institutions from over 40 countries. This often leads to slow decisions. Strictly speaking, W3C standards are only recommendations. That's why they're not always fully supported by all browsers. Equally important, the recommendations sometimes lag behind the pace of innovation on the Web. For example, browsers began supporting CSS opacity long before its incorporation into a W3C standard.

Why CSS has taken so long to be embraced by designers

According to the W3C, the CSS specification was drawn up in response to "pressure from authors for richer visual control." The demand for better control of web pages was certainly there, but browsers in the late 1990s just weren't up to the job. They implemented CSS very poorly or not at all. As a result, only the very brave or foolhardy adopted CSS in the early stages. Nevertheless, the W3C continued work on the specification and brought out a new version, CSS2, in 1998. This retained all the features of CSS1 and added some new ones.

Instead of designers leaping with joy, those brave enough to embrace CSS ended up banging their heads on their keyboards in frustration. The specification was a statement of what the W3C thought browsers ought to do. The reality was completely different. The now-defunct Netscape Navigator 4 (usually referred to simply as Netscape 4) was the most popular browser at the time, with an estimated 80 percent market share in 1997. It supported a lot of CSS, but not very well. Its rival, Microsoft Internet Explorer (IE), also in version 4, was even worse. However, Microsoft put a huge effort into improving its browser, and by the time IE6 was released in 2001, it supported most of CSS—although it was far from perfect.

Microsoft's battle with Netscape completely reversed the browser scene, with IE taking about 90 percent of the market share by 2001-2002. With Netscape in terminal decline, adventurous designers began to use CSS in earnest, but they faced several problems:

- Netscape's original dominance of the browser market left a significant user base resistant to change, particularly in schools and public libraries in the United States. This meant finding ways to style web pages that could still be rendered in Netscape 4 without causing it to crash.

- CSS in IE6 was usable, but it had many bugs and didn't support every feature.

- Although IE was the dominant browser, new ones, such as Firefox, Safari, and Opera, came on the scene aiming at full standards compliance and with better support for CSS.

Even when designers felt they could reasonably stop supporting Netscape 4, they faced a new dilemma with the emergence of the standards-compliant browsers. They could either ignore the standards and design for IE6 or create CSS that worked well in the new browsers and find ways to compensate for the flaws in IE6.

For a long time, instead of fixing the CSS bugs in IE6, Microsoft issued only security updates. However, a combination of security scares and demands for better CSS support eventually resulted in Firefox making considerable inroads into its market share. Firefox is managed by the Mozilla Corporation, an organization that traces its origins to Netscape but is now controlled by the nonprofit Mozilla Foundation. For legal reasons, Firefox underwent several name changes, but within two years of its original release in February 2004, it had taken an estimated 10 percent of the browser market share. Microsoft's response emerged in the form of IE7 in 2006. It still wasn't perfect, but it was followed in March 2009 by IE8, which finally supports the whole of CSS2.1. Firefox, in the meantime, has continued its rise and currently represents nearly one in four of all browsers in use.

ExplainED

The W3C doesn't formally adopt a CSS specification until all parts of it are implemented by two browsers or user agents, such as screen readers for the visually impaired. Because no two browsers ever managed to implement the full CSS2 specification, the W3C dropped some features, added some new ones, and issued a revised specification called CSS2.1 in 2002. More than a decade after the original publication of the CSS2 specification, CSS2.1 still hadn't received formal approval. No wonder web designers have been frustrated with the glacial progress of CSS!

The time for CSS has finally come

After such a dismal history, you might be wondering whether it's worth the effort of learning CSS. The answer is a resounding yes. Within seven months of its release, IE8 represented 18 percent of browsers in use, reducing the combined market share of IE6 and IE7 to roughly 40 percent. The bad news for web designers is that, in the early months at least, IE8's rise was due to people switching from IE7; little dent was made in the market share for IE6, which has annoying CSS bugs. It's fair to say it will take several years before IE6 and IE7 disappear completely from the scene, but the arrival of IE8 and other modern browsers, such as Firefox, Safari, and Opera, means you can now use CSS with far greater confidence than ever before. As long as the website remains usable in older browsers, you don't need to worry if there are some minor differences in display.

AdvancED

Before deploying a website on the Internet, check what it looks like in all the main browsers and on different operating systems. If you don't have access to some browsers or operating systems, ask in an online forum for others to check for you, or subscribe to a browser testing service, such as Browsercam (www.browsercam.com). If you have Dreamweaver CS4 or later, you can use Adobe BrowserLab (http://browserlab.adobe.com/). On Windows, you can also use Expression Web SuperPreview (http://expression.microsoft.com/en-us/dd565874.aspx) to compare how your pages look in IE6 and IE7 or IE8. The version of Expression Web SuperPreview released just as this book was about to go to press also included support for Firefox 3.5, so more browsers might be added in future.

Some designers fret if their site doesn't look exactly the same in each browser. Don't worry about the difference of an odd pixel or two. Most visitors only see your site in one browser. What really matters is that it works and looks acceptable to each visitor.

What are the advantages of CSS?

CSS has three huge advantages, namely:

- Less-cluttered HTML code, making it easier to read and maintain
- The ability to change the look of a whole site by changing a single file
- Greater control over the way page elements look

Let's take a look at each of these in detail.

Write simpler markup

Figure 1-3 shows a simple web page with a heading, three paragraphs, and a link. The download files for this chapter contain two versions of the same page: one styled the old way with presentational HTML (font_tags.html), and the other styled using CSS (css.html). Both look exactly the same in a browser.

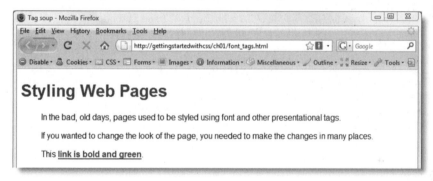

Figure 1-3. Both CSS and old-style presentational tags remain hidden from view in the browser.

The difference between the two versions becomes obvious only when you examine the underlying HTML. This is what the page that uses presentational tags (highlighted in bold) looks like:

```
<!DOCTYPE html PUBLIC "-//W3C//DTD XHTML 1.0 Transitional//EN"
"http://www.w3.org/TR/xhtml1/DTD/xhtml1-transitional.dtd">
<html xmlns="http://www.w3.org/1999/xhtml">
<head>
<meta http-equiv="Content-Type" content="text/html;
charset=utf-8" />
<title>Tag soup</title>
</head>
```

```
<body bgcolor="#FFFFFF" text="#000000" link="#006600"
vlink="#009966" alink="#006600">
<h1><font color="#990000" size="6" face="Arial, Helvetica,
sans-serif">Styling Web Pages</font></h1>
<blockquote>
    <p><font size="3" face="Arial, Helvetica, sans-serif">In the
bad, old days, pages used to be styled using font and other
presentational tags.</font></p>
    <p><font size="3" face="Arial, Helvetica, sans-serif">If you
wanted to change the look of the page, you needed to make the
changes in many places.</font></p>
    <p><font size="3" face="Arial, Helvetica, sans-serif">This
<strong><a href="#">link is bold and green</a></strong>.</font>
</p>
</blockquote>
</body>
</html>
```

The HTML for the version of the page that uses CSS looks like this:

```
<!DOCTYPE html PUBLIC "-//W3C//DTD XHTML 1.0 Transitional//EN"
"http://www.w3.org/TR/xhtml1/DTD/xhtml1-transitional.dtd">
<html xmlns="http://www.w3.org/1999/xhtml">
<head>
<meta http-equiv="Content-Type" content="text/html;
charset=utf-8" />
<title>Styling with CSS</title>
<link href="css/simple.css" rel="stylesheet" type="text/css" />
</head>

<body>
<h1>Styling Web Pages</h1>
<p>In the bad, old days, pages used to be styled using font and
other presentational tags.</p>
<p>If you wanted to change the look of the page, you needed to
make the changes in many places.</p>
<p>This <a href="#">link is bold and green</a>.</p>
</body>
</html>
```

ExplainED

The examples in this book use Extensible HyperText Markup Language (XHTML) 1.0, which is identical to HTML 4.01, except that it follows slightly stricter rules. XHTML was originally intended to replace HTML, but the W3C began work on HTML5 in 2007. Then in July 2009, it announced that work would stop on XHTML 2. This threw the web development community into confusion over which standard they should use, with some people mistakenly believing that XHTML 1.0 was also being abandoned. XHTML 1.0 remains an approved standard, and is still preferred by many developers because of its stricter rules.

At the time of this writing, HTML5 is still only a draft, but the W3C has stated that it will be compatible with both HTML 4.01 and XHTML 1.0. So, it doesn't matter which version you choose. I use "HTML" to refer to all three flavors. The CSS taught in this book will work with all of them.

The markup is much simpler and easier to read. Even if you use an HTML editor that generates the markup for you, there are times when it's necessary to examine the underlying code. The lightweight code used by a well-designed CSS site makes this a pleasure, rather than a perilous journey hacking through masses of tangled code. There's also less of it, so the page loads more quickly and uses less bandwidth.

AdvancED

Just because most people use broadband these days, it doesn't mean that page size is no longer important. Masses of code not only take longer to display in a browser, but the bigger your pages, the more bandwidth you consume. On a popular site, this can cost a lot of money in extra bandwidth charges.

"So, where's the CSS?" you might be asking. It's not in the web page, but in a separate file (called a style sheet), simple.css. The <link> tag highlighted in bold in the <head> of the page tells the browser where to find the styles. The code inside simple.css looks like this:

```
body {
  font-family: Arial, Helvetica, sans-serif;
  color: #000;
```

```
   background-color: #FFF;
}
h1 { color: #900; }
p { margin-left: 40px; }
a:link {
   color: #060;
   font-weight: bold;
}
a:visited { color: #096; }
a:hover, a:active { color: #060; }
```

Don't worry about the meaning of the CSS code yet. You'll learn about the structure of style rules in "How do I write a style rule?" later in this chapter, and you'll be writing your own rules to format text in Chapter 2.

Although it might seem strange to put instructions on how your page should look in a separate file, there's a very good reason for doing so. You can attach the same set of instructions to every page in your website. Unlike presentational HTML markup, which needs to be applied individually to each element, CSS gives you central control over the look of the whole site. What's more, changes to your style sheet are automatically applied to all pages that are linked to it.

AdvancED

When styles are defined in an external style sheet, the browser stores them in the cache on the visitor's computer, so they need to be downloaded only once regardless of how many pages are viewed in your site. This speeds up the display of subsequent pages and reduces bandwidth usage

Turn into a quick change artist

The best way to see the power of CSS in action is to visit www.csszengarden.com. Every page in the site looks completely different (see Figure 1-4), but if you look at the underlying HTML, you'll see that it's actually exactly the same page. What changes the look of the page is the style sheet attached to it.

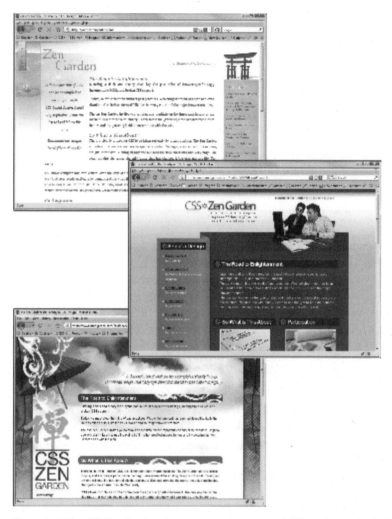

Figure 1-4. The CSS Zen Garden demonstrates the power of CSS to change the look of a website.

The CSS Zen Garden was launched in 2003 by a Canadian web designer named Dave Shea. It was a call to arms to web designers to show what could be done with CSS. He asked designers to submit original visions in the form of style sheets and images. There was one basic rule: no changes could be made to the underlying HTML. In fact, if you look at the site with CSS turned off, every single page looks like Figure 1-5—plain, unadorned text. There are no images in the page itself; they're all added as background images through CSS.

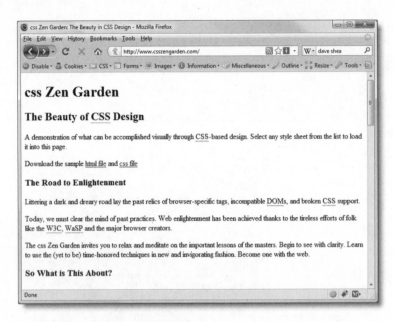

Figure 1-5. Without a style sheet, the CSS Zen Garden is just plain text.

AdvancED

All modern browsers let you view web pages without CSS. In Firefox, select View ➤ Page Style ➤ No Style. *In IE8, select* Page ➤ Style ➤ No Style. *In Opera, select* View ➤ Style ➤ User Mode. *Safari also lets you disable styles, but first you need to enable the* Develop *menu by opening the* Preferences *panel (from the* Safari *menu on a Mac, or the* Edit *menu on Windows). Select the* Advanced *tab, and enable the* Develop *menu. Thereafter, you can turn off CSS in Safari by selecting* Develop ➤ Disable Styles.

The CSS Zen Garden shows how one page can be restyled in many different ways. This is powerful stuff. It means that you can make a site look completely different just by changing the style rules. But just imagine if, instead of one page, you have a site with dozens or hundreds of pages. If the same style sheet is attached to each page, you can change the look of the whole site just by making changes to the style sheet. To take a very simple example, the simple.css style sheet in the previous section contains this style rule:

```
body {
  font-family: Arial, Helvetica, sans-serif;
  color: #000;
  background-color: #FFF;
}
```

This tells the browser to use Arial, Helvetica, or a sans-serif font, and to display the text as black on a white background. In simple2.css, I have changed it like this:

```
body {
  font-family: "Palatino Linotype", "Book Antiqua", Palatino, serif;
  color: #034B61;
  background-color: #EFECCA;
}
```

Changing just these three lines of code changes the entire look of the page. You can see the result in css2.html and in Figure 1-6.

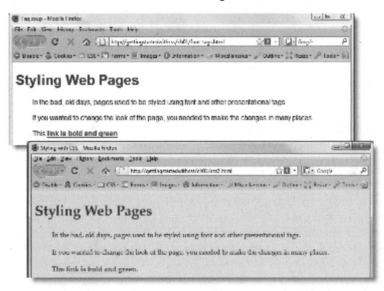

Figure 1-6. Using CSS makes it easier to make global changes to the way a website looks.

Even in just one page, this involves much less work than it would with <font> tags and other presentational HTML markup. But the real difference becomes apparent when the change to the style sheet affects a whole site.

Gain greater control over the look of page elements

The other huge advantage of CSS is that it gives you a finer level of control over the look of different elements on your page. If you add a border to an image or table with HTML markup, you get the same border on all sides. With CSS, you can apply a different border to each side of an element. As shown in Figure 1-7, this lets you create embossed and indented buttons without the need to use images (you can test the page yourself in borders.html in the download files for this chapter).

Figure 1-7. With CSS, you can use different borders to create the illusion of embossed or indented buttons.

The technique is very simple: you add a darker border to the right and bottom, and a lighter border to the other two edges to create an embossed effect. Reversing the colors creates an indented effect.

Incidentally, the two buttons in borders.html are not in a table. Their positions are controlled by adjusting their margins and using a CSS property called float. You'll learn about margins in Chapter 3, and Chapter 4 introduces you to the concept of floating page elements to the left or right of other objects or text. When used in combination with each other, you can flow text around images in a much cleaner way than using the vspace and hspace HTML attributes. Figure 1-8 shows the difference (the original files are image_hspace.html and image_float.html in the download files for this chapter).

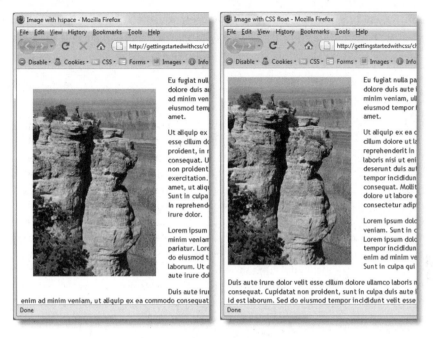

Figure 1-8. HTML presentational markup (left) applies horizontal and vertical space to both sides of an image, whereas CSS (right) gives you individual control over each margin.

In the screenshot on the left of Figure 1-8, the image is positioned the traditional way, using the align, hspace, and vspace attributes of the <img> tag. Used on its own, the align attribute results in each line of the text being jammed right up to the image, so it's necessary to use hspace to give it a bit of breathing space. Adding the vspace attribute is optional, but for this demonstration, I have added 25 pixels of both horizontal and vertical space. The problem is that HTML doesn't let you control which side the space is applied to. As a result, you get 25 pixels of space all around, destroying the clean lines of the layout.

With CSS, though, the ability to control margins independently on each side of an element produces the much smarter result in the screenshot on the right of Figure 1-8. I have applied the same 25 pixels of space to the right and bottom of the image, and just three pixels to the top to bring it into line with the top of the text. There's no extra space on the left of the image, leaving it flush with the following text.

This flexibility extends to background images, which can be positioned with a great degree of accuracy, often producing stunning results, such as the designs in the CSS Zen Garden (see Figure 1-4).

So, how do I use CSS?

Like HTML, CSS is written as plain text. So, you don't need anything more sophisticated than a text editor, such as Notepad or TextEdit, to start writing CSS. However, if you're using an HTML editor to build your web pages, you'll almost certainly find that it provides you with code hints or other features to help create your style rules. Adobe Dreamweaver (www.adobe.com/products/dreamweaver/), the leading professional tool for building websites, has a lot of CSS features, including a dialog box that builds style rules for you. It groups the main CSS properties in logical categories to make them easier for beginners to find (see Figure 1-9). If you prefer to work directly in the code, most HTML editors, including Dreamweaver and Microsoft Expression Web (www.microsoft.com/expression/products/overview.aspx?key=web), offer pop-up code hints similar to those in shown in Figure 1-10. The granddaddy of script editors on the Mac, BBEdit (www.barebones.com/products/bbedit/) uses both code hints and dialog boxes (see Figure 1-11).

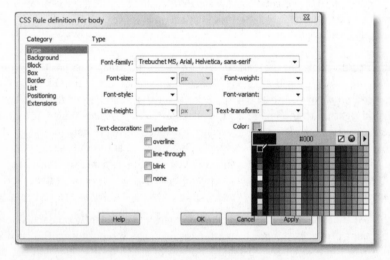

Figure 1-9. Dreamweaver helps build style sheets through a dialog box that lists the main CSS properties.

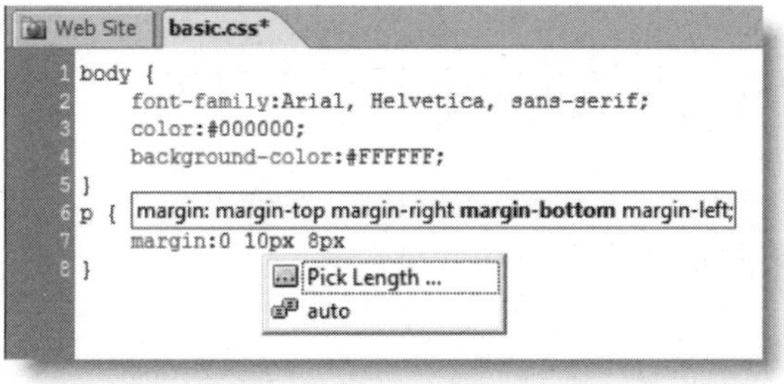

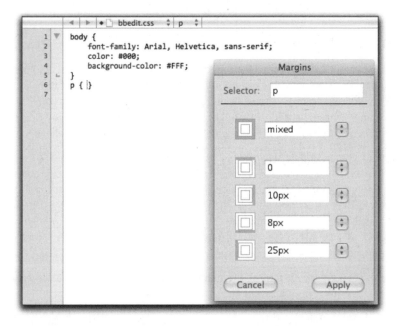

Figure 1-10. Microsoft Expression Web offers CSS code hints.

Figure 1-11. BBEdit uses a mixture of code hints and dialog boxes for CSS.

There are also dedicated CSS editors. Among the most popular are Style Master for Windows and Mac (www.westciv.com/style_master/), Top Style Pro for Windows only (www.newsgator.com/individuals/topstyle/default.aspx), and CSSEdit for Mac (http://macrabbit.com/cssedit/).

ExplainED

Don't worry if I've missed out your favorite HTML or CSS editor. This book is strictly software and operating system neutral. What you use to build your style sheets is unimportant. The emphasis here is on teaching you how CSS works.

Before getting down to the detail of how to write CSS, it's important to understand the principle of the cascade, which we'll look at next.

Why are they called "cascading" style sheets?

The **cascade** in CSS refers to the way that rules are added together and applied cumulatively. Think of the cascade in the literal sense of a waterfall or a river. As a river flows from the mountains to the sea, it starts off as a tiny trickle, but as more water is added through tributaries, it becomes bigger and more powerful. Yet the water in that original trickle is still part of the whole.

CSS works in a similar way. You can create a style rule that trickles down through the whole page. For example, it's common to set the background and text colors in a rule for the body of the page. But lower down, new rules can be added that affect the font or size of the text without changing the color. And just like a river can break into a delta as it reaches the sea, you can break the CSS cascade into different strands, so that a sidebar looks different from the main content or footer of the page.

This might sound mysterious at the moment, but all should become clear by the end of this book. The important things to remember are these:

- **Styles trickle down**: A style rule applied to the <body> affects everything inside the page unless something else overrides it.

- **Styles are cumulative**: Most property values are inherited, so you need apply only new ones.

- **Inherited styles can be overridden**: When you want to treat an element or section of the page differently, you can create more detailed style rules and apply them selectively.

In most cases, the order of your style rules doesn't matter. However, the cascade plays an important role when there's a conflict between rules. As a basic principle, style rules that appear lower down in a style sheet or <style> block override any previous rules in the case of a direct conflict. You'll see an example of this principle in action in "Don't forget the cascade" later in this chapter. But first, I need to show you how to write CSS.

AdvancED

I'm deliberately simplifying things to avoid overburdening you with too much detail at this stage. Chapter 7 explains the rules that determine which style wins in the case of a conflict. For the time being, just remember that a rule that appears after another one can override it.

How do I write a style rule?

Creating a style rule is very simple. Figure 1-12 shows the different parts that make up a style rule, using an example from `simple.css` earlier in the chapter.

Figure 1-12. The anatomy of a style rule

Let's take a look at each part in turn:

- **Selector**: This tells the browser where you want to apply the rule. Figure 1-12 uses the simplest type of selector, a **type selector**, which redefines the default style of an HTML tag. You create a type selector by using the name of an HTML tag without the surrounding angle brackets. This example redefines the style of all <p> tags—in other words, paragraphs. Because they redefine the style of HTML tags, you'll also see type selectors referred to as "tag selectors." You'll learn about other types of selectors as you progress through this book.

- **Declaration block**: This begins with a left curly brace and ends with a right curly brace. You put your style declarations between these braces. Each declaration consists of a property followed by a colon (:) and value, and ends with a semicolon (;).

- **Property**: This is one of the properties defined in the CSS specification. There are nearly 100 visual properties in the current version, CSS2.1. Most have intuitive names. The property in Figure 1-12 affects the left margin of the element being styled. Property names are not case-sensitive, but they are normally written entirely in lowercase. The CSS specification also defines aural properties for use with screen readers for the disabled, but these are beyond the scope of this book.

- **Value**: This is the value you want to apply to the property. Some properties have a fixed list of values that you can choose from. Others let you specify the value yourself, although the value must still adhere to some simple rules. The example in Figure 1-12 sets the value of the left margin to 40 pixels.

There's a full list of all CSS2.1 visual properties and their permitted values in this book's appendix. Each chapter also has handy tables to remind you of the properties used to style different parts of a web page.

Note that the property is separated from the value by a colon (:), and the value is followed by a semicolon (;). Strictly speaking, you can leave out the semicolon after the last declaration in a block or if the block contains only one property/value pair.

AdvancED

Get into the habit of always using a semicolon after the value, even if there's only one declaration inside the declaration block. You might forget to insert it when later adding extra declarations to the same block. A missing semicolon in the middle of a declaration block is a common cause of CSS failing to work as expected. Remember: colon between property and value, semicolon after the value.

The declaration block in Figure 1-12 contains only one property/value pair, but you can define any number of properties in the same declaration block.

AdvancED

Technically speaking, a declaration block with no style declarations between the curly braces is perfectly valid. An empty declaration block does nothing, but you might want to put one in your style sheet to remind you to fix the styles later. You might also want to remove existing styles temporarily when troubleshooting a problem.

Formatting CSS for ease of maintenance

Browsers don't care how you format your style rules. As long as you separate each property from its value by a colon, put a semicolon after the value, and surround declaration blocks with curly braces, the browser ignores any whitespace in your style sheet. However, a consistent layout makes your CSS easier to maintain.

The example in Figure 1-12 uses whitespace to make the rule easier to read, but the following is just as valid:

```
p{margin-left:40px;}
```

Spreading everything out even more like this is also acceptable:

```
p {
  margin-left : 40px ;
}
```

However, the following *will not work*:

```
p {
  margin - left : 40 px;
}
```

Although CSS ignores whitespace in style declarations, you cannot put any spaces in property names. Nor can there be any whitespace in the value between a number and the unit of measurement. Accidentally putting a space between 40 and px renders the rule invalid and prevents it from working.

In simple.css earlier in the chapter, I put rules with a single declaration all on the same line but spaced out rules with multiple declarations like this:

```
body {
  font-family: Arial, Helvetica, sans-serif;
  color: #000;
  background-color: #FFF;
}
```

```
h1 { color: #900; }
p { margin-left: 40px; }
```

Putting rules with a single declaration all on the same line saves space but is probably not so easy to read. It also means that you need to reformat everything if you decide to add another declaration inside a single-line declaration block. Spacing out everything like this is probably easier on the eye, and easier to maintain:

```
body {
   font-family: Arial, Helvetica, sans-serif;
   color: #000;
   background-color: #FFF;
}
h1 {
   color: #900;
}
p {
   margin-left: 40px;
}
```

Adding comments to your CSS

Style sheets can run to hundreds of lines, so it's often a good idea to add comments to your style sheets to remind you what a particular rule or set of rules is for. Anything between /* and */ is treated as a comment in CSS and is ignored by the browser. Comments can be spread over more than one line. You could add comments to the previous example like this:

```
/* Sets the font, text color, and background color for the page.
   These values will be applied to all elements in the page
   unless overridden by subsequent style rules. */
body {
   font-family: Arial, Helvetica, sans-serif;
   color: #000;
   background-color: #FFF;
}
/* Overrides the body rule and colors level 1 headings red */
h1 {
   color: #900;
}
/* Puts a 40-pixel left margin on all paragraphs */
p {
   margin-left: 40px;
}
```

Adding comments to every rule like this is overkill. Too many comments can be just as just as bad as no comments at all.

Comment tags can also be used to disable part of your CSS temporarily. This is a useful technique when experimenting with new ideas or troubleshooting problems. Just put the opening /* and closing */ comment tags around the section that you want to disable. You can disable a single declaration or a whole section at a time. For example, this disables the color and background-color properties in the following rule:

```
body {
  font-family: Arial, Helvetica, sans-serif;
  /* color: #000;
  background-color: #FFF; */
}
```

Just remove the comment tags to restore the rules.

AdvancED

*Comments cannot be nested. As soon as the browser encounters the first */ closing tag, it treats everything else as CSS until it finds another /* opening tag. When disabling rules temporarily, make sure you remove the comment tags from any rules that have already been disabled within the section you're blocking off. The same applies to any comments within the section. Alternatively, add a closing comment tag before each nested opening tag.*

Where do I create my CSS?

Style rules can be defined in three places, namely:

- **External style sheets**: This is the most common and effective way of using CSS. The styles in external style sheets affect all pages to which they're linked. You can link more than one style sheet to a page.

- **A <style> block**: This must go in the <head> of the web page. The style rules are applied only to that page. This can be useful if you want to apply a different set of rules to one page, but as soon as you want to apply the rules to more than one page, they should be moved to an external style sheet.

- **A style attribute**: This goes in the opening tag of an HTML element, so it applies to that element alone. This is the least efficient way to apply CSS and should be avoided. As with all rules, there *is* an exception: some email programs, such as Outlook 2007, don't understand style rules unless they're applied this way. At the time of this writing, Microsoft says it has no plans to change the way it handles CSS in Outlook 2010.

LinkED

See http://msdn.microsoft.com/en-us/library/aa338201.aspx *for details of how Outlook 2007 handles HTML and CSS.*

There's also a fourth way to add CSS to your page, although it's not part of any official standard: using an Internet Explorer conditional comment. I'll explain the purpose of conditional comments and how they work after describing the standard ways of defining styles.

Using external style sheets

Create your style rules in a separate file, and save the file with .css as the file name extension. An external style sheet can be anywhere within your website, but the normal practice is to put all style sheets in a dedicated folder called styles or css.

It's important to note that an external style sheet must *not* contain anything other than CSS style rules or CSS comments. You cannot mix HTML, JavaScript, or anything else in a style sheet. If you do, your styles won't work.

There are two ways to attach an external style sheet to a page: using a <link> tag or a CSS @import rule.

Attaching a style sheet with a <link> tag This is the most common way to attach an external style sheet. The <link> tag must go inside the <head> of the web page. This is how simple.css is linked to css.html in the download files for this chapter:

```
<!DOCTYPE html PUBLIC "-//W3C//DTD XHTML 1.0 Transitional//EN"
"http://www.w3.org/TR/xhtml1/DTD/xhtml1-transitional.dtd">
<html xmlns="http://www.w3.org/1999/xhtml">
<head>
<meta http-equiv="Content-Type" content="text/html;
charset=utf-8" />
<title>Styling with CSS</title>
```

```
<link href="css/simple.css" rel="stylesheet" type="text/css" />
</head>
```

If you're using an HTML editor, such as Dreamweaver or Expression Web, the `<link>` tag is created automatically when you select the option to attach a style sheet. As you can see in the preceding example, it contains three attributes: `href`, `rel`, and `type`. All of them *must* be included. However, even if you're hand-coding, the only one with a value you need to change is `href`, which tells the browser where to find the style sheet.

AdvancED

The rel *attribute accepts two values:* stylesheet *or alternate* stylesheet *(in both cases,* stylesheet *is written as one word). In practice,* stylesheet *is the only one you're ever likely to use. It instructs the browser to load the files in the external style sheet and apply them to the page.*

Using rel="alternate stylesheet" *prevents the browser from loading the styles automatically. However, if you also add a* title *attribute to the* <link> *tag, IE8 and most other modern browsers let users choose which set of styles to load. In theory, this sounds a good idea but is of very little practical value because there's no obvious indication of a choice of styles, except by selecting the appropriate browser menu (*Page ➤ Style *in IE8, and* View ➤ Page Style *in Firefox). More important, the browser doesn't remember your choice. You can test this in* css_alternate.html *in the download files. Change the style in your browser to* Sandy, *and then click the link in the final paragraph. This loads* css_alternate2.html, *which also has a choice of style sheets. When the new page loads, the original styles are applied, not the ones you have just chosen.*

Using an @import rule This technique was frequently used in the past because it was not supported by Netscape 4, so it provided a convenient way to hide styles that caused the browser to crash. Now that Netscape 4 has been consigned to the dustbin of history, there's no real advantage in using @import to link a style sheet directly to a web page. However, I have included it here so you know what it's for if you come across it in an existing site.

The following code shows how `simple.css` is linked to `css_import.html` in the download files using @import:

```
<!DOCTYPE html PUBLIC "-//W3C//DTD XHTML 1.0 Transitional//EN"
"http://www.w3.org/TR/xhtml1/DTD/xhtml1-transitional.dtd">
<html xmlns="http://www.w3.org/1999/xhtml">
```

25

```
<head>
<meta http-equiv="Content-Type" content="text/html;
charset=utf-8" />
<title>Styling with CSS</title>
<style type="text/css">
@import url("css/simple.css");
</style>
</head>
```

As you can see, the @import rule goes inside an HTML <style> block in the <head> of the page. The location of the style sheet is specified by putting it between the parentheses of url(). The quotes around the path to the style sheet are optional.

Again, if you're using an HTML editor, it should create all this code for you automatically.

You can also use @import in an external style sheet to import the styles from another style sheet. This can be useful when you organize your rules in several different style sheets. Instead of linking each style sheet separately to your web pages, you can link just one, which then imports the rules from the other style sheets.

If you do this, the @import rule *must* come before any other style rules in the external style sheet. Also, because it's in an external style sheet, you don't wrap it in an HTML <style> block. The following code shows how you might import rules into one external style sheet from another:

```
@import url("another.css");
/* Other style rules */
body {
  font-family: Arial, Helvetica, sans-serif;
  color: #000;
  background-color: #FFF;
}
```

AdvancED

Using @import *is the only way to import style rules from one style sheet to another. The* <link> *tag can be used only inside the* <head> *of an HTML page. It cannot be used inside another style sheet.*

Using a <style> block

Using an HTML <style> block in the <head> of a page limits the style rules to the current page. Because they're embedded in the page, these are known as **embedded styles**. You should normally use this technique only for styles that you want to limit to a single page. The following code shows how I embedded the styles in image_float.html (see Figure 1-8):

```
<!DOCTYPE html PUBLIC "-//W3C//DTD XHTML 1.0 Transitional//EN"
"http://www.w3.org/TR/xhtml1/DTD/xhtml1-transitional.dtd">
<html xmlns="http://www.w3.org/1999/xhtml">
<head>
<meta http-equiv="Content-Type" content="text/html;
charset=utf-8" />
<title>Image with CSS float</title>
<style type="text/css">
p {
  font-family:"Trebuchet MS", Arial, Helvetica, sans-serif;
  font-size: 85%;
  line-height: 1.3;
}
.floatleft {
  float: left;
  margin-right: 20px;
  margin-bottom: 20px;
  margin-top: 3px;
}
</style>
</head>
```

As you can see, the style rules are written in exactly the same way as in an external style sheet, but they are wrapped in a pair of HTML <style> tags. The opening tag must contain type="text/css".

AdvancED

The @import rule is also wrapped in a <style> block when used to attach a style sheet to a page. If you embed any other styles in the <head> of the page, they must come after the @import rule. Otherwise, the external style sheet will be ignored. Avoid using @import unless really necessary.

Applying a style directly to an HTML element

The final way to apply CSS is by adding a style attribute to the opening tag of an HTML element. This is known as creating an **inline style** and should be avoided unless you need to create styles for an HTML newsletter.

Inline styles use the same properties and values as CSS rules that you put in an external style sheet or embedded in the <head> of a page. The only differences are that you don't need a selector (because the HTML tag itself acts as the selector), and the curly braces are replaced by quotes. For example, you might create the following style rule for <h1> tags:

```
h1 {
  font-family: Arial, Helvetica, sans-serif;
  color: #900;
}
```

To create an inline style, add the style properties and values to the style attribute of the opening tag like this:

```
<h1 style="font-family: Arial, Helvetica, sans-serif; color: #900;">
This Heading Uses an Inline Style</h1>
```

I have inserted spaces in the value of the style attribute for ease of reading, but the following is just as valid:

```
<h1 style="font-family:Arial,Helvetica,sans-serif;color:#900;">
This Heading Uses an Inline Style</h1>
```

Don't forget the cascade

You can attach as many external style sheets to a page as you like. On a complex site, using multiple style sheets can be a good idea, allowing you to organize your style rules into logical categories, such as typography, layout, color, and so on. You can also use a combination of external styles and embedded ones. However, it's important to remember that CSS always applies style rules according to the principles of the cascade. Even if rules are in separate locations, their values are added together. So, if you have separate style sheets for fonts and colors, the rules for <h1> tags will be added together; and if there's a conflict between rules, the value that comes lowest in the cascade normally wins. This means the order in which you attach or embed your styles affects which rule takes precedence in case of a conflict.

AdvancED

If you decide to use @import, remember that the rules are included in the cascade at the point they are imported. Since the @import rule must come before any other rules in an external style sheet, the imported rules are higher in the cascade. So, if you import styles2.css into styles1.css, the rules in styles2.css are applied first. The rules in styles1.css come further down the cascade and override the earlier rules in case of a conflict.

Let's use a simple example to make that clear. The file css_conflict1.html attaches simple.css with a <link> tag and then defines an embedded style for the color of <h1> tags like this:

```
<link href="css/simple.css" rel="stylesheet" type="text/css" />
<style type="text/css">
h1 { color: #006; }
</style>
```

Because the embedded style comes lower down in the cascade, the value of color (#006) overrides the value in simple.css (#900). So, the heading in the page is a deep blue instead of dark red. However, let's move the <link> below the <style> block in css_conflict2.html like this:

```
<style type="text/css">
h1 { color: #006; }
</style>
<link href="css/simple.css" rel="stylesheet" type="text/css" />
```

The result is that the heading is now dark red. The order (or cascade) affects the way the styles are applied.

Inline styles are in the opening HTML tag of the element they apply to. So, they're always the lowest in the cascade and always take precedence.

AdvancED

Although the position of a style rule in the cascade is very important, the type of selector used also plays a big role in determining which rule takes precedence. You'll learn more about this in Chapters 4 and 7.

Using Internet Explorer conditional comments

Versions of Microsoft Internet Explorer prior to IE8 have serious CSS bugs that can destroy your page layout. Of the versions still in common use, IE6 is the worst offender; IE7 is considerably better but does have some problems. Over the years, web designers have resorted to a number of ingenious techniques—or hacks—to hide from Internet Explorer style rules that it doesn't understand. The problem with hacks is that they're nonstandard, difficult to remember, and could break in future browsers. Fortunately, there's a simple solution: using Internet Explorer conditional comments.

ExplainED

If you're new to CSS, feel free to skip this section and come back later when you encounter a bug in Internet Explorer. It's best to get your pages working first in a standards-compliant browser, such as IE8, Firefox 3.5, or Safari 4, before worrying about bugs in older versions of Internet Explorer.

What's great about conditional comments is that they're wrapped in HTML comment tags, so—although they use proprietary code—the markup in your web page remains valid. What's more, everything inside a conditional comment is ignored by other browsers. Only Internet Explorer sees and acts on its contents. The slight drawback with conditional comments is that you cannot put them inside an external style sheet. When using them with CSS, you must put them in the <head> of each web page.

The basic structure of a conditional comment looks like this:

```
<!--[if condition]>
Content that will be seen only by Internet Explorer
<![endif]-->
```

The condition that goes in the opening pair of square brackets determines which version(s) of Internet Explorer use the code inside the conditional comment. Table 1-1 lists the most important values used in building conditions.

Table 1-1. Values used in building IE conditional comments

Value	Meaning
lt	Less than
lte	Less than or equal to
gt	Greater than
gte	Greater than or equal to
IE 6	Internet Explorer 6 (note the space before the number)
IE 7	Internet Explorer 7 (note the space before the number)

If your styles trigger a bug in IE6 or IE7, you can use a conditional comment to add an extra style to compensate for the bug and hide it from all other browsers, including IE8. For example, in Chapter 5, I use the following conditional comment to add an extra style rule that only IE6 or earlier versions will see (don't worry about the meaning of the rule at the moment—it's explained in Chapter 5):

```
<!--[if lte IE 6]>
<style type="text/css">
.highlight1, .highlight2 {
  zoom: 1;
}
</style>
<![endif]-->
```

Notice that the conditional comment contains a complete `<style>` block. Because it uses HTML comment tags, you cannot put it inside an embedded style block.

If you have several style rules that apply only to earlier versions of Internet Explorer, you can put them in an external style sheet and use a conditional comment to link the style sheet to your page like this:

```
<link href="css/normal_styles.css" rel="stylesheet" type="text/css" />
<!--[if lte IE 7]>
<link href="css/ie_styles.css" rel="stylesheet"
type="text/css" />
<![endif]-->
```

All browsers see the styles in normal_styles.css, but only IE7 and earlier take any notice of ie_styles.css. Most of the time, the way you overcome a bug in IE6 or IE7 is by overriding the style seen by other browsers. Therefore, it's important to put the styles in the conditional comment *after* the normal styles.

Limiting which devices use your styles

By default, your style rules are used by all types of media that are capable of displaying them. However, CSS lets you create separate sets of rules and target them at different types of devices by specifying one or more media types. Specifying media types is completely optional, so feel free to skip this section and come back to it later when you're ready.

These days, people don't use just a browser in a desktop or laptop computer to access the Web. They use all sorts of devices: mobile phones, TV, screen readers for the visually impaired, and so on. If your design uses features that aren't supported by a particular type of device, you can restrict which devices use external style sheets or embedded styles by specifying one or more of the media types listed in Table 1-2. One of the most useful is print, which lets you specify separate style rules for how you want your web pages to be printed out, as described in Chapter 12.

Table 1-2. Media types supported by CSS

Type	Use
all	The default value if no media type is specified. Applies the styles to all devices.
braille	Specifies that the styles should be used for Braille tactile feedback devices.
embossed	Applies the styles to paged Braille printers.
handheld	For handheld devices, such as mobile phones.
print	Applies the styles to the pages when they are printed.
projection	Indicates that the styles are for use with a projector.
screen	Specifies that the styles should be used in a visual browser on a desktop or laptop computer.

Type	Use
speech	Intended for speech synthesizers for the visually impaired.
tty	For teletypes, terminals, or portable devices with limited display capabilities. Do not use pixels as a measurement with this media type.
tv	Intended for televisions and similar devices.

The most common way to specify the media type(s) you want to target is by adding the media attribute to the `<link>` or `<style>` tag. This accepts a comma-separated list of media types from Table 1-2 like this:

```
<link href="css/simple.css" rel="stylesheet" type="text/css"
media="screen, handheld, tv" />
```

For embedded styles, use this syntax:

```
<style type="text/css" media="screen, handheld, tv">
/* Embedded styles */
</style>
```

When using @import, the list of media types follows the url() property like this:

```
@import url("css/simple.css") screen, handheld, tv;
```

Note that when used with @import, the media types are not enclosed in quotes.

The important thing to remember is that specifying media types like this prevents the styles from being used by other media types. So, the preceding examples limit the styles to screen, handheld, and tv. Unless you specify other rules, *no* styles will be applied to other media types.

Using the media attribute affects all styles in the external style sheet or `<style>` block. However, you can also use an @media rule to control which rules are used by different media types within a style sheet or `<style>` block. To use an @media rule, add the media type(s) after @media, and wrap the targeted rules in a pair of curly braces. The following code shows separate rules for screen and print media types (you can test the code in css_atmedia.html and css_atmedia.css in the download files):

```
body {
  color: #000;
  background-color: #FFF;
}
```

```
@media screen {
  body { font-family: Arial, Helvetica, sans-serif; }
  h1 { color: #900; }
  p { margin-left: 40px; }
  a:link {
    color: #060;
    font-weight: bold;
  }
  a:visited { color: #096; }
  a:hover, a:active { color: #060; }
}
@media print {
  body { font-family: Georgia, "Times New Roman", Times, serif; }
  p { margin-left: 0; }
  a { color: #000; }
}
```

When viewed onscreen, `css_atmedia.html` looks exactly the same as Figure 1-3, but in *Print Preview* in Firefox, it looks like Figure 1-13.

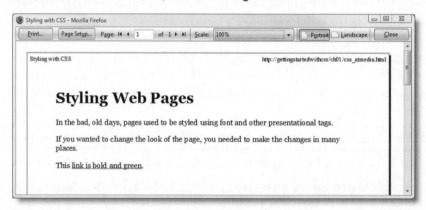

Figure 1-13. CSS lets you define different styles for printing.

The `@media` rules for `screen` and `print` assign different fonts, and change the styles applied to the paragraph margins and links.

All browsers since IE5.5 support `@media` rules. However, mixing rules for different media types in the same style sheet can be confusing and difficult to maintain. Creating separate style sheets using the `media` attribute is usually the preferable option.

AdvancED

Support for the various media types is patchy. The most reliable—and useful—are screen *and* print. *Create one style sheet to style the way your pages look in a browser. Create a separate style sheet to control the same pages when printed out.*

Learning to write CSS well

CSS is amazingly simple, but it can also be phenomenally complex—at times infuriatingly so. The simplicity of CSS lies in the limited number of properties you need to remember. The complexity lies in the fact that you can combine the properties in an infinite number of ways. This makes CSS extremely powerful, but it also means there can be a long learning curve before you begin to feel comfortable.

My advice is not to rush. The way I learned CSS was to add or change one property at a time and view the results in a browser. It was a slow, tedious process, but it helped me understand the interaction of the different properties. Once you appreciate the trickle-down, cumulative effect of the cascade, you'll be amazed at the power of CSS. The time spent will be repaid many times over in increased efficiency and easier maintenance of your websites.

Avoiding common mistakes

CSS beginners are prone to two common diseases known as **classitis** and **divitis**. You won't find either of them in a medical dictionary, but they are widespread among web developers. Once caught, they are notoriously difficult to cure. The style rule in Figure 1-12 uses a type selector, which redefines the default look of an HTML tag. It's the simplest type of selector, yet is often overlooked by beginners who become fixated with another type of selector known as a class. A **class** can be used to apply the same styles to many different elements in a page. You apply a class by adding the class name to the opening HTML tag of the element. This has a comforting, familiar feeling, because you're applying the style directly. However, it's little better than the old method of using <font> tags and other presentational markup that needed to be added directly to every element.

The file `css_classitis.html` in the download files for this chapter shows the type of problem caused by overuse of classes. Every paragraph has an opening tag that looks like this: `<p class="bodyText">`. In Chapter 4, you'll see the important role classes have to play, but this is overkill. As `css.html` proves, you can style paragraphs without the need for any extra markup in the HTML.

The other disease, divitis, tends to afflict designers who relied heavily on table layout. A `<div>` is an HTML device designed to group elements together so they can be styled in a unified way. Unfortunately, many people misinterpret the role of a `<div>`, and wrap everything in a `<div>` before styling it. Again, this usually results in redundant markup.

My aim in this book is to try to help you avoid catching either of these diseases. I suffered from both of them at one stage and know how hard it is to undo bad habits once learned. So, if you have previous experience of CSS, please try to put out of your head all thoughts of using classes or wrapping elements in `<div>` tags, at least for the time being. Classes and `<div>` tags have a vital role to play in CSS, but I want you to learn first about using type selectors and exploiting the cumulative effect of the cascade.

Test your CSS early in several browsers

The whole purpose of CSS is to control the way your web pages look in a browser. Because Internet Explorer is the most widely used browser, over the years many designers have made the mistake of using IE6 or IE7 to test their web pages. After getting everything looking the way they wanted, they finally tested in Firefox, Opera, or Safari, and discovered to their horror that the pages didn't display properly. Unfortunately, the CSS bugs in IE6 and IE7 meant that fixing the problems in the other browsers was much more difficult than if they had designed their styles to work in a more standards-compliant browser to start with. The arrival of IE8 should make things easier for developers, but the Web is constantly changing. The moral of this story is to test early and test often in different browsers—and on different operating systems. Design for browsers that you know to be standards-compliant (IE8 or the most recent versions of Firefox, Safari, Google Chrome, and Opera).

Building a useful toolset for working with CSS

Understanding the effect of a style rule can sometimes be difficult, even for experienced designers. Fortunately, there are some useful tools available that let you inspect the styles not only of your own site but of any public website, giving you a useful insight into how CSS works.

I have already mentioned the *Develop* menu in Safari. You enable it by selecting the check box labeled *Show Develop menu in menu bar* in the *Advanced* tab of the *Preferences* panel. In Safari 4, this gives you access to the *Web Inspector* (see Figure 1-15), a sophisticated panel that lets you analyze how style rules are being applied. You can also use the panel to disable styles temporarily to see what effect it has. The *Web Inspector* panel might look baffling now, but as you come to understand CSS, you'll appreciate just how useful it is.

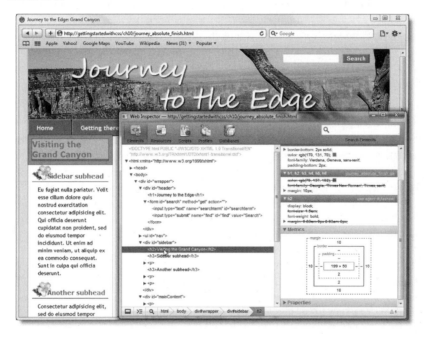

Figure 1-15. The Web Inspector in Safari 4 helps you analyze the effect of style rules with a range of helpful tools.

Similar analysis tools are available in the most recent versions of other leading browsers. You access the *Developer Tools* panel in IE8 through the *Tools* menu or by pressing F12. In Opera 10, select *Tools* ➤ *Advanced* ➤ *Developer Tools*. Firefox doesn't have a built-in panel, but the Firebug and Web Developer Toolbar add-ons are indispensible for working with CSS. Both are free, and can be obtained by selecting *Tools* ➤ *Add-ons* from the Firefox menu. Use the search field in the *Get Add-ons* tab to locate and download Firebug and the Web Developer Toolbar.

Of course, you also need a decent selection of modern browsers for testing: IE8, Firefox, and Safari at the minimum. You can find them easily online using your favorite search engine—and they're all free, so there's no excuse not to use them.

Chapter review

This chapter has given you a brief overview of the reasons behind the development of CSS and why it took so long to become widely adopted by the web development community. Although it will take several years for older browsers with substandard support for CSS to die out, the arguments in favor of using CSS are now overwhelming. Learning how to create styles involves patience and practice, but the effort is more than repaid by the efficiencies offered by CSS. To take just a simple example, changing the color of links with CSS involves a simple change to a single page that affects the whole website.

The most efficient way to use CSS is by creating style rules in one or more external style sheets and attaching them to each page with the <link> tag. You can also embed styles in the <head> of a page if you want to apply special styles only to that page. The third way of applying styles is inline with the style attribute in the opening HTML tag of the element you want to affect. However, inline styles are the least efficient form of CSS and should normally be used only when designing an HTML email.

In the next chapter, you'll start creating your own CSS to style text. This is the quickest way to make a dramatic difference to the look of your pages. It also helps reinforce the basic concept of using the cascade, showing the cumulative effect of styles as they trickle down the structure of a web page and how they can be overridden by styles lower down in a style sheet.

Chapter 2

How Do I Improve the Look of Text and Links?

When designing a website, your first thoughts are usually of images, color scheme, and other decorative elements. The text content probably comes low down on your list of priorities. After all, getting many clients to provide the actual text is like squeezing blood from a stone. Yet, in the vast majority of sites, text is usually the most important element. Visitors are in search of information, and that information is more often than not presented as text.

So, presenting text in a visually pleasing manner is an important part of your design. Not only should the text look good, it must be easy to read—the font needs to be large enough, but not too large, and the text shouldn't look too dense or bunched up. CSS has many properties that affect the appearance of text. Most are very easy to use, and they have an immediate impact on the overall design of a site. Using CSS to style text also introduces you to some important CSS concepts, such as specifying size and applying the same style rules to multiple elements.

As I said in the previous chapter, I don't intend to use CSS classes until Chapter 4, although when styling links you need to use a feature known as pseudo-classes. Don't worry if that sounds like double Dutch; all will be revealed in due course. For most of this chapter, you'll use type selectors to change the default look of HTML tags. This approach should help reinforce the principles of the CSS cascade, as rules trickle down the hierarchy of the HTML structure and are applied cumulatively.

In this chapter, you'll learn how to do the following:

- Define which fonts are used for text.
- Set color values and apply them to text.
- Specify size with pixels, ems, and other units of measurement.
- Automatically transform lowercase to uppercase and vice versa.
- Indent the first line of paragraphs and change the space between lines.
- Target multiple elements and nested elements.
- Style links and change the way they look when moused over.

By the end of this chapter, you should have a good practical knowledge of the basics of CSS, laying the foundation for the rest of the book. Before creating any style rules, let's take a quick look at the text properties available in CSS2.1.

Exploring the CSS text properties

CSS gives you a lot more control over the appearance of text than HTML, through 17 properties plus one shorthand property. Table 2-1 lists all the text properties with a brief description of what each one is for.

ExplainED

A shorthand property lets you specify several properties all at once, rather than individually. For example, instead of three separate rules to specify Arial bold font at 12px, you can use the shorthand property to define them all together. Unfortunately, some shorthand properties are difficult to use. I'll point out which are likely to save time, as well as those that are best avoided.

Table 2-1. Text properties in CSS2.1

Property	Initial Value	Inherited	Description
`color`		Yes	Always refers to text color. The color of other elements is controlled by dedicated properties, such as `border-color` and `background-color`.
`direction`	`ltr`	Yes	Controls the layout for text blocks depending on whether the text is read from left to right (`ltr`) or right to left (`rtl`). Since the default is left to right, this property is of interest only if you are working in a language written from right to left, such as Hebrew, Arabic, or Urdu. For details, see `www.w3.org/TR/CSS21/visuren.html#propdef-direction`.
`font-family`		Yes	Browsers use the fonts on the user's computer, so you should always specify a choice of fonts in order of preference, finishing with a generic font (see Table 2-2).
`font-size`	`medium`	Yes	Sizes can be set using a variety of different methods, as described in "Setting font-size" later in this chapter.
`font-style`	`normal`	Yes	Determines whether the text should be displayed as italics or regular text.
`font-variant`	`normal`	Yes	Determines whether the text should be displayed as small capitals (see Figure 2-10 in "Displaying text in small caps" later in this chapter) or regular text.
`font-weight`	`normal`	Yes	The weight of a font describes the thickness of the lines that make up the characters (such as bold). The CSS2.1 specification offers a wide range of values, but in practice, most browsers display only bold or regular text.
`font`		Yes	Shorthand property that lets you combine `font-style`, `font-variant`, `font-weight`, `font-size`, `line-height`, and `font-family` in a single declaration. Best avoided except by advanced users, as it can be difficult to get right.

Property	Initial Value	Inherited	Description
letter-spacing	normal	Yes	Increases or decreases the horizontal space between characters.
line-height	normal	Yes	Increases or decreases the vertical space between lines.
text-align		Yes	Controls whether text is aligned to the left or right, centered, or justified. The default in English and other Western European languages is left-aligned. This property is also used to align the content of table cells.
text-decoration	none	No	Draws a line under, over, or through text. This property is also used to remove the underline from links and can make text flash on and off.
text-indent	0	Yes	Sets the amount that the first line of text should be indented. Applies to any block of text, including text in a table cell. Applying a negative value creates a hanging indent (see Figure 2-12 in "Indenting the first line of text" later in this chapter).
text-transform	none	Yes	Converts text to initial capitals, all uppercase, or all lowercase.
unicode-bidi	normal	No	Controls how text is displayed when left-to-right and right-to-left languages are displayed in the same document, e.g., English and Arabic or Hebrew. For advanced users only. See www.w3.org/TR/CSS21/visuren.html#propdef-unicode-bidi for details.
vertical-align	baseline	No	Controls the vertical alignment of inline elements and table cells. Cannot be used to control the vertical alignment of block level elements, such as paragraphs.
white-space	normal	Yes	Controls how spaces and word wrapping are handled.
word-spacing	normal	Yes	Computers have no concept of what constitutes a word. This increases or decreases the size of the space character between strings of text.

> **ExplainED**
>
> *All properties can take* inherit *as their value. This sets the value of the property to the same as the parent element. The only time you need to use* inherit *is when a property is marked as not inherited. You can assume that inheritance is automatic if I don't list* inherit *among the permitted values when describing a property in the text.*

Looking at Table 2-1, it doesn't take long to realize that a lot of the properties do the same as their HTML equivalents: color, font-family, font-size, and the shorthand font property work together to fulfill the same role as the <font> tag. Similarly, font-style and font-weight are the equivalent of the <b> and <i> tags, and text-align and vertical-align do the same as the align and valign attributes in many HTML tags. However, CSS goes further by letting you indent the first line of a block of text, control the spacing between letters, words, and lines, as well as automatically transform the letter case. Another point to notice in Table 2-1 is that most of the properties are listed as inherited. This means that the value trickles down through the HTML hierarchy of the page to affect all elements. You'll see how this works when you change the default font for a page in the next section.

Changing the default font and color of text

Throughout most of this book, you'll be working with the page shown in Figure 2-1, which you can find in the download files for this chapter as journey_start.html. The page is totally unstyled, so it uses the browser's default font, and the links are underlined and blue for unvisited links, and purple for visited ones. You'll use this page to experiment with the CSS text properties and begin to turn it into something more elegant.

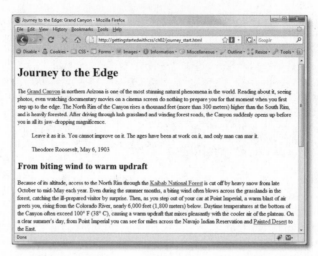

Figure 2-1. The starting point for your journey into CSS—a completely unstyled page with no images

ExplainED

If you want a sneak peek at where this journey is heading, take a look at Figure 12-1 in Chapter 12.

Unless you tell the browser which font to use, most browsers display text in Times New Roman, Times, or a similar font. The actual font depends not only on the browser but also on what's available on the visitor's computer. Understanding this is vital when it comes to setting fonts for a web page. Inexperienced designers frequently create the design of their dreams on their own computer, get it looking just the way they want it, and then proudly upload it to their website. When they see the site on somebody else's computer, they are devastated to find that the really cool font they used for all the text is replaced by boring Times New Roman.

Using font-family to choose a range of alternative fonts

As a designer, you're likely to have lots of fonts on your computer, but visitors to the sites you design probably won't have half as many. If you choose an unusual font for your page, in all likelihood, few of your visitors will ever see the page the way you envisaged. Consequently, you should always choose several alternatives similar to your preferred choice. Sadly, from the designer's perspective, the range of fonts in common use on most computers is rather limited, as Figure 2-2 shows.

Sans-serif fonts

Journey to the Edge	Verdana (both)
Journey to the Edge	Tahoma (Win)
Journey to the Edge	Arial (both)
Journey to the Edge	Trebuchet MS (both)
Journey to the Edge	Helvetica (Mac)
Journey to the Edge	Geneva (Mac)
Journey to the Edge	Lucida Sans Unicode (Win)
Journey to the Edge	Franklin Gothic Medium (Win)
Journey to the Edge	Arial Black (both)
Journey to the Edge	Impact (Win)

Serif fonts

Journey to the Edge	Times New Roman (Win)
Journey to the Edge	Times (Mac)
Journey to the Edge	Sylfaen (Win)
Journey to the Edge	Georgia (both)
Journey to the Edge	Palatino Linotype (Win)

Cursive font

Journey to the Edge	Comic Sans MS (both)

Monospace fonts

Journey to the Edge	Courier New (Win)
Journey to the Edge	Courier (Mac)
Journey to the Edge	Lucida Console (Win)
Journey to the Edge	Monaco (Mac)

Figure 2-2. Examples of the fonts currently most commonly in use on computers

LinkED

See www.codestyle.org/css/font-family/sampler-CombinedResults.shtml *for the most up-to-date list of fonts in common use on computers.*

Uninspiring though the range of fonts shown in Figure 2-2 may be, it's essentially what you need to resign yourself to. None of the fonts listed is guaranteed to be available on every computer, so it's important to specify several alternatives in order of preference in a comma-separated list. Browsers use the first available font listed.

In case none of the fonts in your list is available, you should also specify a generic font family using one of the keywords in Table 2-2. This ensures that visitors to your site see something similar to what you intend, even if they don't see it exactly how you designed it.

ExplainED

A generic font family describes the basic characteristics of a font, such as whether it is decorative, plain, or has characters of identical width. The examples shown in Figure 2-2 are grouped according to their generic font families.

Table 2-2. Generic font families

Name	Description
sans-serif	In typography, serifs are little hooks at the end of strokes. A sans-serif font has no such hooks. The lack of hooks tends to produce a cleaner result on computer screens.
serif	A serif font has little hooks at the end of strokes. The hooks are said to make characters easier to recognize on the printed page but are often indistinct on a computer monitor.
cursive	Cursive fonts look handwritten or done with a calligraphic pen. Although there are many attractive cursive fonts, the only one widely available is Comic Sans MS, which has become so closely associated with poorly designed websites that most professional designers refuse to use it.
monospace	Characters in monospace fonts are all the same width, so the letter *i* occupies the same horizontal space as the letter *m*. This type of font is typically used to display code snippets in online tutorials.
fantasy	This generic font family covers fonts that don't fall into any other category. Examples of fantasy fonts are Jokerman and Ravie.

ExplainED

If you're wondering why CSS doesn't have the ability to embed the fonts of your choice, the original CSS2 specification did have an @font-face rule designed to do just that. However, it was removed from CSS2.1 because of lack of support. Apart from the technical difficulties, most fonts are copyrighted, so embedding them in a web page presents legal difficulties.

The @font-face rule is now part of the CSS3 proposals and is supported by Safari 4 and Firefox. Internet Explorer has supported @font-face since IE5. Unfortunately, it uses a proprietary format for embedding fonts. Until that incompatibility is sorted out, using @font-face remains something to hope for, rather than a practical reality.

That's enough theory for the moment. It's time to roll up your sleeves and begin styling the page in Figure 2-1.

If you are using an ordinary text editor to create your style sheets, make sure the text editor doesn't add an .rtf or .txt file name extension to your pages. Turn on the display of file name extensions in your operating system if necessary.

Setting the default fonts and colors for a page

In this brief exercise, you'll specify the default fonts and colors for the page by creating an external style sheet, defining a style rule for the <body> tag, and attaching the style sheet to the page.

1. Launch the editing software of your choice, and open journey_start.html in the ch02 folder. To enable you to check your own code at different stages of the chapter, the same folder contains copies of the same file numbered journey_01.html, journey_02.html, and so on. These are linked to updated versions of the style sheet in the ch02/css subfolder. How you organize your exercise files is up to you, but I suggest that you create a new folder called workfiles and save journey_start.html as journey.html in the new folder.

2. Test journey.html in a browser. It should look the same as Figure 2-1.

3. Examine the HTML code in journey.html. The main body of the text is marked up using <p> tags. There are one <h1> and two <h2> headings, the quotation and attribution to President Roosevelt are wrapped in a

<blockquote>, and there's a table containing some facts about the Grand Canyon. All the markup is used to convey the structure of the page. The <blockquote> is used to indicate a quotation, not simply because it indents the text, and the table is used for data, not for layout. Note that the text in the left table column is bold and centered not through the use of HTML presentational markup, but because this is how browsers display <th> tags.

4. Create a subfolder called css in your workfiles folder.

5. In the workfiles/css folder, create an empty style sheet, and save it as journey.css. An external style sheet is simply a text file, so it should contain no code at this stage.

6. Type the following code in journey.css:

```
body {
  background-color: #FFF;
  color: #000;
  font-family: "Trebuchet MS", Arial, Helvetica, sans-serif;
}
```

7. This uses a type selector to style the <body> of the page. As I explained in the previous chapter, a type selector consists of the name of an HTML tag without the angle brackets, and it changes the default style for that tag.

8. The body rule contains the following three style declarations:

   • background-color: This sets the background color of the element. The value is set to #FFF, which is the shorthand hexadecimal notation for white (the following section, "Setting color values in CSS," explains in detail how to specify colors, including the use of shorthand hexadecimal values).

   • color: This sets the color of text inside the element. The value #000 is the shorthand hexadecimal for black.

   • font-family: This tells the browser to use Trebuchet MS if it's available on the user's computer. If not, it looks for Arial or Helvetica in that order, and if neither is found, it uses a generic sans-serif font.

ExplainED

When a font name, such as Trebuchet MS, contains spaces, you must enclose the name in quotes. American readers who are used to putting commas inside quotes should note that the comma goes outside. The generic font families listed in Table 2-2 are keywords and must never be in quotes.

9. Save journey.css and switch to journey.html.

10. Attach journey.css to journey.html using a `<link>` tag. You should be able to do this through your editing program, but if you're hand-coding, add the following line of code just before the closing `</head>` tag in journey.html:

```
<link href="css/journey.css" rel="stylesheet"
type="text/css" />
```

11. Save journey.html, and view it in a browser. It should look like Figure 2-3.

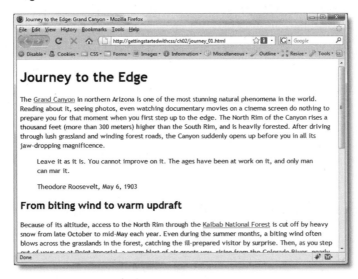

Figure 2-3. Just three lines of CSS have changed the look of all the text.

Check your code, if necessary, against journey_01.html and css/journey_01.css in the ch02 folder of the download files.

If you have used <font> tags in the past or applied CSS classes to every paragraph, I think you'll agree that creating just one rule to style the <body> of the page is a lot easier. Browsers regard the tags in a web page like a family tree. Just like children inherit characteristics from their parents, everything within the same branch of the family tree in a web page normally inherits the style rules from higher up the family tree.

ExplainED

CSS and other web technologies use the analogy of the family tree when referring to the relationship between page elements. In an HTML page, the <html> tag is regarded as the root of the tree. Tags nested inside another tag are called children. Tags nested at a deeper level are called descendants; and tags that are at the same level as each other are called siblings. As you go back up the family tree, tags one level up are called parents, and those at higher levels are ancestors.

Figure 2-4 shows the first part of the page used in the preceding exercise viewed as a family tree. The headings, paragraphs, and <blockquote> elements are all children of the <body> tag. In relation to each other, they are siblings. The two paragraphs inside the <blockquote> tag are its children, and in turn they are descendants of the <body>. Visualizing this family-tree relationship is key to understanding CSS inheritance and the cascade.

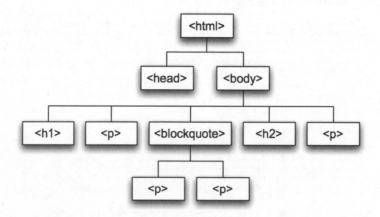

Figure 2-4. CSS treats a web page like a family tree, allowing style rules to cascade down the hierarchy of tags.

Because they're contained inside the <body>, all the text elements inherit the same font and text color. The only exception is the color of the links. Links don't inherit the color of their parent or ancestor element. As you'll see later in this chapter, you use special selectors to style links.

So, to summarize:

- To choose the font for any style rule, use the font-family property. Because you don't know which fonts will be available on the user's computer, set the value of font-family to a comma-separated list of fonts in the order of precedence that you want the browser to use them. Always finish the list with a generic font family from the list in Table 2-2. If any font name contains spaces, surround the name in quotes.

- To set the color of text, use the color property, and set its value to the hexadecimal equivalent of the color. Alternatively, use one of the color keywords in Table 2-3.

Setting color values in CSS

When setting colors in CSS, most of the time you use the hexadecimal notation for the red, green, blue (RGB) values. This is the same as in HTML: the hash character (#) followed by hexadecimal characters (the numbers 0-9 or the letters A-F). Most HTML and graphics editing programs generate the hexadecimal number for you automatically when you use a color picker or eyedropper tool.

In a six-digit hexadecimal number, the first pair of digits represents the red component of the color; the second pair represents the green component, and the final pair the blue component. In CSS, if both digits are identical in all three pairs, for example, #FFFF00 (yellow), you can shorten this to three digits (#FF0). However, if any pair does not contain identical digits, you must use the full six-digit version. So, #008080 (teal) cannot be shortened.

ExplainED

Using hexadecimal notation lets you specify 256 shades each of red, green, and blue, representing more than 16 million colors. In the early days of the Web, monitors didn't have the capability to display so many colors, so it was recommended to use a restricted set of 216 colors that were known as "web-safe." Although old textbooks and online tutorials still refer to web-safe colors, it's no longer necessary to limit yourself to their use.

Hexadecimal is fine for computers, but it can be hard to remember the numbers for common colors. So, the CSS specification defines 17 color keywords, which are listed in Table 2-3 along with their hexadecimal equivalents.

Table 2-3. Color keywords in CSS2.1

Keyword	Hexadecimal Equivalent	Keyword	Hexadecimal Equivalent
aqua	#0FF	olive	#808000
black	#000	orange	#FFA500
blue	#00F	purple	#800080
fuchsia	#F0F	red	#F00
gray	#808080	silver	#C0C0C0
green	#008000	teal	#008080
lime	#0F0	white	#FFF
maroon	#800000	yellow	#FF0
navy	#000080		

There is another way to designate colors if you feel more at home with numeric RGB values. Instead of using hexadecimal notation, you can use rgb(). Inside the parentheses you place the red, green, and blue values as comma-separated numbers in the range of 0–255 or percentages from 0% to 100%. So, for example, red can be represented in all of the following ways:

- 6-digit hexadecimal: #FF0000
- 3-digit hexadecimal: #F00
- keyword: red

- RGB numeric: `rgb(255, 0, 0)`
- RGB percentages: `rgb(100%, 0%, 0%)`

While we're on the subject of color, let's add a touch of color to the headings and style them in a different font.

Selectively applying a different font and color

Black text on a white background is OK for the main body of text, but you normally want to liven up your pages by making headings stand out with a different color and maybe a different font. You can do this easily in CSS by choosing a more specific selector. Up to now, everything inside the `<body>` inherits the same style rules. But you can override those rules by creating type selectors for individual HTML elements. A type selector redefines the HTML element's default look. So, if you create a style rule for `<h1>` elements, that's the way all `<h1>` elements will look. As you progress through this book, you'll learn that type selectors can be overridden by other selectors, but I want to keep things simple for the moment.

Changing the color and font of the headings

In this exercise, you'll see how to override inherited properties by using more specific type selectors. You'll also learn how to apply the same style rules to more than one type of element by grouping selectors together.

1. Continue working with the files from the previous exercise. Alternatively, use `journey_01.html` and `css/journey_01.css` from the download files for this chapter.

2. Open the style sheet, and add the following style rule highlighted in bold:

```
body {
  background-color: #FFF;
  color: #000;
  font-family: "Trebuchet MS", Arial, Helvetica, sans-serif;
}
h1 {
  color: #468966;
  font-family: Georgia, "Times New Roman", Times, serif;
}
```

3. This is a new type selector that changes the default look of `<h1>` tags, setting the text color to green and using a serif font. Note that Times New Roman has spaces in the font name, so it's enclosed in quotes.

53

4. Save the style sheet, and view journey.html in a browser. If you have Georgia installed on your computer, the main heading of the page should now look like Figure 2-5. Even if you don't have Georgia, the heading should be displayed in a serif font and its color should be green. However, all the other text, including the <h2> headings, remains unchanged. The more specific h1 selector has overridden the body selector.

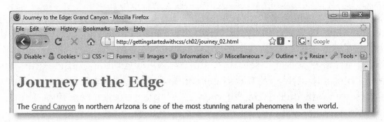

Figure 2-5. The color and font of the <h1> heading is changed by a more specific selector.

5. Copy the h1 style rule that you created in step 2, and paste it below the h1 rule. Change h1 in the rule you have just pasted to h2. The two rules should now look like this:

```
h1 {
  color: #468966;
  font-family: Georgia, "Times New Roman", Times, serif;
}
h2 {
  color: #468966;
  font-family: Georgia, "Times New Roman", Times, serif;
}
```

6. Save the style sheet, and test the page again in a browser. It should now look like Figure 2-6. The <h1> and <h2> headings now use the same font and color.

Figure 2-6. Both sets of headings are now styled the same way.

7. Copying and pasting a style rule like that is an easy way to apply the same set of rules to another element, but it bloats your code unnecessarily. There's a more efficient way of doing it.

8. Delete the h2 rule you created in step 4. Just the body and h1 rules should remain in the style sheet. Now amend the h1 selector by typing a comma after it followed by *h2*. The edited rule should look like this:

```
h1, h2 {
  color: #468966;
  font-family: Georgia, "Times New Roman", Times, serif;
}
```

9. This is called grouping selectors. To **group selectors**, just separate each selector by a comma. I have inserted a space after the comma for readability, but the space is optional. The page you're working on contains only <h1> and <h2> tags, but if you wanted to make sure that the same color and font is applied to all levels of headings, you simply add the others to the selector. In fact, let's do that now.

10. Change the selector to look like this:

```
h1, h2, h3, h4, h5, h6 {
  color: #468966;
```

```
    font-family: Georgia, "Times New Roman", Times, serif;
}
```

11. Save the style sheet, and view journey.html in a browser. It should still look the same as in Figure 2-6.

12. In journey.html, change the second <h2> heading to <h3>.

13. Save the page, and reload it in a browser. Scroll down to the heading you just edited. As shown in Figure 2-7, it should now be smaller, but still have the same color and font as the other two headings.

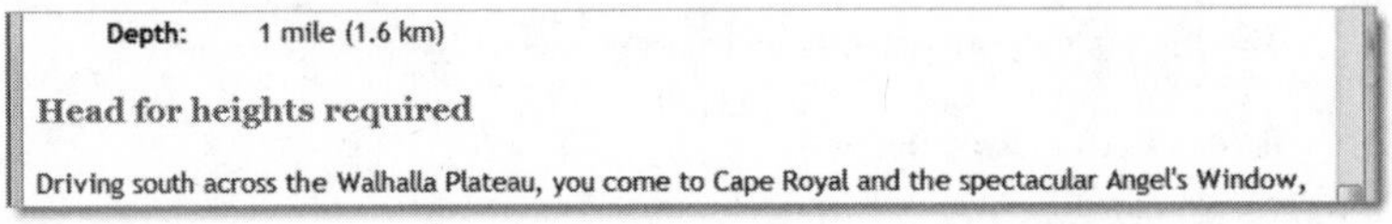

> **Depth:** 1 mile (1.6 km)
>
> **Head for heights required**
>
> Driving south across the Walhalla Plateau, you come to Cape Royal and the spectacular Angel's Window,

Figure 2-7. The same styles are applied to all levels of headings.

You can check your code, if necessary, against journey_02.html and css/journey_02.css in the download files for this chapter.

Changing the size of fonts

Setting the size of fonts in CSS is easy. You give the font-size property a value, and that's it. Unfortunately, that's only half the story.

The problem lies in number of different ways you can specify the value of font-size. According to the CSS specification, apart from inheritance there are four ways, as follows:

- Absolute size keywords
- Relative size keywords
- Length
- Percentage

In practice, it's the last two methods that are normally used, but it's important to mention the other two briefly in case you ever encounter them. Table 2-4 lists the absolute size keywords and their recommended equivalents in the HTML <font> tag's size attribute.

Table 2-4. Absolute size keywords for font-size

Keyword	HTML Size Equivalent
xx-small	1
x-small	
small	2
medium	3
large	4
x-large	5
xx-large	6

Note that x-small doesn't have a recommended HTML equivalent, and there's no keyword that equates to the HTML size 7.

Although these keywords are officially *called* absolute size, there's nothing absolute about them. How browsers interpret the keywords is entirely up to them, and the HTML equivalent is only a recommendation, not a requirement. In effect, they give you very little real control over the way your text is rendered in different browsers.

There are only two relative size keywords: larger and smaller. The relative size relates to the absolute size keywords in Table 2-4 and is one size larger or smaller than the parent element. So, for example, if the font-size of a paragraph is set to medium and the style rule for <a> tags uses font-size: larger;, links within the paragraph should be rendered as large.

Quite honestly, I suggest you think about the absolute and relative keywords as if they were a bad dream—something best forgotten.

For more precise control over the size of fonts, you need to specify the value as a length or a percentage. These two concepts affect most other aspects of CSS, so this is a good time to pause to explain how they work.

Setting length with pixels, ems, and other units of measurement

Length is simply CSS-speak for "a size specified using a unit of measurement." It has nothing to do with the number of words in a paragraph. CSS recognizes the eight units of measurement listed in Table 2-5 for specifying length, three of them relative units and the rest absolute units.

Table 2-5. CSS units of measurement for length (size)

Type	Unit	Description
Relative Units		
	em	A term borrowed from typography, it means the height of the font, usually including whitespace above and below. So, with a 16px font, one em is 16px; with a 24px font, one em is 24px, and so on. Contrary to popular belief, it is not the width of an uppercase *M*.
	ex	Also borrowed from typography, and defined as the height of a lowercase *x*. In practice, most browsers treat ex as half an em.
	px	Pixel. Equivalent to one of the dots that makes up the image on a computer monitor. Pixels are considered relative units because the actual size depends on the monitor resolution.
Absolute units		
	in	Inch (2.54 centimeters).
	cm	Centimeter (0.394 in).
	mm	Millimeter (0.039 in).
	pt	Point. A typographical unit equivalent to 1/72 of an inch (0.353 mm).
	pc	Pica. A typographical unit equivalent to 12 points (4.233 mm).

The CSS specification says absolute units are useful only "when the physical properties of the output medium are known." Since web pages are viewed on a wide range of devices, you have no way of knowing the physical properties of the device an individual visitor is using. The resolution on my 24-inch monitor is completely different from an iPhone. What this means in practice is that the only time you should use absolute units in your CSS is when defining rules for a print style sheet. Inches, millimeters, and points are meaningful to printers but not to web browsers. So, unless you're creating a print style sheet, you're left with just the three relative units to be concerned with.

ExplainED

A lot of old books use points to define the size of fonts. This works, because most browsers simply convert one point to one pixel. However, points should not be used except in print style sheets.

Of the three relative units, ex is the least useful. So, you're now down to just two: em and px. Unfortunately, they have become the focus of endless arguments in the web design community. The reason for all the hostility comes down to—yes, you've guessed it—Internet Explorer. Until the release of IE7, Internet Explorer didn't allow users to resize text if the size was specified in pixels. Well, there was a way, but it was buried so deep in the accessibility preferences that most users would never find it.

This split the design community into two opposing camps: those who wanted absolute control over the size of text from the aesthetic point of view, and those who argued that text should be resizable for the benefit of people with poor eyesight. The size control freaks advocated pixels, conveniently ignoring the fact that Firefox and other browsers allowed text in pixels to be resized. The others advocated ems, because Internet Explorer allowed users to resize text if the size was specified in ems.

The release of IE7 brought an end for the need to argue over the resizing of text, because IE7 incorporated a zoom feature that increases the size of the whole page, so everything remains in proportion. Most modern browsers now zoom by default, rather than increase only the size of text. Still, the legacy of the flame wars has left the design community split in two camps: ems and pixels. So, which should you use?

Both ems and pixels have their advantages and drawbacks, but if you're new to CSS, pixels are undoubtedly easier to understand. Images are measured in pixels, and most designers know the width and height of their monitor in pixels. Even though the pixels on one screen might be smaller than another, 14 pixels will always be 14 pixels on both screens.

Ems, on the other hand, are proportional to the height of the current font. So, if the size of the current font is 14 pixels, one em will also be 14 pixels. But if the font is changed to 20 pixels, one em also becomes 20 pixels. Although this makes calculations more difficult (or even impossible), it does have the advantage that measurements remain in proportion—and therefore in harmony—with the size of your text. Most of the time, I'll use pixels in this book, but I'll show you how to use ems where appropriate.

Whichever unit of measurement you use, the rules are the same:

- There must be *no space* between the number and the unit of measurement: 14px, not 14 px.

- When the value is zero, the unit of measurement is optional: 0em is valid, but 0 is simpler.

Using percentages

Most sizes in CSS, including font-size, can also be expressed as a percentage. The question is: a percentage of what?

In the case of fonts, a percentage indicates size relative to the parent element. If no size for the font has been defined in the parent element, the percentage represents size in proportion to the default. So, if the size of the font in the parent element is 14px, setting font-size in a child element to 85% results in text being displayed at 12px (11.9px rounded up). Similarly, the default size of paragraph text in all browsers is 16px. So, setting font-size for paragraphs to 87% results in 14px text as long as no other style rule has changed the default size.

For all other measurements, percentage is always taken in relation to the size of the parent element.

AdvancED

Be careful when using ems or percentages for font sizes. Because nested elements inherit their size from their parents, you might end up with ever shrinking text. For example, if you set font-size for unordered lists to 70%, the size of text in a nested list becomes 49% (70% of 70%).

Let's get back to styling journey.html.

Changing font sizes

This exercise continues styling the text in the same page as the previous two exercises, and demonstrates how to change the size of fonts using different units of measurement. Continue working with the same files as before. Alternatively, use journey_02.html and css/journey_02.css from the download files for this chapter.

1. Open `journey.css`, and add a new h1 type selector to set the font-size property for the `<h1>` heading like this:

```
h1, h2, h3, h4, h5, h6 {
  color: #468966;
  font-family: Georgia, "Times New Roman", Times, serif;
}
h1 {
  font-size: 220%;
}
```

You need to create a separate style block for the `<h1>` heading, because you don't want the `font-size` property to be applied to all the other heading levels. This shows the cumulative aspect of the cascade in action. The `font-size` property is added to the existing styles defined for `<h1>` tags.

The value has been set to 220%. Browsers regard the default size of `<h1>` tags as 200% (twice the size of ordinary text). So, this makes the heading at the top of the page slightly larger than before. If using percentages with fonts, you need to experiment to see which produces the most pleasing effect.

Because nothing is nested inside the `<h1>` heading, there's no danger of a multiplier effect when using a percentage.

2. Save the change to the style sheet, and test `journey.html` in a browser. You should see the heading at the top of the page is slightly larger, but it's still green and uses the same font.

3. Now, let's change the size of the main text, which is contained in paragraphs. The default size that all browsers use for body text is 16px, which many designers find a bit too large. Instead of using a percentage this time, specify the `font-size` property in pixels by adding the following style block at the bottom of `journey.css`:

```
p {
  font-size: 14px;
}
```

This targets all paragraphs, including those inside the `<blockquote>`, and resets the size of the text to 14 pixels.

4. Save the style sheet, and test `journey.html` again. As Figure 2-8 shows, the text in the table is still the same size as before. It's not inside paragraphs, so the new style doesn't affect it.

Because of its altitude, access to the North Rim through the Kaibab National Forest is cut off by heavy snow from late October to mid-May each year. Even during the summer months, a biting wind often blows across the grasslands in the forest, catching the ill-prepared visitor by surprise. Then, as you step out of your car at Point Imperial, a warm blast of air greets you, rising from the Colorado River, nearly 6,000 feet (1,800 meters) below. Daytime temperatures at the bottom of the Canyon often exceed 100° F (38° C), causing a warm updraft that mixes pleasantly with the cooler air of the plateau. On a clear summer's day, from Point Imperial you can see for miles across the Navajo Indian Reservation and Painted Desert to the East.

Grand Canyon facts

Length:	277 miles (446 km)
Widest point:	18 miles (29 km)
Depth:	1 mile (1.6 km)

Figure 2-8. The paragraph style rule doesn't affect the text in the table.

5. How can we change the text in the table? First, let's take a look at the HTML code:

```
<table width="300" border="0">
  <caption>
    Grand Canyon facts
  </caption>
  <tr>
    <th scope="row">Length:</th>
    <td>277 miles (446 km)</td>
  </tr>
  <tr>
    <th scope="row">Widest point:</th>
    <td>18 miles (29 km)</td>
  </tr>
  <tr>
    <th scope="row">Depth:</th>
    <td>1 mile (1.6 km)</td>
  </tr>
</table>
```

One solution would be to use table as a type selector. That will affect everything inside the table, but I would like to make the text in the <caption> tag look more prominent.

The alternative would be to apply the same font-size to the <th> and <td> tags, thereby leaving the <caption> tag unaffected. However, I'd like to demonstrate the effect of inherited font-size, so let's take the first option and group table with the p selector like this:

```
p, table{
  font-size: 14px;
}
```

6. This makes all the text in the table the same size as in the paragraphs. So the caption is also 14 pixels. Ideally, I want it several pixels larger.

Of course, I could just create a new `caption` selector and choose a size in pixels. But where's the fun in that? Let's experiment with ems.

Add the following style block at the bottom of the style sheet:

```
caption {
  font-size: 1.3em;
}
```

As I explained earlier, ems are proportional to the height of the current font. Because the `<caption>` tag is inside the table, the current font height is 14px. By specifying a `font-size` of 1.3em, this style rule makes the font height 1.3 times bigger than 14px.

7. Save the style sheet, and view `journey.html` in a browser. The table and caption should now look like Figure 2-9.

From biting wind to warm updraft

Because of its altitude, access to the North Rim through the Kaibab National Forest is cut off by heavy snow from late October to mid-May each year. Even during the summer months, a biting wind often blows across the grasslands in the forest, catching the ill-prepared visitor by surprise. Then, as you step out of your car at Point Imperial, a warm blast of air greets you, rising from the Colorado River, nearly 6,000 feet (1,800 meters) below. Daytime temperatures at the bottom of the Canyon often exceed 100° F (38° C), causing a warm updraft that mixes pleasantly with the cooler air of the plateau. On a clear summer's day, from Point Imperial you can see for miles across the Navajo Indian Reservation and Painted Desert to the East.

Grand Canyon facts

Length:	277 miles (446 km)
Widest point:	18 miles (29 km)
Depth:	1 mile (1.6 km)

Figure 2-9. The table text is now the same size as in the paragraphs, but the caption is bigger.

8. Let's verify what has happened. If you multiply 14 by 1.3, the result is 18.2. Pixels can only be whole numbers, so the browser rounds this down to 18px. Replace 1.3em in the caption style rule with 18px, and change its color to match the other headings like this:

```
caption {
  font-size: 18px;
  color: #468966;
}
```

9. Save the style sheet, and test the page again. The caption should still be the same size as in Figure 2-9. The only difference is the change of color.

You can check your code, if necessary, against `journey_03.html` and `css/journey.css` in the download files for this chapter.

As I said earlier, you'll probably find defining the size of text in pixels much easier to start with. The purpose of this exercise has been to show you how ems and percentages also work.

Changing the look of fonts

You'll be relieved to hear that the remaining text properties are much more straightforward. Setting aside the font shorthand property, which is covered at the end of this chapter, three more properties begin with font:

- font-style: Control whether text is italicized.
- font-weight: Make text bolder or lighter.
- font-variant: Convert the text to small caps, if the font supports them. Otherwise, convert the text to uppercase.

Closely related to these is the text-transform property, which changes the letter case of text, converting it to uppercase, lowercase, or initial caps.

The following sections explain how to use each of these properties.

Italicizing text

The font-style property accepts the following three values:

- italic: Italicize the text.
- normal: Remove italics.
- oblique: Use an oblique version of the font, if one exists. Otherwise, render the text as italics.

Since very few fonts used on the Web have oblique versions, italic and normal are the only values you need. The main use for normal is to remove italics from text that you want to emphasize inside a larger block of text that's already italicized.

Making text bolder or lighter

The font-weight property accepts the following values:

- bold: Make the text bold.
- bolder: Make the text bolder in relation to its parent.
- lighter: Make the text lighter in relation to its parent.
- normal: Render the text normally.

- One of nine values increasing in steps of 100 from 100 to 900: 400 equals `normal`, and 700 equals `bold`.

In practice, the only values you are likely to use are `bold` and `normal`. Setting `font-weight` to `normal` is useful when you want to display as normal text an element, such as a `<th>` tag (table heading), that browsers normally render in a bold font.

Displaying text in small caps

The `font-variant` property accepts the following values:

- `normal`: Render text using the same letter case as in the underlying code.
- `small-caps`: Render the text in small caps if supported by the font. Otherwise, transform the text to uppercase.

Small caps display lowercase letters as uppercase, but in a smaller size and with slightly different proportions, as shown in Figure 2-10.

Figure 2-10. In a small caps font, uppercase letters are only slightly taller than lowercase.

Switching between uppercase and lowercase

The `text-transform` property accepts the following values:

- `capitalize`: Convert the first letter of every word to uppercase.
- `lowercase`: Convert all characters to lowercase.
- `uppercase`: Convert all characters to uppercase.
- `none`: Render text in the same letter case as the underlying code.

Using `capitalize` converts to uppercase the first letter after every space. All other characters are unaffected.

The `text-transform` property is inherited, so it affects all child elements. Set the value to `none` in a child element to turn off an inherited text transformation rule.

Now you've seen the properties and their values, let's put them into action.

Adding bold, italics, and small caps

This exercise continues styling journey.html from the previous exercise, showing how to use the font-style, font-weight, font-variant, and text-transform properties to change the look of selected parts of the text. Continue using the same files as before, or use journey_03.html and css/journey.css from the download files for this chapter.

1. Edit the h1 style rule in journey.css to add the font-variant property, and set its value to small-caps like this:

```
h1 {
  font-size: 220%;
  font-variant: small-caps;
}
```

This converts the main heading of the page to look like Figure 2-10.

2. Edit the caption style rule to add the font-style property, and set its value to bold like this:

```
caption {
  font-size: 18px;
  color: #468966;
  font-weight: bold;
}
```

This renders the table caption in a bold typeface.

3. Let's use font-weight again, this time to reverse the way the browser has automatically applied bold to the table headings. Create a new style rule for the <th> tags like this at the bottom of the style sheet:

```
th {
  font-weight: normal;
}
```

AdvancED

You might wonder why I created the table with <th> tags if I was planning to display the text in a normal font. The idea was not just to demonstrate how to remove a bold typeface. The underlying HTML uses <th> tags with the scope attribute making the table more accessible to blind people using a screen reader. HTML defines the structure of your site. CSS is what makes it look the way you want.

4. When creating the caption for the table, I wrote "facts" all in lowercase. On reflection, I think it would probably look better if I gave it an initial capital. Of course, I could just change the text, but let's imagine that I have several tables in my site, and I want to make sure the captions all use initial capitals. CSS to the rescue! Amend the caption style rule like this:

```
caption {
    font-size: 18px;
    color: #468966;
    font-weight: bold;
    text-transform: capitalize;
}
```

5. Finally, I want to display the quotation from President Roosevelt in italics. It's in a paragraph, but I can't add `font-style: italic;` to the paragraph style rule, because that would make all paragraphs italic. If you've done any CSS before, I expect you're probably shouting "use a class!" No, a class isn't necessary. The quotation is in a `<blockquote>` tag, so that's what you need to style. Create a new style rule at the bottom of the style sheet like this:

```
blockquote {
    font-style: italic;
}
```

6. Save the style sheet, and check `journey.html` in a browser. It should now look like Figure 2-11. The top-level heading is in small caps, the quotation is in italics, and the table caption and labels have been transformed.

    You can check your code, if necessary, against `journey_04.html` and `css/journey_04.css` in the download files for this chapter.

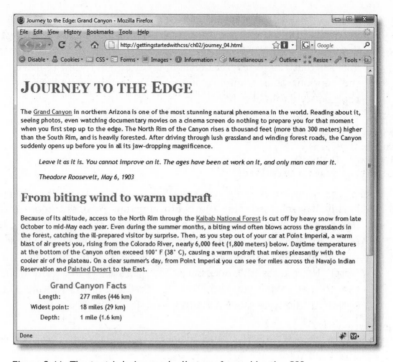

Figure 2-11. The text is being gradually transformed by the CSS.

Aligning and spacing text

Most of the remaining CSS text properties are concerned with the alignment of text and how it's spaced out. The following properties are available:

- `text-align`: Align text horizontally to the left, right, center, or justified.

- `vertical-align`: Align text vertically in relation to an imaginary line box. Also use to adjust the vertical alignment of content in table cells.

- `text-indent`: Indent the first line of a block of text.

- `line-height`: Adjust the vertical spacing between lines in the same block of text.

- `letter-spacing`: Adjust the spacing between each character.

- `word-spacing`: Adjust the spacing between each word.

- `white-space`: Control how whitespace and word wrapping is handled.

The following sections explain how to use each of these properties.

Aligning text horizontally

The `text-align` property accepts the following values:

- `left`: Align text to the left, and leave ragged ends on the right.
- `right`: Align text to the right, and leave ragged ends on the left.
- `center`: Center text, leaving ragged ends on both sides.
- `justify`: Align text on both sides.

Aligning text vertically

When used with text, the `vertical-align` property adjusts the position of text vertically in relation to the text around it. The position is based on an imaginary box representing the current line of text. It accepts the following values:

- `baseline`: Align the text to the same baseline as text in the parent element. This is the default value.
- `middle`: Align the vertical midpoint 0.25em above the baseline of the parent.
- `sub`: Align text to the proper position for a subscript. This does not alter the size of the font.
- `super`: Align text to the proper position for a superscript. This does not alter the size of the font.
- `text-top`: Align the top of the imaginary text box with the top of the text in the parent element.
- `text-bottom`: Align the bottom of the imaginary text box with the bottom of the text in the parent element.
- `top`: Align the top of the imaginary text box in line with the top of the parent's text box.
- `bottom`: Align the bottom of the imaginary text box in line with the bottom of the parent's text box.
- `inherit`: Vertical alignment is not inherited by default, so use this to apply the same value as the parent element.

The `vertical-align` property can also take a length (see "Setting length with pixels, ems, and other units of measurement" earlier in this chapter) or a percentage.

If your mind is boggling at this point, you're not alone. The `vertical-align` property is probably one of the least well understood aspects of CSS. The biggest misconception about vertical-align is that it can be used to adjust the vertical position of block elements, such as paragraphs. *It can't.* The only time vertical-align can be used in that way is when controlling the vertical alignment of the content in a table cell. Except in a table, vertical-align is used *only* for inline elements, such as text and images.

Consequently, vertical-align is probably the least useful of the CSS text-related properties. I have included it here mainly to warn you that it doesn't do what you might have expected. I'll return to vertical-align in Chapter 9, where it is much more useful in relation to tables.

Indenting the first line of text

The text-indent property takes a length or a percentage and indents the first line of text in each block by the amount specified. When the value is a percentage, the indentation is a percentage of the containing block's width.

If you specify a negative value for text-indent, it creates a hanging indent with the first line protruding to the left, as shown in Figure 2-12.

> Because of its altitude, access to the
> October to mid-May each year.
> grasslands in the forest, catchi
> Imperial, a warm blast of air gre
> Daytime temperatures at the b
> mixes pleasantly with the coole
> miles across the Navajo Indian

Figure 2-12. Hanging indent

You need to be careful when creating a hanging indent, because text-indent shifts the beginning of the first line to the left. If you're not careful, this can result in part of your text being hidden. When taking the screenshot for Figure 2-12, I needed to add extra style rules to journey.css. Without them, the first word of the paragraph was hidden beyond the left border of the browser window.

ExplainED

Don't be confused by the name of text-indent. *You can't use it to indent an entire block of text. You do that by defining margins, which are covered in Chapter 3.*

Adjusting the vertical space between lines of text

If you have studied typography or printing, you'll be familiar with the concept of **leading**, which sets the amount of space between lines in a block of text, such as a paragraph. Too little space and everything looks cramped and is hard to read. Too much space and the reader's eye wanders, making reading equally difficult.

The CSS equivalent of leading is `line-height`. This property accepts a length, percentage, or number. You can also use the keyword `normal` to reset line-height to its default value.

Because of the way `line-height` is calculated and applied by browsers, the most consistent results are achieved by using a number *without* a unit of measurement like this:

`line-height: 1.3;`

The default value applied by browsers varies but is normally in the range of 1.0-1.2.

Negative values are not permitted. You can use positive values less than 1, but anything smaller than about 0.6 results in lines overlapping each other.

Adding or removing space between words

The `word-spacing` property controls the amount of horizontal space between words. It accepts a length. A positive value adds space by the specified amount. A negative value reduces space by the specified amount. Because it's an inherited property, the same value is applied to all child elements. Set `word-spacing` to `normal` to reset its value in a child element.

Increasing or decreasing the space between letters

The `letter-spacing` property controls the amount of horizontal space between letters. In print terminology, this is known as **tracking**. It works the same way as `word-spacing` by adding or subtracting the specified amount from the default value.

Controlling whitespace and line wrapping

Browsers automatically close up sequences of spaces, ignore new lines in HTML, and wrap text at the right edge. The white-space property gives you control over the handling of whitespace and new lines. It accepts the following values:

- normal: This is the default value and is used to cancel any inherited value.

- pre: Preserve all spaces and new lines in the HTML.

- nowrap: Prevent the browser from automatically wrapping text.

- pre-wrap: Preserve sequences of whitespace and new lines, but automatically wrap text when the border is reached (see Figure 2-15 in the following exercise).

- pre-line: Close up sequences of whitespace as in normal text, but honor new lines (see Figure 2-16).

Using white-space: pre; has a similar effect to using <pre> tags in HTML, but with the advantage of preserving the current font. It's useful for displaying poetry without the need to insert <br /> tags at the end of each line.

Using white-space: nowrap; is useful for preventing the text in table cells from wrapping onto a new line.

The pre-wrap and pre-line values give a finer level of control over the handling of whitespace and new lines.

Let's see some of these properties in action by updating journey.html from the previous exercises.

Adjusting spacing and alignment of the text

This exercise builds on the previous exercises by using all the alignment and spacing properties described in this section, with the exception of vertical-align. You'll also learn how to target nested elements. Continue using the same files. Alternatively, use journey_04.html and css/journey.css from the download files for this chapter.

1. Let's begin by centering the main heading. Edit the h1 style rule like this:

```
h1 {
  font-size: 220%;
  font-variant: small-caps;
  text-align: center;
}
```

2. Next, justify the main text in the paragraphs. So far, the only style rule specifically for paragraphs is grouped with the table type selector. So, you need to create a new style block at the bottom of the style sheet like this:

```
p {
  text-align: justify;
}
```

3. Add the text-indent property to the same style block and set the value to 30px. This will indent the first line of each paragraph by 30 pixels. Amend the p style rule like this:

```
p {
  text-align: justify;
  text-indent: 30px;
}
```

4. While you're at it, give the paragraphs a bit more breathing space between each line by adding line-height to the rule like this:

```
p {
  text-align: justify;
  text-indent: 30px;
  line-height: 1.4;
}
```

5. Before going any further, save the style sheet, and check your handiwork in a browser. If you have a large monitor, I expect you won't notice anything particularly odd. But if you resize your browser window to 800 pixels, you should see something like Figure 2-13.

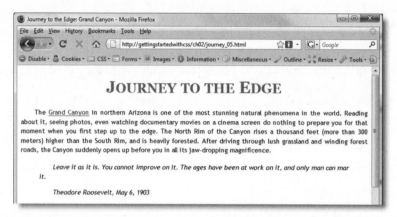

Figure 2-13. The text-indent property also affects the paragraphs inside the <blockquote> element.

The `text-indent` property that you added in step 3 affects all paragraphs including those inside the `<blockquote>` element. There's nothing particularly wrong with this, but the beauty of CSS is that you can target your style rules precisely. Let's eliminate the indent in the `<blockquote>`.

I suspect that some of you with previous experience of CSS are thinking "Now he's going to use a class." Wrong.

6. The way to target nested elements is to use what's called a **descendant selector**. Using the analogy of a family tree, an element nested inside another is called a child element. The paragraphs inside the `<blockquote>` element are children of the `<blockquote>`. In other words, they are its descendants.

   To create a descendant selector, simply add a space after the parent selector, followed by the child selector. In this case, the parent is `blockquote` and the child is `p`. So, the descendant selector becomes `blockquote p`. You already have a `blockquote` style rule, which you can edit to target accurately the paragraphs in the `<blockquote>`. Change the `blockquote` style rule like this:

```
blockquote p {
  font-style: italic;
  text-indent: 0;
}
```

This resets the value of text-indent to its default, which is 0. You could add px after the 0, but it's not necessary. Zero is zero. The unit of measurement doesn't matter.

If you test the page again, you'll see that the Roosevelt quote has moved 30 pixels to the left.

7. Time to tidy up the table. Amend the th style rule like this to align the labels to the right:

```
th {
  font-weight: normal;
  text-align: right;
}
```

8. Adjusting the space between words and letters is a tricky business. Getting just the right amount takes not only a good eye but a lot of experimentation. It's also worth remembering that the results will look different if the user doesn't have your main choice of font. After several tries, I felt happy with the following settings for the main heading of the page:

```
h1 {
  font-size: 220%;
  font-variant: small-caps;
  text-align: center;
  word-spacing: 0.2em;
  letter-spacing: 0.05em;
}
```

This is one of the cases where using ems usually gives more satisfactory results than pixels, because an em is directly related to the size of the font. As you can see, you can use decimal fractions of an em. The leading zero before the decimal point is optional, but I prefer to use it for ease of reading.

9. To wrap up this exercise, let's experiment with the white-space property. The HTML code for the Roosevelt quotation is split over two lines like this:

```
<p>Leave it as it is. You cannot improve on it.
The ages have been at work on it, and only man can mar it.</p>
```

Amend the blockquote p style rule to use white-space: pre; like this:

```
blockquote p {
  font-style: italic;
  text-indent: 0;
  white-space: pre;
}
```

10. Save the style sheet, and test the page in a browser. It should look like Figure 2-14.

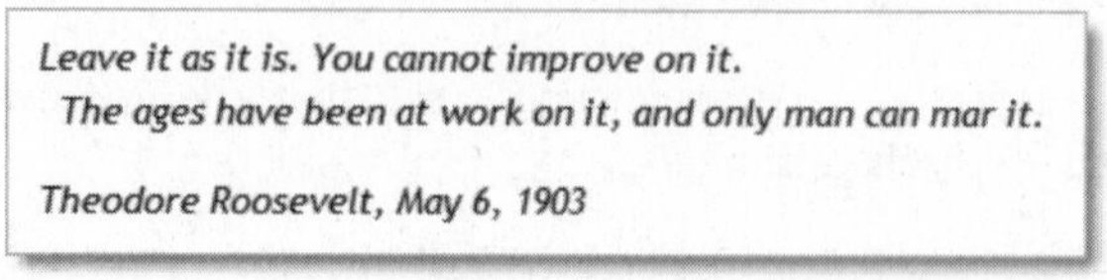

> *Leave it as it is. You cannot improve on it.*
> * The ages have been at work on it, and only man can mar it.*
>
> *Theodore Roosevelt, May 6, 1903*

Figure 2-14. Both the new line and two spaces at the beginning of the second line have been preserved.

As you can see, the new line and spaces in the underlying HTML have been preserved. However, unlike the `<pre>` HTML tag, the font hasn't been converted to monospace.

11. Change `pre` to `pre-wrap`, save the style sheet, and test the page again. The effect is the same. However, if you add a large amount of filler text at the end of the quote and test the page, you'll see that the original line break and spaces are preserved, but the rest of the text is wrapped normally, as shown in Figure 2-15.

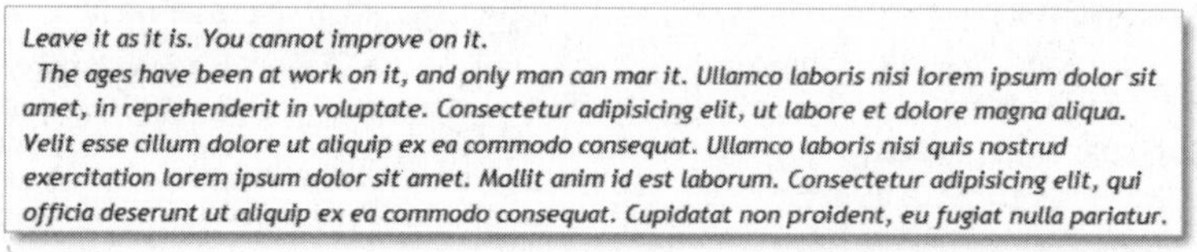

> *Leave it as it is. You cannot improve on it.*
> * The ages have been at work on it, and only man can mar it. Ullamco laboris nisi lorem ipsum dolor sit amet, in reprehenderit in voluptate. Consectetur adipisicing elit, ut labore et dolore magna aliqua. Velit esse cillum dolore ut aliquip ex ea commodo consequat. Ullamco laboris nisi quis nostrud exercitation lorem ipsum dolor sit amet. Mollit anim id est laborum. Consectetur adipisicing elit, qui officia deserunt ut aliquip ex ea commodo consequat. Cupidatat non proident, eu fugiat nulla pariatur.*

Figure 2-15. The effect of pre-wrap is to preserve line breaks and spaces but wrap text normally.

12. Change `pre-wrap` back to `pre`, and test again. This time the extra text stays on the second line and spawns a long horizontal scrollbar.

13. Finally, change `pre` to `pre-line`, and test again. The two spaces at the beginning of the second line should have been removed, and the text should now look like Figure 2-16.

14. Delete the extra text at the end of the Roosevelt quote, and save the page. You can check your code, if necessary, against `journey_05.html` and `css/journey_05.css` in the download files for this chapter.

> *Leave it as it is. You cannot improve on it.*
>
> *The ages have been at work on it, and only man can mar it. Ullamco laboris nisi lorem ipsum dolor sit amet, in reprehenderit in voluptate. Consectetur adipisicing elit, ut labore et dolore magna aliqua. Velit esse cillum dolore ut aliquip ex ea commodo consequat. Ullamco laboris nisi quis nostrud exercitation lorem ipsum dolor sit amet. Mollit anim id est laborum. Consectetur adipisicing elit, qui officia deserunt ut aliquip ex ea commodo consequat. Cupidatat non proident, eu fugiat nulla pariatur.*

Figure 2-16. Using pre-line removes extra whitespace and wraps text normally but preserves new lines.

ExplainED

The pre-wrap *and* pre-line *values for* white-space *are supported by the most recent versions of browsers, such as IE8 and Firefox 3.5. Earlier browsers that don't recognize these values ignore the style rule and wrap the text as normal without preserving whitespace or new lines.*

Styling text links

Links are the driving force of the Web. The ability to jump from one page to another, often located on a server on the opposite side of the world, is what makes the Web such a powerful resource. Although they're familiar to everyone today, in the early days of the Web, they were a new idea. So, to make them stand out, it was decided to underline links and color them a vivid blue. You still need links to stand out—or at least be discoverable. Otherwise, no one would realize they're links. However, blue underlined text frequently spoils the look of an otherwise harmonious color scheme. So, styling links is an important aspect of CSS.

HTML allows you to change the color of links with the link, vlink, and alink attributes of the <body> tag, but CSS goes much further. Not only can you change the color of links, you can remove the underline and control how a link looks when the mouse pointer passes over it. What's more, you can also control the look of links separately in different parts of the same page. So, you can have links in a navigation menu styled completely differently from links in the main body of the page, and yet another style in a sidebar or footer.

I'll show you how to create different styles of links in the same page in Chapter 7. In this chapter, I'll concentrate on the basics of styling links.

Just remember it's a love-hate relationship

No, I haven't gone mad. Love-hate—or LoVe-HAte if you prefer—is the mnemonic most web designers use to remember the rules of styling links with CSS. Links are created using the <a> tag in HTML, so you can use a type selector to control the look of links. For example, the following rule makes links bold and red:

```
a {
  font-weight: bold;
  color: red;
}
```

That's fine as far as it goes, but it means that links will look the same, regardless of whether they have been visited. It's usual to give a visual clue that a link has been visited; the browser default is purple. It's now also expected to give another visual clue when the mouse passes over a link, in addition to the default behavior of the cursor turning into a hand. The problem is that these different states are controlled by the browser; there's nothing in the HTML that indicates when the mouse is hovering over a link, or that the link has been visited.

The answer is what CSS calls pseudo-classes. As I explained briefly in the last chapter, a class can be used to apply a style to several elements in a page by adding the class attribute and the name of the class to each element's opening tag. But you can't change the class once the page has been loaded, because it's embedded in the HTML code. A **pseudo-class** defines how you want an element to look dependent on its interactive state. So, if the mouse is hovering over a link, the browser applies the appropriate pseudo-class, which is called, aptly enough, :hover. As soon as the mouse is no longer over the link, the browser removes the :hover pseudo-class and applies the appropriate pseudo-class depending on whether the link has been visited or not. At the point of being clicked, a link is considered to be active, so there's also an :active pseudo-class to represent this state. You don't need to worry about the technical details of how it works; all you need to do is create style rules for the pseudo-classes.

The selector for a pseudo-class is made up of the ordinary type selector followed by the name of the pseudo-class, which always begins with a colon (:). The most important pseudo-classes for links are as follows:

- a:link: Unvisited link
- a:visited: Visited link
- a:hover: Link when the mouse is over it
- a:active: Link at the point of being clicked

Love-hate refers to the first letter of each one—*L* for :link, *V* for :visited, and so on. It's not simply an easy way to remember the names of the pseudo-classes; it also reminds you of the order they must appear in your style sheet. The cascade depends on this order being preserved. So, if your links don't behave as expected, check the order of the pseudo-classes.

Before creating some link styles, there's just one more thing you need to know: how to control underlines.

Controlling underlines

The text-decoration property is the CSS way of adding or removing underlines to text. In fact, it can do more than just that. It accepts the following values:

- none: Remove underlines or cancel any inherited text-decoration rules.
- underline: Underline the text.
- overline: Add a line above the text.
- line-through: Add a line through the center of the text.
- blink: Blink the text on and off (browsers are not required to support this).
- inherit: This property is not inherited, so use this to apply the same value as the parent element.

Because underlined text has become so closely associated with links on the Web, text-decoration is used mainly in connection with links. Many designers remove the underline from unvisited and visited links but restore it as a visual clue when the mouse passes over the link. However, you can sandwich the link with lines above and below by using both underline and overline in the same style declaration like this:

text-decoration: underline overline;

Using text-decoration: line-through; has the effect of striking out text. It's the recommended replacement for the deprecated <s> and <strike> HTML tags.

Blinking text seemed cool when it was first introduced in the 1990s. Making text blink once or twice to draw attention to it is fine, but there's no way to control the duration of blinking with text-decoration. Use it only if you want to drive your visitors mad!

Now you know how to style links, let's put that knowledge to practical use by returning to journey.html.

Making the links harmonize with the page

The following exercise continues working with the same pages as in the previous exercises and demonstrates how to style the different states of links using pseudo-classes. Continue working with the same files as before. Alternatively, use journey_05.html and css/journey_05.css from the download files for this chapter.

1. How you style links is a matter of taste, but I prefer to remove the underline from links and make them stand out in a bold font and distinctive color. The color will change according to the state of the link, but the bold font will apply to all states. The underline will be restored when the mouse hovers over the link, but the basic state requires no underline. So, the basic rule needs to set font-weight and text-decoration. Add a new type selector for the <a> tag at the bottom of the style sheet like this:

```
a {
  font-weight: bold;
  text-decoration: none;
}
```

2. Next, set the colors for the unvisited and visited states. Add the following rules below the rule you created in step 1:

```
a:link {
  color: #B64926;
}
a:visited {
  color: #FFB03B;
}
```

This colors unvisited links a rusty brown that's typical of the Grand Canyon, while visited links use a lighter color closer to orange.

3. For the hover state, I'm going to use a darker brown and sandwich the link between lines above and below. Since the active state occurs only when the link is being clicked, I'll use the same style by grouping the a:hover and a:active selectors like this:

```
a:hover, a:active {
  color: #8E2800;
  text-decoration: underline overline;
}
```

4. That's all there is to it. Save the style sheet, and test the page in a browser. The links now harmonize with the other styles, and when you

mouse over one of the links, it should look like the first link in Figure 2-17.

You can check your code, if necessary, against journey_06.html and css/journey_06.css in the download files for this chapter.

Figure 2-17. You can use CSS to give a clear visual clue when a link is moused over.

Making full use of the cascade

Take a closer look at the code used in the previous exercise to style the links in journey.html. It consists of the following dozen or so lines:

```
a {
  font-weight: bold;
  text-decoration: none;
}
a:link {
  color: #B64926;
}
a:visited {
  color: #FFB03B;
}
a:hover, a:active {
  color: #8E2800;
  text-decoration: underline overline;
}
```

When I help people in online forums, I often come across style rules that are much longer than this. Yet they achieve nothing more than these few lines. Many beginners—and some who should know better—tend to put every property in each rule. So, for example, their a:link rule would look like this:

```
a:link {
    font-family: "Trebuchet MS", Arial, Helvetica, sans-serif;
    font-size: 14px;
    color: #B64926;
    font-weight: bold;
    text-decoration: none;
}
```

The same pattern is repeated in the a:visited, a:hover, and a:active rules. Not only is this totally unnecessary, it also makes style sheets more difficult to maintain. The code becomes longer, making it difficult to locate the properties you want to change. Say you decide to use a different set of fonts or change the size of the font, this duplication of style declarations means that you need to make the same change in every style block. There's a danger you'll miss one, resulting in your styles not being applied the way you intended.

The key to writing efficient, easy-to-maintain CSS is to create rules only for properties that change. Set the basic styles at the top of the HTML hierarchy, and let them trickle down. In the style sheet that you have built through the exercises in this chapter, the font-family for the links is set in the body rule; the font-size in the p, table rule; and the font-weight and text-decoration in the a rule. As a result, the only things that need to be set in the pseudo-class rules are the color changes and the text-decoration for a:hover, a:active.

Using the font shorthand property

CSS shorthand properties let you combine several style declarations into one. Often, this saves a lot of typing and the rules for creating the shorthand version are generally quite simple. I have left this section to the last because, in my opinion, the font shorthand property is the exception to the rule. It's difficult to use. If you're a beginner, I suggest that you skip this section and just note that it's here for future reference. There's nothing you can do with the font shorthand property that you can't do with the properties you have already learned about.

The font shorthand property combines the following properties:

- font-style (optional)
- font-variant (optional)

- font-weight (optional)
- font-size
- line-height (optional)
- font-family

What makes this shorthand property so difficult is that, not only are the first three items optional, they can be presented in any order. However, the remaining items must come in the prescribed order. If you declare line-height, it must be separated from font-size by a forward slash. Take, for example, the following style rule:

```
p {
  font-style: italic;
  font-weight: bold;
  font-size: 14px;
  line-height: 1.4;
  font-family:"Trebuchet MS", Arial, Helvetica, sans-serif;
}
```

You can convert that to shorthand like this:

```
p {
  font: bold italic 14px/1.4 "Trebuchet MS",Arial,Helvetica,sans-serif;
}
```

Notice that I reversed the order of font-style and font-weight, which is perfectly valid. The shorthand version is shorter and relatively easy to read. However, I find that the code completion features in most HTML editors make it much quicker to use the more explicit declarations.

A common mistake is to leave out everything except the font-family. The following example *will not work*:

```
/* BAD EXAMPLE */
p {
  font: "Trebuchet MS", Arial, Helvetica, sans-serif;
}
/* END BAD EXAMPLE */
```

Remember that font is not a synonym for font-family. It's an easy mistake to make, because of the association with the old <font> tag.

Chapter review

So, there you have it—a page that has been styled without using a single class (well, apart from the pseudo-classes). Everything has been done by using type selectors to change the default look of HTML elements. The only change to the HTML code has been the `<link>` tag to attach the style sheet.

This chapter has covered a lot of ground, and you might find it difficult to absorb everything at a single sitting, but the description of each text property has been designed for you to refer to later. It has also covered some of the most important features of CSS, such as how to apply the same rules to several elements by grouping selectors together, and how to target nested elements with descendant selectors. Finally, you were introduced to pseudo-classes, specialist types of selectors that style links depending on their interactive state. As you increase your knowledge of CSS, you'll come to realize that one of the most important skills lies in choosing the correct type of selector. The other important skill is to make use of the cascade, setting properties as far up the HTML hierarchy as possible, and letting them trickle down to child elements, changing only those properties that you want to be styled differently lower down in the chain.

The page looks a lot better, but if you have been working on a large monitor, you'll know that the text spreads right across the page. This not only looks bad, it makes the text almost impossible to read, because the human eye cannot scan text that spreads too far horizontally.

You'll start to put that right in the next chapter, which deals with setting widths and controlling margins. CSS gives you independent control over the margin on each side of every page element, allowing you to lay out your pages with considerable flexibility.

Chapter 3

How Can I Improve the Layout of My Text?

Take a look at any page. It doesn't matter whether it's on the Web, in a newspaper, or even in this book. Something that should become fairly obvious is that all pages are laid out as a grid. Headings and paragraphs form blocks that are always aligned in a regular pattern. The grid might not be visible on the page, but the underlying structure is there all the same.

That's why tables became so popular for page layout in the days before CSS could be relied upon. The problem with tables is that, to get the degree of control you want, it's frequently necessary to merge cells and nest tables inside other table cells. Designers who became experts at table layout created some brilliant designs, but the underlying code was usually very complex. Make a mistake, and everything falls down like a house of cards.

CSS takes a different approach, treating everything on the page as a box. The **box model**, as it's known, lies at the heart of CSS. The basic concept is simple enough: each box is surrounded by space (margins); you can also have space inside the box (padding); and you can put a border around the box, as well as give it a background. However, the implementation can be tricky to understand. So, instead of throwing everything at you in one go, I have decided to break everything down into more digestible chunks. The focus of this chapter is on adjusting the margins surrounding complete HTML elements, such as headings, paragraphs, and so on. Then in the next chapter, I'll show you how to flow text around images, before moving on to describe the remaining aspects of the box model in Chapters 5 and 6.

In this chapter, you'll learn about the following:

- Using <div> and <span> to group elements
- Zeroing the margins on the page body
- Inspecting margins with Firebug and other CSS developer tools

- Understanding how vertical margins overlap or collapse
- Centering page content
- Applying a different style to the first paragraph after a heading
- Organizing style sheets for easier maintenance

Before diving into the details of working with margins, it's important to understand how a browser treats HTML markup.

Sliding boxes and blocks

As a child, you probably played with one of those maddening yet fascinating sliding block puzzles. You know the type—all the blocks are interlocked inside a tray (see Figure 3-1). There's just one empty space, and you have to slide the blocks around until they're all in the right order. If you think of each of those blocks as an HTML tag and its contents, it gives you a pretty good idea of how CSS (and JavaScript) manipulate the elements on your page to produce the layout you want. An important difference is that CSS lets you change the size of the blocks, giving you much more freedom in your design.

Figure 3-1. Elements on a web page are blocks that can be moved around like a sliding puzzle.

HTML defines most tags as either block-level or inline. A **block-level element** begins on a new line, sits as far left as possible, and fills the available horizontal space. It also forces the next element onto a new line of its own. An **inline element**, on the other hand, doesn't begin on a new line or force what follows onto a new line. Inline elements sit alongside whatever precedes and follows them, and the line wraps automatically when there's no further space on the right. The <a>, <em>, and <strong> tags are examples of inline elements, as is the text content of a block-level element, such as a paragraph. The vertical distance between each line is determined by the line-height property, which was covered in the last chapter. However, this is overridden if any of the inline elements are too tall to fit.

Surprisingly, images are considered inline elements, which is why text is aligned to the bottom of an image when you first insert it into a web page, as shown in Figure 3-2. HTML uses the align, hspace, and vspace attributes to flow text around images, but as you'll learn in Chapter 4, CSS uses a combination of the float and margin properties to achieve the same effect with greater flexibility and elegance.

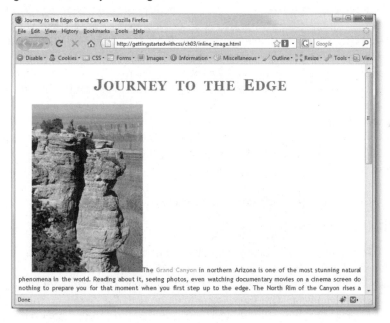

Figure 3-2. HTML treats images as inline elements, so you need special techniques to flow the text around the edge.

Even though inline elements don't force a new line before or after themselves, they still adhere to the CSS box model. That means you can apply margins, padding, and borders to any block-level or inline element, altering both the element's position and look.

ExplainED

The main exceptions to the block-level and inline classification are table rows and cells, which have rules of their own. Chapter 9 deals with these issues in detail. However, as you'll see later in this chapter, tables—as opposed to their constituent parts—are treated as block-level.

The sliding block puzzle analogy is useful because the tray and interlocking pieces constrain how you can move each block. What controls the position of HTML elements within a web page is known as the **flow** of the document. The flow of a web page is simply the order in which the HTML elements appear in the source code. Browsers lay out each element in turn, applying your styles or the default properties. This is why it's so important to understand what the underlying HTML of your pages looks like. The box model lets you change the space around elements, but where that space is inserted and how it affects the surrounding elements depends on where the element is within the flow of the document. Some CSS properties, such as float (the main subject of the next chapter), affect the normal flow, but how they do so depends on where the element lies within the page. So, if you're a designer who never looks at the underlying markup of your pages, now is the time to start changing your habits. Otherwise, you'll find your efforts with CSS just as frustrating as the child's puzzle.

Two HTML tags that are the friends of CSS: <div> and <span>

The HTML specification contains two elements, <div> and <span>, described as grouping elements. Unlike <p>, <h1>, or <blockquote>, they don't have a clearly defined role in the structure of the document. They're there for you to do whatever you want with them in conjunction with CSS. Although this sounds rather vague, the idea is that you can use them to group other elements together and style them as a single unit. A <div> creates a new block-level element that contains as many block-level and inline elements as you like, while a <span> can contain only inline elements.

The use of `<div>` and `<span>` will become clearer when you start using classes and ID selectors in the next chapter. However, the basic principle is that you can use `<div>` tags to divide your page into distinct sections, such as the page heading, sidebar, main content, and so on. You can use `<span>` tags to group several words to style them in a particular way. Later in this chapter, you'll use a `<div>` tag to group together all the page elements and center them in the browser window.

ExplainED

There's a common misconception that the `<div>` tag creates an absolutely positioned "layer" on the page. The misunderstanding arose from a well-intentioned but misguided attempt by Dreamweaver in the days before CSS had gained widespread acceptance to make page layout easier through the use of inline styles and absolute positioning. Dreamweaver has since changed the way it applies absolute positioning, a subject I have left until Chapter 10 because of its complexity. Nevertheless, the myth continues that a `<div>` has some sort of magical properties. It doesn't; a `<div>` simply groups other elements into a single block.

How CSS controls margins

Margins are horizontal and vertical space around an element. CSS lets you control the margin independently on each side, so there are four properties—one for each side—and a shorthand property, as listed in Table 3-1.

The first things to note about Table 3-1 are that margins are never inherited and the initial value of each property is 0. The lack of inheritance is a good thing, because it means you can control margins independently without worrying about affecting other elements on the page. However, the initial value is potentially confusing. Although the default CSS value is 0, all browsers add their own default margins to every page element. You can verify this by launching a browser and comparing journey_06.html and no_margins.html in the download files for this chapter. The first file is the page as it looked at the end of the exercises in the previous chapter. As you can see in Figure 2-17, there is space around each heading and paragraph. In no_margins.html, I have explicitly set the margins of each element to 0. The result is shown in Figure 3-3—everything is bunched up unnaturally.

Table 3-1. CSS margin properties

Property	Initial Value	Inherited	Description
margin	0	No	Shorthand property. Can take between one and four values, as described in "Using the margin shorthand property" later in this chapter.
margin-bottom	0	No	Sets the bottom margin. Adjacent vertical margins collapse, as described in the text.
margin-left	0	No	Sets the left margin. Horizontal margins never collapse.
margin-right	0	No	Sets the right margin. Horizontal margins never collapse.
margin-top	0	No	Sets the top margin. Adjacent vertical margins collapse, as described in the text.

AdvancED

*Some web developers use what is known as a **reset style sheet** to eliminate not only default margins but also any other inconsistencies introduced by different browser defaults. The idea is to create a level playing field, but it has the disadvantage that you need to set all the rules again explicitly. I find that many of the browser defaults have been created for a reason and prefer to adjust only those values where I want to achieve a special effect. To learn more about reset style sheets, see* http://meyerweb.com/eric/tools/css/reset/.

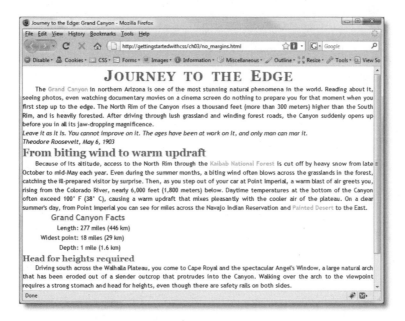

Figure 3-3. Without the default margins applied by browsers, page elements look crowded too close together.

The other point to note is that adjacent vertical margins collapse. This is an important concept to grasp.

Understanding how vertical margins collapse

Every element has a top margin and a bottom margin, even if it's set to zero. When block-level elements follow one another, adjacent vertical margins collapse or overlap each other. What this means is quite simple. In the download files for this chapter, you'll find a page called margin_collapse.html. In the external style sheet, I have set the margin-bottom property of all headings to 50px and the margin-top property of all paragraphs to 25px. Although this adds up to 75 pixels, the vertical margin between each heading and the following paragraph is only 50 pixels. The smaller margin collapses, leaving only the larger of the two. Figure 3-4 uses the Firebug extension for the Firefox browser to demonstrate the way the margins are handled. On the left of the figure, the 50-pixel bottom margin of the main heading is highlighted, with the 25-pixel top margin of the first paragraph highlighted on the right.

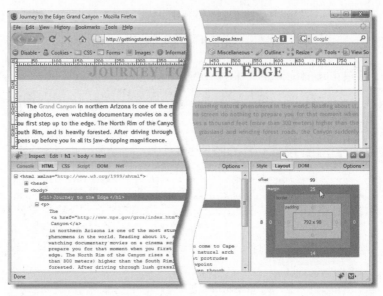

Figure 3-4. The Firebug extension for Firefox gives a visual demonstration of how adjacent vertical margins collapse.

LinkED

Firebug is one of the most useful tools in a web developer's armory. Not only is it an invaluable aid to inspecting and testing CSS, but it also helps with debugging JavaScript and network problems. If you don't have Firebug, get it from http://getfirebug.com/, *where you'll also find details of how to use it.*

Firebug works only in Firefox. You can also get a JavaScript file called Firebug Lite from http://getfirebug.com/lite.html *to simulate a subset of Firebug features in other browsers. However, as mentioned in Chapter 1, IE8, Safari 4, and Opera have built-in developer tools that perform similar tasks. Browsers differ in the way they render CSS, so you will probably need all of them at one time or another.*

Most of the time, it's only two adjacent elements that you need to think about. However, there are occasions when more than two margins come together and collapse. One such scenario is with an unordered or ordered list. Both the list and its <li> elements can have separate rules for margins. So, if you have a list followed by a paragraph, the vertical margin between the final list item and the paragraph is determined by whichever element has the biggest margin. To give a concrete example, if the list items have a bottom margin of 10px, the list has bottom margin of 5px, and the paragraph has a top margin of 0, the vertical margin between the list and the paragraph is *not* 5px, but 10px.

This behavior affects only top and bottom margins. Margins on the left or right *never* collapse.

Setting margin values

Margins can be set using either a length (see "Setting length with pixels, ems, and other units of measurement" in Chapter 2) or a percentage. For pages displayed in a browser, this means pixels, ems, or a percentage. Most of the time, you'll find pixels the easiest to work with. Percentages are computed in relation to the parent element. For example, if you have a paragraph inside a <div> that's 500px wide, and you set the paragraph's left margin to 10%, it creates a 50px margin. In other words, it offsets the paragraph 50 pixels from the left of the <div>.

Margin properties also accept the keyword auto, which tells the browser to calculate the margin automatically. However, for the browser to be able to do so, the element *must* have a width. The width can be set either in the HTML (for example, through the width attribute of an image or table) or in CSS. To set the width of an element in CSS, you simply use the width property, which accepts a length or a percentage.

ExplainED

Setting the width of an element in CSS is simple enough. However, the way that CSS handles both width and height is a little more complicated. I'll return to this subject in Chapter 6.

Because margins are not inherited, you can also use inherit as the value. However, it's more usual to set an explicit value.

You can set values for all four margins in a single declaration with the margin shorthand property. Before describing its use, let's get some practice working with the other margin properties.

Using margins to improve page layout

Most of the rest of this chapter is devoted to hands-on exercises with journey.html from the previous chapter. You can continue working with the same files as before. Alternatively, use as your starting point journey_06.html and css/journey_06.css in the download files for this chapter.

Removing the default margins from your pages

If you load journey.html into a browser, you'll notice that there's a slight gap between the left side of the browser window and the text (see Figure 2-17 in the previous chapter). Also, the main heading is set down from the top of the page. This is because browsers automatically add an 8-pixel margin all round the page. Most of the time, this default margin is unimportant, but it does make a difference if you want to use as part of your design images that go right to the edge of the page. So, it's a good idea to eliminate this default margin.

Removing the default page margin

This exercise removes the default page margin and uses Firebug to examine the effect of the default margins on the page's main heading. If you don't have Firebug, you can use the *Developer Tools* in IE8 or Opera 10, or the *Web Inspector* in Safari 4. However, I recommend that you download Firebug from the URL I gave earlier and install it in Firefox. In my experience, it's the most useful of the CSS analysis tools currently available.

1. Because you want the same value applied to all four margins, this is a good opportunity to use the margin shorthand property. Open the style sheet, and amend the body style rule like this:

```
body {
    background-color: #FFF;
    color: #000;
    font-family: "Trebuchet MS", Arial, Helvetica, sans-serif;
    margin: 0;
}
```

   The margin shorthand property is described in detail at the end of this chapter, but when used with a single value like this, it applies the same value to all sides. Since the value is 0, no unit of measurement is needed.

2. In practice, that's all you need. However, older versions of the Opera browser used padding on the <body> tag. So, it's common to set padding to zero too. Amend the style rule like this:

```
body {
  background-color: #FFF;
  color: #000;
  font-family: "Trebuchet MS", Arial, Helvetica, sans-serif;
  margin: 0;
  padding: 0;
}
```

3. Save the style sheet, and load journey.html into Firefox. It should look like Figure 3-5. The gap between the left and right sides of the paragraphs and the browser window has clearly gone, but the heading is still some way from the top.

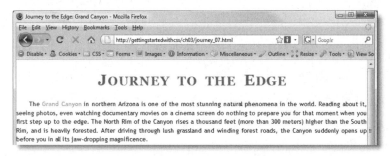

Figure 3-5. Removing the default page margin removes the gap on the left and right, but the heading is still offset from the top.

4. To find out why the gap at the top is so big, click the Firebug icon at the bottom right of the browser window. Then select the *HTML* and *Layout* tabs, as shown in Figure 3-6.

ExplainED

If you are using IE8, press F12 to launch the Developer Tools *panel, and select the* HTML *and* Layout *tabs the same as in Firebug.*

If you are using Safari 4, select Develop ➤ Show Web Inspector. *Then select the* Elements *tab, and expand the* Metrics *section on the right of the panel.*

If you are using Opera 10, select Tools ➤ Advanced ➤ Developer Tools. *Then select the* DOM *and* Layout *tabs.*

All work almost identically to Firebug and provide similar information.

Figure 3-6. Firebug lets you examine the size of the default margins around the <h1> tag.

5. Expand the HTML tree in the *HTML* tab, and select the <h1> tag. The *Layout* tab displays a graphical representation of the box model of the selected element as a series of nested boxes. The outmost box represents the margins on each side, with numbers indicating the size of the margin in pixels. As you might be able to see in Figure 3-6, there's a 23-pixel margin on both the top and bottom of the heading. The left and right margins are zero.

ExplainED

The Developer Tools *panel in IE8 displays the top and bottom margins as* 0.67em. *This is nowhere near as helpful as Firebug, the Safari 4* Web Inspector, *or the Opera 10* Developer Tools *which all display the value in pixels.*

6. Firebug and the analysis tools in IE8 and Safari 4 (but not Opera 10) let you temporarily disable style rules to see how they affect the layout. Make sure the <h1> tag is still selected in the *HTML* or *Elements* tab. This ensures that the appropriate style block is displayed. In Firebug or the IE8 *Developer Tools* panel, select the *Style* tab (to the left of *Layout*).

    If you're using the Safari 4 *Web Inspector* panel, expand the *Styles* section on the right, and then expand the top section labeled *h1*.

7. In Firebug, position your mouse pointer to the left of the font-size declaration, and click once. This inserts a red circle with an oblique bar alongside the rule, and grays out the property and its value, as

shown in Figure 3-7. This indicates that it has been temporarily disabled.

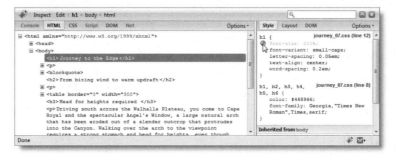

Figure 3-7. The Style tab in Firebug lets you disable style rules temporarily.

In the IE8 *Developer Tools* panel, you disable style rules temporarily by deselecting the check box to the left of the property name.

The Safari 4 Web Inspector panel works slightly differently. Check boxes appear to the right of style declarations only when your cursor is over the relevant section on the right of the panel (see Figure 3-8). When the check boxes appear, deselect the one alongside the rule(s) you want to disable temporarily.

AdvancED

The *Safari 4* Web Inspector *panel also reveals the browser's default styles. The text might be too small to read in Figure 3-8, but the final* h1 *section in the* Styles *section on the right is labeled* user agent stylesheet. *The* font-size *property is struck out in this section because its value is overridden by the* h1 *type selector in* journey.css.

If you ever want to find out the default styles for an element, fire up the Web Inspector *panel in Safari 4. Of course, it won't tell you the default styles for other browsers, but knowing what one browser does by default often provides the information you need.*

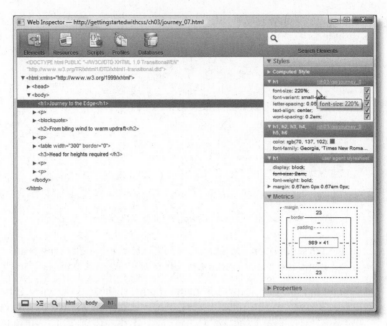

Figure 3-8. In the Safari 4 Web Inspector panel, check boxes to disable styles temporarily appear when you mouse over the relevant section.

8. Switch back to the *Layout* tab or *Metrics* section. You should see that the top and bottom margins are now 21 pixels. (The IE8 *Developer Tools* panel still displays *0.67em*, but you can see that the *Offset* has changed from 24 to 21 pixels.) In other words, the default margins the browser has applied to the <h1> element are directly proportional to the size of the font.

9. Reenable the `font-size` rule by clicking the icon in Firebug or reselecting the check box in the other analysis tools.

10. Close your CSS analysis tool, and return to the style sheet in your editing program. Amend the style block that applies to all headings by adding a 10-pixel top and bottom margin like this:

```
h1, h2, h3, h4, h5, h6 {
  color: #468966;
  font-family: Georgia, "Times New Roman", Times, serif;
  margin-top: 10px;
  margin-bottom: 10px;
}
```

11. Save the style sheet, and test journey.html again. The top-level heading should now be closer to the top of the page, and the gap between the heading and first paragraph should also have closed up a little.

You can check your code, if necessary, against journey_07.html and css/journey_07.css in the download files for this chapter.

ExplainED

To simplify the instructions in future exercises, I will give instructions for only one of the CSS analysis tools. They all work in a very similar way, so once you have become accustomed to using one, you should find no difficult working with the others.

Don't use an onscreen pixel ruler to measure the vertical difference between the bottom of the heading and the top of the first paragraph. As I explained in Chapter 2, the size of a font includes whitespace above and below the characters. If it didn't, lines of text would be too close together to read. When applying top and bottom margins to blocks of text, there's always a small amount of extra whitespace. However, there's no extra whitespace around nontext items, such as images.

Centering page content

As you learned in the previous chapter, centering text involves using the text-align property and setting its value to center. However, with block-level elements, you use the left and right margins to control their horizontal position. If you set both margins to the same value, the object is centered. At first glance, this might seem like a lot more work than using HTML <center> tags or align="center". You might need to center many items, all of different widths. No problem—CSS does it all for you.

As long as the element you want to center has a declared width, you simply set the values of margin-left and margin-right to auto. Mission accomplished.

You can also use this technique to center the content of your page. Simply wrap everything inside the <body> tags in a <div>, and set its left and right margins.

Let's put the theory into practice.

Using margins to center page content

This exercise continues from the previous one, showing how to center the table, the block quotation, and the page itself using both automatic and specific left and right margins. Continue working with the same files as before. Alternatively, use journey_07.html and css/journey_07.css from the download files for this chapter.

1. Technically speaking, tables aren't block-level elements (they're table elements—surprise, surprise), but they are treated as such when applying margins to their outer edges. The table in journey.html has a width of 300 (pixels) declared in its opening HTML tag. Because it has a declared width, you can use auto to calculate the left and right margins automatically. Create the following new style block at the bottom of journey.css:

```
table {
  margin-left: auto;
  margin-right: auto;
}
```

That's all there is to it—the table is now centered.

2. Let's do the same for the Roosevelt quotation. Add the following style block at the foot of the style sheet:

```
blockquote {
  margin-left: auto;
  margin-right: auto;
}
```

3. Save the style sheet, and test journey.html in a browser. It should look like Figure 3-9. The table is centered, but the Roosevelt quote is still at the left side of the browser window.

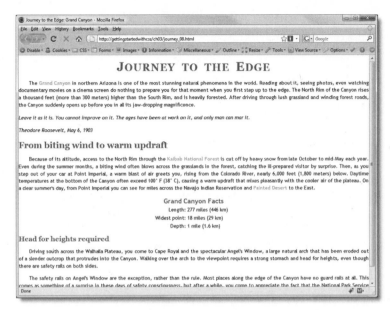

Figure 3-9. Setting the left and right margins to auto works only if the element has a declared width.

I did that deliberately to remind you that an element *must* have a declared width for the browser to be able to calculate the left and right margins automatically. Forgetting the width is a common mistake that even experienced designers occasionally make.

4. Return to the style sheet, and add a width to the blockquote style rule like this:

```
blockquote {
  margin-left: auto;
  margin-right: auto;
  width: 38%;
}
```

I have set the width property to 38%. When you use a percentage for width, CSS calculates it relative to the parent element. The <blockquote> is inside the <body> element, so the value is calculated as 38% of the <body>—in other words, 38% of the full page.

5. Save the style sheet, and test the page again. The quote should now be centered as shown in Figure 3-10.

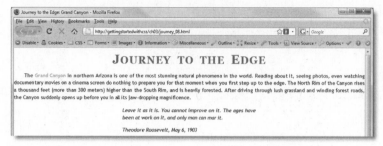

Figure 3-10. The quote is centered now it has a declared width.

6. The problem with the page is that the text still stretches right across the browser window. One way you could fix that is to give the paragraphs a width and center them, but that leaves the subheadings, which you probably don't want centered. The solution is to use a `<div>` to group together all the elements inside the `<body>`, and use its margins to center the page content.

    Dive into the HTML code of `journey.html`, and add an opening `<div>` tag immediately after the opening `<body>` tag like this:

```
<body>
<div>
  <h1>Journey to the Edge</h1>
```

7. Put the closing `</div>` tag immediately before the closing `</body>` tag like this:

```
. . . responsible for their own safety.</p>
</div>
</body>
```

8. On its own, the `<div>` makes no difference to the way the page looks in the browser. You need to create a style rule for it. Add the following to the bottom of the style sheet:

```
div {
  margin-left: 15%;
  margin-right: 15%;
}
```

9. Save the style sheet, and test `journey.html` in a browser. The page content should be nicely centered. Change the size of the browser window. The page content remains centered, but the width changes in relation to the size of the browser, as shown in Figure 3-11.

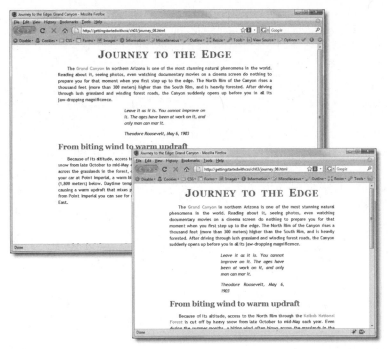

Figure 3-11. Setting the left and right margins to a percentage creates a liquid layout that resizes with the browser window.

Although the `<div>` doesn't have a declared width, the browser calculates it from the left and right margins. Controlling the width of content like this is known as a **liquid layout**.

Notice, too, how the `<blockquote>` expands and contracts as you change the size of the window. Its parent element is no longer the `<body>`, but the `<div>`. So, it takes its width as a proportion of the horizontal space occupied by the `<div>`.

10. Liquid layouts were popular in the days of smaller monitors, but the page still looks unacceptable in a fully expanded browser on a 24-inch monitor. It's better to give the `<div>` a fixed width. Amend its style rule like this:

```
div {
  width: 720px;
  margin-left: auto;
  margin-right: auto;
}
```

This sets the width property to 720px, which fits comfortably into a browser on an 800 × 600 resolution monitor, leaving a small margin on both sides, and is centered on a larger resolution monitor, as shown in Figure 3-12.

Figure 3-12. A fixed-width layout keeps lines of text the same length regardless of the size of the browser window.

11. Using div as a type selector works here because there's only one <div> on the page, but the same styles would apply to any other <div> tags that you might want to add. Most of the time when using <div> tags to group elements together, you need to give each <div> a unique identity with the id attribute, and create a style rule that applies only to that <div>.

Edit the opening `<div>` tag to give it an ID like this:

```
<div id="wrapper">
```

12. Change the `div` selector of the style rule to `#wrapper` like this:

```
#wrapper {
    width: 720px;
    margin-left: auto;
    margin-right: auto;
}
```

To style an element that has an ID, prefix the ID with the hash sign (#), and use it as the selector. I'll come back to ID selectors and their use in detail in Chapter 4.

13. Save both pages, and test `journey.html` again. It should look exactly the same as before.

You can check your code against `journey_08.html` and `css/journey_08.css` in the download files for this chapter.

Using margin-left to indent text

In addition to centering block-level elements and tables, the horizontal margins can be used to indent paragraphs or position elements just where you want them to be in relation to their surroundings. In the past, the `<blockquote>` tag was frequently used to indent text. Apart from using a tag for a purpose that was never intended, the big limitation of `<blockquote>` is that it created a 40-pixel margin on both sides of the text. If you nested `<blockquote>` tags, the text in the center steadily became narrower and narrower. Using CSS margins eliminates that problem, because you can use just `margin-left` and set its value to the exact amount you want.

It's also a good idea to set your own top and bottom margins for paragraphs to give you better control over the way they stack on top of each other. Opinions vary on the best way to do this, but my preference is to set `margin-top` to 0, and then choose a value for `margin-bottom` that suits the overall look of the page.

So, let's continue our practical exploration of margins with `journey.html`.

Indenting paragraphs

This exercise shows how to adjust the margins around paragraphs to indent them and control the amount of whitespace between consecutive paragraphs. You'll also learn how to style the first paragraph after a heading differently.

Continue working with the files from the previous exercise. Alternatively, use as your starting point journey_08.html and css/journey_08.css from the download files for this chapter.

1. Let's break free of the 40-pixel straightjacket imposed by using `<blockquote>` for indented text. Set the value of margin-left for paragraphs to 45px like this:

```
p {
  text-align: justify;
  text-indent: 30px;
  line-height: 1.4;
  margin-left: 45px;
}
```

2. Save the style sheet, and test journey.html in a browser. It should look like Figure 3-13.

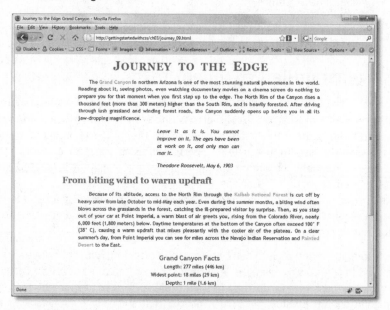

Figure 3-13. Indenting the paragraphs has also affected the text in the `<blockquote>`.

As you can see from the position of the paragraphs in relation to the subheadings, the paragraphs are now indented 45 pixels from the left. The problem is that the same rule has been applied to the paragraphs inside the `<blockquote>` element. That's one thing that needs to be fixed.

Another aesthetic problem is that the indentation of the first line of each paragraph after a heading doesn't look quite right. A common typographical convention is to indent the first line only of subsequent paragraphs. So that's another issue that needs to be fixed.

3. Fixing the first item is easy. Reset the paragraphs' left margin in the blockquote p rule like this:

```
blockquote p {
  font-style: italic;
  text-indent: 0;
  white-space: pre-line;
  margin-left: 0;
}
```

4. Fixing the second item is also easy. There are two ways to do it. The one that's most likely to be chosen by people with previous experience of CSS is a class, but I don't want to do it that way. It's not that I'm class prejudiced—far from it. Classes are very useful, and you'll start using them in the next chapter. However, to use a class, you need to add the class attribute to every HTML element that you apply it to. Never add extra code to the HTML, if you can avoid it.

What I want to do is style every paragraph that immediately follows a heading. CSS has the perfect selector for just such a situation. It has a rather grand sounding name: **adjacent sibling selector**, but it's just a humble plus (+) sign. This is how you use it:

- Both elements must have the same parent.
- Separate the first element from the following one with a plus sign.

So, to style the first paragraph after an <h1> heading, the selector becomes h1 + p. To style the first paragraph after an <h2> heading, you use h2 + p. The current page has paragraphs that you want to style differently when they come immediately after <h1>, <h2>, and <h3> headings. So, this is the style rule that you need to create:

```
h1 + p, h2 + p, h3 + p {
  text-indent: 0;
}
```

Remember that text-indent, which was covered in Chapter 2, indents only the first line in a block of text. So, this rule removes only the first line indent. It doesn't affect the 45-pixel indent created in step 1.

ExplainED

The adjacent sibling selector is not supported by IE6. I don't think it matters a great deal if visitors using this outdated browser see indented text on the first line of each paragraph. However, if you still have a lot of visitors using IE6, you can't use the adjacent sibling selector for styles that have a big impact on your design. For such cases, you will probably need to use a class or an ID selector, both of which are described in detail in the next chapter.

In CSS3, the adjacent sibling selector has been renamed adjacent sibling combinator, so you might see it called that in some places. The only difference is in the name.

5. Save the style sheet, and test journey.html again. As shown in Figure 3-14, the first line of the first paragraph after each heading is no longer indented, but the second paragraph after the <h3> heading is not affected.

Head for heights required

Driving south across the Walhalla Plateau, you come to Cape Royal and the spectacular Angel's Window, a large natural arch that has been eroded out of a slender outcrop that protrudes into the Canyon. Walking over the arch to the viewpoint requires a strong stomach and head for heights, even though there are safety rails on both sides.

  The safety rails on Angel's Window are the exception, rather than the rule. Most places along the edge of the Canyon have no guard rails at all. This comes as something of a surprise in these days of safety consciousness, but after a while, you come to appreciate the fact that the National Park Service has left the Grand Canyon unspoiled as much as possible. Footpaths are clearly marked and well-made. Visitors are left responsible for their own safety.

Figure 3-14 The adjacent sibling selector makes it possible to style the first paragraph after a heading differently.

6. All that remains to fix the look of the paragraphs is to change the top and bottom margins to gain greater control over the way they stack on top of each other. Since subsequent paragraphs have the first line indented, the space between paragraphs looks too big. By default, browsers leave a space equivalent to the height of one line of text—in other words, one em. Roughly half that amount would be better, so amend the paragraph rule like this:

```
p {
  text-align: justify;
  text-indent: 30px;
```

```
line-height: 1.4;
margin-left: 45px;
margin-top: 0;
margin-bottom: 0.4em;
}
```

7. Save the style sheet, and test `journey.html` again. The text should now look much more elegantly laid out. Of course, you might not agree with me. Experiment with your own margin values until you get the page looking the way you think looks best.

    If you want to compare your code with mine, check your pages against `journey_09.html` and `css/journey_09.css` in the download files for this chapter.

Using negative margins

CSS permits the use of negative values for margins. This means that you can reduce the gap between elements, or move an element further to the left—the opposite of indenting. When using negative margins, you need to be careful, because doing so could result in elements overlapping as in `negative_overlap.html` in the download files for this chapter. The top margin of the table has been set to -55px. As Figure 3-15 shows, the table has moved up to overlap the preceding paragraph.

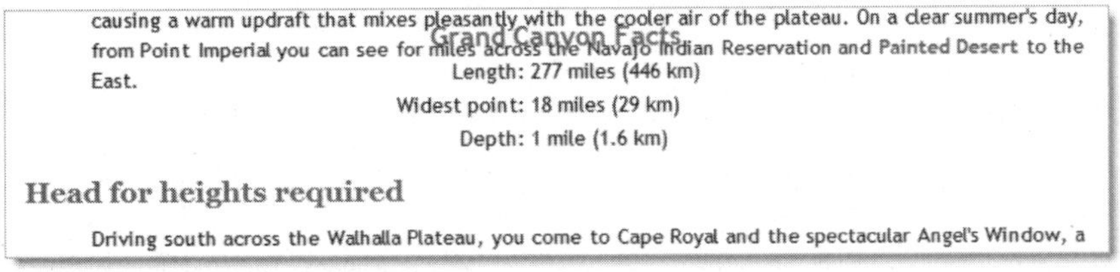

causing a warm updraft that mixes pleasantly with the cooler air of the plateau. On a clear summer's day, from Point Imperial you can see for miles across the Navajo Indian Reservation and Painted Desert to the East.

Grand Canyon Facts

Length: 277 miles (446 km)

Widest point: 18 miles (29 km)

Depth: 1 mile (1.6 km)

Head for heights required

Driving south across the Walhalla Plateau, you come to Cape Royal and the spectacular Angel's Window, a

Figure 3-15. Negative margins can cause elements to overlap.

ExplainED

In Firefox 3.0 and 3.5, applying the negative top margin to the table has an unexpected side-effect. It moves the table, but not the caption, even though the caption is an integral part of the table. Other modern browsers treat the caption correctly. Always test your designs in a range of browsers.

Of course, getting elements to overlap might be exactly what you want. If so, go for it. However, the normal way to overlap elements is to use CSS positioning, a more advanced subject that I have left until Chapter 10.

Another common use for negative margins is to move items off the screen. This can be useful when you want to hide from visual browsers an accessibility feature designed for screen readers for the visually disabled. For example, it's common to add a link to the page's main content just before a navigation menu. This enables the user of a screen reader to skip the navigation, rather than having to listen to the menu repeated ad nauseam on each page. It's a vital feature for disabled visitors to a site, but you don't want it displayed to everyone else. Giving the link a negative left margin of several thousand pixels banishes it out of sight, but it's still recognized by the screen reader. However, again you need to be careful about how this affects the rest of your layout. In hidden_heading.html, I have given the top heading a margin-left value of -9000px. This hides the heading, but the rest of the text doesn't move up to take its place, as you can see in Figure 3-16.

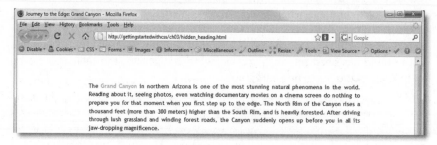

Figure 3-16. The heading has been moved offscreen with a negative margin, but it still occupies the vertical space.

This is because the default behavior of block-level elements is to occupy all available horizontal space and force the next element onto a new line. You'll learn how to change this default behavior in the next chapter by using the float property. However, one way to move the text up to the top of the page is to give the h1 style rule a negative top margin of approximately 45 pixels.

ExplainED

If you remove the comments from the margin-top *declaration in the* h1 *style rule in* hidden_heading.css, *the text will move to the top of the page. Note that this is an occasion where the position of the style rule plays a crucial role. The preceding* h1, h2, h3, h4, h5, h6 *style rule sets* margin-top *to* 10px *for all headings. Because the* h1 *rule comes lower in the cascade, it overrides the value for* margin-top *and resets it to* -45px *for the* <h1> *tag only. If the order of the style blocks is reversed, the negative value for the* <h1> *tag is overridden.*

Also note that when setting margin-left *to* -9000px, *there is no comma in the number. You cannot use the thousands separator with numbers in CSS.*

In Chapter 11, I demonstrate an alternative way of hiding a "skip to navigation" link for screen readers that avoids the problem demonstrated in Figure 3-16.

Applying margins to inline elements

Throughout this chapter, I have concentrated on working with block-level elements, such as paragraphs and headings, because that's where margins play the most important role in page layout. However, inline elements can also have margins, but they work slightly differently from how you might expect. Figure 3-17 shows the middle section of inline_margins.html from the download files for this chapter. The style rules for the page have applied a 40-pixel margin to all sides of the links. As you can see, the margin has been applied to the left and right sides of each link, but this has no effect on the paragraph's line-height property.

From biting wind to warm updraft

Because of its altitude, access to the North Rim through the   Kaibab National Forest   is cut off by heavy snow from late October to mid-May each year. Even during the summer months, a biting wind often blows across the grasslands in the forest, catching the ill-prepared visitor by surprise. Then, as you step out of your car at Point Imperial, a warm blast of air greets you, rising from the Colorado River, nearly 6,000 feet (1,800 meters) below. Daytime temperatures at the bottom of the Canyon often exceed 100° F (38° C), causing a warm updraft that mixes pleasantly with the cooler air of the plateau. On a clear summer's day, from Point Imperial you can see for miles across the Navajo Indian Reservation and   Painted Desert   to the East.

Figure 3-17. Vertical margins on inline text elements are ignored.

Figure 3-18 shows the margins being inspected in Firebug. You can see that the 40-pixel margin has actually been applied to each side of the link, but the vertical margins are ignored by the browser. This is not a bug, but the expected behavior.

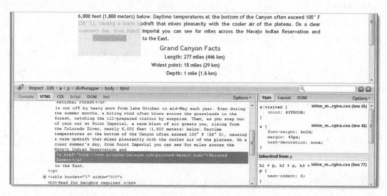

Figure 3-18. Firebug confirms that the vertical margins have been applied to the link.

It's a different story with images, though. Images are also inline elements, but top and bottom margins do affect the layout of surrounding elements, as you'll see in the next chapter.

AdvancED

Trying to remember all the rules and exceptions can be confusing. Keep it simple, and just remember that top and bottom margins have no effect on inline text.

Keeping your style sheet manageable

In the exercises up to now, I have told you to add new style blocks at the bottom of the style sheet. In some respects, it's a good strategy, because each new style rule that you create comes further down the cascade. As a result, the new rule takes precedence in the event of a conflict. However, as you continue to add rules, there comes a time when chaos threatens to take over. The style sheet that you have been working on in the exercises is nearly 80 lines long—more if you have been adding a space between each style block. Style sheets often come to several hundred lines. On a really sophisticated site, there might be considerably more. So, you need to develop a strategy to organize your style rules. Otherwise, maintenance becomes a nightmare.

One common technique is to put all rules relating to typography together, followed by separate sections that represent different parts of the layout. If some rules are used only in one part of the site, you might create a separate style sheet and link it only to those pages that actually need it.

Another strategy for keeping style sheets manageable is to use shorthand properties wherever possible. In the previous chapter, I warned you that the font shorthand property is difficult to use; but once you understand the margin shorthand property, you'll find it easy to read—and much quicker to type.

Before reorganizing the style sheet, let's see how the margin shorthand property works.

Using the margin shorthand property

As Table 3-1 says, the margin shorthand property takes between one and four values. This is how it works:

- **One value:** Applies equally to all four sides.
- **Two values:** The first one applies to the top and bottom, and the second one to the left and right.
- **Three values:** The first one applies to the top, the second one to the left and right, and the third one to the bottom.
- **Four values:** The values are applied in clockwise order starting from the top.

Confused? Don't be. Take my advice, and forget about using three values. Concentrate on one, two, and four. The way to remember the rest is simple:

- Always start at the top.
- Go clockwise.

If there's only one value, it's easy—it applies to the top and all other sides.

If there are two values, the first one applies to the top. Then, going clockwise, the next one applies to the right side. The same two values are repeated in the same order as you continue going round the clock. So, the first one is applied to the bottom, and the second one to the right.

If there are four values, you start at the top, and go clockwise to the right, bottom, and left. Some designers use the mnemonic TRouBLe to remember this, but I think that clockwise is much simpler.

So, let's tidy up the style sheet for journey.html by converting the existing single-side properties.

Converting margin properties to shorthand

Continue using the same files as in the preceding exercise. Alternatively, use journey_09.html and css/journey_09.css in the download files for this chapter.

1. The first style block, body, already uses the margin shorthand property, so there's nothing to do there. The next style rule applies to all headings and looks like this:

```
h1, h2, h3, h4, h5, h6 {
  color: #468966;
  font-family: Georgia, "Times New Roman", Times, serif;
  margin-top: 10px;
  margin-bottom: 10px;
}
```

This applies a 10-pixel margin to both the top and bottom of each heading. The shorthand version must always provide a value for each side, so you need a value for left and right. But since you don't want a horizontal margin, set left and right to 0. Top and bottom are the same, as are left and right, so you need just two values.

2. Amend the rule like this:

```
h1, h2, h3, h4, h5, h6 {
  color: #468966;
  font-family: Georgia, "Times New Roman", Times, serif;
  margin: 10px 0;
}
```

3. The next style block to use a margin property is this:

```
blockquote p {
  font-style: italic;
  text-indent :0;
  white-space: pre-line;
  margin-left: 0;
}
```

This sets only the left margin. Don't even think about how you deal with the other three sides. This is a case where you're interested only in the one margin, because it overrides the general rule for paragraphs. Using the margin-left property is exactly what you want. Leave it alone.

114

4. The next rule is, in fact, the general rule for paragraphs, which looks like this:

```
p {
  text-align: justify;
  text-indent: 30px;
  line-height: 1.4;
  margin-left: 45px;
  margin-top: 0;
  margin-bottom :0.4em;
}
```

This sets specific values for all margins, except `margin-right`. When you don't know what value to apply, you can use the keyword `auto`. However, there is no right margin on the paragraphs, so `0` is the correct value. Change the rule like this:

```
p {
  text-align: justify;
  text-indent: 30px;
  line-height: 1.4;
  margin: 0 0 0.4em 45px;
}
```

Going clockwise, this sets the top and right margins to `0`, the bottom margin to `0.4em`, and the left margin to `45px`. If you replace the second value with `auto`, the result is the same.

5. The last three style blocks that set margins are all used to center elements by setting the left and right margins to `auto`.

```
table {
  margin-left:auto;
  margin-right:auto;
}
blockquote {
  margin-left:auto;
  margin-right:auto;
  width:38%;
}
#wrapper {
  width:720px;
  margin-left:auto;
  margin-right:auto;
}
```

In the case of the wrapper `<div>`, you definitely want the top and bottom margins to be `0`, but rather than agonizing over what to use for the table and blockquote rules, set them to `0`, too. If you don't like the resulting vertical space between them and the adjacent elements, you can adjust it later. Amend the three rules like this:

```
table {
  margin: 0 auto;
}
blockquote {
  margin: 0 auto;
  width:38%;
}
#wrapper {
  width:720px;
  margin: 0 auto;
}
```

6. Save the style sheet, and test journey.html in a browser. There is a tiny reduction in the vertical space around the Roosevelt quote, but everything else remains the same. This is the advantage of collapsing vertical margins. Even though you didn't check the top and bottom margins on the <table> and <blockquote> elements, the vertical margins of the adjacent elements filled in the gap. As long as the adjacent elements have a suitable margin, the layout is often not disturbed.

You can check your code, if necessary, against journey_10.html and css/journey_10.css in the download files for this chapter.

AdvancED

Using shorthand properties reduces the amount of code in your style sheets. So, in theory at least, websites that use CSS shorthand load more quickly than ones that use the individual properties. In practice, the difference is likely to be far too short to notice. Use the coding style that makes you feel comfortable. If you have difficulty remembering the rules for shorthand properties, use the individual properties until you gain more experience with CSS.

Organizing your style rules for easier maintenance

Designers adopt different strategies for organizing their style sheets. There's no "right way" to do it. However, there is a wrong way. . .

When reordering style blocks, you must remember the effect of the cascade. Some people simply put all their style rules in alphabetical order, and then wonder why their pages suddenly don't work the way they intended. In Chapter 2, I warned you about the need for the pseudo-classes for links to be in the order :link, :visited, :hover, :active (LoVe-HAte). Put them in alphabetical order, and your links will always look as though they have been visited. They won't change even when the mouse is hovered over them.

When reordering style blocks, you can go directly into the code to cut and paste. Alternatively, some editing programs let you drag and drop your rules. In Dreamweaver CS3 or above, open the *CSS Styles* panel and select *All* mode. In Expression Web, use the *Manage Styles* task pane. In both programs, select the style block that you want to move, and hold down the left mouse button. As you drag the style block, a line appears, indicating where the rule will be moved to. When you're in the right position, release the mouse button to move the rule (see Figure 3-19).

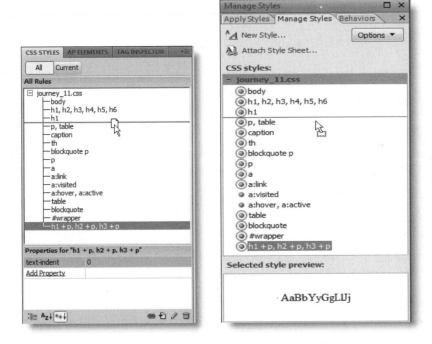

Figure 3-19. Both Dreamweaver (left) and Expression Web (right) let you reorganize your styles through drag and drop.

117

Rather than go through the style sheet step by step, I'll leave you to decide how to reorganize the style rules for easier maintenance. The following listing shows how I reorganized journey.css (it's css/journey_11.css in the download files for this chapter). Notice how I have added CSS comments to identify different sections of the style sheet indicating what the rules are for.

```css
/* Page infrastructure */
body {
  background-color:  #FFF;
  color:  #000;
  font-family:  "Trebuchet MS", Arial, Helvetica, sans-serif;
  margin: 0;
  padding: 0;
}
#wrapper {
  width: 720px;
  margin: 0 auto;
}
/* Headings */
h1, h2, h3, h4, h5, h6 {
  color: #468966;
  font-family: Georgia, "Times New Roman", Times, serif;
  margin: 10px 0;
}
h1 {
  font-size: 220%;
  font-variant: small-caps;
  text-align: center;
  word-spacing: 0.2em;
  letter-spacing: 0.05em;
}
h1 + p, h2 + p, h3 + p {
  text-indent: 0;
}
/* Main text */
p, table {
  font-size: 14px;
}
p {
  text-align: justify;
  text-indent: 30px;
  line-height: 1.4;
  margin: 0 0 0.4em 45px;
}
a {
  font-weight: bold;
  text-decoration: none;
}
a:link {
  color: #B64926;
}
```

```
a:visited {
  color: #FFB03B;
}
a:hover, a:active {
  color: #8E2800;
  text-decoration: underline overline;
}
blockquote {
  margin: 0 auto;
  width: 38%;
}
blockquote p {
  font-style: italic;
  text-indent: 0;
  white-space: pre-line;
  margin-left: 0;
}
table {
  margin: 0 auto;
}
caption {
  font-size: 18px;
  color: #468966;
  font-weight: bold;
  text-transform: capitalize;
}
th {
  font-weight: normal;
  text-align: right;
}
```

At the moment, I have put the rules for the `<blockquote>` and `<table>` elements in the "Main text" section. If I start adding more rules for these elements, I will probably create new sections for them. Most editing programs highlight comments in a different color from the rest of the code, so adding them makes it easier to find the section you're looking for when you come back to a style sheet in several months' time.

Chapter review

This chapter has introduced you to margins, the first part of the CSS box model that governs the layout of elements on a web page. Margins create the vertical and horizontal space around an element. Since all block-level elements and tables have a `margin` property that can be applied independently to each side, you can do a great deal to influence the layout of your pages. The main thing to remember is that vertical margins of adjacent elements collapse, whereas horizontal margins are always preserved. Inline elements can also have margins, but top and bottom margins around inline text are ignored.

Negative margins are permitted. This can be useful for adjusting the position of an element, or even removing it completely from the visual display. Negative margins can be used in imaginative ways to lay out pages, as you'll see in Chapter 11.

This chapter showed you how to use Firebug and other CSS analysis tools to examine margins and how they overlap. Once you start pushing elements around by adjusting their margins, they are likely to affect the position of other elements. So, it's always a good idea to test your styles at frequent intervals during development. If you change a rule or value and see that it's had an unexpected effect on your design, you know immediately what the culprit is.

You also learned how to use the adjacent sibling selector (a + sign between two selectors) to target the first paragraph after a heading. This can be used with any two elements, where you want to treat the second element a special way when it immediately follows the first one. Finally, the chapter discussed the need to organize style sheets in a logical way for ease of maintenance. When reordering style rules, remember to preserve the cascade by putting rules that override others lower down in the style sheet.

In the next chapter, you'll continue working with margins as you explore the float property, which changes the behavior of images and block-level elements, allowing you to move them to the left or right and position other elements alongside. I'll also introduce the concept of using classes and ID selectors to apply styles.

Chapter 4

How Can I Flow Text Around Images?

It's time to bring the sample page alive with some images. The reason I have not used images so far is because HTML treats images as inline elements. As you saw in the previous chapter, inserting an image in a block of text forces the text to align with the bottom of the image. In order to get the text to flow around the image, you need to use the CSS property called float. In principle, using float is very simple, and it can be used on any HTML element, not just images. You float the element to the left or right, and everything moves up to fill the vacated space alongside, as illustrated in Figure 4-1.

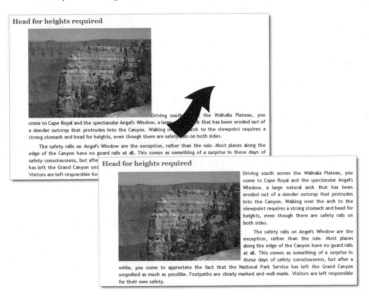

Figure 4-1. The CSS float property is used, among other things, to wrap text around images.

This chapter will have you flowing text around images in next to no time. That's the good news. . .

As so often in life, things aren't always as simple as they first seem. Although it's the text that has floated up to fill the space alongside the image, you apply the float property to the image, and not the text. What happens is that the floated object—in this case, the image—floats to one side to make room for whatever follows. That's how the text automatically resumes its normal width when it comes to the bottom of the image. Floating elements can have unexpected consequences for the unwary. So, after showing you the basic use of the float property, I'll go deeper into the effect that it has on the flow of the document. Don't let that put you off. Most of the time, using float is very easy.

Because you frequently need to float more than one element, now is the time for me to start using CSS classes. A class is simply a different type of CSS selector. The main difference is that you need to add the class attribute to the opening tag of the HTML element(s) that you want to use the styles defined in the class. I'll also show you how to use an ID selector to style unique elements in a page.

In this chapter, you'll learn how to do the following:

- Create a class and apply it to an HTML element.
- Float images to the left and right, and flow text around them.
- Prevent headings and other elements from moving up alongside images.
- Correct problems caused by floating elements.
- Create ID selectors to style unique elements.
- Add a caption to a floated image.

As you'll see in later chapters, you can use float with many different parts of a web page, but I'm going to concentrate on images in this chapter, because they demonstrate just about everything that you need to know about this property. Because floating images is such a common task, it makes sense to create two basic classes in your style sheet to move images to the left and right. Before doing that, I need to explain what classes are and how you create them.

CSS classes 101

Classes tend to be one of the first things that most people learn about CSS. As a result, they start using them indiscriminately, and end up with complex code that's difficult to maintain. Wherever possible, you should use type selectors to create your basic styles. Classes come into their own when you want to apply a different style or set of styles to several elements on a page. Say, for example, you have defined a basic style for all paragraphs using the p type selector, but you want certain paragraphs to use a different font. A class selector lets you define that different style and then apply it to the selected paragraphs. If that sounds rather vague, all should become clear with a practical example.

Creating and applying CSS classes

A CSS class looks the same as all the style rules you have created so far. The only difference is the selector. Instead of using the name of an HTML tag, you choose your own names for classes. You can call a class anything you like, but it's recommended to use names that describe what the style is for. A good example of a class name is warning. It tells you that anything styled with that class is intended as a warning. A bad example is boldRed. Sure, it tells you that anything styled with it is going to be in bold, red text. But what happens if you decide that all warnings should be black on a yellow background? You either end up with a class name that no longer describes its purpose, or you need to change the class name in every single place you have used it.

When choosing a class name, you must follow the following rules:

- No spaces are permitted.
- The only punctuation characters permitted are the hyphen (-) and the underscore (_).
- The name cannot begin with a number or a hyphen followed immediately by a number.

AdvancED

If you're using a language other than English, you'll be delighted to know that, as long as your pages are encoded as UTF-8, you can use accented characters in your class names. In fact, you can also use Chinese characters or other Asian scripts. When using characters other than A–Z, a–z, or 0–9 in an external style sheet, put @charset "utf-8"; at the top of the style sheet to indicate that it uses UTF-8 encoding.

When you create a class in a style sheet or `<style>` block in the `<head>` of a page, you precede the class name with a period or dot (.).

So, to create the style rules for the warning class with bold, red text, this is what goes in your style sheet:

```
.warning {
  font-weight: bold;
  color: #F00;
}
```

To apply this rule to a paragraph, you add the class attribute to the opening HTML tag with the name of the class as its value. However, you use the name on its own, without the leading dot, like this:

```
<p class="warning">Please correct the highlighted errors.</p>
```

If you are hand-coding everything, this involves going into the HTML code and adding the class attribute manually. However, most popular HTML editing programs let you apply classes through the user interface. In Expression Web, either select the object to which you want to apply the class or position your cursor inside it. Then, select the class from the *Apply Styles* task pane, as shown in Figure 4-2.

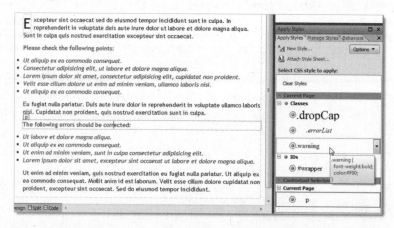

Figure 4-2. Use the Apply Styles task pane in Expression Web to apply a class.

The process is very similar in versions of Dreamweaver since MX 2004. Select the element to which you want to apply the class, or position your cursor inside it; and then select the class name from the *Class* menu in the Property inspector. Both Dreamweaver and Expression Web display the names of classes that affect fonts in a similar style to that applied by the class. This makes them easier to recognize, particularly if you have a style sheet with a lot of styles.

That's all there is to know about creating and applying a class. If you would like to practice, the example file shown in Figure 4-2 is `warning_start.html` in the download files for this chapter. The finished version is `warning.html`, which has the `warning` class applied to two paragraphs. The following styles are embedded in a `<style>` block in the `<head>` of both pages (there are other styles, but these are the relevant ones):

```
body {
    font-family: "Trebuchet MS", Arial, Helvetica, sans-serif;
    font-size: 14px;
    color: #000;
    background-color: #FFF;
}
p {
    margin: 0 auto 0.75em 30px;
}
.warning {
    font-weight: bold;
    color: #F00;
}
```

In `warning_start.html`, all paragraphs are styled the same. However, in `warning.html`, the two paragraphs are bold and red. As always, the cascade adds the rules together, so the `warning` paragraphs still share the same styles where there is no conflict, but the `color` property overrides the value inherited from the `body` rule. The `font-weight` property doesn't cause any conflict, but its value is added to the style, rendering them in bold.

ExplainED

Class selectors are case-sensitive. If class styles don't work, the first thing to do is check that the spelling of the class *attribute in the HTML tags matches the class selector in your style sheet. For example, if your style sheet uses* .warning, *putting* class="Warning" *in your HTML won't work. As far as browsers are concerned, "Warning" is not the same as "warning." Er, you have been warned.*

Now you know how to make classes, it's time to float.

Using float to flow text around images

Working with `float` doesn't require you to commit lots of CSS properties to memory. In fact, there are just two, as listed in Table 4-1.

Table 4-1. CSS Float Properties

Property	Initial value	Inherited	Description
float	none	No	Floats an element to the left or right of its parent element. Can be used on all elements, except absolutely positioned ones (see Chapter 10). When applied to an inline element, such as an image, the element is treated as a block.
clear	none	No	Prevents block-level elements from flowing alongside a floated element, and pushes them down below the floated element.

The float property accepts the following values:

- left: Float the element to the left, and flow text and other elements around its right side.
- right: Float the element to the right, and flow text and other elements around its left side.
- none: Prevent the element from floating. This is the default value.

Since float is not inherited, you can also use inherit to force inheritance from the parent element. For most practical purposes, the only values that need concern you are left and right. The purpose of none is in case you need to override the value of float. As you'll see in later chapters, the float property isn't used only with images. You might have a situation where most <li> elements are floated left with the following rule:

```
li {
  float: left;
}
```

For <li> elements that you don't want to float, you could create the following class:

```
.dontFloat {
  float: none;
}
```

ExplainED

If you're wondering whether this is a very likely scenario, the answer is "no." Floating `<li>` elements is quite common—it's how you create a navigation bar (see Chapter 8). However, you would probably use a more specific selector to target the elements you want to float, thereby avoiding the need to create the dontFloat *class.*

Some of the permitted values for CSS properties are rather like fire extinguishers. Most people will never use one in their whole lifetime, but if the occasion ever arises where you need one, you're sure glad it was there. That's why none *is an acceptable value for* float. *You might just need it one day, but in all probability, you won't.*

I'll deal with clear later. First, let's put float to work.

Creating generic classes to position images

The float property moves an element to the left or right and flows the following content around the opposite side. It works in exactly the same way as the HTML align property—in other words, there is no gap between the image and the text flowing along its side. To give the image some breathing space, you need to add a margin to the side that content is flowed around. So, if the image is floated left, you need to add a right margin to the image; and if it's floated right, the margin needs to be on the left.

In my experiments, I have found an 8-pixel margin separates images and text quite well. I also find it useful to add a small top and bottom margin to the image, usually about 3 pixels. So, in my style sheets, I normally create the following two classes to position images:

```
/* Image alignment */
.floatleft {
  float: left;
  margin: 3px 8px 3px 0;
}
.floatright {
  float: right;
  margin: 3px 0 3px 8px;
}
```

Both classes use the margin shorthand property, which—as you learned in Chapter 3—lists the values in clockwise order starting from the top. So, the 8px in the floatleft class represents the right margin, and in the floatright class, it's the left margin.

How do I center an image?

The float property moves an element to the left or right. It cannot be used to center an image. If you think about it for a moment, it actually makes sense. The float property has two effects: it moves the element, and flows the remaining content around its side. Imagine how difficult it would be to read continuous text that flowed along both sides of an image.

Although you might not have realized it, you learned how to center an image in the previous chapter. As long as it has a defined width, you can center any block-level element by setting its left and right margins to auto. If you're creating well designed web pages, every image will have its width declared in the <img> tag. So, you can create another class to center images and other objects like this:

```
.imgcentered {
  margin: 3px auto;
  display: block;
}
```

Images are inline elements, so setting the left and right margins to auto has no effect on its own. You need to use the CSS display property to get the browser to treat it as a block-level element by setting its value to block. You'll learn more about the display property in Chapter 8.

That had nothing to do with floating, but it's a question that gets asked so often, it was a worthwhile diversion. Now, back to floating images and flowing text around them.

Aligning images with CSS classes

The exercises in this chapter continue using journey.html and css/journey.css from the previous two chapters. If you have been doing the exercises in the order they appear in this book, you can continue using the same files. If you want to jump in at this point or start with fresh files, use as your starting point journey_11.html and css/journey_11.css in the download files for this chapter. The finished versions for each exercise are also in the download files to enable you to check your progress.

This exercise shows how to position images to the left or right of text, as well as in the center.

1. If you haven't already done so, add the floatleft, floatright, and imgcentered class definitions to the bottom of journey_css.

```
/* Image alignment */
.floatleft {
  float:left;
  margin:3px 8px 3px 0;
}
.floatright {
  float:right;
  margin:3px 0 3px 8px;
}
.imgcentered {
  margin:3px auto;
  display:block;
}
```

Don't forget the dot (period) in front of each class name. There must be no space between the dot and the name.

2. Insert forest_grassland.jpg from the images folder at the beginning of the paragraph under the <h2> heading that reads *From biting wind to warm updraft*.

3. Apply the floatleft class to the image either by inserting class="floatleft" directly into the <img> tag or by using your HTML editor to do it for you. The HTML code should look similar to this:

```
<h2>From biting wind to warm updraft</h2>
  <p><img src="../images/forest_grassland.jpg" alt="Kaibab National ↵
Forest" width="325" height="208" class="floatleft" />Because of. . .
```

ExplainED

It doesn't matter which order the attributes appear inside the <img> tag. The important thing to remember is that you don't use the dot in front of the class name when assigning it as the value of the class attribute inside an HTML tag.

4. Save the page and style sheet, and test journey.html in a browser. The image should be on the left with the text flowing around its right side, as shown in Figure 4-3.

Figure 4-3. The image is floated to the left, and the text that flows around the sides is offset by the margins.

If you want a wider or narrower margin between the image and the text, adjust the second value of the margin shorthand property in the floatleft class definition. You can also adjust the first and third values to change the vertical position of the image in relation to the text. As long as the final value remains 0, the left side of the image will remain flush with the main body of the paragraph.

5. Change the class applied to the image from floatleft to floatright. Save and test the page again. This time the image should be on the right, as shown in Figure 4-4.

Figure 4-4. Floating the image to the right flows the text around the left side.

Again, adjust the margins if you want to change the size of the gap between the text and the image. This time, it's the fourth value of the margin shorthand property that controls the horizontal space between the image and the text. Also note that the gap is evenly spaced because the style rule for paragraphs justifies the text. If the text is left-aligned, the gap between text and image will appear more ragged.

6.   The image doesn't need to be at the beginning of the paragraph for you to float it. Move the image to the start of the second sentence (the one beginning "Even during the summer. . ."). Save the page, and test it again. It should now look similar to Figure 4-5.

Figure 4-5. Browsers differ in the way they position images floated in the middle of a block of text.

When the floated element is in the middle of inline content, such as text, the browser positions the top of the floated element as high as possible, but never higher than the point where it appears in the underlying HTML. Browsers don't always agree on where this should be. The screenshot on the left of Figure 4-5 was taken in Firefox 3.0. As you can see, the top of the image is on the line below the words "Even during the summer. . ." In IE8, it's aligned with the line in which the image was inserted, as shown on the right of Figure 4-5.

7.   Finally, change the class to imgcentered, and test the page again. This time, the image should be centered, as shown in Figure 4-6.

131

From biting wind to warm updraft

Because of its altitude, access to the North Rim through the Kaibab National Forest is cut off by heavy snow from late October to mid-May each year.

Even during the summer months, a biting wind often blows across the grasslands in the forest, catching the ill-prepared visitor by surprise. Then, as you step out of your car at Point Imperial, a warm blast of air greets you, rising from the Colorado River, nearly 6,000 feet (1,800 meters) below. Daytime temperatures at the bottom of the Canyon often exceed 100° F (38° C), causing a warm updraft that mixes pleasantly with the cooler air of the plateau. On a clear summer's day, from Point Imperial you can see for miles across the Navajo Indian Reservation and Painted Desert to the East.

Figure 4-6. The float property cannot center elements, so the text is broken at the point the image is inserted.

As you can see, the text is broken at the point the image was inserted into the text, so you need to put the image at a place where it's convenient to break the text, such as at the end of a sentence.

You can check your code, if necessary, against journey_12.html and css/journey_12.css in the download files for this chapter.

What happens when the image is taller than the text?

When you center an image in the middle of text, you know exactly what's going to happen—the following text is pushed down below the image. But what about a floated image that doesn't have enough text to flow alongside? Most of the time, it's not a problem. When you float an image inside a paragraph, it's not only the text in the containing paragraph that's flowed around the image. Subsequent paragraphs are also moved upward to fill the space, as shown in Figure 4-7.

Head for heights required

Driving south across the Walhalla Plateau, you come to Cape Royal and the spectacular Angel's Window, a large natural arch that has been eroded out of a slender outcrop that protrudes into the Canyon. Walking over the arch to the viewpoint requires a strong stomach and head for heights, even though there are safety rails on both sides.

The safety rails on Angel's Window are the exception, rather than the rule. Most places along the edge of the Canyon have no guard rails at all. This comes as something of a surprise in these days of safety consciousness, but after a while, you come to appreciate the fact that the National Park Service has left the Grand Canyon unspoiled as much as possible. Footpaths are clearly marked and well-made. Visitors are left responsible for their own safety.

Figure 4-7. The text in the following paragraph is also flowed around the side of the floated image.

However, there are times when this automatic upward movement can play havoc with your layout, as you can see in Figure 4-8.

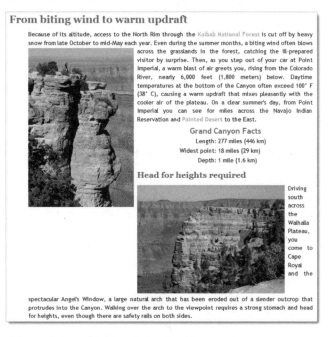

From biting wind to warm updraft

Because of its altitude, access to the North Rim through the Kaibab National Forest is cut off by heavy snow from late October to mid-May each year. Even during the summer months, a biting wind often blows across the grasslands in the forest, catching the ill-prepared visitor by surprise. Then, as you step out of your car at Point Imperial, a warm blast of air greets you, rising from the Colorado River, nearly 6,000 feet (1,800 meters) below. Daytime temperatures at the bottom of the Canyon often exceed 100° F (38° C), causing a warm updraft that mixes pleasantly with the cooler air of the plateau. On a clear summer's day, from Point Imperial you can see for miles across the Navajo Indian Reservation and Painted Desert to the East.

Grand Canyon Facts
Length: 277 miles (446 km)
Widest point: 18 miles (29 km)
Depth: 1 mile (1.6 km)

Head for heights required

Driving south across the Walhalla Plateau, you come to Cape Royal and the spectacular Angel's Window, a large natural arch that has been eroded out of a slender outcrop that protrudes into the Canyon. Walking over the arch to the viewpoint requires a strong stomach and head for heights, even though there are safety rails on both sides.

Figure 4-8. A tall floated image affects all subsequent layout.

Obviously, one solution is to make sure you have sufficient content to flow alongside your images. However, you can't always predict such things. So, you need a way to prevent this type of layout disaster. The answer is the clear property.

Using clear to force elements below a floated image

The float property's partner in crime, clear, takes the same values as float, plus one more, namely:

- left: Force the element to a new line below any left-floated elements.

- right: Force the element to a new line below any right-floated elements.

- both: Force the element to a new line below any left- or right-floated elements.

- none: Floats act normally. This is the default value but can also be used to cancel the clear property when creating a rule that inherits from another.

Since clear is not inherited, you can also use inherit to make a child element act the same way as its parent, but most of the time, you are likely to use left, right, or both.

The clear property is simple to use, as you'll see in the following exercise.

Preventing headings from flowing alongside images

This exercise shows how to prevent the layout problems shown in Figure 4-8. Continue using the same files as in the previous exercise. Alternatively, use journey_12.html and css/journey_12.css in the download files for this chapter.

1. Insert angels_window.jpg at the beginning of the first paragraph after the heading that reads *Head for heights required*, and apply the floatleft class to the image.

2. Save the page, and test it in a browser. It should look like Figure 4-7.

3. Replace forest_grassland.jpg with cape_royal.jpg, and set its class to floatleft.

4. Save the page, and test it again in a browser. It should now look like Figure 4-8. As you can see, the image is much taller. This results in not only the table, but also the <h3> heading and the following paragraph being flowed around the right side of the image. It also demonstrates what happens when two elements floated the same way come alongside each other.

ExplainED

When an element is floated, the float *property prevents it from being overlapped by other elements. So the image of Angel's Window moves up and as far left as it can go, but the presence of the tall image prevents it from moving all the way across to the left side of the page.*

Although Figure 4-8 looks a mess, this behavior is useful, because it means that you can float several elements in the same direction, and get them to line up in a row. This, in fact, is how you create a horizontal navigation bar from an unordered list. As you'll see in Chapter 8, each list item is floated left, and styled to look like a button.

5. To fix the problem, edit the style sheet to add the clear property to the selector that groups all the headings. Set its value to left, like this:

```
h1, h2, h3, h4, h5, h6 {
  color: #468966;
  font-family: Georgia, "Times New Roman", Times, serif;
  margin: 10px 0;
  clear: left;
}
```

6. Save the page, and test it again, preferably in Firefox with Firebug installed or in Safari 4. The heading, together with the following paragraph and image, should now be below the tall image, and flush with the left side of the page. However, you'll probably notice that the gap between the bottom of the image and the heading is rather narrow.

7. Open Firebug or the Safari 4 *Web Inspector* panel, select the *HTML* tab, and expand the page hierarchy to reveal the <h3> tag. When you hover your mouse pointer over the heading, the margins should be highlighted, as shown in Figure 4-9. Unfortunately, the IE8 and

Opera 10 *Developer Tools* panels don't highlight margins in the same way, so they're not quite so useful in this case.

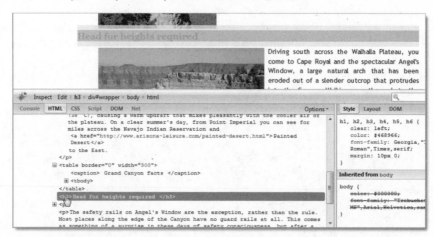

Figure 4-9. Floated elements appear to ignore the top margin of cleared elements.

ExplainED

It comes as a surprise that the 10-pixel margin on the top of the heading overlaps the bottom of the floated image. This isn't a bug; it's what the CSS specification says should happen.

What you see highlighted in Figure 4-9 is the margin declared in the style sheet. The browser actually applies a much bigger top margin to the heading to push it down just past the floated image, but it doesn't add the declared margin as well. Consequently, the gap between the tall image and the heading is not the 10 pixels you might have been expecting, but the 3 pixels on the bottom of the floated image. In fact, if the image didn't have a bottom margin, there would be no gap at all.

What this means is that if you want a minimum gap between the bottom of a floated element and the top of a cleared one, you must put that amount of margin on the bottom of the floated element.

For the purposes of this exercise, I'm not going to change the bottom margin of the floated image, because I'm using it only to demonstrate how the clear property affects margins.

8. Change the class of the tall image to `floatright`, and test the page again. This time, it should look like Figure 4-10.

Figure 4-10. Using clear: left doesn't affect images floated to the right.

This demonstrates two points: using `clear` with a value of `left` has no influence on anything that is floated to the right, and when elements are floated to opposite sides, content rises to fill any gap between them.

9. This layout doesn't look too bad, but the purpose of this exercise is to experiment with `clear`. So, change the value of `clear` from `left` to `both`.

10. Test the page again. As you might expect, the top of the `<h3>` heading is now in line with the bottom edge of the tall image. You would get the same effect in this particular layout by using `right` as the value for `clear`. However, using `both` ensures that headings are pushed down below floated images regardless of which side they are floated to.

You can check your code, if necessary, with journey_13.html and css/journey_13.css in the download files for this chapter.

What if an element is too wide to sit alongside a float?

As you can see in Figures 4-8 and 4-10, the *Grand Canyon Facts* table moved up alongside the tall image. That's because the table is only 300 pixels wide. So, there's plenty of room for it to sit alongside a 250-pixel wide image. However, what happens if the table is too wide to fit in the space alongside the image?

As you might expect, it automatically drops below the floated element to the first available space where it will fit. You can see this in wide_table.html in the download files for this chapter (see Figure 4-11), where I have added a border to the table and increased its width to 600 pixels.

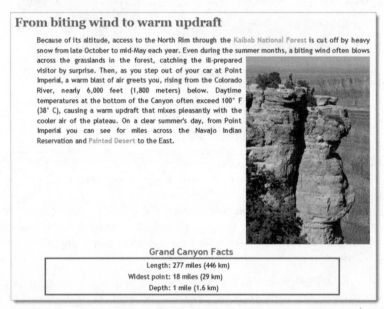

Figure 4-11. When an element is too wide to fit alongside, it is automatically moved down below the floated element.

It's the width of the table, not clear, that has forced it down below the image. While that seems fairly logical, what might come as a surprise is how CSS treats the <blockquote> element when it's alongside a floated element.

What happens to margins alongside a float?

Because of the way the 300-pixel table sat comfortably alongside the floated image, and was centered in the available space, you would be tempted to think that the margins of all block-level elements are treated that way. Unfortunately, you would be wrong.

The reason the table was centered is because the CSS specification says that when a table appears alongside a floated element, the table's borders must not overlap the floated element. In this sense, it's treated the same way as another floated element. As Figure 4-8 shows, when two images are floated in the same direction, the second image doesn't overlap the first one but sits alongside if there's sufficient space. Of course, if there isn't enough room, it drops below the first one and floats as far as it can in the designated direction. So, tables and floats never overlap. It's a different story with other block-level elements.

This concept can be quite difficult to grasp when working purely with style rules. Fortunately, Firebug and the Safari 4 *Web Inspector* panel give a visual representation of how the browser handles block-level elements alongside floats. So, roll up your sleeves. It's time to start experimenting again.

Adjusting the margins of the quote alongside a floated image

In this exercise, you'll use Firebug or the Safari 4 *Web Inspector* panel to examine how the width and margins of the Roosevelt quote are treated when it's alongside a floated image. Unfortunately, this exercise does not work with the IE8 or Opera 10 *Developer Tools* panels. For the sake of brevity, the instructions refer only to Firebug.

Continue working with the same files as the previous exercise. Alternatively, use journey_13.html and css/journey_13.css in the download files for this chapter.

1. Move the tall image, cape_royal.jpg, from the second paragraph to the beginning of the first paragraph (alongside the words "The Grand Canyon. . ."), and set its class to floatleft.

2. Save the page, and test it in Firefox or Safari 4. It should look like Figure 4-12.

JOURNEY TO THE EDGE

The Grand Canyon in northern Arizona is one of the most stunning natural phenomena in the world. Reading about it, seeing photos, even watching documentary movies on a cinema screen do nothing to prepare you for that moment when you first step up to the edge. The North Rim of the Canyon rises a thousand feet (more than 300 meters) higher than the South Rim, and is heavily forested. After driving through lush grassland and winding forest roads, the Canyon suddenly opens up before you in all its jaw-dropping magnificence.

Leave it as it is. You cannot improve on it. The ages have been at work on it, and only man can mar it.

Theodore Roosevelt, May 6, 1903

Figure 4-12. Unlike the table, the quote hasn't been centered.

Instead of being centered, the <blockquote> has been left-aligned, just like the preceding paragraph. Why has this happened? You might be tempted to think it's because the width of the <blockquote> is declared as a percentage, and the browser has failed to calculate the automatic margins on the left and right. It's a reasonable assumption, but it's wrong.

3. Before using Firebug to inspect what's happening, change the width in the blockquote style rule from 38% to 600px like this:

```
blockquote {
    margin: 0 auto;
    width: 600px;
}
```

4. Save the style sheet, and reload journey.html in the browser. Surely, the <blockquote> element will have been forced below the image? Wrong.

    The text in the quote is wider, but it's still up there alongside the image. Time to open Firebug, and find out what's going on.

5. Expand the code in the *HTML* tab of Firebug, and locate the <blockquote> element. As you hover your mouse pointer over the element, Firebug highlights its position in the top half of the browser

window. As Figure 4-13 shows, the 600-pixel width of the `<blockquote>` overlaps the floated image. However, the text inside the `<blockquote>` is pushed aside. You can also see that the element is, in fact, centered. If you think it's slightly off-center, don't forget there's a 45-pixel offset on the paragraph containing the floated image.

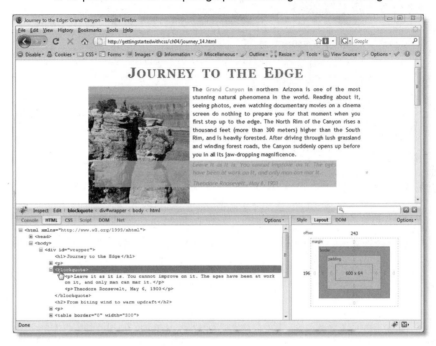

Figure 4-13. Firebug reveals why the quote hasn't been pushed below the image.

6. Although the treatment of the `<blockquote>` seems odd, it begins to make more sense if you select the paragraph above, and see how it's highlighted by Firebug. As shown in Figure 4-14, Firebug highlights the full width of the paragraph in one color (normally light blue) and its margins are highlighted in a different color (normally yellow). The only difference is that the margins of the `<blockquote>` element aren't highlighted because they're calculated automatically by the browser, rather than being defined in the style rule.

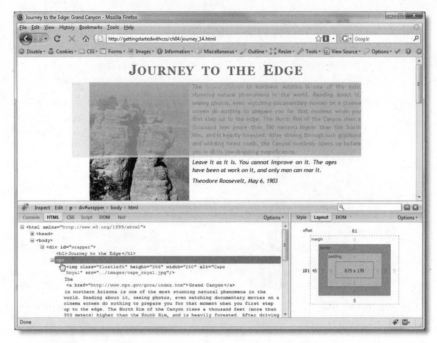

Figure 4-14. Although the content is displaced by the float, the block-level element still occupies its normal place.

What this means is that, with block-level elements, it's only the content that is shifted left or right, depending on the direction of the float. *The element itself remains unchanged.*

AdvancED

This treatment of block-level elements alongside floated elements has important consequences when the block-level element has a background or border. The background and/or border are drawn underneath the floated element unless you take appropriate steps to counter this behavior. Backgrounds and borders are the subject of the next chapter, so I'll leave that issue until then.

7. To center the `<blockquote>` element, you need to do a little calculation. The page content is enclosed in a wrapper `<div>` 720 pixels wide. You want to center the `<blockquote>` element in the

space to the right of the floated image. The image is 250 pixels wide, but it's inside a paragraph that has a 45-pixel left margin, and the image itself has an 8-pixel right margin. That means the space available to the right of the image can be calculated as follows:

```
720 - (45 + 250 + 8) = 417
```

The width property of the blockquote style rule is currently set at 38% of the parent element—in other words, 38% of 720 pixels. That's 723.6 pixels, which needs to be rounded up to 725px to create an even margin of 71px on both sides.

So, the left margin of the <blockquote> element needs to be 71px plus the left margin of the paragraph (45px), image width (250px), and image right margin (8px):

```
71 + 45 + 250 + 8 = 374
```

8. Edit the blockquote style rule like this:

```
blockquote {
  margin: 0 71px 0 374px;
  width: 275px;
}
```

9. Save the style sheet, and reload the page in the browser. The <blockquote> should now be nicely centered in the space alongside the image. The only problem is that it's too close up against the preceding paragraph.

10. Fix the vertical position of the <blockquote> by setting its top margin to 50px like this:

```
blockquote {
  margin: 50px 71px 0 374px;
  width: 275px;
}
```

The page should now look like Figure 4-15 (note that I have added forest_grassland.jpg back into the second paragraph to add some balance to the page).

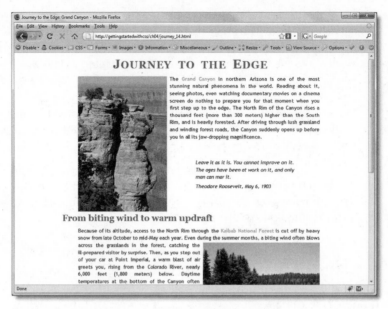

Figure 4-15. Calculating the size of the left margin results in the quote being correctly positioned alongside the floated image.

You can check your code, if necessary, against journey_14.html and css/journey_14.css in the download files for this chapter.

Phew! That involved a bit of working out, but as you'll discover with CSS, there are times when you need to sit down with pencil and paper to calculate the necessary dimensions. Hopefully, though, this should also demonstrate the high degree of control that CSS gives you over the layout of page elements.

In a real-world situation, you wouldn't use the blockquote type selector to position the Roosevelt quote like this, because the same properties would apply to all <blockquote> elements in pages linked to the same style sheet. This particular quote is a unique element that needs to be treated in a unique way. That calls for a new type of selector: the ID selector.

Using ID selectors to style unique elements

You briefly came across the use of ID selectors in the previous chapter when you gave the <div> that wraps around the page content the ID, wrapper. Using an ID selector is easy. The ID identifies the element that you want to style differently from any other element. The ID must follow the same naming rules as a class, namely:

- No spaces are permitted.
- The only punctuation characters permitted are the hyphen (-) and the underscore (_).
- The ID cannot begin with a number or a hyphen followed immediately by a number.

To distinguish ID selectors from classes, you precede the ID with the hash sign (#) instead of a dot. You add the ID to the element's opening tag using the id attribute. As with a class, you use just the name inside the HTML tag (leaving off the hash sign). So, to create an ID selector for the Roosevelt quote, you add a style block to the style sheet like this:

```
#tr_quote {
  /* Style rules go here */
}
```

The ID goes in the opening <blockquote> tag like this:

```
<blockquote id="tr_quote">
```

So, what's the difference between a class and an ID—apart from the dot and hash?

Deciding whether to use a class or an ID

The whole point of CSS selectors is to identify the elements to which style rules should be applied. You started off in Chapter 2 with type selectors, which redefine the appearance of HTML tags. Then you targeted elements more precisely with descendant selectors (e.g., blockquote p) and the adjacent sibling selector (h1 + p). Class and ID selectors add to this arsenal.

The main use for ID selectors is to mark out specific areas of your page, for example, the page header, main navigation, main content, sidebar, footer, and so on. A class, on the other hand, is used to apply the same style to different parts of the page that aren't related to each other. The way to decide which to use is simple:

- If you're likely to use the same style on several unrelated elements, use a class.
- If the element is unique within the context of a page or represents a unified section of the page, use an ID.

The floatleft, floatright, and imgcentered classes you created earlier in this chapter are good examples of styles that are likely to be used on several elements within the same page. However, the Roosevelt quote needs special treatment. Its width and margins depend entirely on the size of the image floating alongside. Technically speaking, you *could* use a class to style it, but applying the same style rules to another element wouldn't make much sense. Using an ID selector tells you, "These are the styles for a specific element and no other."

Another advantage of ID selectors is that many page elements use IDs for other purposes, such as working with JavaScript to hide or display page elements. Because the id attribute is already inside the HTML tag, you don't need to add extra code to the page.

AdvancED

ID selectors take precedence over classes and type selectors when there's a conflict between style rules. Working out the exact order of precedence is a subject that I'll come back to in Chapter 7 when you have more experience of selectors.

The golden rule with IDs is that you should never use the same ID more than once on each page. So, you can have a header ID on every page, but only once on each one.

Now that you know the basics of creating an ID selector, let's update journey.html.

Converting the blockquote styles

In this brief exercise, you'll add an ID to the Roosevelt quote and change the style rules, so that they target only a specific element. Continue working with the files from the previous exercises. Alternatively, use journey_14.html and css/journey_14.css from the download files for this chapter.

1. Add the ID, tr_quote, to the opening <blockquote> tag like this:

```
<blockquote id="tr_quote">
  <p>Leave it as it is. You cannot improve on it.
```

On its own, this makes no difference to the way the quote is displayed.

2. Switch to the style sheet, and locate the style rules that affect the `<blockquote>`. There are two of them like this:

```
blockquote {
  margin: 50px 71px 0 374px;
  width: 275px;
}
blockquote p {
  font-style: italic;
  text-indent: 0;
  white-space: pre-line;
  margin-left: 0;
}
```

The first one sets the margins and width for this particular quote, so you definitely need to convert the first one to use the ID selector, #tr_quote. However, the second one is much more generic. If you convert that to use the ID selector, you would need to create the same rule again for any other `<blockquote>` elements elsewhere in the same site. So, we'll leave that one alone.

3. Amend the selector for the first style block like this:

```
#tr_quote {
  margin: 50px 71px 0 374px;
  width: 275px;
}
blockquote p {
  font-style: italic;
  text-indent: 0;
  white-space: pre-line;
  margin-left: 0;
}
```

4. Save both pages, and view `journey.html` in a browser. It should look exactly the same as before (see Figure 4-15).

You can check your code, if necessary, against `journey_15.html` and `css/journey_15.css` in the download files for this chapter.

147

ExplainED

The important lesson to take away from this exercise is that it's not necessary to put all the style rules for an element in a single selector. Even though you have added an ID to the `<blockquote>`*, it doesn't prevent it from using the styles defined by the generic* `blockquote p` *selector. As long as there is no conflict between the properties, the cascade adds everything together. Learning to combine rules like this is the key to writing flexible CSS. Put the basic rules in type selectors, and use the more specialized selectors to override them when necessary.*

Adding a caption to an image

Moving images to the left or right and flowing text around the side is one of the main uses of the `float` property; but it's important to realize that you can use `float` with other elements, too. You'll see more examples of floating as you progress through this book, but to round out this chapter, I want to show you how you can easily adapt the `floatleft`, `floatright`, and `imgcentered` classes to add a caption to an image—something that requires complex markup with HTML.

As I explained in Chapter 3, HTML provides two tags, `<div>` and `<span>`, designed to group elements together for styling. As you might remember, `<div>` creates a block-level element, while `<span>` is used for inline elements. To add a caption to an image, all that's necessary is to wrap the image and the caption in one of these tags, and then float the `<div>` or `<span>`. So, which should you use? Either is technically correct, because images and text are inline elements, but a floated element is treated as a block. However, I have chosen to use `<span>`. This has the advantage that you can use it to float an image and its associated caption in the middle of a paragraph. You can't put a `<div>` inside a paragraph. So, using `<span>` in this case gives you more flexibility.

Let's add some captions to the images in `journey.html`.

148

Captioning images

This exercise shows how to add captions to floated images and style them so they stand out from the surrounding text. It also demonstrates how you can use an inline style to control the width of a caption. Continue working with the files from the previous exercise. Alternatively, use journey_15.html and css/journey_15.css from the download files for this chapter.

1. The caption you're going to add to the first image is *Grand Canyon at Cape Royal*. To force the caption onto a new line underneath the image, you need to add a line break (<br />), and then wrap both the image and caption in a <span>. Finally, you need to remove the floatleft class from the image, and apply it to the <span>. The resulting HTML should look like this:

```
<p><span class="floatleft"><img src="../images/cape_royal.jpg" alt= ↵
"Cape Royal" width="250" height="366" /><br />Grand Canyon at Cape ↵
Royal</span> The <a href="http://www.nps.gov/grca/index.htm">Grand ↵
Canyon</a> in northern Arizona. . .
```

2. If you test the page now, you'll see the caption floated along with the image. However, to make it stand out like a caption, it needs to be bold and centered. Fixing that with the font-weight and text-align properties is easy, but you'll want to apply the same values to the floatright and imgcentered classes as well. Instead of adding them to each class separately, create a group selector for all three classes like this:

```
.floatleft, .floatright, .imgcentered {
  font-weight:bold;
  text-align:center;
}
```

Grouping all three class selectors in a comma-separated list applies the same properties to each of them, and the cascade takes care of adding the values to the existing class style rules.

3. Save the page and its associated style sheet, and test journey.html in a browser. The caption should now be properly styled under the first image, as shown in Figure 4-16.

JOURNEY TO THE EDGE

The Grand Canyon in northern Arizona is one of the most stunning natural phenomena in the world. Reading about it, seeing photos, even watching documentary movies on a cinema screen do nothing to prepare you for that moment when you first step up to the edge. The North Rim of the Canyon rises a thousand feet (more than 300 meters) higher than the South Rim, and is heavily forested. After driving through lush grassland and winding forest roads, the Canyon suddenly opens up before you in all its jaw-dropping magnificence.

Leave it as it is. You cannot improve on it. The ages have been at work on it, and only man can mar it.

Theodore Roosevelt, May 6, 1903

Grand Canyon at Cape Royal

From biting wind to warm updraft

Figure 4-16. You can easily add a caption by wrapping the image and text in a <span> and floating them together.

4. Repeat step 1 to add captions to the other two images, using floatleft and floatright as appropriate. Make the captions brief: *Kaibab National Forest* for the second image, and *Angel's Window* for the third image.

5. Test journey.html again in a browser to make sure that all three captions are displayed correctly.

6. Now change the second caption to read *The approach to the North Rim of the Grand Canyon through Kaibab National Forest.*

7. Save and test the page again. The long caption spreads across the page, destroying the position of both the image and the text flowed around it (see Figure 4-17). The problem is that, while the image has a declared width, there is nothing to control the width of the <span>.

From biting wind to warm updraft

Because of its altitude, access to the North Rim through the Kaibab National Forest is cut off by heavy snow from late October to mid-May each year. Even during the summer months, a biting wind often blows across the grasslands in the forest, catching the ill-prepared visitor by surprise. Then, as you step out of your car at Point Imperial, a warm blast of air greets you, rising from the Colorado River, nearly 6,000

The approach to the North Rim of the Grand Canyon through Kaibab National Forest

feet (1,800 meters) below. Daytime temperatures at the bottom of the Canyon often exceed 100° F (38° C), causing a warm updraft that mixes pleasantly with the cooler air of the plateau. On a clear summer's day, from Point Imperial you can see for miles across the Navajo Indian Reservation and Painted Desert to the East.

Figure 4-17. With nothing to control its width, the caption spreads across the page.

8. Unless all your images are the same width, you can't add the width property to the classes. This is one of the rare instances when I think it is justified to use an inline style. The image, forest_grassland.jpg is 325 pixels wide. Amend the opening <span> tag to add the width property as an inline style, and set its value to match that of the image like this:

```
<span class="floatright" style="width:325px">
```

9. Save the page, and test it again in a browser. The caption should now be wrapped neatly beneath the image, as shown in Figure 4-18.

From biting wind to warm updraft

Because of its altitude, access to the North Rim through the Kaibab National Forest is cut off by heavy snow from late October to mid-May each year. Even during the summer months, a biting wind often blows across the grasslands in the forest, catching the ill-prepared visitor by surprise. Then, as you step out of your car at Point Imperial, a warm blast of air greets you, rising from the Colorado River, nearly 6,000 feet (1,800 meters) below. Daytime temperatures at the bottom of the Canyon often exceed 100° F (38° C), causing a warm updraft that mixes pleasantly with the cooler air of the plateau. On a clear summer's day, from Point Imperial you can see for miles across the Navajo Indian Reservation and Painted Desert to the East.

The approach to the North Rim of the Grand Canyon through Kaibab National Forest

Grand Canyon Facts
Length: 277 miles (446 km)
Widest point: 18 miles (29 km)
Depth: 1 mile (1.6 km)

Figure 4-18. Giving the <span> a declared width brings the caption under control.

You can check your code, if necessary, against journey_16.html and css/journey_16.css in the download files for this chapter.

Using inline styles is generally considered bad practice, because it's the least flexible way of adding styles to a page, and it clutters the HTML markup with presentational information. The alternative would be to give the <span> an ID and use an ID selector to set its width. So, the opening <span> tag would look like this:

```
<span class="floatright" id="forest_grassland">
```

And this would be added to the style sheet:

```
#forest_grassland {
  width: 325px;
}
```

However, this not only involves more code but makes maintenance much more difficult, because the information about the width is removed from the markup surrounding the image. If you change the image, you will probably need to change the ID as well as its associated style block. On a single page, it might be acceptable, but in a large site, it would rapidly become a nightmare. Sometimes, it's necessary to make compromises to achieve the most workable result.

To avoid the need for an inline style like this, it's a good idea to keep your captions short. The caption shown in Figure 4-16 begins to affect the layout in Firefox when the text size is increased more than three steps. If you think that's a problem, add an inline style to set the width, create a shorter caption, or put a line break in the existing one. However, if you expect users to increase the text size by more than three steps, your text is probably too small to start with.

Chapter review

Floating elements to the left or right is an important CSS layout technique. The basic principles are simple:

- The floated element moves as far left or right as permitted by its containing element.
- Floated elements cannot overlap each other.

- Subsequent content moves up to fill the available space alongside the floated element.
- The `clear` property prevents elements from moving up alongside a float.

However, using the `float` property can also have unexpected consequences. While the table was automatically centered alongside a floated element, the Roosevelt quote was treated quite differently. This is because tables cannot overlap floated elements. However, when other block-level elements move up to fill the horizontal space alongside a floated element, the dimensions of the block-level element remain unchanged. Only the content is shifted sideways to prevent it from overlapping the float. As a result, you needed to calculate the width of the horizontal space alongside the floated image and adjust the margins of the Roosevelt quote to recenter it.

This chapter also introduced you to two important selectors: classes and IDs. A class is a useful device for applying a style to multiple elements on a page, whereas an ID is used to apply styles to unique elements. Although both classes and IDs play important roles in CSS, you should resist the temptation to overuse them. First, make full use of type selectors and other devices, such as the adjacent sibling selector that you used in the previous chapter to style the first paragraph after a heading (h1 + p, h2 + p, h3 + p). Classes and IDs rely on the addition of the `class` or `id` attribute to the opening HTML tag, increasing the amount of code you need to maintain. So, use them sparingly.

The next chapter looks at how to add backgrounds and borders to highlight elements on your web pages and improve visual interest. You'll also see what happens when a floated element appears alongside an element that has a background or border.

Chapter 5

How Do I Add Backgrounds and Borders to Improve the Look of My Page?

The secret of good web design is drawing the visitor's eyes to important parts of the page. Images, borders, and background colors all help to break up the page and focus attention. The images you inserted in the exercises in the previous chapter not only look attractive, they tell the visitor what the Grand Canyon looks like. But images can also serve another purpose—decorative touches that please the eye and give a unified look to the site. Rather than littering the HTML markup with purely decorative images, it's preferable to add them as background. Although some HTML tags allow you to add background images, the options are very limited. CSS, on the other hand, gives you an amazing amount of control over the location and appearance of background images.

Borders also provide visual guides, separating sections of a page or highlighting important information. In HTML, borders are an all or nothing option—the same border is applied to all four sides of an element. But CSS gives you full control, allowing you to set a different color, style, and width for each side, should you wish to do so. You can even add a border to just one side.

In this chapter, you'll learn how to do the following:

- Apply individual background colors to different parts of a page.
- Add background images and control their position accurately.
- Control the look of borders around images and text.
- Get rid of blue borders around image links.
- Prevent borders and backgrounds from running under floated elements.

The basics of adding backgrounds and borders are simple—deceptively so. These two aspects of CSS contain some surprises, so don't be tempted to rush this chapter.

Controlling backgrounds with CSS

CSS has six properties that handle backgrounds, as listed in Table 5-1. Five of them deal with individual aspects of an element's background, and the remaining one is a shorthand property that lets you define all values in a single declaration.

Table 5-1. CSS Background Properties

Property	Initial Value	Inherited	Description
background-attachment	scroll	No	Determines whether a background image remains in a fixed position or scrolls with the page.
background-color	transparent	No	Sets the background color of an element. The default value allows the background color and image of the parent element to show through.
background-image	none	No	Sets an image as the element's background. In CSS2.1, only one image can be attached to an element.
background-position	0% 0%	No	Determines the horizontal and vertical position of the background image. The default is at the top left of the element.
background-repeat	repeat	No	Determines whether the background image should tile if it's smaller than the element. Tiling can be suppressed or limited to either the horizontal or vertical axis.
background	See individual properties	No	Shorthand property.

Apart from background-color, all of the individual properties are concerned with background images. Since color is the easiest to handle, let's tackle that first.

Changing the background color of an element

As you might expect, the background-color property takes as its value a color, which can be expressed in any of the ways described in "Setting color values in CSS" in Chapter 2, namely:

- A 3- or 6-digit hexadecimal number
- One of the 17 color keywords listed in Table 2-3
- An rgb() value specifying the red, green, and blue values as comma-separated numbers in the range of 0–255 or percentages from 0% to 100%

Technically speaking, the background-color property is not inherited, so you can use the inherit property to use the same color as the parent element. However, the default value is transparent. As you'll see when you start experimenting with backgrounds, this means that the parent's background properties show through unless you specify a different value.

Seeing is believing. So, let's get on right away with an exercise. As in previous chapters, I'm going to continue working with journey.html. If you have completed the exercises in the preceding chapter, you can continue working with the same files. But if you want to jump in at this point, or just need fresh files, use journey_16.html and css/journey_16.css in the download files for this chapter.

Setting different background colors for page elements

This exercise demonstrates how the background of a parent element shows through all child elements, except when the background-color property of a child element is set independently. The exercise also shows the effect of margins on backgrounds. To understand the effect of margins on backgrounds, it's a good idea to use a CSS analysis tool, such as Firebug or the Safari 4 *Web Inspector* panel. The IE8 and Opera 10 *Developer Tools* panels don't highlight margins, so I suggest you use Firefox or Safari 4 for this exercise.

1. Browsers now use white as the default background for web pages (ancient browsers used a dirty gray), but you should always set the background-color property for the <body> explicitly, even if you want to use white. In fact, this was the first style rule you created in

157

Chapter 2. Change it now to an olive color by amending the body style block like this:

```
body {
  background-color: #EFECCA;
  color: #000;
  font-family: "Trebuchet MS", Arial, Helvetica, sans-serif;
  margin: 0;
  padding: 0;
}
```

This changes the background of the entire page. Although background-color is not inherited, its default value is transparent. So, the olive color shows through everywhere.

2. Add the background-color property to the #wrapper style rule, and set its value to white like this:

```
#wrapper {
  width: 720px;
  margin: 0 auto;
  background-color: #FFF;
}
```

3. Save the style sheet, and load journey.html into a browser. The page should look like Figure 5-1.

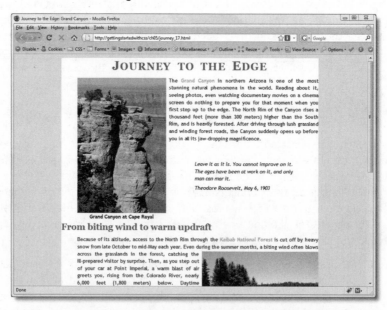

Figure 5-1. The wrapper <div> now has a different background color from the body.

Giving the #wrapper style rule a different value for background-color has overridden the olive color of the body rule. However, there are several problems. There's no breathing space between the left side of the wrapper <div> and the <h2> and <h3> headings. Similarly, there's no breathing space between the paragraphs and the right side. But worst of all, there's about 10 pixels of olive background showing at the top and bottom of the page.

4. Sorting out the left and right sides is easy. You just need to adjust the margins of the headings and paragraphs. First, fix the headings. Locate the rule that controls their margins. It looks like this:

```
h1, h2, h3, h4, h5, h6 {
  color: #468966;
  font-family: Georgia, "Times New Roman", Times, serif;
  margin: 10px 0;
  clear: both;
}
```

As you might remember from Chapter 3, when the margin shorthand property is followed by two values, the first value applies to the top and bottom, and the second value applies to the left and right sides. So, this rule means there is a 10-pixel margin on the top and bottom of each heading but no margin on either side.

5. Change the margin shorthand property to just a single value of 10px. This applies the same value all the way round, ensuring a nice breathing space on the left. Applying the same value to the right doesn't visibly affect the current page, but it also ensures a similar amount of breathing space even if you have a long subheading that wraps onto another line.

6. Now, fix the right margin of the paragraphs. The p style block uses the margin shorthand property with four values. So, it's the second value that you need to change to affect the right margin (remember, margin shorthand begins at the top and goes clockwise). Change the rule like this:

```
p {
  text-align: justify;
  text-indent: 30px;
  line-height: 1.4;
  margin: 0 10px 0.4em 45px;
}
```

159

7. Save the style sheet, and reload journey.html in the browser. The breathing space on both sides looks OK, but what about that olive gap at the top and bottom?

8. Open Firebug or the Safari 4 *Web Inspector* panel, and expand the HTML structure to reveal the <h1> heading. When you hover the mouse pointer over the heading in the CSS analysis tool, you can see the 10-pixel margin highlighted all around it in the browser, as shown in Figure 5-2.

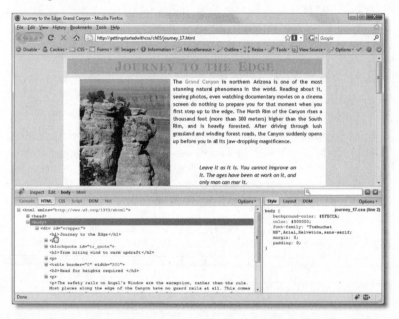

Figure 5-2. Using a CSS analysis tool like Firebug reveals that the top margin of the heading is causing the gap.

This is one of those strange mysteries of collapsing vertical margins. The top margin of the wrapper <div> is 0, but the heading has a top margin of 10px. Instead of the heading's top margin pushing it 10 pixels inside the <div>, as you might expect, the two margins are combined and push the <div> 10 pixels away from the top of the <body>.

9. The <h1> heading already has a style block that sets properties that don't apply to the other headings. So, you can fix this problem by adding the margin-top property with a value of 0 like this:

```
h1 {
    font-size: 220%;
    font-variant: small-caps;
    text-align: center;
    word-spacing: 0.2em;
    letter-spacing: 0.05em;
    margin-top: 0;
}
```

In this case, you use the property for a single side, and not the shorthand version, because you want to override only one value, and keep the rest.

10. Save the style sheet, and reload journey.html in the browser. The gap should now have disappeared. The gap at the bottom of the page is caused by the bottom margin of the final paragraph, but I'm not going to bother fixing that, because I'll be changing the bottom of the page later in this chapter.

11. I want to the Roosevelt quote stand out a bit more. This will be achieved gradually throughout the chapter, but the first step is to change the #tr_quote style block like this, and give it a pale yellow background:

```
#tr_quote {
    margin: 50px 71px 0 374px;
    width: 275px;
    background-color: #FFFEF1;
}
```

12. Save the style sheet, and reload journey.html in the browser. Look at the quote very closely. The background color is flush with the left side of the text, but there's a slight gap on the right. You can verify this by hovering your mouse pointer over the first paragraph of the quote in the HTML structure of your CSS analysis tool to highlight its margins in the browser window. As Figure 5-3 shows, the right side of the text is offset from the right edge of the background color.

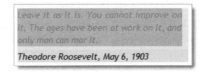

Leave it as it is. You cannot improve on it. The ages have been at work on it, and only man can mar it.

Theodore Roosevelt, May 6, 1903

Figure 5-3. There's a 10-pixel right margin on the paragraphs inside the <blockquote>.

161

One way to fix this is to increase the margins on the other sides. For the time being, though, I want to get rid of the right margin on the paragraphs inside the `<blockquote>`. It was added in step 6 when you added breathing space between the main paragraphs and the right side of the wrapper `<div>`. You can see the difference in Figures 5-1 and 5-2. In Figure 5-1, the first line ends with the word "it," but it has been moved to the beginning of the second line in Figure 5-2.

13. Fix the right margin by adding the `margin-right` property to the `blockquote p` style block, and setting its value to `0` like this:

```
blockquote p {
  font-style: italic;
  text-indent: 0;
  white-space: pre-line;
  margin-left: 0;
  margin-right: 0;
}
```

The gap between the text and the background color should have disappeared, and the layout of the text should look the same as in Figure 5-1.

You can check your code, if necessary, against `journey_17.html` and `css/journey_17.css` in the download files for this chapter.

As you have just seen, adding a background color is simple, but margins can have unexpected effects on where the background is displayed. Let's quickly recap what this exercise has demonstrated.

- If an element has no background color of its own, the background of its parent element shows through.

- Once you apply a different background color to a child element, the new color becomes the background of any subsequent children.

- When you added a background color to the wrapper `<div>`, you needed to add horizontal margins to the headings and paragraphs to move them away from the sides of the `<div>`.

- The top margins of the `<h1>` heading and wrapper `<div>` combined, pushing the `<div>` away from the top of the page and leaving an olive strip.

ExplainED

Background colors and images fill only the element to which they are applied. They do not stretch into the margins surrounding the element. That's why the olive background applied to the <body> remains visible on either side of the wrapper <div>. It also explains why the top margin of the <h1> heading produced an olive strip at the top of the page. The heading's margin was added to the top of the <div>, and because the background doesn't stretch into margins, the <body> background showed through until you removed the margin.

Creating the breathing space between the sides of the <div> and the text was achieved by adding horizontal margins to the headings and paragraphs. This didn't expand the background color of the <div>. Instead, the headings and paragraphs moved inward to let the background color show through their margins. That's why the text in the Roosevelt quote wrapped the words at the end of each line: there was less space for the text until you removed the right margin.

If you already have experience of CSS, you'll know the padding property offers another way to adjust the space between content and the background color. I'm deliberately leaving the padding property out of the equation at the moment, because it has a counterintuitive effect on width and height. All will be revealed in the next chapter.

Now let's take a look at background images.

Adding a background image

At the moment, the file that you have been working with in the exercises, journey.html, contains three images that have been added using the HTML <img> tag. These are an integral part of the page, designed to illustrate the accompanying text, and could be regarded as foreground images. However, a lot of images used in websites are there for purely decorative purposes. When using an image for decoration, it's generally a good idea to use CSS. There are several advantages to doing so, namely:

- Text or other content can appear in front of background images.
- Using CSS avoids cluttering your HTML code with purely decorative elements.

- With an external style sheet, the same decorative elements appear automatically on all pages.
- To change the images, you simply change the style sheet, rather than edit every page.
- CSS lets you control the position of background images accurately.
- All browsers in widespread use, except IE6, support background images that remain in position when the rest of the page scrolls.

As the name suggests, background-image is the property that adds a background image to an element. It accepts three possible values, namely:

- url(): The path to the image goes between the parentheses.
- none: Default value. No background image.
- inherit: Like background colors, background images show through, but they are *not* inherited. Using inherit tells the browser to apply the same image as an independent background. So, the result won't necessarily look the same as simply showing through.

When adding the path to the image between the parentheses of url(), you can optionally surround it in single or double quotes. You can also leave whitespace around the path name. The following are all valid:

```
background-image:url(../../images/flower1.png);
background-image:url('../../images/flower1.png');
background-image:url("../../images/flower1.png");
background-image:url(  ../../images/flower1.png  );
```

The only time it's mandatory to use quotes around the path name is if it contains spaces. However, you should *never* use spaces in file or folder names for a website.

ExplainED

Both Mac OS X and modern versions of Windows permit spaces in the names of files and folders, making it easy to create user-friendly file structures. This has resulted in many inexperienced web developers using spaces in names on their websites, blissfully unaware of the fact that spaces are not permitted in URLs. Also many websites are hosted on Linux or Unix servers that don't permit spaces in names. That's why you see %20 in some URLs. It's the way HTML editors encode spaces to prevent the URL from breaking, but it looks ugly and amateurish. If you want to use multiple words in folder and file names, join them with a hyphen or underscore. Better still, keep names short and easy to type.

When you add a background image to an element, by default, the browser places the image at the top left of the element and automatically tiles (repeats) the image both horizontally and vertically to fill all available background space, as shown in Figure 5-4.

Figure 5-4. By default, browsers tile background images to fill all available space.

The background image of a single flower has been applied to the body style rule like this:

```
body {
  background-color: #EFECCA;
  color: #000;
  font-family: "Trebuchet MS", Arial, Helvetica, sans-serif;
  margin: 0;
  padding: 0;
  background-image: url(../../images/flower1.png);
}
```

As you can see, the image is automatically repeated to fill the background of the entire page. You can test it in image_repeat.html in the download files for this chapter. If you expand the width of the browser, you'll see the flower is repeated under the wrapper <div> as the width of its left and right margins is increased.

165

Sometimes, this automatic tiling is what you want. However, in this case, I think you'll agree that it's overkill. Fortunately, CSS gives you control over this default behavior.

Controlling how background images repeat

The property that controls the way background images are repeated is called background-repeat. It accepts the following values:

- repeat: This is the default value. Repeat the image both horizontally and vertically to fill all available background space.

- repeat-x: Repeat the background image horizontally only.

- repeat-y: Repeat the background image vertically only.

- no-repeat: Display the image once only.

- inherit: The background-repeat property is not automatically inherited, so this applies the same value as in the parent element.

The download files contain examples of background-repeat used with different values. Since repeat is the default value, I haven't used it in image_repeat.html, but the result would be the same as Figure 5-4.

Figure 5-5 and image_repeat-x.html show what happens when repeat-x is added to the body style rule like this:

```
body {
  background-color: #EFECCA;
  color: #000;
  font-family: "Trebuchet MS", Arial, Helvetica, sans-serif;
  margin: 0;
  padding: 0;
  background-image: url(../../images/flower1.png);
  background-repeat: repeat-x;
}
```

Figure 5-5. Setting background-repeat to repeat-x tiles the background image across the horizontal axis only.

Figure 5-6 and `image_repeat-y.html` in the download files show what happens when `background-repeat` is changed to `repeat-y`.

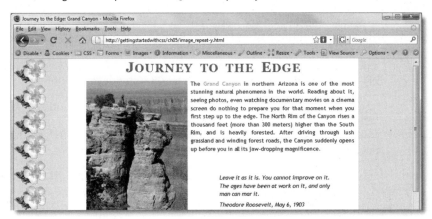

Figure 5-6. Setting background-repeat to repeat-y tiles the background image down the vertical axis only.

Figure 5-7 and `image_no-repeat.html` in the download files show the effect of changing `background-repeat` to `no-repeat`.

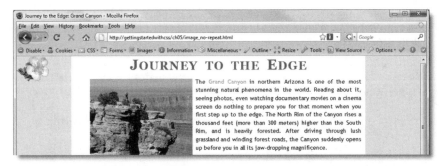

Figure 5-7. Using no-repeat displays the background image just once.

When you scroll `image_no-repeat.html`, the background image remains in its current position relative to the rest of the content, and rapidly disappears out of view. However, modern browsers let you fix the background image in relation to the browser viewport.

Fixing a background image in relation to the browser viewport

To fix the background in position, use the background-attachment property, which is supported by all browsers in widespread use, except IE6. The property accepts the following values:

- fixed: Fix the background image in relation to the browser viewport.

- scroll: Fix the background image in relation to the page content. This is the default value.

- inherit: The background-attachment property is not inherited, so this tells the browser to use the same value as the parent element.

Because scroll is the default value, you need to use background-attachment only when you want to fix the background image in relation to the browser viewport. The body style rule in image_fixed.html in the download files sets background-attachment to fixed like this:

```
body {
  background-color: #EFECCA;
  color: #000;
  font-family: "Trebuchet MS", Arial, Helvetica, sans-serif;
  margin: 0;
  padding: 0;
  background-image: url(../../images/flower1.png);
  background-repeat: no-repeat;
  background-attachment: fixed;
}
```

As Figure 5-8 shows, the image of the flower remains at the top left of the browser window even when you scroll down the page.

Figure 5-8. The background image remains at the top left of the browser window when the page is scrolled.

168

What if you don't like the position of the background image? CSS has thought of that, too.

Adjusting the position of a background image

The last of the background-related properties, `background-position`, gives you precise control over the position of a background image. It accepts up to two values expressed in any combination of the following ways:

- Lengths (pixels, ems, etc.)
- Keywords (see Table 5-2)
- Percentages

This can make `background-position` rather confusing at first, but the following section should make things clear. Table 5-2 explains the keywords and their equivalent values expressed as percentages.

Table 5-2. Keywords and Percentage Values for background-position

Axis	Keyword	Percentage Equivalent
Horizontal		
	left	0%
	center	50%
	right	100%
Vertical		
	top	0%
	center	50%
	bottom	100%

When defining `background-position`, you can use one or two values.

- If you use only one value, the other value is automatically set to center or 50%.
- If you use two values, and *both* are keywords, they can be in either order. Otherwise, the first value controls the horizontal position, and the second controls the vertical position.

Still confused? One of the joys of CSS is that it offers a lot of flexibility, but that often comes at the expense of clarity. Let's try a few examples, starting with a single keyword like this:

```
background-position: left;
```

This puts the background image halfway down the left side.

The following rule centers the background image at the top:

```
background-position: top;
```

This centers the background image exactly within the element:

```
background-position: center;
```

ExplainED

It's important to realize that background-position *works independently of* background-repeat. *Unless you also set* background-repeat *to* no-repeat, *the image will still fill the entire background. The difference is that it will start from the specified position, and tile in all directions. If you set* background-repeat *to* repeat-y, *it will fill the entire vertical axis. Tiling along an axis always goes in both directions. The purpose of using* background-position *with an image that repeats is to control its balance, instead of tiling it from the top left corner.*

When using two keywords, they can be in either order, so the following definitions are both valid ways of putting the bottom right of the background image at the bottom right of the element:

```
background-position: bottom right;
background-position: right bottom;
```

When using two values, unless *both* are keywords, the horizontal value must come first. For example, the following fails in most browsers:

```
background-position: bottom 25px; /* WRONG */
```

Although there's no doubt that bottom indicates the vertical axis, the horizontal value *must* precede the vertical one like this:

```
background-position: 25px bottom; /* CORRECT */
```

This puts the left of the background image 25px from the left side of the element, with its bottom edge at the bottom of the element.

If you use a length on its own, the background image is placed that distance from the left of the element and centered vertically. So, the following rule places the left edge of the image 25 pixels from the left side of the element and centers it vertically:

```
background-position: 25px;
```

Two lengths are calculated from the top-left corner of the background image. So, take the following rule:

```
background-position: 20px 10px;
```

This puts the top left corner of the background image 20px from the left side of the element and 10px from the top.

Percentages are calculated not only in relation to the background but also in relation to the image itself, for example:

```
background-position: 50% 50%;
```

This centers the image exactly in the background, because a position 50% across the image's horizontal and vertical axes is placed 50% across the horizontal and vertical axes of the background. So, using percentages gives you very precise control over the position of a background image without the need for complex calculations.

Hopefully, that has clarified some of the confusion. The best way to understand this sort of thing is to experiment.

Now that you know all about background images, let's add some to journey.html.

Inserting background images

This exercise adds and positions background images on the main heading, Roosevelt quote, and bottom of the wrapper <div> in the page used in the previous exercises. Continue working with the same files. Alternatively, use as your starting point journey_17.html and css/journey_17.css in the download files for this chapter.

1. The images folder contains two versions of the flower used in Figures 5-4 to 5-8, one roughly twice the size of the other. I want to use the larger image, flower1.png, to tuck under the first letter of the <h1> heading. So amend the h1 style block like this:

```
h1 {
  font-size: 220%;
```

```
    font-variant: small-caps;
    text-align: center;
    word-spacing: O.2em;
    letter-spacing: O.O5em;
    margin-top: O;
    background-image: url(../../images/flower1.png);
    background-repeat: no-repeat;
}
```

If necessary, amend the path to the image to match your site structure. I have used a path relative to the style sheet, but you can also use a path relative to your site root, like this:

```
background-image:url(/images/flower1.png);
```

2. Save the style sheet, and load journey.html into a browser. As Figure 5-9 shows, the bottom of the flower is cut off. This is because the background image is taller than the <h1> element.

Figure 5-9. The background image is cut off because it's taller than the heading.

One solution would be to create a smaller image, but that would defeat the purpose of the exercise. You need to make more room for the background to fit in. Increasing the bottom margin of the heading won't work (try it), because—as I explained earlier—backgrounds don't stretch into an element's margins.

3. The answer is to give the heading the same height as the background image, which is 61px. Amend the h1 style block like this:

```
h1 {
    font-size: 220%;
    font-variant: small-caps;
    text-align: center;
    word-spacing: O.2em;
    letter-spacing: O.O5em;
    margin-top: O;
    background-image: url(../../images/flower1.png);
    background-repeat: no-repeat;
    height: 61px;
}
```

4. If you check the page now, you should see the background image is no longer cut off. So, all that remains is to reposition it horizontally by adding the `background-position` property to the style rule like this:

```
h1 {
    font-size: 220%;
    font-variant: small-caps;
    text-align: center;
    word-spacing: 0.2em;
    letter-spacing: 0.05em;
    margin-top: 0;
    background-image: url(../../images/flower1.png);
    background-repeat: no-repeat;
    background-position: 70px;
    height: 61px;
}
```

Because I have used only one value, this moves the background image 70px to the right. The vertical position is automatically set to `center`.

5. Before checking the page, let's add the smaller flower to the bottom right of the Roosevelt quote. Change the #tr_quote style block like this:

```
#tr_quote {
    margin: 50px 71px 0 374px;
    width: 275px;
    background-color: #FFFEF1;
    background-image: url(../../images/flower2.png);
    background-repeat: no-repeat;
    background-position: 97% 95%;
}
```

This uses percentages to position the flower. Using 100% 100% would put it as far as possible in the bottom right corner, but I think it looks better slightly offset at 97% horizontal and 95% vertical.

6. Save the style sheet, and reload `journey.html` in the browser. It should look like Figure 5-10.

The small flower looks great in the corner of the quote, but the position of the heading needs to be slightly tweaked. However, I'm going to leave that until the next chapter, when we delve into the mysteries of the `padding` property.

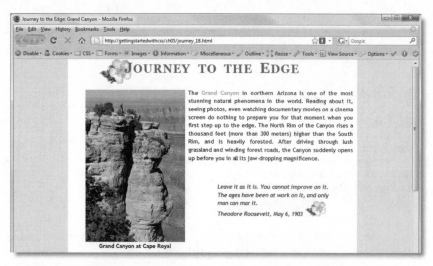

Figure 5-10. Background images add decorative interest to a page.

7. To round off this exploration of background images, let's fix the problem of the olive stripe at the bottom of the page, and give it a dramatic touch by adding a background image of the Grand Canyon.

   Insert an empty paragraph at the bottom of the page inside the wrapper <div>, and give the paragraph an ID of footer.

8. Create a style block using the ID selector, #footer, and set the value of margin-bottom to 0. It's not important where you put the style block inside the style sheet, but the footer will eventually become part of the page structure, so I suggest putting after the #wrapper:

```
#wrapper {
  width: 720px;
  margin: 0 auto;
  background-color: #FFF;
}
#footer {
  margin-bottom: 0;
}
```

   This eliminates the olive stripe at the bottom of the page by removing the 0.4em bottom margin on the paragraph.

9. As you saw with the flower at the top of the page, the visibility of a background image is constrained by the height of the element to which it's applied. The background image of the Grand Canyon is 251px high, so there's no point adding it as the background of the

footer paragraph. The paragraph isn't tall enough, so the background will be cut off unless you put a lot of material in there.

However, as long as no other background is defined, the background of a parent element shows through, thanks to the default transparent value of background-color. So, that means you can apply the background image to the wrapper <div>, and it will show through the other elements inside the <div>.

Change the #wrapper style block like this:

```
#wrapper {
  width: 720px;
  margin: 0 auto;
  background-color: #FFF;
  background-image: url(../../images/grand_canyon.jpg);
  background-repeat: no-repeat;
  background-position: bottom;
}
```

I have made the background image of the Grand Canyon 1200px wide. That's much wider than the page currently needs, but it gives scope for expanding the width of the wrapper <div> later. It needs to go at the bottom of the <div>, so I have used the keyword, bottom. The most interesting part of the image is the center, but you don't need to declare a horizontal position, as the browser automatically uses center when you supply only a vertical keyword.

10. If you test the page now, you'll see the text comes down too far over the background image. So, add a height of 120px to the #footer style block:

```
#footer {
  margin-bottom: 0;
  height: 120px;
}
```

This is a lot neater than the usual trick of adding a lot of empty paragraphs. It's also a temporary measure until you learn about the padding property in the next chapter.

11. Save the style sheet, and reload journey.html in a browser. The bottom of the page should now look like Figure 5-11. The background image fades at the top so that it blends with the background of the wrapper <div>, while the last couple of sentences remain readable over the dramatic image.

You can check your code, if necessary, against journey_18.html and css/journey_18.css in the download files for this chapter.

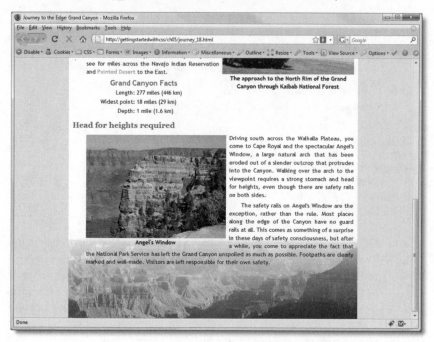

Figure 5-11. A background image at the bottom of the page transforms a previously bland design.

Using the background shorthand property

The background shorthand property lets you define all five background properties in a single declaration. Any value that is omitted is automatically set to its default value. The #wrapper style block currently looks like this:

```
#wrapper {
  width: 720px;
  margin: 0 auto;
  background-color: #FFF;
  background-image: url(../../images/grand_canyon.jpg);
  background-repeat: no-repeat;
  background-position: bottom;
}
```

To save space in your style sheet, you can rewrite it like this:

```
#wrapper {
  width:720px;
```

```
  margin:0 auto;
  background: #FFF url(../../images/grand_canyon.jpg) no-repeat bottom;
}
```

Separate the values with spaces. They can be in any order, apart from the values that specify the position of the background image, which must follow the same rules as the individual background-position property. In other words, if you want to specify the horizontal and vertical position of the background image, the horizontal value must come first unless you use two keywords.

My personal preference is to use the individual properties. Although it involves more typing, I think the individual properties make the style sheet easier to understand.

There is also a hidden danger lurking in the background shorthand property. As I said earlier, any value that is omitted from the shorthand property declaration is automatically set to its default value. It's easy to slip into the habit of using just background to define the background color.

Figure 5-12 and journey_bad_shorthand.html in the download files show what happens when the #wrapper style block is rewritten using the background shorthand property to set the color after the individual properties:

```
#wrapper {
  width: 720px;
  margin: 0 auto;
  background-image: url(../../images/grand_canyon.jpg);
  background-repeat: no-repeat;
  background-position: bottom;
  background: #FFF; /* This overrides the individual properties */
}
```

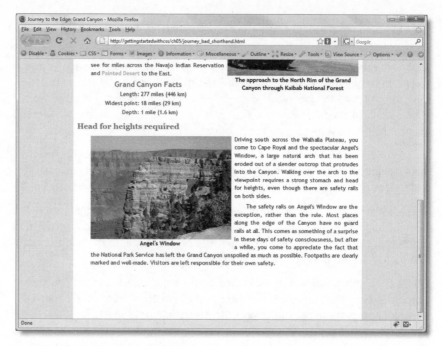

Figure 5-12. Careless use of the background shorthand property results in the background image not being displayed.

ExplainED

Although there aren't many background properties to remember, there are quite a lot of things to remember about using them. One of the main things to watch out for when working with backgrounds is the effect of vertical margins. As you saw in the exercises, margins on elements at the top or bottom of a <div> can extend beyond the <div>, pushing it away from its expected position and revealing a different background. Fortunately, Firebug and the Safari 4 Web Inspector panel can highlight margins, making it easier to debug such problems. Other things that can catch you out are the way background images tile, and mastering the complexities of background-position.

So much for backgrounds—let's take a look at borders.

Controlling borders with CSS

CSS provides individual control over each border, allowing you to set its color, style, and width. As a result, there are a lot of border-related properties, all of which are listed in Table 5-3.

Table 5-3. CSS Border Properties

Property	Initial Value	Inherited	Description
border-top-color	Text color	No	Defines the color for the top border. If no color is defined, the border uses the same color as would be used for the element's text.
border-right-color	Text color	No	Same as the previous property for the right border.
border-bottom-color	Text color	No	Same as the previous property for the bottom border.
border-left-color	Text color	No	Same as the previous property for the left border.
border-top-style	none	No	Defines the style for the top border. A style must be set for the border to appear.
border-right-style	none	No	Same as the previous property for the right border.
border-bottom-style	none	No	Same as the previous property for the bottom border.
border-left-style	none	No	Same as the previous property for the left border.
border-top-width	medium	No	Defines the width of the top border.
border-right-width	medium	No	Defines the width of the right border.
border-bottom-width	medium	No	Defines the width of the bottom border.

179

Property	Initial Value	Inherited	Description
border-left-width	medium	No	Defines the width of the left border.
border-color		No	Shorthand property that defines the color of all four borders.
border-style		No	Shorthand property that defines the style of all four borders.
border-width		No	Shorthand property that defines the width of all four borders.
border-top		No	Shorthand property that defines the top border.
border-right		No	Shorthand property that defines the right border.
border-bottom		No	Shorthand property that defines the bottom border.
border-left		No	Shorthand property that defines the left border.
border		No	Shorthand property that defines the color, style, and width of all borders. When used, the same values are applied to all four borders.

As you can see, there are a lot of shorthand properties. They take a little getting used to, but they work in a similar way to the margin shorthand property and can save a lot of typing on a complex layout.

There are two other CSS properties that relate to borders: border-collapse and border-spacing. They apply only to tables, which are a special case, and we'll cover them separately in Chapter 9.

Setting a border color

Setting a border color is very simple. You can use one of the individual properties, such as `border-top-color`, to set the color of a specific side or the shorthand `border-color` to set the colors for all four sides. If you don't specify a color, the browser should automatically use the same color as would be used for text in the same element. However, some browsers don't always do this, so it's better to specify the border color explicitly, even if you want to use the same color as the text.

Color values can be expressed in any of the following ways:

- A 3- or 6-digit hexadecimal number
- One of the 17 color keywords listed in Table 2-3
- An `rgb()` value specifying the red, green, and blue values as comma-separated numbers in the range of 0–255 or percentages from 0% to 100%

In addition to a color, you can also use `transparent` as the value. This preserves the border width, but lets the underlying content show through.

When using the `border-color` shorthand, you can specify one, two, three, or four values. These follow exactly the same rules as for the `margin` shorthand property, namely:

- **One value**: Applies equally to all four sides.
- **Two values**: The first one applies to the top and bottom, and the second one to the left and right.
- **Three values**: The first one applies to the top, the second one to the left and right, and the third one to the bottom.
- **Four values**: The values are applied in clockwise order starting from the top.

As with the `margin` shorthand property, I suggest you forget about using three values. Just remember to start at the top and move in a clockwise direction.

Setting a border style

You can choose from eight border styles: `dashed`, `dotted`, `double`, `groove`, `inset`, `outset`, `ridge`, and `solid`. Examples of how each style is displayed in Firefox 3.0 are shown in Figure 5-13.

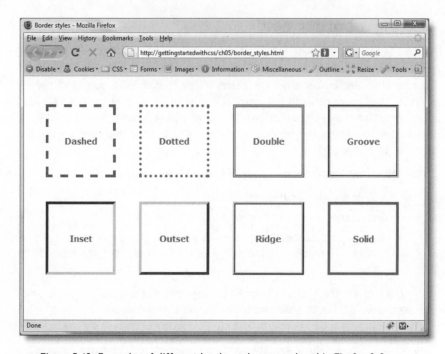

Figure 5-13. Examples of different border styles as rendered in Firefox 3.0

You can also test border_styles.html in the download files for this chapter. View the file in different browsers to see how they render the styles. Also experiment by changing the value of the border-width property in the div style block. You'll notice that there are sometimes considerable differences in what each browser displays. Borders need to be tested carefully if you want to avoid disasters in your design, particularly when using wide borders.

In addition to the styles already listed, you can also specify none, hidden, or inherited. The hidden value is used exclusively with tables and is discussed in Chapter 9. Although none is the default value, it is also useful for suppressing an unwanted border.

Specify the border style using one of the individual properties, such as border-top-style, or the border-style shorthand property. Like border-color, border-style takes one, two, three, or four values, and applies them in the same way.

Setting a border width

You can define the width of a border using a length, such as pixels or ems, or one of the following keywords: thin, medium, or thick. The CSS2.1 specification doesn't lay down an equivalent value for these keywords, so the result you get is likely to differ from browser to browser.

Specify the width using one of the individual properties, such as border-top-width, or the border-width shorthand property. The shorthand property accepts up to four values, which are applied in the same way as described earlier for border-color.

The important thing to realize about the width of borders is that they are added *outside* the element to which they are applied. While this sounds logical enough, it has a major impact on calculations concerning width and height.

ExplainED

Many a designer is caught out by forgetting—or not realizing—that the width of any border is added to the size of the element. The Roosevelt quote is currently 275 pixels wide, but if you add a 5-pixel border all round, its total width increases to 285 pixels. This affects the calculations you did in the last chapter to adjust its margins and center it alongside the floated image.

Using border shorthand properties

Because every element has four sides, adding a border involves typing out up to twelve properties if you use the individual ones. For example, to add a 5-pixel solid, green border to every image requires this massive style block:

```
img {
    border-top-color: #468966;
    border-top-style: solid;
    border-top-width: 5px;
    border-right-color: #468966;
    border-right-style: solid;
    border-right-width: 5px;
    border-bottom-color: #468966;
    border-bottom-style: solid;
    border-bottom-width: 5px;
    border-left-color: #468966;
    border-left-style: solid;
    border-left-width: 5px;
}
```

Obviously, typing out the individual properties all the time is a major chore, so the shorthand properties are great time-savers. Using the `border-color`, `border-style`, and `border-width` shorthand properties reduces the previous style block to this:

```
img {
    border-color: #468966;
    border-style: solid;
    border-width: 5px;
}
```

In fact, because the same values are applied to all four sides, you can reduce it even further by using the `border` shorthand property:

```
img {
    border: #468966 solid 5px;
}
```

When using the `border` shorthand property, it doesn't matter which order you place the values. Just separate them with at least one space. For a uniform border around all sides of an element, using the `border` shorthand property is best choice.

So why have all the individual properties and six other shorthand properties? It's because CSS recognizes that you don't always want the same border on every side. In fact, you might not even want a border on every side. CSS gives you the freedom to put a border along just one side, for example, as a divider between columns. In such cases, using the individual properties or the other shorthand properties makes sense.

Using borders to simulate embossing and indenting

The border styles include `inset` and `outset`, which give the impression of an indented or embossed border. However, browsers tend to use quite different colors to achieve these effects, so it's usually better to create your own style rules to get exactly the colors you want. Figure 5-14 shows this in action in border_shorthand.html, which you can find in the download files for this chapter.

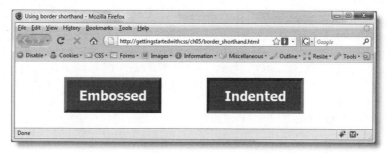

Figure 5-14. The large range of border shorthand rules makes it easy to use different styles and colors.

The embossed <div> on the left uses the following shorthand rules:

```
#embossed {
  border-top: #5C9D9D solid 6px;
  border-right: #003636 solid 6px;
  border-bottom: #003636 solid 6px;
  border-left: #5C9D9D solid 6px;
}
```

This defines the color, style, and width for the border on each side. However, the style and width is the same for each one. So, you can save yourself a bit of typing by using the border shorthand property to declare them for all sides, and then use the border-color shorthand property to define the color for each side, which is how I did it for the indented <div>:

```
#indented {
  border: solid 6px;
  border-color: #003636 #5C9D9D #5C9D9D #003636;
}
```

In this example, the border-color shorthand property has four values. So, starting at the top and going in a clockwise direction, they define the top, right, bottom, and left colors. As you can see from both the code and Figure 5-14, the top and left colors are the same, as are the right and bottom ones.

Don't worry if you find the shorthand properties confusing. Just use the individual properties until you feel more comfortable with CSS. You'll find it easier to make the transition from individual properties to the shorthand versions if you follow the same order as the shorthand: top, right, bottom, left. Another useful technique is to create the style you want with the individual properties, and then convert it to shorthand. Comment out the longhand version while you build the shorthand one. If anything goes wrong, you can comment out the shorthand and revert to your original version. Experimenting like this helps build your knowledge and confidence.

Understanding how borders affect layout

Adding borders to elements in your pages is easy. What's not so easy is remembering the impact that adding a border has on your layout. As mentioned earlier, the width of borders is added to the width and height of an element. So, if you have a 5px border all round, the element will be 10px wider and taller than any declared width and height. This often means recalculating existing margins once you add a border.

Let's add a few borders to journey.html.

Adding borders

This exercise shows you how to add borders to individual sides of elements as well as all around them. It also demonstrates the effect that adding borders has on the layout of your page. Continue working with the files from the preceding exercise. Alternatively, use journey_18.html and css/journey_18.css from the download files for this chapter.

1. The transition between the page's olive background and the white of the center section looks somehow incomplete. Adding a border to the

left and right sides of the wrapper <div> should give it more definition. However, a border on the top and bottom would look too heavy. This is a case for the border-left and border-right shorthand properties. Add them to the #wrapper style block like this:

```
#wrapper {
    width: 720px;
    margin: 0 auto;
    background-color: #FFF;
    background-image: url(../../images/grand_canyon.jpg);
    background-repeat: no-repeat;
    background-position: bottom;
    border-left: 2px solid #D8D0AC;
    border-right: 2px solid #D8D0AC;
}
```

2. Save the style sheet, and load journey.html into a browser. The new style rules have added a narrow border along either side of the center section in a slightly darker shade of olive. The effect is subtle, but I think it improves the look of the page.

3. Experiment with other styles and widths, or choose a different color if you prefer. You'll notice that you need to set the width to at least 4 or 5 pixels for some of the styles to display correctly. Notice also how the color changes when you choose groove, ridge, inset, or outset.

   Because the wrapper <div> has a fixed width and its left and right margins are set to auto, it doesn't matter how wide a border you add, the <div> remains centered—provided, of course, that the border is the same width on both sides.

4. Let's see what happens when you add a border to the images. Create a new style rule at the bottom of the style sheet using img as a type selector:

```
img {
    border: #468966 double 5px;
}
```

5. Save the style sheet, and reload the page in the browser. Look at the two images that are floated left. The border has been added to them, and the content flowing around them has been moved across to make room. Everything looks just fine.

6. Now, take a close look at the image floated right. The border has been added, but the image is jammed up against the right edge of the wrapper <div>. Figure 5-15 shows a comparison of the position of the image before and after the border was added.

187

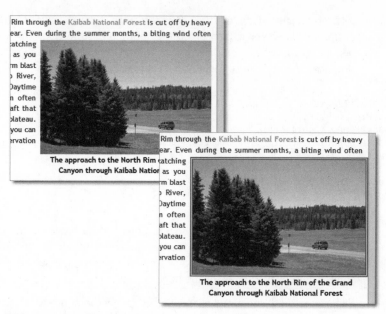

Figure 5-15. Adding the border has caused the image to shift.

What's going on here? Cast your mind back to the first exercise in this chapter, where you added a 10-pixel right margin to the paragraphs to create some breathing space between the text and the right side of the wrapper `<div>`. The image is now flush with the side of the `<div>`. In other words, it has shifted 10 pixels to the right. The border that you added to the images in step 4 is 5px all round. So, that amount on each side accounts for the extra 10 pixels. What it doesn't explain is why this image hasn't realigned itself with the rest of the paragraph.

The answer is that the image is wrapped in a `<span>` to float it together with the caption. This image has a particularly long caption, so I gave the `<span>` an inline style in the previous chapter to make it the same width as the image (325px). However, with the border, the image is now 335px wide. As a result, the `<span>` is still floating only the same distance as before, and the extra 10 pixels are protruding from its right side.

7. Amend the inline style for the `<span>` to set its width to 335px like this:

```
<span class="floatright" style="width:335px"><img ↵
src="../images/forest_grassland.jpg"
```

8. Save the page, and reload it in a browser. The right border of the image should now be aligned with the right edge of the text.

9. However, let's say you want the border to go round the caption as well. Cut the border style definition from the img style block, and paste it into the group selector that defines the text properties for the captions. The styles should now look like this:

```
.floatleft, .floatright, .imgcentered {
    font-weight: bold;
    text-align: center;
    border: #468966 double 5px;
}
img {

}
```

This leaves the img style block with no rule definitions, but that's perfectly valid.

10. Save the style sheet, and reload journey.html in the browser. The border fits snugly around the two images floated left, but there's now a 5px gap on either side of the image that's floated right, as shown in Figure 5-16.

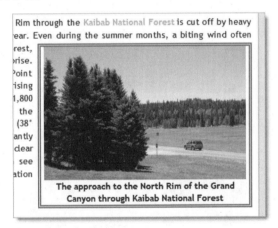

Figure 5-16. The <span> is now too wide for the image.

The reason for this is that the border is no longer around the image, but around the <span>. Since the <span> is floated, the browser automatically adjusts the surrounding text to take account of the border. However, the internal width of the <span> is now 10px too

189

wide for the image. To get rid of the gap, you need to set the width of the <span> back to the same as that of the image, 325px.

11. To conclude this investigation of the effects of borders and margins, add the following border styles to the Roosevelt quote:

```
#tr_quote {
  margin: 50px 71px 0 374px;
  width: 275px;
  background-color: #FFFEF1;
  background-image: url(../../images/flower2.png);
  background-repeat: no-repeat;
  background-position: 97% 95%;
  border: solid 30px;
  border-top-color: #CAC7B0;
  border-right-color: #606249;
  border-bottom-color: #606249;
  border-left-color: #CAC7B0;
}
```

This uses the border shorthand property to set the style and width for all four sides. I have deliberately chosen a very wide border to demonstrate how borders affect the calculations for margins. The other four style rules define the color for each side: a lighter color for the top and left, and a darker one for the right and bottom sides, creating an embossed effect.

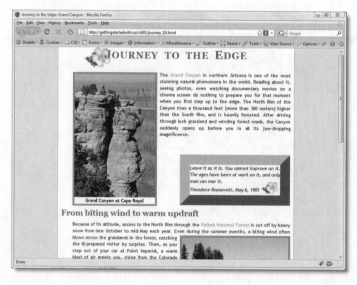

Figure 5-17. The exaggeratedly wide border demonstrates the impact borders have on margins.

12. Save the style sheet, and reload journey.html in the browser. As Figure 5-17 shows, adding a 30px border to the quote results in it being no longer centered alongside the floated image.

    The quote was centered alongside the image in the previous chapter by calculating its left and right margins. However, the 30 pixels have been added to the outside of the quote, pushing it down and to the right. The interesting thing to note is that the explicit right and left margins don't result in the quote and its border being squashed. The left margin is respected, and the right margin is ignored.

13. The current width is far too much, so reduce it to 3px. At the same time you need to recalculate the margins. Because you're adding a 3px border to the quote, you need to reduce its top, right, and left margins by the same amount. The bottom margin was already 0, so you don't need to change that. However, the quote is floated alongside an image that has an extra 5px border on either side. So, you need to take that into account, too.

    The space inside the wrapper <div> is still 720px, because *its* borders are added outside. So, to calculate the space available to the right of the image, you need to subtract the following amounts from 720px:

    - Left margin: 45px
    - Left border on floated element: 5px
    - Image: 250px
    - Right border on floated element: 5px
    - Right margin on floated element: 8px

    That adds up to 313px. So, the space to the right of the floated element is 407px. The <blockquote> is 275px wide, but it now has a 3px border on every side, so its overall width is 281px.

    To keep the quote centered in that space, it needs a 63px margin on both sides. But remember that the left margin of a block-level element alongside an element that has been floated left stretches under the floated element. So, you need to add the 313px to this figure to get the correct left margin (376px). Figure 5-18 shows how I arrived at this result.

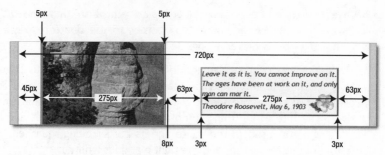

Figure 5-18. You need to add up all the dimensions to arrive at the correct value for the margins around the quote.

The amended styles look like this:

```
#tr_quote {
  margin:47px 63px 0 376px;
  width: 275px;
  background-color: #FFFEF1;
  background-image: url(../../images/flower2.png);
  background-repeat: no-repeat;
  background-position: 97% 95%;
  border: solid 3px;
  border-top-color: #CAC7B0;
  border-right-color: #606249;
  border-bottom-color: #606249;
  border-left-color: #CAC7B0;
}
```

14. Save the style sheet, and reload the page in the browser. The quote should now have a slimmer border and be correctly positioned.

    There's currently no breathing space between the text and the border. You could fix that by adjusting the margins of the blockquote p style rule, but I plan to use the padding property in the next chapter. So, leave it for now.

    You can check your code, if necessary, against journey_19.html and css/journey_19.css in the download files for this chapter.

I suspect that some readers might be shaking their head in disbelief at this stage. Controlling the layout of a page with CSS often involves fiddly calculations, and it's not always easy to see what causes a particular effect. That's why it's important to understand the interaction between the different aspects of the CSS box model. Up to now, you have dealt with margins and borders. In the next chapter, the final piece of the jigsaw will fall into place: padding. Once you understand how all three work together, much of the confusion should fall away, and you'll begin to appreciate how much real control CSS gives you. Using a CSS analysis tool like the Safari 4 *Web Inspector* panel or Firebug also helps visualize what the browser is doing behind the scenes.

ExplainED

If you test journey_19.html *in IE6, you'll see that it adds the* 45px *left margin inside the border around the images and captions floated left. Older browsers often have CSS bugs that affect layout. The purpose of this book is to teach you the basic principles of CSS as implemented by standards-compliant browsers, rather than to engage battle with every bug—and there are a lot of them—in IE6. However, this particular layout problem will be solved by changes made to the image styles in Chapter 7.*

Before moving onto the next chapter, I need to tidy up a few loose ends regarding backgrounds and borders.

How do I get rid of the blue border around link images?

When you use an image as a link, browsers automatically surround the image with a blue border. In the early days of the Web, this was a useful visual device indicating that the image was a link. However, using images as links is now commonplace, and the blue border tends to destroy the visual harmony of a page.

The traditional way of getting rid of the border was to add border="0" in the <img> tag. CSS provides a much simpler method. Just add the following rule to your style sheet:

```
a img {
  border: none;
}
```

This is another example of a descendant selector, which you first encountered with blockquote p in Chapter 2. A descendant selector targets an element that is nested inside another—in other words, a child element. The blockquote p selector targets paragraphs inside a <blockquote>; a img targets images inside an <a> tag.

Adding this simple rule to your style sheet removes the blue border from every link image in your site—provided, of course, the style sheet is attached to every page that uses images as links.

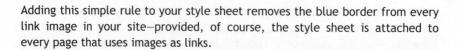

Strictly speaking, to target a child element, you should use a child selector, which uses a greater than symbol between the two basic selectors like this: a > img. *However, IE6 doesn't understand child selectors, so you need to use a descendant selector instead.*

A child selector applies only to elements nested one level deep, whereas a descendant selector targets elements nested at any level. When dealing with elements nested only one level deep, child selectors are more efficient, but lack of support in IE6 makes their use impractical in a public website.

How do I prevent backgrounds and borders from displaying under floats?

A rather surprising feature of backgrounds and borders is that, when they are used on an element alongside a float, they stretch underneath the float. This isn't a bug, but as designed. In fact, it's quite logical when you consider the way margins are handled alongside floats. Logical or not, it can look quite strange. So, you need a way of dealing with this behavior.

Figure 5-19 demonstrates the problem. The image in the first paragraph is floated left. The second paragraph has a background color, and the third paragraph has a border. To show what's happening, I have put a 20px margin on the left and right sides of the floated image. You can examine the code yourself in floats.html in the download files for this chapter.

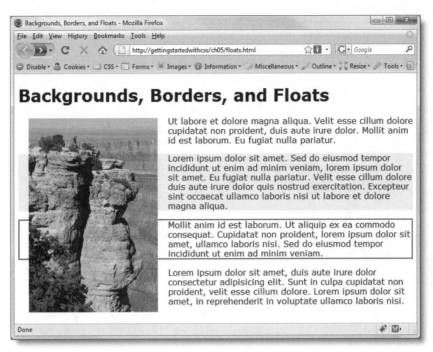

Figure.5-19. The default behavior of backgrounds and borders is to stretch behind floated elements.

Fortunately, preventing the background and border from stretching underneath the floated element is very easy. You just add the `overflow` property to the styles that define the background and border and set its value to `hidden` like this (the code is in `floats_overflow.html`):

```
.highlight1 {
  background-color: #FF3;
  overflow: hidden;
}
.highlight2 {
  border: #063 2px solid;
  overflow: hidden;
}
```

As Figure 5-20 shows, the background and border are now flowed alongside the floated image, just like the text.

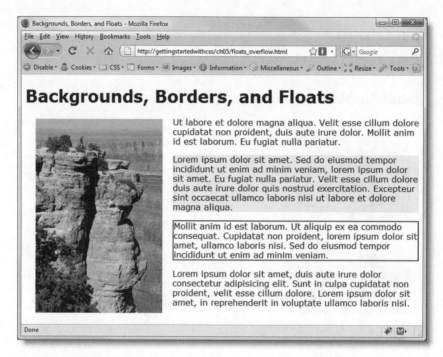

Figure 5-20. Setting the overflow property to hidden stops the background and border stretching under the floated image.

Setting the overflow property to hidden works in all modern browsers. As you might have guessed, IE6 spoils the party. You can fix this problem by adding the Microsoft proprietary property, zoom, to the style rule, and setting its value to 1. Because it's not standard CSS, you might want to put this in a Microsoft conditional comment inside the <head> of your web page after any embedded styles or links to external style sheets. As explained in Chapter 1, the advantage of a conditional comment is that it's inside HTML comment tags. So, other browsers—and the W3C validator—ignore it. This is how I added the proprietary style rule in floats_overflow.html:

```
<!--[if lte IE 6]>
<style type="text/css">
.highlight1, .highlight2 {
  zoom: 1;
}
</style>
<![endif]-->
```

OK, I know I said I wasn't going to deal with every IE6 bug, but this one is so simple to squash.

LinkED

Visit www.quirksmode.org/css/condcom.html *to find out more about Microsoft conditional comments.*

Chapter review

CSS makes the addition and precise positioning of background images very easy. Borders are also easy to style once you get used to the initially bewildering number of border properties. What's not so easy is understanding how backgrounds and borders interact with margins. Adding a background or border to an element usually impacts the rest of the page layout. Background colors and images do not stretch into the margins surrounding an element, allowing the surrounding background to show through. Most of the time, this is what you want, but the overlapping margins at the top and bottom of the wrapper <div> resulted in an unwanted stripe of the <body> background being displayed.

You also saw how adding a border to an element often necessitates the recalculation of margins or width. Understanding the rules governing width and height is one of the trickiest aspects of CSS. By the time you reach the end of the next chapter, you should be a master.

Chapter 6

How Do I Solve the Mysteries of Width and Height?

By now, you should know that the addition of a border affects the margins surrounding an element. Borders are added outside the element, increasing its overall width and height. However, that's not the only thing that goes outside an element—so does padding. As the name suggests, padding is a sort of buffer zone between the contents of an element and its surroundings. Figure 6-1 shows the Roosevelt quote from the exercise file from the preceding chapters without padding and with it added.

Figure 6-1. Padding adds space between the content and border.

The screenshot on the left shows the quote as it looked at the end of Chapter 5. There is no space between the text and the border, except at the bottom. The gap between the final paragraph and the border is created by the 0.4em bottom margin on each paragraph. I could have increased the other margins around the paragraphs to create the space in the screenshot on the right, but I didn't. The paragraphs don't have a declared width, so increasing their margins would have left less room for the text. Instead, I added padding to the #tr_quote style rule for the <blockquote> element. As you can see, the <blockquote> on the right is both wider and taller. However—and this is the part that confuses most people—the width property of the <blockquote> in both screenshots has the same value: 275px.

There's no trickery involved. Both screenshots were taken in the same browser at the same time on the same monitor. The point is that width and height in CSS refer to the *content*. Padding, borders, and margins are all added *outside* the content. So, although the width property of both elements is set in the style sheet at 275px, the overall size of the quote on the left is 281px (275px + 3px of border on each side), and the quote on the right is 301px (275px + 10px of padding on each side + 3px of border on each side). Once you understand the distinction between the *declared* width or height of an element and its *overall* width or height including padding and borders, the mysteries of width and height in CSS begin to fade.

This chapter brings together the four pieces of the CSS box model—content, padding, borders, and margins—and their effect on width and height calculations. In particular, you'll learn about the following:

- How to control space between the content of an element and its borders
- Deciding whether to choose padding or margins
- Controlling the minimum and maximum dimensions of an element
- Scaling images automatically depending on browser width
- Simulating min-width and max-width in IE6
- What to do when content spills out of its container
- Using the overflow property to keep a floated element inside a background
- Displaying a message to warn users of older browsers about display problems

First, let's review the principles of the CSS box model.

Padding—the final piece of the CSS box model

As I mentioned in Chapter 3, the **box model** lies at the heart of CSS. In theory, the box model is very simple, but many people find it confusing. The purpose of this section is to clarify how it works and remove any cause for confusion. Figure 6-2 summarizes the CSS box model.

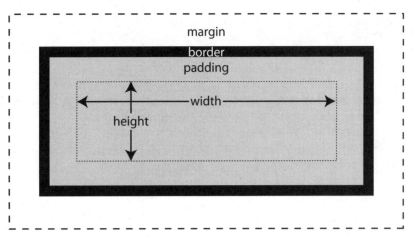

Figure 6-2. How the CSS box model works

What most people find difficult to understand is that, although padding goes inside the border, it is added outside the element to which it applies. Since the border is also added outside, the overall width and height of the element are increased by the size of any padding and border. When you look at a diagram like Figure 6-2, it seems obvious. However, when you're staring at a style sheet scratching your head, it's easy to forget that adding 10px of padding around 300px-wide element has made it 320px wide. Add a 1px border and a 25px left margin, and the space it occupies has suddenly grown to 346px.

ExplainED

If you think this way of calculating width and height is counterintuitive, you're not alone. In the early days of CSS, Microsoft thought that the width and height of a box should be measured from the outside of one border to the outside of the opposite border. So, it included the border *and* padding *properties inside the box. In the Microsoft box model, a 300px-wide element with 10px of padding and a 1px-border measured 300px across, leaving 278px for the content. However, this was an incorrect interpretation of the CSS specification, and Microsoft switched to the correct box model in IE6.*

To prevent sites that used the old, incorrect interpretation from breaking, browsers adopted the practice of rendering CSS in what's known as **quirks mode** when a web page lacks a complete DOCTYPE declaration. This treats the padding and border properties as included in the width and height values of elements. So, why not omit the DOCTYPE declaration and make your life easier? Quirks mode is likely to cause other problems and might not be supported by future browsers. You'll soon get used to the box model, and sticking to the official standards makes it easier for others to help you if you run into problems.

LinkED

To learn more about quirks mode, web standards, and browser support for CSS, visit Peter-Paul Koch's excellent website at www.quirksmode.org/css/quirksmode.html.

Choosing between margins and padding

Both margins and padding have the effect of creating space around an element. So, which should you use? Sometimes, there appears to be no difference, but when an element has a border, the choice is clear. If you want space between the border and the element, you must use padding, because margins are always outside the border. There are other important differences between margins and padding, namely:

- **Background**: Margins are transparent, and show the background of the parent element. Padding shares the same background as the element itself.
- **Adjacent elements**: Adjacent vertical margins collapse, and only the largest value is applied. Padding never collapses.

So, if you want the background to stretch beyond the element, padding is the one to choose. Padding also preserves the distance between elements.

Using padding to add space around elements

You apply padding in very much the same way as margins and borders. Padding can be added to almost any element. However, the only table elements that can have padding are the table itself and individual table cells. Table 6-1 lists the properties used for padding.

Table 6-1. CSS Padding Properties

Property	Initial Value	Inherited	Description
padding-top	0	No	Adds padding to the top of an element
padding-right	0	No	Adds padding to the right side of an element
padding-bottom	0	No	Adds padding to the bottom of an element
padding-left	0	No	Adds padding to the left side of an element
padding	0	No	Shorthand property that accepts between one and four values

All properties listed in Table 6-1 accept a length, such as pixels or ems; a percentage; or the keyword inherit. The padding shorthand property works exactly the same way as the margin shorthand property, namely:

- **One value**: This applies equally to all four sides.
- **Two values**: The first one applies to the top and bottom, and the second one to the left and right.
- **Three values**: The first one applies to the top, the second one to the left and right, and the third one to the bottom.
- **Four values**: The values are applied in clockwise order starting from the top.

My advice, as before, is to forget about using three values. Just remember to start at the top and move around the element in a clockwise direction: top, right, bottom, left. With two values, the first applies to the top, and the second one to the right; then repeat the values continuing in a clockwise direction, applying the first one to the bottom, and the second one to the left.

Although you can use a percentage value for padding, it works in a very unusual way. It's so unusual, I recommend you stick to pixels or ems for padding. For the insatiably curious, the sidebar explains why.

ExplainED

If you create a paragraph, set its width to 400px, *and give it* 10% *padding, you probably expect the padding on the left and right to be* 40px, *and the top and bottom padding to be based on the height of the paragraph. It's a reasonable assumption, but it's wrong. When you use a percentage for padding, the value is based on the width of the parent element—even for top and bottom padding. If the paragraph is inside a* <div> *that has a width of* 600px, *the* 10% *padding on all sides will be* 60px.

If the paragraph doesn't have an outer container (or parent), the padding is calculated as a percentage of the page width. So, at 800 × 600 *resolution, the padding is approximately* 75px; *and at* 1280 × 800, *it's approximately* 124px. *In both cases, browser chrome accounts for the value being slightly less than* 10%.

If you want to check this out, load padding_percentage.html *in the download files for this chapter into a browser. As you resize the browser window, you will see the yellow background of the paragraph expand and contract, indicating that the percentage is based on the window size, and not on the width of the paragraph to which the padding has been applied.*

Let's update journey.html, the file that has been used in the exercises in the previous chapters, to see how padding affects various elements.

Creating space around text with padding

This exercise demonstrates how to adjust the space around different text elements using padding and illustrates the effect padding has on width and height measurements. It also shows how the display property can be used to create an inline block, thereby changing the way padding is handled. If you have been working through all the exercises in order, continue working with your existing files. Alternatively, use as your starting point journey_19.html and css/journey_19.css in the download files for this chapter.

1. In Chapter 5, you saw that the 10-pixel margin on top of the `<h1>` heading pushed the wrapper `<div>` away from the top of the page, revealing a stripe of olive background color. Removing the margin got rid of the olive stripe, but the heading is too high on the page. To move it down, add `padding-top` with a value of `13px` to the h1 style block like this:

```
h1 {
  font-size: 220%;
  font-variant: small-caps;
  text-align: center;
  word-spacing: 0.2em;
  letter-spacing: 0.05em;
  margin-top: 0;
  background-image: url(../../images/flower1.png);
  background-repeat: no-repeat;
  background-position: 70px;
  height: 61px;
  padding-top: 13px;
}
```

2. Save the style sheet, and test `journey.html` in a browser. Figure 6-3 shows the heading before and after adding the padding. The addition of padding moves the heading down not only in relation to the page but also to the background image of the flower.

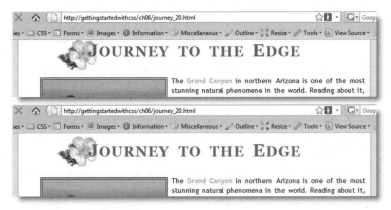

Figure 6-3. Adding padding improves the position of the heading, but it also increases the overall height (below).

The only problem is that adding 13 pixels of padding has increased the overall height of the heading by the same amount, pushing the subsequent content lower. You'll fix that in a moment, but first try a little experiment to see the difference between margin and padding.

3. Change the final property in the h1 style block from padding-top to margin-top like this:

```
h1 {
    font-size: 220%;
    font-variant: small-caps;
    text-align: center;
    word-spacing: 0.2em;
    letter-spacing: 0.05em;
    margin-top: 0;
    background-image: url(../../images/flower1.png);
    background-repeat: no-repeat;
    background-position: 70px;
    height: 61px;
    margin-top: 13px;
}
```

This creates two conflicting values for margin-top, but the lower one overrides the first one, so the value applied will be 13px.

4. Save the style sheet, and reload journey.html into the browser. The top of the page should now look like Figure 6-4.

Figure 6-4. Using margin rather than padding lets the body background show through.

The heading is still the same distance from the top of the page, but using a top margin instead of padding results in the background of the parent element—in other words, the <body>—showing through.

5. The obvious way to deal with the extra height is to deduct the 13px padding from the 61px height of the <h1> heading. However, doing so has a potential drawback, illustrated in Figure 6-5, which shows what happens if someone uses the browser controls to increase the size of the text.

Figure 6-5. Giving elements a fixed height can cause serious problems when text is enlarged by the user.

Admittedly, the design is beginning to fall apart when text is enlarged this much, but someone with really poor eyesight is far less interested in how beautiful your page looks than in actually being able to read the content. Giving the heading a fixed height—in fact, giving a fixed height to any text element—reduces the accessibility of your site. The answer is to remove the height and add some padding to the bottom of the heading.

ExplainED

These days, most browsers have a zoom feature that increases everything in proportion, making fixed heights for text less of a problem. However, users have the option to turn off the zoom feature and increase only the size of text, which is how I took the screenshot in Figure 6-5. Because you have no control over how people will choose to view your sites, fixed heights for text should be avoided.

Delete the height property from the h1 style block, and change the final line like this:

```
h1 {
    font-size: 220%;
    font-variant: small-caps;
    text-align: center;
    word-spacing: 0.2em;
    letter-spacing: 0.05em;
    margin-top: 0;
    background-image: url(../../images/flower1.png);
    background-repeat: no-repeat;
    background-position: 70px;
    padding: 13px 0;
}
```

This uses the padding shorthand property with two values to add 13 pixels of padding to the top and bottom of the heading, and no padding on either side. If anyone increases the text size, the height of the heading will now expand automatically, leaving the text perfectly legible.

6. Next, let's add 10 pixels of padding around the Roosevelt quote. You can do this with the padding shorthand property and a single value. However, since padding increases the overall width of the element, you also need to adjust the margins around the quote. Otherwise, it will no longer be centered and will appear lower down on the page. Amend the #tr_quote style block like this:

```
#tr_quote {
  margin: 37px 58px 0 361px;
  width: 275px;
  background-color: #FFFEF1;
  background-image: url(../../images/flower2.png);
  background-repeat: no-repeat;
  background-position: 97% 95%;
  border: solid 3px;
  border-top-color: #CAC7B0;
  border-right-color: #606249;
  border-bottom-color: #606249;
  border-left-color: #CAC7B0;
  padding: 10px;
}
```

This is quite a simple change. You have added 10px padding to each side, so it's necessary to remove the same amount from each margin, except the bottom one, which remains 0. If you test the page now, the quote should look the same as the right screenshot in Figure 6-1 at the beginning of this chapter.

7. Finally, let's tackle the footer. At the moment, it simply has a fixed height of 120px, designed to make room for the background image of the Grand Canyon to show through. The background image is actually applied to the wrapper <div>, but it will remain visible as long as you don't apply a different background to the footer or anything inside it.

Begin by adding a design credit inside the footer paragraph:

```
<p id="footer">Design: Getting StartED with CSS</p>
```

The bottom of the page now looks like Figure 6-6. The footer paragraph is indented, and there's nothing to set it off from the rest of the text.

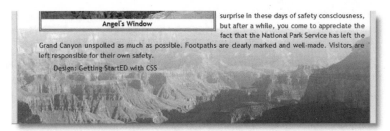

Figure 6-6. The footer paragraph needs to be distinguished from the preceding text.

8. If you apply a background color to the footer paragraph, it will cover the entire width and height, obscuring the image of the Grand Canyon. I want to move the design credit to the bottom right of the page, so the text color will need to be reversed to make it legible against the dark background. Wrap the design credit in a <span>, and give it a class called reversed (you'll create the class style block shortly):

```
<p id="footer"><span class="reversed">Design: Getting StartED with ↵
CSS</span></p>
```

9. The footer paragraph is indented because all paragraphs that don't immediately follow a heading have text-indent set to 30px. So, reset that to 0 in the #footer style block, and create the reversed class like this:

```
#footer {
  margin-bottom: 0;
  height: 120px;
  text-indent: 0;
}
.reversed {
  color: #FFF0A5;
  background-color: #333;
  padding: 3px 5px;
}
```

This gives the design credit yellow text reversed out of a dark background. The padding shorthand property adds 3px of padding to the top and bottom, and 5px on the left and right, making sure there's a small amount of breathing space between the edge of the background color and the text. The problem is that the text is still too high on the page.

209

10. The way to move the design credit to the bottom of the page while keeping the background image of the Grand Canyon visible in its current position is to add a large top margin to the #footer style block. Margins are transparent, so the background of the parent element shows through. However, adding a top margin means reducing the height or eliminating it altogether. Delete the height property from the #footer style block, and add a top margin of 110px. The style block should look like this:

```
#footer {
  margin-top: 110px;
  margin-bottom: 0;
  text-indent: 0;
}
```

11. Save the style sheet, and reload journey.html in the browser. Take a close look at the bottom of the page. As Figure 6-7 shows, the design credit has not only been pushed to the bottom of the page, a tiny strip of the olive background has reappeared.

3px gap →

Figure 6-7. The padding on the bottom of the <span> pushes the wrapper <div> away from the bottom of the page.

Time to start pulling your hair out? Not really. What has happened is that the padding on the bottom of the <span> has overlapped the bottom of the wrapper <div>, and pushed it away from the bottom of the page. This is one of those weird features of inline text elements. Adding padding or margins to the top or bottom of an inline text element doesn't increase the line height; it just spills over to whatever is above or below. Fortunately, there is a cure.

12. Add the display property to the reversed class style block, and set its value to inline-block:

```
.reversed {
  color: #FFF0A5;
  background-color: #333;
```

```
    padding: 3px 5px;
    display: inline-block;
}
```

The display property is described in detail in Chapter 8. All you need to understand at this stage is that setting the display property to inline-block changes the way the <span> is displayed. Although it remains inline, it's treated like a block-level element. Unlike an inline element, the top and bottom padding of an inline block are treated as part of its overall height, so it no longer overlaps surrounding elements. As a result, the 3-pixel gap at the bottom of the page is removed.

13. Even better, you can now move the <span> away from the bottom of the page by giving it a bottom margin of its own. While you're at it, align the footer paragraph to the right, and give it a 10px right margin. Change the style rules like this:

```
#footer {
    margin:110px 10px 0 auto;
    text-align:right;
    text-indent:0;
}
.reversed {
    color: #FFF0A5;
    background-color: #333;
    padding: 3px 5px;
    display: inline-block;
    margin-bottom: 10px;
}
```

The #footer style block now uses the margin shorthand property, leaving the top and bottom values at 110px and 0 respectively, and setting the right margin to 10px. The left margin is set to auto, because you don't know exactly how wide it needs to be.

14. Save the style sheet, and reload journey.html in the browser. The bottom of the page should now look like Figure 6-8.

211

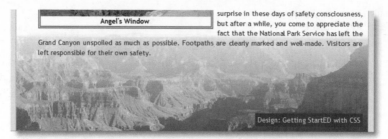

Figure 6-8. The design credit sits close to the bottom right corner, with the background image in its correct position.

You can check your code, if necessary, with journey_20.html and css/journey_20.css in the download files for this chapter.

ExplainED

Changing the <span> to an inline block has given you considerable freedom over its look and position. The 10px margin on the bottom of the <span> has the effect of moving the design credit away from the bottom of the page without triggering a strip of olive background as before. This is because an inline block is normally placed on the text baseline of its parent element—in this case the footer paragraph. Adding a bottom margin to an inline block simply raises it from the text baseline and has no effect on surrounding elements. Don't worry if you find this confusing. I'll come back to the display property in detail in Chapter 8.

Hopefully, this exercise helped clarify the difference between margins and padding. The principal advantage of padding is that it extends the background beyond the edges of an element, whereas margins are always transparent, letting the background of the parent element show through. You might also have noticed that, once I brought padding into the mix, I got rid of the fixed heights I used in the previous chapter. Browsers permit users to resize text, so using a fixed height for any text content runs the risk of destroying your layout and potentially making it unreadable.

Controlling width and height

In addition to the width and height properties you have already met, CSS has four related properties, as described in Table 6-2.

Table 6-2. CSS Width and Height Properties

Property	Initial Value	Inherited	Description
width	auto	No	Sets the width for an element. Can be applied to any element, except inline text elements, or table rows. If no value is specified, the element expands horizontally as far as possible to accommodate the element's content.
max-width	none	No	Sets a maximum width for an element. Percentages are calculated in relation to the parent element.
min-width	0	No	Sets a minimum width for an element. Percentages are calculated in relation to the parent element.
height	auto	No	Sets the height for an element. Can be applied to any element, except inline text elements, or table columns. If no value is specified, the element expands vertically as far as possible to accommodate the element's content.
max-height	none	No	Sets a maximum height for an element. Percentages are calculated in relation to the parent element.
min-height	0	No	Sets a minimum height for an element. Percentages are calculated in relation to the parent element.

Most browsers in widespread use support all six properties, but IE6, which still refuses to lie down and die, supports only width and height.

The important thing to note is that the default value for both the width and height properties is auto. In other words, the element expands and contracts to make room for the content. The default for min-width and min-height is 0, whereas the default for max-width and max-height is none. Although these sound just two ways of saying the same thing, 0 means "there is no minimum," and none means "there is no maximum." So, unless you specify a minimum, the element will collapse to nothing if it has no content. If you specify no maximum, the element will expand horizontally or vertically as far as it can to accommodate its content.

All six properties accept values expressed as a length (for example, pixels or ems) or as a percentage. When a percentage is used, the width or height is calculated as a percentage of the parent element's width or height.

Using the width property in combination with horizontal margins, borders, and padding gives you considerable control over the layout of your web page. However, the height property tends to create problems for layout unless you use it very carefully.

Using a fixed height

The problem with setting a fixed height for an element is that browsers allow users to change the size of text. Most modern browsers have a zoom feature that scales everything in proportion, but users can override it and choose to scale only text. Figure 6-5 earlier in this chapter shows what happens in a modern browser when enlarged text spills out of a fixed-height element. Consequently, you should exercise great care before using the height property.

ExplainED

Some older browsers ignore the height *property when content becomes too large to fit. However, this is incorrect behavior, and you cannot rely on it happening in modern, standards-compliant browsers.*

In my experience, the only time you should declare a specific height is when the content of the element also has a fixed height, for example an image or Flash movie. It's also important to set the height of an element if you want to use a nonrepeating background image, as in the following exercise.

Using a single background image with text

This exercise shows how to use a large image as the background for text. The height property is needed to ensure that the whole image is displayed, regardless of how much content is inside the element that uses the background.

1. For a change, this exercise doesn't use journey.html. So, close it if necessary, and create a new file called height.html in your work folder.

2. In the <body> of the page, create a pair of <div> elements, one nested inside the other like this:

```
<body>
<div id="wrapper">
  <div id="header"></div>
</div>
</body>
```

3. Create some basic style rules to set the colors of the page background and text. Also zero the page margins and padding, and make the wrapper <div> 720px wide and centered. Since this is a one-off exercise, you can embed the styles in a <style> block in the <head> of the page like this:

```
<style type="text/css">
body {
  background-color: #FFF;
  color: #000;
  margin: 0;
  padding: 0;
}
#wrapper {
  width: 720px;
  margin: 0 auto;
}
</style>
```

4. Use tree_and_sky.jpg as the background image for the header <div> by creating a new ID selector like this:

```
<style type="text/css">
body {
  background-color: #FFF;
  color: #000;
  margin: 0;
  padding: 0;
}
#wrapper {
```

215

```
  width: 720px;
  margin: 0 auto;
}
#header {
  background-image: url(../images/tree_and_sky.jpg);
}
</style>
```

Adjust the path to the image to match your own site hierarchy.

5. Save the page, and test it in a browser. Don't panic if you see a blank page, because that's exactly what you should see. The header <div> has no content, so it collapses to nothing. The fact that it has a 720 × 479 background image makes no difference. Without a defined height, the background is invisible.

6. Add the height property to the #header style block, and set its value to 479px:

```
#header {
  background-image: url(../images/tree_and_sky.jpg);
  height: 479px;
}
```

7. Reload the page into the browser. It should now look like Figure 6-9.

Figure 6-9. The full background image is displayed once you give the element a height.

If the image is missing, make sure you have the correct file path to the image. If necessary, check your code against height_01.html in the download files for this chapter.

8. Of course, you could have put the image directly inside the header <div> in the HTML markup, but using it as a background means that you can put other content inside the <div>.

Add an <h1> heading inside the header <div>:

```
<div id="container">
  <div id="header">
    <h1>Our Climate<br />
    is Changing</h1>
  </div>
</div>
```

9. Now, use some of the text properties you learned in Chapter 2 to give the heading some punch. You also need to use the margin and padding-top properties to move the heading into a better position. Create a type selector for the <h1> tag like this:

```
h1 {
  color: #FFF;
  font-family:"Arial Black", Gadget, sans-serif;
  font-size:40px;
  text-indent: -60px;
  margin: 0 auto 0 80px;
  padding-top: 35px;
}
```

This sets the text color to white, and uses a large, bold font. I have given the text-indent property a negative length to create a hanging indent. As you might remember from Chapter 2, using a negative length for text-indent can result in the text moving outside its parent element. So, it's necessary to compensate for this by adding a large left margin. In this case, I have used 80px. However, the top margin of the heading needs to be 0. Otherwise, it pushes the header <div> away from the top of the page. So, to push the heading down, I have set padding-top to 35px.

This set of style rules produces the effect shown in Figure 6-10.

Figure 6-10. The heading is positioned over the image using a combination of margin, padding, and text-indent.

10. Next, add a short paragraph of text after the `<h1>` heading, but still inside the header `<div>`. You can type anything you like or use the paragraph in `height_01.txt` in the download files for this chapter:

```
<div id="header">
  <h1>Our Climate<br />
  is Changing</h1>
  <p>Although some people still dispute the causes of climate change,
there is no doubt that weather patterns have become more erratic.
Violent hurricanes have become a regular occurrence; crops are
vulnerable to drought; and floods threaten people's homes more
frequently than ever before.</p>
</div>
```

11. This needs to be positioned to fit inside the area of open sky at the bottom left of the background image. This is easily done with the `margin` property. The bottom margin on the `<h1>` heading has been set to 0, so you can use a pixel ruler or guides in your editing software to work out the approximate margins needed, and then fine tune them in your CSS. To style this paragraph, I'm going to use an adjacent sibling selector (see Chapter 3 and this book's appendix) like this:

```
h1 + p {
  margin: 150px 275px auto 20px;
```

```
    color: #FFF;
    font-weight: bold;
}
```

This styles the first paragraph that comes immediately after an `<h1>` heading. It should now look like Figure 6-11.

Figure 6-11. The position of the paragraph in relation to the image is controlled entirely by setting its margins.

12. The page is beginning to look quite attractive. Add some more text to the page after the header `<div>`, but still inside the wrapper `<div>`. There's some dummy text for you to use in `height_02.txt` in the download files for this chapter:

```
frequently than ever before.</p>
  </div>
  <h2>What can we do about it?</h2>
  <p>Sed do eiusmod tempor. . .</p>
  <p>Excepteur sint occaecat. . .</p>
</div>
```

The page now looks like Figure 6-12.

Figure 6-12. The background image with text overlaid makes a strong impact at the top of the page.

13. In spite of the page's good looks, there are a couple of problems. To begin with, what happens if the image is missing or the user visits with images disabled in the browser? Because the text is white, the heading and the first paragraph disappear completely. The answer is to give the header <div> a background color as well as the background image. Amend the #header style block like this:

```
#header {
  background-image: url(../images/tree_and_sky.jpg);
  height: 479px;
  background-color: #719AD0;
}
```

This gives the <div> a sky blue background color. As long as the background image is displayed, it covers the background color. However, if the image is missing for any reason, the page remains readable, as shown in Figure 6-13.

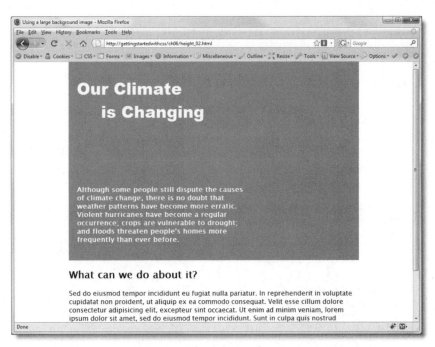

Figure 6-13. Using a background color ensures the text remains legible even if the background image is missing.

14. The other main problem is what happens if a user enlarges the text. In some older browsers, the header <div> will expand vertically to accommodate the larger content. Although this keeps the text visible, it results in the background image being repeated. To avoid this, it's a good idea to add the background-repeat property and set it to no-repeat. The white text then displays over the background color. It's not ideal, but the content remains accessible. So, amend the #header style rule like this:

```
#header {
  background-image: url(../images/tree_and_sky.jpg);
  background-repeat: no-repeat;
  height: 479px;
  background-color: #719AD0;
}
```

15. In modern, standards-compliant browsers, the text spills out of the fixed-height <div> and becomes illegible against the white background. The solution is to add the overflow property, and set its value to auto like this:

```
#header {
    background-image: url(../images/tree_and_sky.jpg);
    background-repeat: no-repeat;
    height: 479px;
    background-color: #719AD0;
    overflow: auto;
}
```

When the text is its normal size, the page displays normally, as shown in Figure 6-12. However, if the user expands the text so that it no longer fits in the header <div>, the browser automatically adds a vertical scroll bar to the <div>, making the content accessible, as shown in Figure 6-14.

Figure 6-14. The overflow property turns the <div> into a scrollable area if the content is too large to fit.

Normally, I would not recommend putting text in scrollable areas, but it's certainly preferable to text that's no longer accessible. In this case, the only people likely to see a scroll bar are those who have opted to enlarge the text.

You can check your code, if necessary, against height_02.html in the download files for this chapter.

I'll return to the overflow property later in this chapter. Before that, let's take a look at a practical use for the minimum and maximum width and height properties.

Using minimum and maximum lengths to scale images and text

Back in the days when most people were accessing the Web with small monitors—640 × 480 resolution was very common in the early days—the problem was trying to cram as much as possible in a tiny space. Things didn't change much when the average resolution increased to 800 × 600, but the arrival of 1024 × 768 monitors signaled a moment of liberation. Designers began to create layouts that expanded automatically on a bigger screen. Instead of measuring widths in pixels, using percentages was all the rage. Fluid layout was born. It worked well until liquid crystal displays and bigger resolutions became the norm rather than the exception. My main monitor is 1920 × 1200—and they get much bigger than that. A fluid layout that looks good at smaller resolutions often becomes unreadable on a bigger screen, because the text spreads too far across for the eye to scan easily. As a result, fixed-width layouts have come back into fashion—until everyone changes again.

One thing that could influence future fashions is the ability to set minimum and maximum widths. When IE6 was the dominant browser, there was little point using the `min-width`, `max-width`, `min-height`, and `max-height` properties, because it didn't support them. Now that IE6 is on its way out, these properties are likely to attract greater attention.

AdvancED

Although IE6 doesn't support the minimum and maximum properties in CSS2.1, you can use a Microsoft proprietary solution to achieve a similar effect. This involves using a JavaScript expression in a separate style rule hidden in an Internet Explorer conditional comment. The technique is demonstrated after the following exercise.

As their names suggest, these properties set a minimum or maximum value, so `min-width` and `max-width` shouldn't be used in the same style rule as `width`, except when `width` is defined as a percentage. Similarly, `min-height` and `max-height` should be used with `height` only when it's specified as a percentage.

The minimum and maximum properties calculate the size of an element in the same way as the `width` and `height` properties. In other words, they represent the size of the *content*. Padding, borders, and margins are added to their values. Because text can be enlarged, using `max-height` with elements that

223

contain text is risky. However, `min-height` can be useful in ensuring that an element doesn't shrink beyond a specified size.

A rather neat technique is using `min-width` and `max-width` to scale images.

Scaling images and text

The following exercise uses `min-width` and `max-width` to scale an image in proportion to its containing text block. If you just want to inspect the code, it's in `scaling_image.html` in the download files for this chapter.

1. Create a new file called `scaling_image.html` in your work folder, and add some basic styles for the `<body>` in the `<head>` of the page. This is what I used:

```
<style type="text/css">
body {
  background-color: #FFF;
  color: #000;
  margin: 0;
  padding: 0;
  font-family: "Trebuchet MS", Arial, Helvetica, sans-serif;
}
</style>
```

2. The traditional way to create a fluid layout is to create a wrapper for the page content and give it a percentage width, such as 80%. This means the page content expands and contracts to fill four-fifths of the browser viewport. However, on a large monitor this results in a page 1500 pixels wide or even bigger if the browser is fully expanded. To avoid this problem, set a minimum and maximum width for the wrapper like this:

```
<style type="text/css">
body {
  background-color: #FFF;
  color: #000;
  margin: 0;
  padding: 0;
  font-family: "Trebuchet MS", Arial, Helvetica, sans-serif;
}
#wrapper {
  min-width: 600px;
  max-width: 960px;
}
</style>
```

3. Because the wrapper `<div>` doesn't have a fixed width, you can't use `auto` for the left and right margins. The alternative is to use a percentage. I'm going to use 15%. Since `max-width` is set to 960px, the wrapper `<div>` will remain centered until the browser viewport exceeds 1371px. Beyond that size, the browser will maintain the 15% left margin, but the right margin will get progressively wider. If keeping the page centered is vital, you should avoid setting `max-width` on the wrapper `<div>`. However, for the purposes of this exercise, I'm not going to worry about the page being slightly off-center on a large monitor. Amend the #wrapper style block like this:

```
#wrapper {
  min-width: 600px;
  max-width: 960px;
  margin: 0 15%;
}
```

4. In the `<body>` of the page, create a `<div>` with the ID wrapper, and put a heading and some text inside. You can use the dummy text in `scaling_image.txt` in the download files for this chapter.

5. At the start of the first paragraph, insert `lasvegas.jpg` from the images folder. The image is 600px wide and 374px high. If your editing program inserts the `width` and `height` attributes automatically, delete them from the `<img>` tag, and give the image an ID of vegas. The code should look similar to this:

```
<h1>Desert Theme Park for Adults</h1>
<p><img src="../images/lasvegas.jpg" alt="Las Vegas" id="vegas" />
They say that what happens. . .
```

6. Create a style rule for the vegas ID to float the image left, and give it some margins to separate it from the text like this:

```
#vegas {
  float: left;
  margin: 3px 2% 3px 0;
}
```

I have made the right margin of the image a percentage, so it will also expand and contract automatically with the size of the wrapper `<div>`.

7. Because the image has no size specified in the `<img>` tag, it will automatically display at its full width of 600px. However, this is also the minimum width of the wrapper `<div>`. To control the size of the image, set its `width` property to 65%:

```
#vegas {
  float: left;
  margin: 3px 2% 3px 0;
  width: 65%;
}
```

When using a percentage for width or height, the value is calculated as a percentage of the width or height of the parent element. In this case, the image's parent—the paragraph—has no specified width, so it automatically stretches across the full width of the wrapper <div>. When the wrapper <div> is at its minimum width, the paragraph will also be 600px wide. This means the image's width will be 65% of 600px—in other words, 390px. However, the maximum width of the wrapper <div> is 960px, which will result in the image being displayed 624px wide. This is bigger than the image's natural size, so could result in distortion. To prevent this from happening, add the max-width property to the #vegas style block, and set its value to 600px:

```
#vegas {
  float: left;
  margin: 3px 2% 3px 0;
  width: 65%;
  max-width: 600px;
}
```

You could also add the min-width property, but there's not much point, because the image should stop scaling when the wrapper <div> reaches its minimum width.

8. Save the page, and test it in a browser. As shown in Figure 6-15, the size of the image scales in relation to the overall width of the page. The finished file is scaling_image.html in the download files for this chapter.

AdvancED

In the preceding exercise, I used an ID selector for the image. This involves adding extra HTML markup. All browsers in widespread use, except IE6, support attribute selectors, which identify elements by examining the value of an HTML attribute. In this case, you can use img[src$="vegas.jpg"] to identify the image by the last part of its src attribute. The $= operator means "ending with." You can examine the code in scaling_image_adv.html in the download files for this chapter. See this book's appendix for more information about attribute selectors.

Figure 6-15. Using a percentage width in conjunction with max-width makes it possible to scale images without distortion.

As you can see, using `min-width` and `max-width` is easy. You use `min-height` and `max-height` in the same way.

ExplainED

Although using a percentage width in combination with the `max-width` property produces scalable images, the image needs to be larger than normal. This increases file size and bandwidth usage. If you want to display a higher resolution image, it might be preferable to put the larger image in a separate page, or use one of the many JavaScript lightbox techniques to load it on demand.

The problem with these properties is the lack of support in IE6. However, you can achieve almost the same result with the help of a Microsoft dynamic property—or CSS expression. This uses a JavaScript conditional statement to calculate the value of a property dynamically. Although conditional CSS sounds an attractive idea, Microsoft has already abandoned its use in IE8. So, the technique described in the following exercise is of limited value, since it works only in IE6. If you don't need to support `min-width` and `max-width` or their height equivalents in IE6, skip straight to the next section.

Fixing the minimum and maximum widths for IE6

This brief exercise adapts `scaling_image.html` from the preceding exercise and shows how to simulate the `min-width` and `max-width` properties in IE6 using a CSS expression wrapped in a conditional comment to hide it from other browsers.

1. Continue working with `scaling_image.html` from the preceding exercise. Alternatively, use the version in the download files for this chapter.

2. A CSS expression uses a Microsoft proprietary JavaScript function called `expression()` to calculate the value of a property. Its basic syntax looks like this:

property: expression(*condition ? value if true : value if false*);

If you're familiar with JavaScript, you'll recognize this as the conditional (or ternary) operator. To set minimum and maximum values, set two conditions. The first condition goes before the question mark, and tests whether the browser window is narrower than the minimum. The second condition for the maximum goes after the colon, and is tested only if the first one equates to `false`. So, you end up with two conditional operators like this:

property: expression(*condition ? value if true : condition ? ↵
value if true : value if false*);

If you're not a JavaScript geek, this can be difficult to understand. Just copy the code that follows, and substitute your own values.

Because IE6 doesn't support `min-width` and `max-width`, you need to find out how wide the browser window is, and use that value to set the `width` property of the element you want to control. In IE, the width of the browser window is accessed with `document.body.clientWidth`.

Add the following <style> block wrapped in an IE conditional comment between the existing style block and the closing </head> tag:

```
</style>
<!--[if IE 6]>
<style type="text/css">
#wrapper {
  width: expression(document.body.clientWidth < 780 ? "600px" : ⏎
document.body.clientWidth > 1370 ? "960px" : "auto");
}
</style>
<![endif]-->
</head>
```

The first line of the conditional comment targets this style block at IE6 only. Other browsers, including IE7 and IE8 will ignore everything inside.

The style rule sets the width property of the wrapper <div> using the expression() function. The JavaScript code between the parentheses performs the following calculation:

- If the browser window is less than 780px wide, set width to 600px.
- If the browser window is wider than 1370px, set width to 960px.
- In all other cases, set width to auto.

3. If you test this page in IE6, you'll see that it simulates max-width perfectly. Where it fails is when the browser window is opened at 800 × 600. The 15% margins override the computed value. You can deal with this by setting narrower margins in the same conditional comment. It then applies the minimum width correctly.

You can check your code against scaling_image_ie6.html in the download files for this chapter.

So, as you see, with a bit of effort, it's possible to get IE6 to use minimum and maximum widths. However, it's questionable how far you would want to go in fixing problems in a browser that is declining in importance.

To end this chapter, let's take a quick look at what to do when the content is too wide or too high for its container.

How do I stop content spilling out of its container?

CSS offers several methods of controlling the visibility of content. You have already met one of them—the overflow property. I used it in the second exercise in this chapter ("Using a single background image with text"), to spawn a vertical scrollbar on the header <div> when the text is enlarged and no longer fits within the fixed height. Table 6-3 lists the CSS properties used to control the visibility of content.

The clip and overflow properties perform similar functions in that they determine what should be displayed when an element is too big for its container. However, the clip property applies only to absolutely positioned elements, an advanced CSS subject that I'll deal with in Chapter 10.

Table 6-3. CSS Properties that Control Visibility of Content

Property	Initial Value	Inherited	Description
clip	auto	No	Clips the overflow of an absolutely positioned element (see Chapter 10).
display	inline	No	Changes the default display of an element, for example, turns an inline element, such as an image, into a block-level one. It can also prevent an element from being displayed and remove it from the flow of the document. See Chapter 8 for a full description.
overflow	visible	No	Controls the display of content that is too big for its containing element. Applies to block-level elements, table cells, and inline blocks.
visibility	visible	Yes	Controls visibility without affecting the flow of the document.

I plan to deal with the display property in detail in Chapter 8, but I have included it here because one of its functions is to control visibility, but in a very different way from the visibility property. All should become clear shortly. First, let's deal with overflow.

Controlling overspill with the overflow property

As its name suggests, the overflow property instructs browsers how to handle content that's too big for its container. It accepts one of the following values:

- auto: Tells the browser to add scrollbars to the element only if the content is too large
- hidden: Hides all content that spills out of the container

- scroll: Tells the browser to add scrollbars even if the content fits the container
- visible: Default value that lets the extra content spill out of the container

By default, browsers let content spill out of their containing element, so it's not necessary to set overflow to visible unless you want to override a previous style rule. Since overflow is not inherited, you can also use the inherit keyword to force inheritance.

Figure 6-16 shows how each of the overflow values are rendered by a browser. The files used to generate the screenshots are available in the download files for this chapter: overflow_default.html, overflow_hidden.html, overflow_scroll.html, overflow_auto1.html, and overflow_auto2.html.

The top screenshot in Figure 6-16 illustrates the danger of using a fixed height for a text container. Although IE6 ignores the fixed height and pushes everything further down the page, in all other modern browsers the overspill overlaps any subsequent content.

Note also the difference between scroll and auto. If you set overflow to scroll, the browser generates scrollbars even if the content fits easily inside the container, as shown in the screenshot on the right in the second row of Figure 6-16. On the other hand, auto generates scrollbars only when needed, as shown in the bottom row of Figure 6-16.

Setting overflow to auto is the most versatile option. However, the beauty of CSS is that it gives you a variety of options, allowing you to choose the one that most fits your needs. The overflow property also has a useful side-effect with floated elements.

overflow: visible;

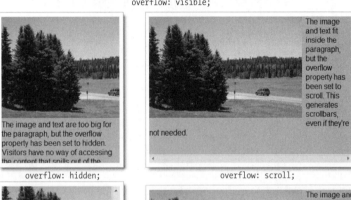

overflow: hidden;   overflow: scroll;

overflow: auto;   overflow: auto;

Figure 6-16. The overflow property can handle oversized material in several different ways.

AdvancED

Modern browsers offer even more options. All browsers currently in widespread use, with the exception of IE6, support the proposed CSS3 properties, overflow-x *and* overflow-y, *which respectively control the horizontal and vertical axes separately. The CSS3 proposal hasn't been finalized, but the current implementations accept the same values as the CSS2.1* overflow *property.*

Using overflow as an alternative to clear with floated elements

A problem with floated elements is that they are removed from the normal flow of the document. As a result, they protrude from a containing element that uses a background, as shown in Figure 6-17 (you can find the code in float_bg.html in the download files for this chapter). How do you get the background to stretch so it includes the whole of the floated element?

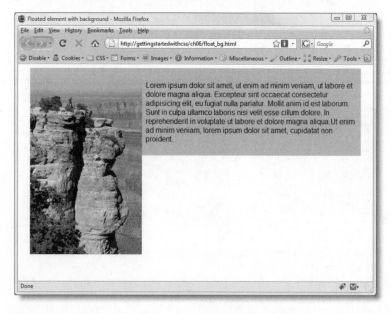

Figure 6-17. If there isn't sufficient content, floated elements protrude from their containing element.

The normal way to get around this problem is to add an empty element, such as a <div> at the end of the content, and apply the clear property to it. You can see how this is done in clear_float_bg.html in the download files for this chapter. However, this has the disadvantage of adding unnecessary HTML markup to your page.

The alternative is to add the overflow property to the style rule that sets the background color and set its value to auto or hidden. The style rule for the container <div> in overflow_float.html has been amended like this:

```
#container {
  width: 720px;
  margin: 0 auto;
  padding: 10px 10px 10px 0;
  background-color: #CCC;
  overflow: auto;
}
```

This produces the result shown in Figure 6-18.

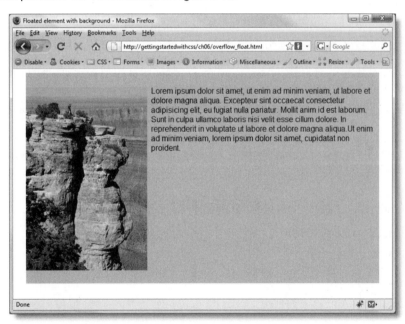

Figure 6-18. Adding the overflow property and setting its value to auto or hidden stretches the background to enclose the floated element.

AdvancED

This example uses an image, but the same technique applies to the parent of any floated element. As you'll see in the next chapter and Chapter 11, the float *property is used extensively to create sidebars. You can use this technique to ensure that both elements share the same background. However, it's important not to give the parent element a declared height. If you do so, setting* overflow *to* auto *or* hidden *works in the normal way, generating scrollbars or hiding content that's too big to fit its container.*

Understanding the difference between visibility and display

The visibility property accepts the following three values:

- collapse: Use only with tables (see Chapter 9).
- hidden: Hide the content, but leave it in the document flow.
- visible: Display the content.

The visibility property is used mainly with JavaScript to show and hide page elements. The important thing to understand about it is that the visibility property doesn't affect the flow of the document. If you set visibility to hidden, the element is not displayed, but the browser still leaves space for it. Figure 6-19 and visibility.html in the download files for this chapter illustrate the effect.

The code in visibility.html is the same as in overflow_float.html, but with the addition of a class called hideMe, which has been applied to the image.

The class looks like this:

```
.hideMe {
  visibility: hidden;
}
```

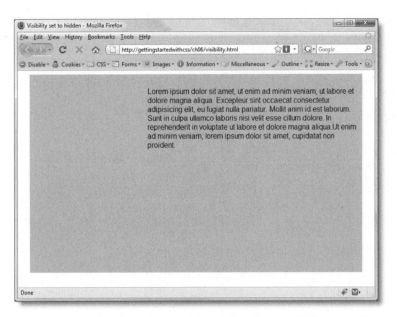

Figure 6-19. Setting visibility to hidden leaves the space normally occupied by the element.

ExplainED

You can apply more than one class to an element. Just separate the class names by a space in the class *attribute like this:* class="floatleft hideMe". *This applies both the* floatleft *and* hideMe *classes to the same element.*

The normal rules of precedence apply if there's a conflict between multiple classes applied this way. The basic rule is that the style lower down the style sheet takes precedence. The next chapter explains in detail why this simple rule doesn't always apply and how to work out precedence in such cases.

The visibility property is inherited, so any nested elements are treated the same way.

You can also affect the visibility of an element with the display property, but the effect is completely different. One of the many values accepted by the display property is none—and when it says "none," it really means it. When you use display: none; the element is removed completely from the flow of the document. The browser treats it as though it doesn't exist—although it remains visible in the page's source code.

In display_none.html in the download files for this chapter, the hideMe class has been changed like this:

```
.hideMe {
  display: none;
}
```

This has the effect shown in Figure 6-20.

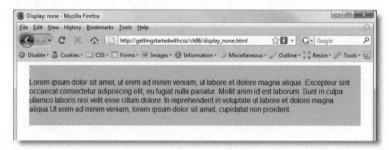

Figure 6-20. Setting the display property to none removes the element completely from the display.

"What's the point of not displaying something?" you might ask. The main use of display: none; is to hide content until the user triggers a JavaScript event, such as selecting a radio button in an online form, or clicking a button or link.

ExplainED

Controlling CSS with JavaScript is beyond the scope of this book.

You can also use display: none; to display a message to users of old browsers encouraging them to upgrade. No, that's not a misprint. This is how it works. . .

Displaying a message to users of old browsers

Old browsers like IE6 don't support everything in the CSS2.1 specification. This can be a pain, as you saw with min-width and max-width earlier in this chapter. Until this old browser finally fades from the scene, you need to jump through hoops to make your pages work in IE6. Alternatively, you can accept the fact that your pages won't look quite the same. Many designers take the attitude that it's reasonable to provide a two-tier service, dealing only with major display problems in IE6 and ignoring ones that don't affect the usability of the site.

You can take advantage of IE6's incomplete support for CSS2.1 to create a message that will be hidden from everyone using a more modern browser. The technique is to use a selector that IE6 doesn't recognize to apply the display property with a value of none to the message. Because IE6 and other old browsers don't recognize the selector, they ignore it, and display the message. Modern browsers understand what's going on and hide the message.

The file old_browser.html in the download files for this chapter is the same as height_02.html from one of the exercises earlier in this chapter. It has a <div> with the ID, oldBrowser, at the top of the page. The <style> block contains the following rule:

```
div[id="oldBrowser"] {
  display: none;
}
```

The selector div[id="oldBrowser"] is simply an alternative way of writing #oldBrowser, but IE6 isn't in on the secret, so it displays the message as shown in Figure 6-21. Modern browsers, including IE7, hide the message.

Figure 6-21. IE6 doesn't understand the selector, so it displays the upgrade message.

239

ExplainED

As Figure 6-21 shows, the div[id="oldBrowser"] *selector isn't the only thing IE6 doesn't recognize. The first paragraph isn't properly styled because IE6 doesn't support the adjacent sibling selector (*h1 + p*) that was used in the exercise earlier in this chapter. How much support you want to devote to IE6 is entirely up to you. However, if you do want to improve this page for IE6 users, you can take advantage of the fact that there's only one paragraph in the header* <div> *and use an ID descendant selector (*#header p*). Using IDs to apply styles to different sections of a page is the main subject of the next chapter.*

Chapter review

This chapter put the final piece in the jigsaw of the CSS box model: padding. Once you understand the CSS box model, you have basically cracked CSS. The counterintuitive aspect of the box model is the way width and height are calculated. The width and height properties refer to the size of an element's content. Everything else—padding, borders, and margins—are added *outside*. The only exception is when you use an incomplete DOCTYPE declaration at the beginning of the page or leave it out altogether. This switches most browsers into quirks mode. Even if you find using the box model difficult, resist the temptation to use quirks mode. It's a hack, and like most hacks, it could easily backfire on you one day.

Padding and margins frequently have a similar effect on the space between elements, but they differ in two important respects. The background of the element extends into padding, but not into its margins. Also, padding is always rendered, whereas the vertical margins of adjacent elements collapse to the height of the largest margin.

You also learned what happens when content is too large for its containing element. By default, modern browsers let the content spill out, but it overlaps subsequent elements. Setting a fixed height on elements that contain text is particularly risky, because text can be resized by the user. In most circumstances it is preferable to avoid setting the height property, but you can use the overflow property to hide overspill or generate scrollbars. Width and height can also be controlled by using the min-width, max-width, min-height, and `max-height` properties to prevent an element from going below a minimum size or exceeding a maximum one.

Finally, you learned the difference between setting the `visibility` property to `hidden` and the `display` property to `none`. Both techniques hide content, but the former leaves an empty space in place of the hidden content, whereas the latter removes the content entirely from the document display.

You're now halfway through this book, but you have already covered the vast majority of CSS2.1 properties. Apart from properties that style lists (covered in Chapter 8), the only ones that remain deal with advanced or little used aspects of CSS. Much of the rest of this book builds on what you have already learned and increases your knowledge of CSS selectors. In the next chapter, you'll take a more in-depth look at descendant selectors as a means to give distinct styles to different sections of a page.

Chapter 7

How Do I Create Differently Styled Sections?

Way back in Chapter 1, I warned you that it's easy to slip into the habit of overusing CSS classes. If you examine the style sheet used in this book's main case study (you can find it in css/journey_20.css in the download files for this chapter), you'll see that it uses classes very sparingly. Instead, I have relied on using type selectors to redefine the default look of HTML tags. I have also used the adjacent sibling selector—such as h1 + p, which styles a paragraph only if it comes immediately after an <h1> heading—to target certain elements without the need to add class attributes to the HTML markup. Other selectors used so far include ID selectors, descendant selectors, and pseudo-classes.

Learning which selectors to use takes time and experience, but it helps keep your HTML code clean and much easier to maintain. In this chapter, I plan to explore the use of descendant selectors further, particularly in combination with ID selectors. Using IDs to identify different sections of your page gives you great control over the way they are styled. Up to now, the case study page, journey.html has consisted of a single column. In this chapter, I'll show you how to transform the page by dividing it into four sections so that it looks like Figure 7-1.

In this chapter, you will learn how to

- Create a sidebar that can easily be switched from left to right.
- Style links and other elements differently in one section of a page.
- Avoid problems with floated elements in older browsers.
- Understand which style rules take precedence in case of a conflict.

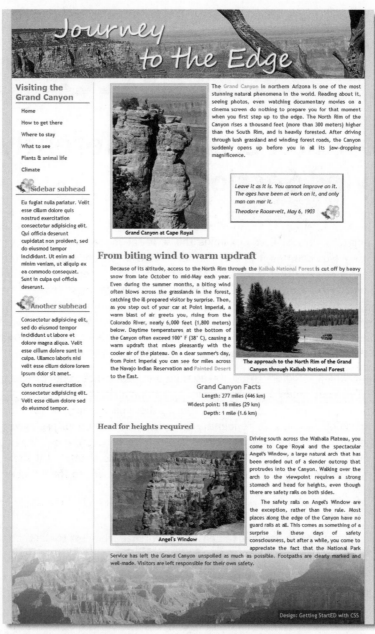

Figure 7-1. How the page looks with the addition of a new heading and sidebar.

This will be very much a hands-on chapter, putting into practice many of the techniques you have learned in previous chapters. It should also help you understand the process of adjusting an existing page to accommodate a change in design.

Adding a sidebar

Adding a sidebar to a single-column layout is a fairly simple process, but it can have some unexpected effects, particularly in older versions of Internet Explorer. If the problems were confined to IE6, I might be tempted to gloss over them, but they also affect IE7, which is likely to retain a significant proportion of the browser market share for several years after the publication of this book. Fortunately, the techniques required for dealing with the problems in IE6 and IE7 don't require any hacks, and the pages render correctly in standards-compliant browsers, including IE8 and other browsers in widespread use.

Creating a sidebar is very similar to positioning an image—you float it to the left or the right. The main difference is that you add a wide margin to the side of the main column to create a space for the sidebar. As you saw in "What happens to margins alongside a float?" in Chapter 4, the margin on the same side as a floated image goes under the image. In Chapters 4 and 5, this behavior caused a bit of a headache, because of the need to recalculate the margins for the Roosevelt quote. However, when it comes to creating sidebars, it's a great asset. By making the margin at least as wide as the sidebar, you effectively create two columns. The sidebar floats to one side, and sits in the margin, while the margin keeps the main content in its own column. As you can see in Figure 7-1, the main column is a constant width. Without the margin, the final section would spread right across the page because the floated sidebar is considerably shorter.

You'll soon see how it works. It's time to roll up your sleeves and start flexing your CSS muscles.

Creating a two-column layout with the float property

This exercise continues working with journey.html, the main case study file from previous chapters. If you have completed each exercise in turn, you can continue working with your existing files. Alternatively, use as your starting point journey_20.html and css/journey_20.css in the download files for this chapter.

1. To make room for the sidebar, widen the wrapper <div> from 720px to 940px by amending the width property in the #wrapper style rule:

```
#wrapper {
  width: 940px;
  margin: 0 auto;
  background-color: #FFF;
  background-image: url(../../images/grand_canyon.jpg);
  background-repeat: no-repeat;
  background-position: bottom;
  border-left: 2px solid #D8D0AC;
  border-right: 2px solid #D8D0AC;
}
```

This changes the position of the <h1> background image, but that's not important, because you'll replace the heading later. The background image at the bottom of the wrapper <div> is 1200px wide, so the extra width simply reveals more of the image at the foot of the page. When creating background images, it's often a good idea to make them wider than necessary in case you decide to change the design later.

2. To create the sidebar, you need to add a new <div> immediately after the <h1> heading in the HTML code. Give the new <div> the ID, sidebar, and insert some placeholder text:

```
<h1>Journey to the Edge</h1>
<div id="sidebar">
  Sidebar goes here
</div>
```

3. Also wrap all the remaining content, except the footer paragraph, inside another <div>, and give it the ID, mainContent. Both new <div> elements are nested inside the wrapper <div> like this:

```
<div id="wrapper">
  <h1>Journey to the Edge</h1>
  <div id="sidebar">
    Sidebar goes here
  </div>
  <div id="mainContent">
    <p><span class="floatleft"><img src="../images/cape_royal.jpg". . .
    . . . responsible for their own safety.</p>
  </div>
  <p id="footer"><span class="reversed">Design: Getting StartED with ↵
CSS</span></p>
</div>
```

This effectively divides your page into four sections: the <h1> heading at the top, the sidebar, a <div> for the main content, and the footer paragraph. Each of these can now be styled independently, as well as using the generic styles already defined in the style sheet. Although it's common practice to wrap each section in a <div>, it's not essential if the section is self-contained, as are the <h1> heading and footer paragraph.

4. In step 1, you widened the wrapper <div> by 220px, so to keep the rest of the layout unchanged, that's how wide the sidebar should be. However, I want to add a 1px border between the sidebar and the main content. Since CSS adds borders outside the declared width of an element, you're left with just 219px. You also need to float the sidebar <div> to the left. Create an ID selector for the sidebar <div> like this (in the download files, I put it immediately after the #wrapper style block):

```
#sidebar {
  width: 219px;
  float: left;
}
```

5. The next decision is where to put the border. The border running down one side of an element will stretch only as far as the element itself. So, if the sidebar content is much shorter than the main content, a border on the right of the sidebar will stretch only part of the way down the page. If you want it to go all the way down, you need to put it on the left of the main content. Both are perfectly acceptable design solutions. Which you choose depends on what you think looks better. I'm going to put it along the side of the main content. That means the <div> that holds the main content needs a left margin the same width as the sidebar: 219px. Add the following style block immediately after the one you created in the previous step:

```
#mainContent {
  width: 720px;
  border-left: #D8D0AC solid 1px;
  margin: 0 0 0 219px;
}
```

If you were to put the border on the right of the sidebar, the left margin of the <div> that holds the main content would need to be 220px (219px for the sidebar, plus 1px for the border).

6. Save the page and the style sheet, and load journey.html into a standards-compliant browser. It should look similar to Figure 7-2.

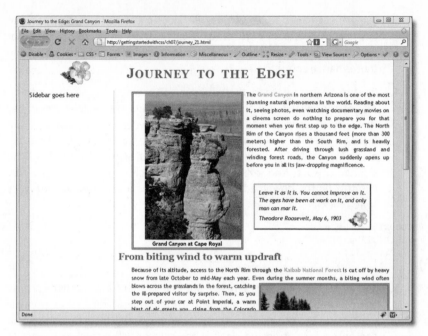

Figure 7-2. The left margin on the main content makes room for the floated sidebar.

A gap has appeared between the first image and its border. That's because the first paragraph no longer follows immediately after the <h1> heading, so the adjacent sibling selector (h1 + p) no longer works. Let's fix that.

7. There are several ways to handle this problem. The one I'm going to use involves a pseudo-class called :first-child, which is supported by all browsers in widespread use except IE6. You were introduced to the concept of pseudo-classes when styling links in Chapter 2. With links, a pseudo-class determines how the link looks depending on its interactive state—whether the mouse is hovering over it or whether it has been visited. The :first-child pseudo class applies the style to an element only if it is the first child of its parent. The paragraph that you want to style is the first child of the <div>, so this pseudo-class fits perfectly.

Amend the style rule that suppresses the text-indent property on paragraphs that follow headings like this:

```
h1 + p, h2 + p, h3 + p, #mainContent p:first-child {
  text-indent:0;
}
```

The `#mainContent p:first-child` selector applies the style to a paragraph only if it's the first child of the element that has the `mainContent` ID. In other words, if the paragraph is the very first thing inside the main content `<div>`, it takes this style. However, if anything else precedes the paragraph inside the `<div>`, the style doesn't apply.

Using a pseudo-class avoids the necessity for adding to the HTML the extra markup associated with an ordinary class. The disadvantage of the `:first-child` pseudo-class is that the style is no longer applied if the element ceases to be the first child of its parent.

ExplainED

Take a moment to let the concept of the `:first-child` *pseudo-class sink in. Although it's being used here to apply to the first paragraph inside the main content* `<div>`, *the* `:first-child` *pseudo-class doesn't mean "the first of its kind." It means "the first element nested inside another." CSS3, the next version of CSS, has a new pseudo-class called* `:nth-of-type()` *that permits you to select the first, second, or third paragraph and so on, but it's currently not widely supported.*

8. If you test the page after adding this pseudo-class, the gap shown in Figure 7-2 disappears in all current browsers except IE6. One way to fix this for IE6 would be to replace the group selector in step 7 with an ordinary class and apply the class to each paragraph that contains a floated image. However, I'm going to make some improvements to the image styles later in this chapter that render this unnecessary.

   You can check your code, if necessary, against `journey_21.html` and `css/journey_21.css` in the download files for this chapter.

Now that you have created the space and container for the sidebar, you need to add some content to it and give it some styles. Although the styles in a sidebar should harmonize with the rest of the page, it's common to add some different touches.

Giving the sidebar different styles

The purpose of creating a <div> for the sidebar is not only to create a block-level element that can be floated but also to give it an ID, which allows you to control the styles of everything within the <div> independently from the rest of the page. In Chapter 2, I introduced you to the concept of descendant selectors when creating a different style for the paragraphs inside the <blockquote>. The selector looked like this:

blockquote p

A descendant selector consists of two or more selectors separated by a space, and targets elements nested inside one another. The selector for the nested element(s) is on the right, while the selector for the parent element is on the left. So, in this case, the descendant selector, blockquote p, targets all paragraphs nested at any level inside a <blockquote> element. This combines two type selectors (ones that redefine the default look of HTML tags).

However, descendant selectors are used more frequently in combination with ID selectors. You saw an example of this in the previous exercise with #mainContent p:first-child. Adding the :first-child pseudo-class makes this a very specific selector, but if you remove the pseudo-class, you're left with #mainContent p, which is a descendant selector that targets all paragraphs nested inside an element that has the ID mainContent.

ExplainED

Even though the original content of journey.html *is now inside a* <div> *with an ID, you don't need to change the existing style rules. The* p *type selector still governs the way the paragraphs look. However, a new style rule that uses the descendant selector* #mainContent p *affects only paragraphs nested inside that* <div>. *It has no effect on paragraphs inside the sidebar or footer. In fact, after the main content has been styled using type selectors, the usual approach is to target other areas using descendant selectors that incorporate their IDs. So, in this case study, you'll start by creating descendant selectors for the sidebar.*

As always, the best way to understand is to try things out in practice. Let's continue working with journey.html. Unfortunately, before you can start styling the sidebar, you need to deal with some bugs in Internet Explorer.

Dealing with IE float bugs

Older versions of Internet Explorer, including IE7, have a number of bugs related to the `float` property. This exercise demonstrates what happens when you put a fixed-width element alongside a floated element in IE6 and shows how to deal with the problem. Continue working with the files from the preceding exercise. Alternatively, use `journey_21.html` and `css/journey_21.css` in the download files for this chapter.

1. In the HTML markup, wrap the placeholder text in the sidebar in a pair of `<h1>` tags like this:

```
<div id="sidebar">
  <h1>Sidebar goes here</h1>
</div>
```

   Later, you'll change this to an `<h2>` heading, because a page should normally have only one `<h1>` heading. However, the larger heading makes it easier to see the problems that Internet Explorer has with floats.

2. Save the page, and test it in a modern, standards-compliant browser, such as Firefox, Safari 3 or 4, or IE8. It should look similar to Figure 7-3.

Figure 7-3. Without creating separate styles for the sidebar, the heading picks up the same style as the main page heading.

   Not surprisingly, the heading takes on the same style as at the top of the page. The only difference is that the text goes completely over the background image because of the sidebar's limited width.

3. If you have access to IE6 or Expression Web SuperPreview, test the page in that browser or IE6 mode. Oh dear, it looks like Figure 7-4.

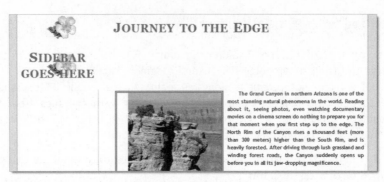

Figure 7-4. Bugs in IE6 expand the content of the sidebar, forcing the main content below it.

IE6 has several complex bugs that affect the width of floated elements when other elements appear alongside. The simplest solution, which works across all browsers without the need to resort to complex calculations or hacks, is to remove the fixed width from the #mainContent style rule.

4. Delete the width property from the #mainContent style block. If you test the page in IE6, you'll see the content in the first paragraph moves back up in line with the sidebar heading. However, the Roosevelt quote is forced down below the image of Cape Royal in IE6. This is again because of float problems. The solution is to change the right margin in the #tr_quote style block from a fixed size to auto like this:

```
#tr_quote {
  margin: 37px auto 0 361px;
  width: 275px;
  background-color: #FFFEF1;
  background-image: url(../../images/flower2.png);
  background-repeat: no-repeat;
  background-position: 97% 95%;
  border: solid 3px;
  border-top-color: #CAC7B0;
  border-right-color: #606249;
  border-bottom-color: #606249;
  border-left-color: #CAC7B0;
  padding: 10px;
}
```

Removing the fixed right margin solves the problem in IE6. Strictly speaking, it doesn't eliminate the bug. The bug results in the quote being slightly to the right of its correct position, but the difference is too small to be noticed. Removing the `width` property from the `#mainContent` style block and the fixed value of the right margin on the Roosevelt quote make no difference to how standards-compliant browsers handle the page, so it's a win-win situation.

You can check your code, if necessary, against `journey_22.html` and `css/journey_22.css` in the download files for this chapter.

Although it's important to understand the CSS box model and know how to calculate the overall width of elements, you can avoid a lot of layout problems by using margins and padding without declaring a specific width. Block-level elements not only automatically expand to fill the available horizontal space, they also contract if the space is, for some reason (such as a bug), smaller than expected.

LinkED

If you're interested in the details of the many bugs that affect older versions of Internet Explorer and floats, visit www.positioniseverything.net/explorer.html. The two most serious problems with floats are called the doubled float-margin bug and the three-pixel text jog. Other IE float bugs include the peekaboo and guillotine bugs.

Now that all main browsers are lining up the sidebar and main content correctly, it's time to create some different styles for the sidebar.

Creating different heading and link styles

This exercise shows how to style the headings and links differently in the sidebar, using descendant selectors. Continue working with the files from the previous exercise. Alternatively, use `journey_22.html` and `css/journey_22.css` in the download files for this chapter.

1. Change the `<h1>` heading in the sidebar to an `<h2>` heading, and add some dummy links in a series of paragraphs. The HTML code should look something like this:

```
<div id="sidebar">
  <h2>Visiting the Grand Canyon</h2>
  <p><a href="#">Home</a></p>
  <p><a href="#">How to get there</a></p>
  <p><a href="#">Where to stay</a></p>
```

```
  <p><a href="#">What to see</a></p>
  <p><a href="#">Plants &amp; animal life</a></p>
  <p><a href="#">Climate</a></p>
</div>
```

2. Save the page, and test it in a browser. It should look similar to Figure 7-5.

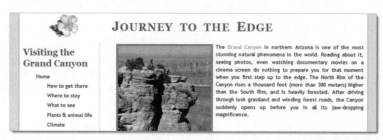

Figure 7-5. The sidebar heading, paragraphs, and links all share the same styles as the rest of the page.

The heading doesn't look out of place, but the paragraph styles result in all except the first one being indented. To distinguish the sidebar from the rest of the page, you need to create some new styles. However, as you can see, everything in the sidebar shares the styles of the rest of the page, so the only styles you need to define are for those properties you want to change. Otherwise, you can let inheritance do its work.

3. Let's start by giving the <h2> heading a distinctive style. This is the style block that's currently styling the heading:

```
h1, h2, h3, h4, h5, h6 {
  color: #468966;
  font-family: Georgia, "Times New Roman", Times, serif;
  margin: 10px;
  clear: both;
}
```

The margins are fine, but change the text color and font by creating a new descendant selector called #sidebar h2 with the following properties and values:

```
/* Sidebar styles */
#sidebar h2 {
  color: #AA8346;
  font-family: Verdana, Geneva, sans-serif;
}
```

Where you put the new style block is a matter of personal preference. Some designers like to keep all related styles together. My preference is to keep the page infrastructure styles together, so the `#wrapper`, `#sidebar`, `#mainContent`, and `#footer` rules are in one section at the top of the style sheet, but the descendant selectors for each section are separate lower down. In the download files, I have created a new section at the bottom of the style sheet.

4. The different color and font look OK, but the size of the font is rather overpowering for the sidebar. I'm going to add `<h3>` headings later on, so convert the `#sidebar h2` selector into a group selector for `<h3>` headings, too; and add a separate style block to set the size of the `<h2>` heading. The styles at the foot of the style sheet should now look like this:

```css
/* Sidebar styles */
#sidebar h2, #sidebar h3 {
  color: #AA8346;
  font-family: Verdana, Geneva, sans-serif;
}
#sidebar h2 {
  font-size: 20px;
}
```

I'll come back to the headings later. Next, let's fix the links.

5. All the links are in paragraphs and currently follow the original style rules. The first paragraph after the heading is not indented, but all the subsequent ones are. Not only does this make the links look odd but the width of the sidebar makes the indenting wasteful. So, let's redefine the margins and indentation for all paragraphs in the sidebar. Create the following new style block at the bottom of the style sheet:

```css
#sidebar p {
  margin: 0 10px 0.75em 25px;
  text-indent: 0;
}
```

This puts a 10px margin on the right of each paragraph, and a 25px margin on the left. The distance between each paragraph is increased from 0.4em to 0.75em. This is necessary to separate the paragraphs more clearly once the indentation is removed.

6. To make the links in the sidebar completely different from those in the rest of the page, add the following rules to the bottom of the style sheet:

```css
#sidebar a:link {
```

```
  color: #466A89;
}
#sidebar a:visited {
  color: #82B0D5;
}
#sidebar a:hover, #sidebar a:active {
  color: #FFF;
  background-color: #466A89;
}
```

This colors the sidebar links deep blue. A lighter blue is used for visited links, and the text changes to white reversed out of dark blue when you hover the mouse over a link.

7. Save the style sheet, and test journey.html in a browser. When you hover over one of the links, you can see there's a white line underneath the text, as shown in Figure 7-6.

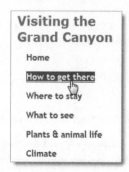

Figure 7-6. The links still inherit the text-decoration property from the main styles.

The white line is inherited from the style rules that control the main links. It's important to realize that using descendant selectors to apply different styles doesn't wipe the slate clean. Any properties that are not explicitly overridden by the descendant selector are inherited from the more general rule.

8. To get rid of the white line, set text-decoration to none in the :hover and :active pseudo-classes like this:

```
#sidebar a:hover, #sidebar a:active {
  color: #FFF;
  background-color: #466A89;
  text-decoration: none;
}
```

9. To make the sidebar headings more distinctive, add a 2px solid border to the bottom. To create a little space between the border and the

text, also add 2px of padding to the bottom. Amend the group selector for the <h2> and <h3> headings like this:

```
#sidebar h2, #sidebar h3 {
  color: #AA8346;
  font-family: Verdana, Geneva, sans-serif;
  padding-bottom: 2px;
  border-bottom: 2px solid;
}
```

I haven't given the border a color, so it automatically uses the same color as the text.

10. The sidebar doesn't have any other content at the moment, but let's create the styles for <h3> headings. I'm going to use the same background image of the flower as in the Roosevelt quote. Add the following style block to your style sheet:

```
#sidebar h3 {
  font-size: 16px;
  background-image: url(../../images/flower2.png);
  background-repeat: no-repeat;
  background-position: left;
  padding: 20px 0 4px 40px;
}
```

If necessary, adjust the path to flower2.png.

11. Add at least one <h3> heading and a paragraph after the links in the sidebar. You can use the dummy text in sidebar_text.txt in the download files for this chapter. Save the page and the style sheet, and reload journey.html into a browser. It should look similar to Figure 7-7.

Oops! Another problem caused by floating the sidebar. In Chapter 4, you added the clear property to the group selector for all headings, and set its value to both. This prevented the headings riding up alongside the floated images. However, it's now preventing the heading in the main column from sitting alongside the content in the floated sidebar. The more content you put in the sidebar, the further down the page the heading will go.

If this happens only occasionally, you could create a class that sets the clear property to none, and apply it to affected elements. In this case study, though, you need to delete the clear property from the h1, h2, h3, h4, h5, h6 style block.

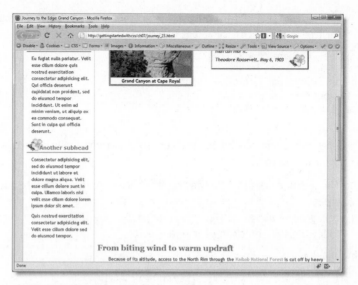

Figure 7-7. The sidebar is floated, so the heading in the main content has been pushed down by the clear property.

12. After removing the `clear` property, save the style sheet, and reload `journey.html` in the browser. As you can see in Figure 7-8, you have exchanged one problem for another.

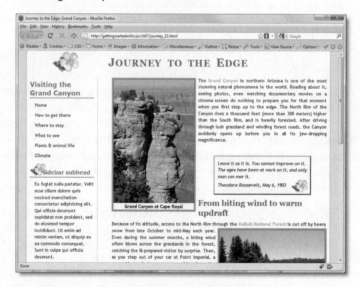

Figure 7-8. The heading is now too far up the page.

Removing the clear property results in the heading riding up alongside the image of Cape Royal. Never fear, the solution is simple.

13. The Roosevelt quote currently has a bottom margin of 0, so the heading has nothing to prevent it from rising as high as it can go. To push the heading back into place, just change the bottom margin in the #tr_quote style block to 70px like this:

```
#tr_quote {
  margin: 37px auto 70px 361px;
  width: 275px;
  background-color: #FFFEF1;
  background-image: url(../../images/flower2.png);
  background-repeat: no-repeat;
  background-position: 97% 95%;
  border: solid 3px;
  border-top-color: #CAC7B0;
  border-right-color: #606249;
  border-bottom-color: #606249;
  border-left-color: #CAC7B0;
  padding: 10px;
}
```

14. When you test the page, everything should now be back in its proper place. You can check your code, if necessary, against journey_23.html and css/journey_23.css in the download files for this chapter.

ExplainED

When I showed this case study to a colleague with an expert eye for design, his immediate reaction was that the page did not have enough text to flow around the images. Of course, he was right. However, the purpose of this case study is not to create the perfect design but to explore the problems you are likely to encounter when using CSS for layout. By keeping the text short, I have deliberately exaggerated the issues with floating so that you know how to cope with them when they arise in your own designs.

Adding an accessible page heading

The page that you have been working on has a simple text heading in an <h1> tag. It serves its purpose and has a small background image to add some visual interest. However, visual designers are often unhappy with not being able to specify exactly which font is used. Until a reliable method of embedding fonts in web pages becomes available, the most common technique for creating visually attractive page headings is to use an image editor, such as Adobe Photoshop or Adobe Fireworks, to add text directly to a header image.

The problem with doing this is that the text becomes part of the image and cannot be read by search engines or assistive technology for the visually impaired. With CSS, however, it's easy to combine a header image with an <h1> heading and move the heading off screen. By doing so, you provide a top-level heading for search engines to index and assistive technology to read, while at the same time offering a visually pleasing header to most users.

Adding a header image

The following exercise shows you how to add a banner heading to the page and move the text heading off screen. Continue working with the files from the preceding exercise. Alternatively, use journey_23.html and css/journey_23.css in the download files for this chapter.

1. Wrap the existing <h1> heading in journey.html in a <div> and give it the ID, header:

```
<div id="header">
  <h1>Journey to the Edge</h1>
</div>
```

2. The header image, journey_header.jpg is 176px high. Create an ID selector for the header <div>, set the height property to the same as the height of the image, and set the image as its background like this:

```
#header {
  height: 176px;
  background-image: url(../../images/journey_header.jpg);
  background-repeat: no-repeat;
}
```

This results in the existing heading being superimposed on the new header.

3. The current h1 style block looks like this:

```
h1 {
  font-size: 220%;
  font-variant: small-caps;
  text-align: center;
  word-spacing: 0.2em;
  letter-spacing: 0.05em;
  margin-top: 0;
  background-image: url(../../images/flower1.png);
  background-repeat: no-repeat;
```

```
  background-position: 70px;
  padding: 13px 0;
}
```

The styles are no longer necessary, so replace them with a single rule setting the left margin of the heading to -9000px:

```
h1 {
  margin-left: -9000px;
}
```

4. Save the page and the style sheet, and test them in a browser. As Figure 7-9 shows, there's an olive strip at the top of the page.

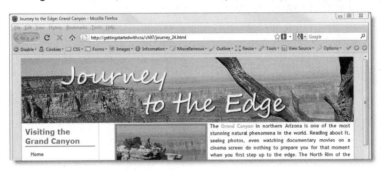

Figure 7-9. Even though the <h1> heading is off screen, the browser renders its top margin.

Hopefully, by now you won't need me to tell you where the gap has come from. By default, browsers add margins to text elements, such as headings and paragraphs. Even though the <h1> heading has been banished thousands of pixels off screen, its top margin stretches across the whole of the header <div>.

5. To get rid of the gap, set the <h1> tag's top margin to 0:

```
h1 {
  margin-left: -9000px;
  margin-top: 0;
}
```

Alternatively, use the margin shorthand property like this:

```
h1 {
  margin: 0 0 0 -9000px;
}
```

6. That solves the problem of the gap at the top of the page, but the clear edge of the new header image reveals an imbalance between the

261

top of the sidebar and the main content. The <h2> heading in the sidebar has a 10px margin all round. You need to add the same margin to the top of the first paragraph in the main content. The rule that you created at the beginning of this chapter to control the text-indent on the first paragraph in the main content looks like this:

```
h1 + p, h2 + p, h3 + p, #mainContent p:first-child {
  text-indent:0;
}
```

Adding the 10px top margin to this style block could have an adverse impact on the other paragraphs, so create a separate style block using the #mainContent p:first-child selector:

```
h1 + p, h2 + p, h3 + p, #mainContent p:first-child {
  text-indent:0;
}
#mainContent p:first-child {
  margin-top: 10px;
}
```

7. If you test the page now, everything should be correctly lined up as shown in Figure 7-10.

Figure 7-10. The accessible heading and the top of the page are now correctly aligned.

You can check your code, if necessary, against journey_24.html and css/journey_24.css in the download files for this chapter.

AdvancED

I used the banner heading as a background image, but many designers insert this sort of image directly in the HTML. Either is perfectly acceptable, although it's arguable that decorative images shouldn't be inside the page markup. The advantage of putting a banner image in the HTML markup is that browsers will display any alternate text (as long as you put some in the alt *attribute) if the image is missing for any reason. The banner heading will also normally be printed out, as it's an integral part of the page. Browsers don't print out background images unless the user explicitly selects that option.*

So far, so good. You're beginning to feel pleased with having created a sidebar. What happens when your boss or client comes along and says, "I like it, but I think the sidebar would look better on the right"?

Switching the sidebar to the other side

Laying out a page with CSS can be time-consuming and even frustrating, but some things are incredibly easy. Switching a sidebar to the other side of the page is just one of those. All that's necessary is to switch the direction of the float, change the margin on the static column, and switch the side of any border.

Here's how it's done.

Moving the sidebar to the right

This exercise moves the sidebar from the left of the page to the right. Continue working with the files from the previous exercise. Alternatively, use journey_24.html and css/journey_24.css in the download files for this chapter.

1. Change the value of the float property in the #sidebar style rule from left to right:

```
#sidebar {
  width: 219px;
  float: right;
}
```

2. Change the border in the `#mainContent` rule from `border-left` to `border-right`, and switch the `219px` margin from left to right like this:

```
#mainContent {
   border-right: #D8D0AC solid 1px;
   margin: 0 219px 0 0;
}
```

When editing the `margin` shorthand property, don't forget to set the value for the left margin to `0`.

3. Save the style sheet, and test the page in a browser. Voilà! The sidebar is on the right, as shown in Figure 7-11.

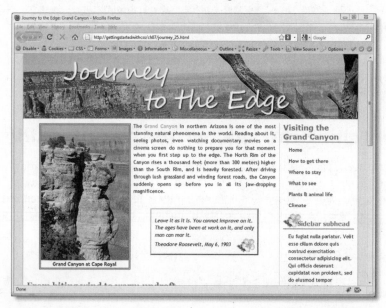

Figure 7-11. Switching the sidebar to the other side is done by changing a few properties.

You can check your code, if necessary, against `journey_25.html` and `css/journey_25.css` in the download files for this chapter.

It's at times like this that you realize how your efforts learning CSS have paid off. Switching the sidebar from left to right was accomplished without the need to make any changes to the HTML markup. Everything was done by changing the values of just a handful of properties in the style sheet.

As the final design touch for this chapter, I want to use another descendant selector to improve the way the picture captions are created. This not only makes the HTML markup cleaner, but also solves a problem in IE6.

Improving the image captions

You added captions to the images in Chapter 4 by wrapping each image in a <span> tag. However, to force the caption onto a new line underneath the image, it was necessary to use a line break (<br />) tag like this:

```
<p><span class="floatleft"><img src="../images/cape_royal.jpg" alt=
"Cape Royal" width="250" height="366" /><br />Grand Canyon at Cape
Royal</span> The <a href="http://www.nps.gov/grca/index.htm">Grand
Canyon</a> in northern Arizona. . .
```

This works, but the left margin on the paragraphs has the unfortunate effect of creating a gap of the same size between the image and its left border in IE6 (see Figure 7-12).

Figure 7-12. IE6 adds the paragraph's left margin to the image, destroying the effect of the border.

At the same time as correcting that problem, it would be nice to get rid of the line break tag. Both can be achieved very easily by using a descendant selector to target images inside an element styled with either the floatleft or floatright class. The selector looks like this:

```
.floatleft img, .floatright img
```

Don't get confused by the comma and the periods (dots). A class selector always begins with a dot, so .floatleft is the selector for the floatleft class. Adding a space followed by img targets any <img> tag inside a floatleft class. The comma simply groups the two descendant selectors: .floatleft img and .floatright img.

The other part of this solution is to use the display property to change the way the image is handled, turning it into a block, thereby automatically forcing the caption onto the next line *without* the need for a line break tag. The next chapter discusses the display property in detail.

Using a descendant selector for captioned images

The following exercise updates the styles and HTML for the captioned images. You can continue working with the files from the preceding exercise. However, I prefer the sidebar on the left, so the completed download files for this exercise are based on journey_24.html and css/journey_24.css.

1. Add the following group descendant selector and style rule to the style sheet:

```
.floatleft img, .floatright img {
  display: block;
}
```

   In the download files, I placed it with the other image alignment rules, just above the sidebar styles.

2. In the HTML code, remove the <br /> tag immediately after the <img> tag for the three floated images. The code for the first one should look like this:

```
<span class="floatleft"><img src="../images/cape_royal.jpg" alt="Cape ↵
Royal" width="250" height="366" />Grand Canyon at Cape Royal</span>
```

3. If you save both pages and test journey.html in a browser, it should look the same as before. However, if you test it in IE6, converting the image to display as a block removes the gap previously incorrectly inherited from the paragraph's left margin.

4. Just one final tweak. . . Now there's a lot more going on in the page, the border around the images looks a bit too heavy. Add a small amount of padding, and change the color and width of the border like this:

```
.floatleft, .floatright, .imgcentered {
  font-weight: bold;
  text-align: center;
```

```
padding: 2px;
border: #66A986 double 4px;
}
```

5. To compensate for this change, you need to adjust the value for the left margin in the #tr_quote style block from 361px to 363px. The padding adds a total of 4 pixels to the overall width, but the border has been reduced by 1px on each side, resulting in the need to increase the left margin of the Roosevelt quote by 2px.

6. Save the style sheet, and test journey.html in a browser again. The change is subtle (see Figure 7-13), but I think it improves the look. You can check your code, if necessary, against journey_26.html and css/journey_26.css in the download files for this chapter.

The Grand Canyon in northern Arizona is one of the most stunning natural phenomena in the world. Reading about it, seeing photos, even watching documentary movies on a cinema screen do nothing to prepare you for that moment when you first step up to the edge. The North Rim of the Canyon rises a thousand feet (more than 300 meters) higher than the South Rim, and is heavily forested. After driving through lush grassland and winding forest roads, the Canyon suddenly opens up before you in all its jaw-dropping magnificence.

Leave it as it is. You cannot improve on it. The ages have been at work on it, and only man can mar it.

Theodore Roosevelt, May 6, 1903

Grand Canyon at Cape Royal

Figure 7-13. A lighter, narrower border with padding improves the look of the images.

How do I tell which styles will be applied?

Most of the emphasis in previous chapters has been on choosing which CSS properties to use for a particular effect. Understanding how the properties work is an important skill, but it's only half the story. The other half is choosing the right selector—and it's arguably a more difficult skill to acquire than understanding the properties.

A review of selectors in CSS2.1

Let's take a quick look at the selectors you have used so far:

- **Type selectors:** A type selector uses the name of an HTML tag without the angle brackets, and redefines the default look of the tag. For this reason, type selectors are sometimes called "tag selectors." For example, p defines the style of <p> tags.

- **Class selectors:** A class selector applies style rules to elements that have the equivalent class attribute in their opening HTML tag. The same class can be applied to multiple elements in the same web page. The selector is created by prefixing the class name by a period. For example, the .floatleft class selector applies to all elements that have class="floatleft" in the opening tag.

  Multiple classes can be applied to the same element by separating the class names by a space in the class attribute, for example, class="floatleft hideMe".

- **Pseudo-classes:** A pseudo-class doesn't rely on a class attribute in the HTML markup but is applied automatically by the browser depending on the position of the element or its interactive state. Examples include a:visited, which applies to visited links; a:hover, which applies to links when the mouse pointer is over them; and :first-child, which applies to an element that is the first child of its parent. (See Chapter 2 for a detailed explanation of the link pseudo-classes; the :first-child pseudo-class is covered earlier in this chapter.)

- **ID selectors:** An ID selector applies style rules to elements that have the equivalent id attribute in their opening HTML tag. IDs must be unique, so you should never apply the same id attribute to more than one element on the same page. It's OK to apply the same ID on different pages, as long as it's used only once on each page. The selector is created by prefixing the ID with the hash sign. For example, #tr_quote applies to the element that has id="tr_quote" in its opening tag.

- **Descendant selectors:** A descendant selector targets elements nested inside another. The selector that identifies the parent (or containing) element(s) is followed by a space and the selector that identifies the nested element(s). For example, #sidebar p targets paragraphs nested inside the element that has the ID, sidebar.

- **Adjacent sibling selectors**: An adjacent sibling selector uses the plus (+) sign to target elements that follow immediately after a specific type of element. Both elements must be siblings—in other words, at the same level of the HTML hierarchy. For example, h1 + p applies styles to a paragraph that immediately follows an <h1> heading with no other tags or text in between. In the draft CSS3 specification, this has been renamed the adjacent sibling combinator, but its function remains unchanged.

- **Attribute selectors**: An attribute selector uses the value of an existing attribute within an element's opening HTML tag to apply a style rule. For example, input[type="submit"] looks for an <input> tag that contains type="submit" in its opening tag—in other words, a submit button.

You have also seen how to group selectors as a comma-separated list to apply the same rules to different elements. For example, the following style block applies the same rules to all headings from <h1> through <h6>:

```
h1, h2, h3, h4, h5, h6 {
  color: #468966;
  font-family: Georgia, "Times New Roman", Times, serif;
  margin: 10px;
}
```

This is simply a convenient way to avoid the need to create the same style block with individual selectors.

With the exception of IE6, all browsers currently in widespread use support the selectors covered so far in this book. Unfortunately, IE6 doesn't support the adjacent sibling and attribute selectors, considerably reducing their usefulness for the foreseeable future.

The remaining selectors in CSS2.1 that I haven't yet covered are as follows:

- **Universal selector**: This is represented by an asterisk (*). It selects any element. I haven't covered it, because it's normally omitted. For example, *.floatleft selects any type of element that uses the class floatleft. However, it has the same meaning as .floatleft on its own, so there is no advantage in using it. The universal selector is often used to create hacks to hide styles from older browsers. For example, IE6 doesn't recognize child selectors (covered next), so a child selector using * will be ignored by IE6 but recognized by more standards-compliant browsers. The universal selector is also useful in conjunction with attribute selectors (see this book's appendix for examples).

269

- **Child selectors:** A child selector is similar to a descendant selector, except that the nested element must be a direct child of the parent. If the element is nested at a deeper level, the selector no longer applies. The relationship is indicated by a greater-than sign (>). For example, blockquote > em applies to all <em> elements directly nested in a <blockquote>, but not to <em> elements inside <p> tags within a <blockquote>.

- **Pseudo-elements:** There are four pseudo-elements, namely:

    - :first-letter: This applies a style to the first letter of the first line inside a block-level element, as long as nothing else precedes it. For example, p:first-letter can be used to style the first letter of each paragraph. It's supported by all browsers in widespread use, including IE6.

    - :first-line: This applies a style to the first line of text in a block-level element. For example, p:first-line styles the first line of each paragraph. The length of the line is entirely dependent on the browser display. If the text is resized by the user, causing it to rewrap, the style applies only to the text that forms the new first line. It cannot be used to select specific words (use a <span> instead). It's supported by all browsers in widespread use, including IE6.

    - :before: This is used in conjunction with the content property to generate content before an element (see Chapters 8 and 12). It's not supported by IE6 or IE7.

    - :after: This is used in conjunction with the content property to generate content after an element (see Chapters 8 and 12). It's not supported by IE6 or IE7.

AdvancED

I have used HTML terminology to describe the various selectors, because this book concentrates on CSS in web design. However, CSS can be used with any structured markup language, such as XML.

The general principle of the CSS cascade is that rules are applied cumulatively. So, what you have seen in this chapter is the way that the p style block affects all paragraphs, but the descendant selector, #sidebar p, adds extra rules that affect only paragraphs inside the sidebar, and in some cases overrides the original p style.

In Chapter 1, I explained that the cascade gives priority to style definitions that are declared lower down in the style sheet. So, you would be justified in thinking that #sidebar p overrides the p style block because it comes after it in journey.css. It's a reasonable assumption on the basis of the information I have given you so far, but in this case, the position of the style rule has nothing to do with it. In CSS, not all rules are equal. Fortunately, it's easy to work out which rules are more powerful than others.

Using specificity to work out which rule wins

Specificity is one of those technical words that tend to set the eyes of many designers rolling. It sounds daunting, and the official way of calculating specificity is admittedly odd; but in reality, it's quite easy.

To borrow an expression from the betting community, specificity is how you work out which style rule is a "dead cert" to win the race. The difference is that this method really works. You'll never lose your shirt backing a winner identified through specificity.

Specificity is quite simply a way of adding up a score to work out which style rule wins in the case of a conflict. The highest score wins. There are two ways of calculating specificity: the easy way and the official way.

Specificity the easy way

The easy way of calculating specificity is to use the following scoring system:

- Inline style: 1000
- ID selector: 100
- Class, pseudo-class, or attribute selector: 10
- Type selector or pseudo-element: 1

You simply assign a score to each part of the selector and add them up—the highest total wins in the case of a conflict of rules.

Table 7-1 lists some examples from css/journey_26.css in the download files for this chapter. The third column (Score) shows the specificity of each selector calculated the easy way. The final column shows the official method of calculation, which is explained in the following section.

Table 7-1. Calculating Specificity

Selector	Components	Score	Specificity
a:link	Type selector and pseudo-class	11	0,0,1,1
#sidebar a:link	ID, type selector, and pseudo-class	111	0,1,1,1
p	Type selector	1	0,0,0,1
blockquote p	Two type selectors	2	0,0,0,2
#mainContent p:first-child	ID, type selector, and pseudo-class	111	0,1,1,1
h1, h2, h3, h4, h5, h6	Six type selectors grouped together	1	0,0,0,1

Note that the score of the final example in Table 7-1 is 1, not 6. Grouping selectors as a comma-separated string is simply a shorthand way of declaring a separate style block for each selector. If you group different types of selectors, you need to calculate the specificity for each one separately. For example, in one of the exercises in this chapter, you grouped #mainContent p:first-child with three adjacent sibling selectors like this:

h1 + p, h2 + p, h3 + p, #mainContent p:first-child

Each of the adjacent sibling selectors has a score of 2, but #mainContent p:first-child has a score of 111. Grouping them together has no effect on their specificity.

As you should be able to see from Table 7-1, blockquote p is more specific than the p type selector on its own. It also has a higher score. Consequently, it doesn't matter which comes first in the style sheet; the higher specificity of blockquote p means that it will override any properties in the p style block. However, it's important to remember that a rule with a higher specificity score does not wipe the slate clean. In the case study, paragraphs nested inside the <blockquote> share the same text-align and line-height values as all other paragraphs, because the blockquote p style block does not override them.

An inline style has a value of 1000, so it always wins in the case of a conflict. Again, this affects only any properties that are being overridden.

272

For most practical purposes, this is all you need to calculate specificity. However, it's worth mentioning the official way, because it's used by some popular editing programs, such as Dreamweaver, as shown in Figure 7-14.

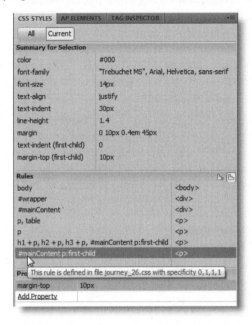

Figure 7-14. The CSS Styles panel in Dreamweaver displays specificity using the official format.

Specificity the official way

The official way of calculating specificity in CSS2.1 is to use a series of comma-separated numbers like this:

- Inline style: 1,0,0,0
- ID selector 0,1,0,0
- Class, pseudo-class, or attribute selector: 0,0,1,0
- Type selector or pseudo-element: 0,0,0,1

Each set of numbers is added up separately. As you can see in Table 7-1, this makes no practical difference to the result. The selector #sidebar a:link adds up to either 111 or 0,1,1,1. What's the point with the commas? In theory at least, you could have a selector that made up from eleven type selectors and pseudo-elements, and another selector that uses a single class and nothing else.

Using the easy method, the first selector has a score of 11, and the second has only a score of 10. So, the first selector wins. Wrong.

Using the official method, the first selector has a specificity of 0,0,0,11, and the second one has a specificity of 0,0,1,0. What determines specificity is not only a higher value, but where it appears in the comma-separated series. The third number from the left in the first example is 0, whereas in the second example it's 1, which is greater than 0. So, the second example has higher specificity. The fourth number would be taken into account only if both had the same value for the third number.

If that makes your brain hurt, don't worry. The likelihood of creating a selector that has more than nine elements with the same score is remote. If you do start creating such monsters, you need to reconsider your design strategy. CSS tends to go wrong when you overcomplicate things. It's complex enough without deeply nested selectors. *Keep your selectors as simple as possible.*

Chapter review

I hope you have found this a useful chapter. Dividing a page into sections and assigning an ID to each section gives you the freedom to apply different styles through the use of descendant selectors. Also, combining the float property with a deep margin makes it possible to create columns. Modern browsers handle floats in their stride, but older versions of Internet Explorer have considerable problems. Fortunately, they can usually be overcome by removing the fixed width on the static column alongside the floated one. The addition of the sidebar to the case study makes the page look more like a regular website.

Finally, you learned how to calculate specificity, which determines the precedence of style rules. In general terms, ID selectors are more powerful than classes, and type selectors are the weakest of all. However, more powerful selectors override only those properties that are explicitly declared. If a style with higher specificity doesn't work the way you expected, it probably means it's inheriting a property from another style, as happened with text-decoration when styling the links for the sidebar.

In the next chapter, I'll show you how to style lists and implement one of the most popular uses for unordered lists—creating a navigation bar. A key component of this technique is using the display property to change the fundamental way HTML elements are handled by the browser.

Chapter 8

How Do I Style Lists and Navigation Menus?

HTML provides tags for three different types of lists: unordered (<ul>), ordered (<ol>), and definition (<dl>). Unordered lists are normally displayed as a series of bullet points; ordered lists are numbered; and definition lists are presented as a word or phrase followed its definition, indented on the following line. Figure 8-1 shows examples of all three (the code is in lists_01.html in the download files for this chapter).

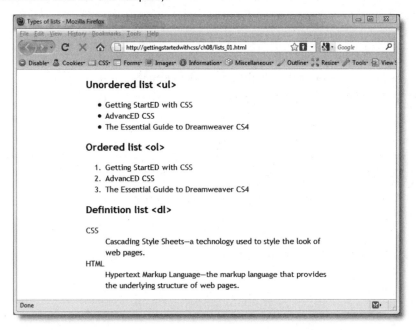

Figure 8-1. The three types of lists supported in HTML

CSS regards the components of definition lists simply as block-level elements, so it has no special properties to deal with them. You style definition lists with text properties, padding, margins, borders, and backgrounds as required. Unordered and ordered lists use the same properties, but CSS provides extra ones to control the bullets or numbers alongside each list item.

Using these extra properties in combination with the CSS display property, it's easy to convert an unordered list into a navigation menu, as you'll learn how to do later in this chapter. Many designers now regard this as the preferred way to build navigation for their sites. However, unlike using tables for layout, this isn't simply a design trick. Even without any styling, a bulleted list is a logical and visually acceptable way of presenting a series of links to other parts of a website. A series of nested lists provides a structured outline of a website's hierarchy, with the top level indicating the site's main sections, and the nested lists acting as submenus.

In this chapter, you'll look first at the properties used for styling unordered and ordered lists, and then at creating a navigation bar. In particular, you'll learn how to

- Control the type of bullets and numbers used for a list.
- Decide whether the bullet or number is displayed as a hanging indent.
- Replace standard bullets with your own images.
- Change the default display type of an HTML element.
- Create a navigation bar from an unordered list.
- Use the !important keyword to ensure a style is applied.
- Automatically generate number sequences on other HTML elements.

The final section of this chapter tackles an advanced aspect of CSS—generated content—which is not supported by IE6 or IE7. However, everything else is supported by all browsers and is essential reading.

First, let's take a look at the properties that control the look of the bullets and numbers

Styling unordered and ordered lists

CSS has three individual properties and a shorthand property designed to style bulleted and numbered lists. They are listed in Table 8-1.

Table 8-1. List Properties in CSS

Property	Initial Value	Inherited	Description
list-style-image	none	Yes	Allows you to use your own image in place of an automatically generated bullet. CSS gives you no control over its position.
list-style-position	outside	Yes	Controls whether the bullet or number is displayed as a hanging indent (default), or nested inside the list item (see Figure 8-5).
list-style-type	disc	Yes	Determines the symbol used as a bullet or number. By default, unordered lists use a solid disc, and ordered lists use 1, 2, 3 followed by a period (dot).
list-style	See individual properties	Yes	Shorthand property.

Because list-style-image gives you no control over the image's position, it's often preferable to use a background image instead, as I'll show you shortly. Let's start with list-style-type and list-style-position.

Changing the symbol or number

The list-style-type property accepts a large number of keywords as its value. Three of them—disc, circle, and square—are intended for unordered lists. The remaining 11 keywords—decimal, decimal-leading-zero, lower-roman, upper-roman, lower-greek, lower-latin, upper-latin, armenian, georgian, lower-alpha, and upper-alpha—are intended for ordered lists. Figure 8-2 and lists_02.html in the download files for this chapter show the output of each keyword.

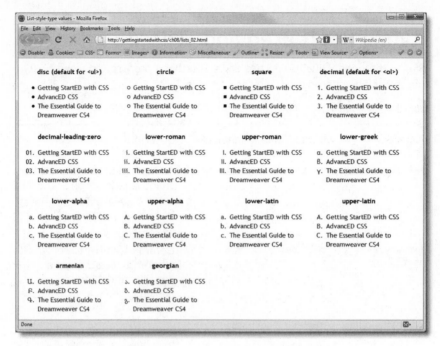

Figure 8-2. Examples of the output of the list-style-type keywords

As you can see in Figure 8-2, lower-alpha and lower-latin are synonymous, as are upper-alpha and upper-latin. Modern browsers, including IE8, now support all keywords for ordered lists. Older browsers display the default decimal style (1, 2, 3) for keywords they don't recognize.

ExplainED

The symbols displayed by ordered lists are determined solely by the value of list-style-type. *Page encoding has no effect. The screenshot in Figure 8-2 was taken using* UTF-8 *encoding, but the page looked identical when tested with a variety of encodings. For example,* lower-alpha *and* upper-alpha *always displayed the letters* a, b, c *and* A, B, C; *and* armenian *and* georgian *displayed traditional Armenian and Georgian numbering even with page encoding that doesn't support either of those alphabets. The ability to display the full range of symbols depends on the fonts installed, but most modern computers have at least one Unicode font, which should be capable of doing so.*

If you use disc, circle, or square with an ordered list, the symbol is displayed instead of the number or letter. However, it doesn't work the other way round. Using one of the keywords for an ordered list with an unordered list results in the default disc (solid circle) being displayed.

If you think there are a lot of keywords, you might be surprised to know that there were six more in the original CSS2 specification: cjk-ideographic, hebrew, hiragana, hiragana-iroha, katakana, and katakana-iroha. The first of these displays numbers as Chinese characters used in Chinese, Japanese, and Korean, while the last four are traditional Japanese counting systems. These six keywords were removed from CSS2.1 because of lack of support in browsers and were moved to the CSS3 proposal. Ironically, the W3C's rather unusual approval process has resulted in most browsers now supporting them. This is because at least two browsers must implement the whole of the specification before it can finally be approved. Since the keywords have been moved to the CSS3 proposal, it simply means that some browsers are already advancing with support for the next version of CSS. Figure 8-3 and lists_03.html in the download files for this chapter show the output in Firefox 3.5 of the six keywords plus another one from the CSS3 proposal, upper-greek.

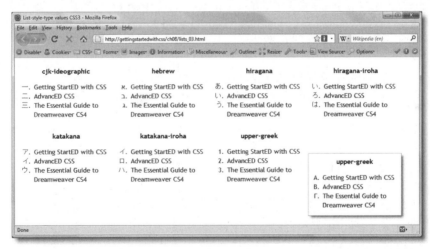

Figure 8-3. Some of the counting systems proposed for CSS3 are already supported.

IE8 doesn't support the six Asian and Hebrew counting systems moved from CSS2.1 to CSS3, but it does support upper-greek (see the inset at the bottom right of Figure 8-3).

LinkED

If and when CSS3 is finally approved, browsers will be expected to support a bewildering number of keywords for list-style-type. *The latest proposals are at* www.w3.org/TR/css3-lists/#list-content.

In addition to all these keywords is perhaps the most important one: none. This enables you to suppress the symbol or number, which opens up the way to convert a list into a navigation bar. For advanced users, you can also use it to display sophisticated nested numbering systems, as described later in this chapter.

The left column in Figure 8-4 and lists_04.html show the default behavior of browsers when lists are nested. With unordered lists, browsers automatically change the symbol for each new level of nesting. However, ordered lists keep track of the current number, starting again at 1 when moving to a deeper level, and resuming the sequence when backing out of a nested list. Although this is convenient, the numbers are difficult to follow because each level of nesting uses the default decimal value for list-style-type. The list on the right of Figure 8-4 uses descendant selectors to apply different values to the list-style-type property, resulting in something much more readable.

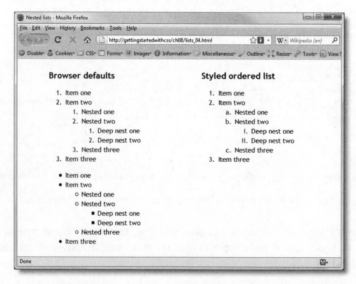

Figure 8-4. Using different values for list-style-type makes nested ordered lists more readable.

To style the series of nested lists on the right of Figure 8-4, I assigned the ID, styled, to the top level list and created the following rules:

```
#styled ol {
  list-style-type: lower-alpha;
}
#styled ol ol {
  list-style-type: lower-roman;
}
```

I used an ID because I wanted to show the difference between the browser default and a styled list. However, in normal circumstances, you would almost certainly want all nested lists to be styled the same way, so you would use an ordinary type selector for the top-level ordered list instead of #styled like this:

```
ol ol {
  list-style-type: lower-alpha;
}
ol ol ol {
  list-style-type: lower-roman;
}
```

The top-level ordered list takes the default decimal value, so it does not need to be declared. The first descendant selector, ol ol, targets ordered lists nested one level deep; and the second one, ol ol ol, targets ordered lists nested at the next level.

Changing the position of the symbol

The list-style-position property accepts just two values, namely:

- inside: This tucks the bullet or number inside the list item, so that it is flush with the left edge in left-to-right languages.
- outside: This is the default position, which positions the bullet or number outside the list item like a hanging indent.

Figure 8-5 and lists_05.html in the download files for this chapter demonstrate the difference between the values, which is self-explanatory.

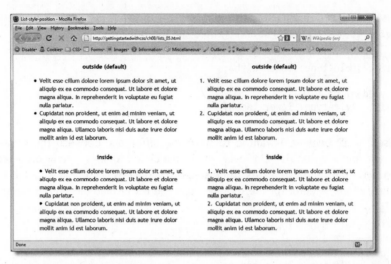

Figure 8-5. The list-style-position property determines whether the bullet or number is inside or outside the list item.

Replacing the symbol with your own image

The list-style-image property allows you to replace the symbol with an image of your own. It works with both unordered and ordered lists, but the same image is used for every list item.

Using this property is very simple. It takes one value: url(), with the path to the image between the parentheses.

In lists_06.html in the download files for this chapter, the small image of a flower has been used as the image by creating the following style rule:

```
ul {
  list-style-image: url(../images/flower2.png);
}
```

As Figure 8-6 shows, the bottom of the image has been aligned with the baseline in the first line of text in each list item. The list-style-image property provides no way to control the position of the image. A better solution is to suppress the automatic symbol, and use a background image instead.

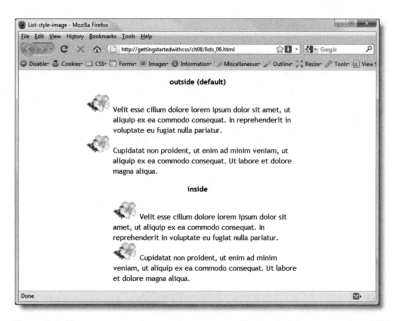

Figure 8-6. You can use an image of your own as the symbol for an unordered list.

When using `list-style-image`, it's recommended that you leave `list-style-type` at its default value (or choose another one), rather than setting it to `none`. This ensures that a symbol is still displayed even if the image is missing or the user is browsing with images turned off.

Using a background image for greater control

The inability to control the position of an image displayed using `list-style-image` means that you need to design your own symbols for unordered lists with considerable care and test them in a range of browsers to make sure they look acceptable. The alternative is to suppress the default symbol by setting `list-style-type` to `none`, and use a background image (backgrounds were covered in detail in Chapter 5).

This is demonstrated in `lists_07.html`, which styles each list item using a descendant selector like this:

```
ul li {
  list-style-type: none;
  background-image: url(../images/flower2.png);
  background-repeat: no-repeat;
  background-position: left 8px;
  padding-left: 70px;
```

```
    padding-bottom: 0.75em;
}
```

To ensure that the background image appears to the left of each list item, it's necessary to add a large amount of padding on the left. The advantage of using this technique is that you can use the `background-position` property to position the symbol exactly where you want it. Figure 8-7 shows the result.

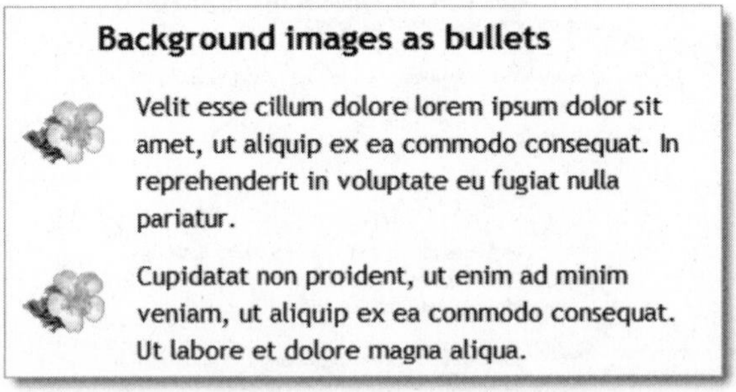

Background images as bullets

 Velit esse cillum dolore lorem ipsum dolor sit amet, ut aliquip ex ea commodo consequat. In reprehenderit in voluptate eu fugiat nulla pariatur.

 Cupidatat non proident, ut enim ad minim veniam, ut aliquip ex ea commodo consequat. Ut labore et dolore magna aliqua.

Figure 8-7. Using background images for list items gives you much greater control over the position of the image.

However, you need to be careful when using this technique, because the background image is likely to be cut off if it's too big for some list items, as shown in Figure 8-8 (the code is in `lists_08.html`).

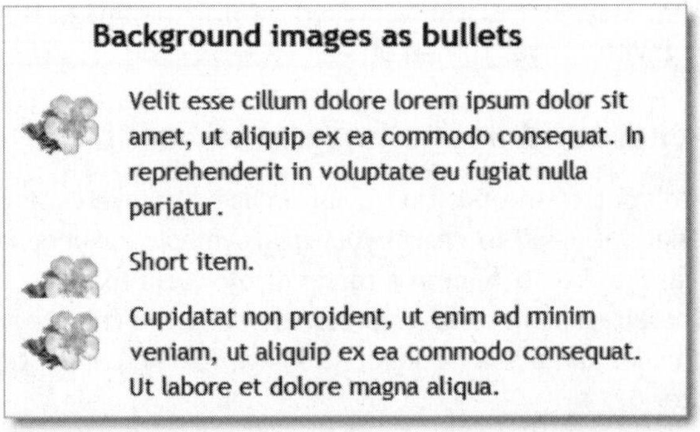

Background images as bullets

 Velit esse cillum dolore lorem ipsum dolor sit amet, ut aliquip ex ea commodo consequat. In reprehenderit in voluptate eu fugiat nulla pariatur.

 Short item.

 Cupidatat non proident, ut enim ad minim veniam, ut aliquip ex ea commodo consequat. Ut labore et dolore magna aliqua.

Figure 8-8. Watch your style rule doesn't result in the background image being cut off.

I got around this problem in `lists_09.html` by adding the `min-height` property (see Chapter 6) to the style rule like this:

```
ul li {
    list-style-type: none;
```

```
    background-image: url(../images/flower2.png);
    background-repeat: no-repeat;
    background-position: left 8px;
    padding-left: 70px;
    padding-bottom: 0.75em;
    min-height: 45px;
}
```

As you can see in Figure 8-9, the result is not ideal, because the text remains aligned with the top of the flower. However, it's certainly preferable to having the flower cut off. If you're likely to use short items in this sort of list, you need to choose the size of the image carefully.

Background images as bullets

 Velit esse cillum dolore lorem ipsum dolor sit amet, ut aliquip ex ea commodo consequat. In reprehenderit in voluptate eu fugiat nulla pariatur.

 Short item.

 Cupidatat non proident, ut enim ad minim veniam, ut aliquip ex ea commodo consequat. Ut labore et dolore magna aliqua.

Figure 8-9. Using min-height prevents the image from being cut off.

AdvancED

Instead of using min-height, *which is not supported by IE6, you could adjust the top and bottom padding of each list item. This is more difficult, because the padding would be added to all items. Of course, you could create a class to add extra padding to affected items. There are many ways to solve problems. Choosing the most appropriate one depends on your design.*

Using the list-style shorthand property

The list-style shorthand property is easy to use. It accepts the same values as the individual list-style-type, list-style-position, and list-style-image properties. You can define all three values, separated by a space, or just one or two. Any value that is omitted uses the default value for its equivalent individual property as listed in Table 8-1. In other words: no image, the symbol or number outside the list item, and a `disc` (solid circle) for unordered lists and `decimal` (1, 2, 3) for ordered lists.

For example, the following style rule uses the `list-style` shorthand property to display unordered lists using a `square` symbol inside the list item:

```
ul {
  list-style: square inside;
}
```

The following rule tells the browser to use an image called green_dot.png outside the list item, and substitute it with a `square` if the image is not available or images are turned off:

```
ul {
  list-style: url(../images/green_dot.png) square;
}
```

I'll come back later in this chapter to more advanced topics with styling the numbering of ordered lists, but let's now turn to the use of the `display` property as a prelude to converting an unordered list into a navigation bar.

Changing layout with the display property

As I explained in Chapter 3, HTML defines most elements as being inline or block-level. The other main types are table and list elements. These default types determine how an element is displayed and which CSS properties can be applied to it. However, the `display` property lets you throw the rule book out of the window and redefine how an element is handled. You have seen this at work occasionally in previous chapters when I used the `display` property to convert images—normally inline elements—into block-level ones and when I converted the design credit in the footer paragraph into an inline block.

The `display` property accepts any of the values listed in Table 8-2. The property is not inherited, so you can also use the `inherit` keyword to inherit the value used by the parent element. Note, however, that when `display` is set to `none`, it affects the entire contents of the element, including all children.

Table 8-2. Values Supported by the Display Property

Value	Level of Support	Description
block	All	Treats the element as block-level.
inline	All	Treats the element as inline.
inline-block	Fair	Treats the element as a single block, but displays it inline in a similar way to the default handling of an image. Unlike inline text elements, the block's height and vertical padding and margins affect the line-height of the line in which it is displayed. IE6 and IE7 support this value only on elements that HTML defines as inline. Not supported in Firefox 2.
list-item	All	No practical value to web designers. It simply defines the default way of displaying `<li>` items. Although you can apply it to other elements, they still need to be wrapped in `<ul>` or `<ol>` tags. However, using anything other than `<li>` elements directly inside `<ul>` or `<ol>` tags produces invalid HTML. If you want to use paragraphs in a list, put them inside `<li>` tags.
none	All	Removes the element and *all* its contents completely from the display and flow of the document (see "Understanding the difference between visibility and display" in Chapter 6). Although the display property is not inherited, everything inside the element is removed. You *cannot* override none by setting a different value in a child element.

Value	Level of Support	Description
run-in	Poor	Treats a block-level element as a run-in headline. In other words, the element begins on a new line of its own, but the first line of a following block-level element runs straight on. Currently supported only by IE8 and Opera.
table, inline-table, table-row, table-cell, table-caption, table-column, table-column-group, table-row-group, table-header-group, table-footer-group	Poor	Causes the element to behave like the equivalent table element. Not supported in IE6 or IE7. Supported in all other browsers in widespread use, although with some minor problems in Safari 3 and Chrome 1. "Table-related display—the future of layout?" in Chapter 11 demonstrates how these values can be used to create a multicolumn page layout.

All browsers currently in widespread use, including IE6 and IE7, support block, inline, and none. There is also reasonably good support for inline-block, but the other values are currently not supported widely enough to be usable in a public website.

The use of none was described in Chapter 6. You saw in Chapter 7 how setting the display property for an image to block forces the text for its caption onto the next line. You'll see another practical use for block later in this chapter—turning a link into a button. So, let's take a quick look at the other main values for the display property: inline and inline-block.

Setting display to inline

Figure 8-10 shows what happens when the display property is set to inline for headings and paragraphs like this (the code is in display_01.html in the download files for this chapter):

```
h1, h2, p {
  display: inline;
}
```

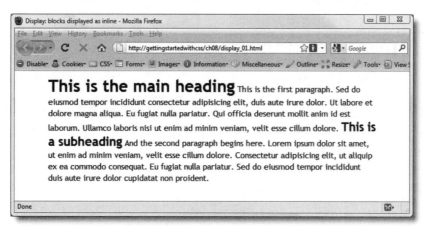

Figure 8-10. Headings and paragraphs, which are normally displayed as blocks, run together when display is set to inline.

Setting display to inline-block

Setting the `display` property to `inline-block` results in the element being displayed inline, but sharing the characteristics of a block-level element. Although this sounds like a contradiction in terms, the meaning should become clear from Figure 8-11, which shows two `<spans>` with identical properties. The only difference between them is that the second `<span>` has its `display` property set to `inline-block`.

The code for Figure 8-11 is in `display_02.html` in the download files for this chapter. The style rules affecting the two `<span>` elements look like this:

```
span {
  font-weight: bold;
  background-color: #6CF;
  padding: 12px;
  border: #000 solid 2px;
  margin: 20px;
  width: 100px;
  vertical-align: super;
}
#block {
  display: inline-block;
}
```

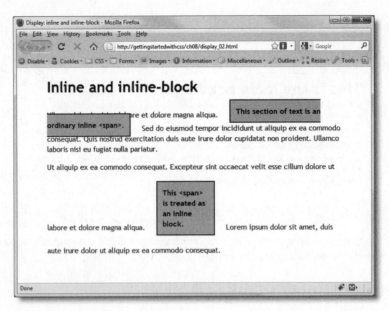

Figure 8-11. An inline-block is displayed inline but shares the characteristics of a block-level element.

Note how the first <span> is split across two lines. Although the padding and border properties are applied to it, the values of margin and width are ignored, because they do not affect inline text elements. However, by setting the display property of the second <span> to inline-block, the margin and width properties are applied in the same way as to any other block-level element. Displaying the second <span> element as an inline block also affects the line height of the surrounding text to make room for the block. No adjustment is made for the first <span>, which results in the background color and border overlapping the text on the surrounding lines. The text on the preceding line is partially obscured by the background and border, but the background and border go beneath text on the subsequent line.

ExplainED

As explained in Chapter 2, the vertical-align *property applies only to inline elements—such as text and images—or the content of table cells. The vertical position is based on an imaginary box surrounding the text in both the element to which the style is applied and its parent. Because the text in both* <span> *elements is the same size as the surrounding text, the only values that make any difference to the vertical position of the first* <span> *in* display_02.html *are* super *and* sub, *which align the text in the correct position for a superscript or subscript respectively. This also explains why the background color and border of the second* <span> *extend below the surrounding text. The bottom line of text in the inline block is in the correct position for a superscript. The* padding, border, *and* margin *are added after the text is positioned. If you change the value of* vertical-align *to* middle, *the inline block will be centered vertically in relation to the surrounding text.*

Creating a navigation bar from a list

Several years ago, the only way to create an attractive navigation bar was to design everything in a graphics editor. If you wanted a rollover effect, you needed to create at least two images for each menu button. I always seemed to nudge something accidentally, and ended up with text out of alignment, meaning I had to start all over again. It was back to the drawing board each time you wanted to make a change to the menu.

The snazziest menus still use images, but CSS has made life a lot easier, because you can often use the image elements as backgrounds and handle all the text with HTML and CSS. Thanks to the display property, you can change the way links are displayed, turning them into large, clickable blocks. Add some different color borders, and before you know it, a humble link looks like an embossed button.

Unordered lists are the ideal container for navigation links, because they can be nested, allowing you to create a hierarchy of top-level items with individual submenus. To animate submenus as flyouts, you currently need to use JavaScript, which is beyond the scope of this book. So, in this chapter, I'm going to deal only with single-level navigation bars. However, the CSS techniques involved are the same for any level of navigation system.

291

Creating a vertical text-based navigation bar

Converting an unordered list into a vertical navigation bar is easy, because you don't need to worry about long menu items. As long as the horizontal space allocated to the navigation bar is wide enough to accommodate two words of average length, long text simply wraps onto another line, and the style rules create a taller button. Assuming you want the navigation bar to fill the entire width of its container element, the process involves the following steps:

1. Remove the bullet symbol and all margins and padding from the unordered list.

2. Remove all margins from the list items.

3. Set the display property of the links to block.

4. Style the links with padding, background color, and borders.

That's all there is to it. So, let's put the theory into practice.

Converting the links in journey.html into a vertical navigation bar

This exercise takes journey.html, the file that has been used as the main case study in previous chapters, and converts the links at the top of the sidebar into a vertical navigation bar. If you have been doing all the exercises in the order they appear in this book, you can continue working with your existing files. Alternatively, use as your starting point journey_26.html and css/journey_26.css in the download files for this chapter. As you proceed through this exercise, it's a good idea to save your files frequently and view the results in a browser to see the changes as they happen.

1. Save your files as journey_vert.html and css/journey_vert.css. Also make sure that the new style sheet is attached to the HTML page you have just saved by changing the <link> tag in the <head> of the page like this:

```
<link href="css/journey_vert.css" rel="stylesheet" type="text/css" />
```

2. Close the original page to make sure you don't alter it by mistake. You will need to use it as the starting point for the next exercise, which shows how to create a horizontal navigation bar.

3. With journey_vert.html open in your editing program, convert the series of links in paragraphs at the top of the sidebar into an

unordered list. Give the unordered list the ID, nav. The HTML code should look like this:

```
<h2>Visiting the Grand Canyon</h2>
  <ul id="nav">
    <li><a href="#">Home</a></li>
    <li><a href="#">How to get there</a></li>
    <li><a href="#">Where to stay</a></li>
    <li><a href="#">What to see</a></li>
    <li><a href="#">Plants &amp; animal life</a></li>
    <li><a href="#">Climate</a></li>
  </ul>
<h3>Sidebar subhead</h3>
```

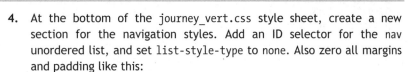

A lot of designers feel they need to wrap their navigation menu in a <div>, but it's not necessary. An unordered list is a block-level element. All it needs for styling is an ID.

4. At the bottom of the journey_vert.css style sheet, create a new section for the navigation styles. Add an ID selector for the nav unordered list, and set list-style-type to none. Also zero all margins and padding like this:

```
/* Vertical navigation bar */
#nav {
  list-style-type: none;
  margin: 0;
  padding: 0;
}
```

5. Make sure the individual list items don't have any margins by adding the following rule:

```
#nav li {
  margin: 0;
}
```

6. Next comes the style rule that makes this technique work so well. Add a rule to set the display property of links inside the nav unordered list to block. The rule looks like this:

```
#nav a {
  display: block;
}
```

Figure 8-12 demonstrates the effect. The screenshot on the left shows a link before adding this style rule; the screenshot on the right shows the same link afterward. The entire width of the link is clickable and adopts its background attributes.

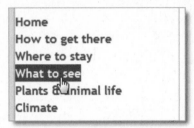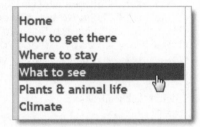

Figure 8-12. Setting a link's display property to block makes the whole element clickable.

7. The navigation bar now works, but needs styling. Begin by adding some padding to the link like this:

```
#nav a {
  display: block;
  padding: 0.5em 10px 0.5em 20px;
}
```

This adds 0.5em padding at the top and bottom, 10px on the right, and 20px on the left.

8. To make the links look like buttons, you need to add background colors for the normal and hover states like this:

```
#nav a:link, #nav a:visited {
  color: #FFF;
  background-color: #AA8346;
}
#nav a:hover, #nav a:active {
  background-color: #CDB187;
}
```

This turns the links into solid blocks of color, as shown in Figure 8-13.

Figure 8-13. The links are now displayed as solid blocks of color.

9. To make the links look like embossed buttons, you need to add a light color as the top and left borders, and a darker color as the bottom and right borders.

AdvancED

The easiest way to choose the most appropriate colors for the borders of links you want to make look like embossed buttons is to use a graphics editor. Create a rectangle of the same color as the links, and apply an embossed effect. Then use the graphics editor's eyedropper tool to get the hexadecimal numbers for the border colors. Make a note of them, and use them in your style sheet for a perfectly harmonized effect.

Add the main border colors to the #nav a style rule like this:

```
#nav a {
  display: block;
  padding: 0.5em 10px 0.5em 20px;
  border-top: #C9B089 2px solid;
  border-left: #C9B089 2px solid;
  border-right: #5B4625 2px solid;
  border-bottom: #5B4625 2px solid;
}
```

10. To give the links an inverted embossed look when the mouse is hovering over them, reverse the colors for the top-left and bottom-right borders in the #nav a:hover, #nav a:active rule:

```
#nav a:hover, #nav a:active {
  background-color: #CDB187;
  border-top-color: #5B4625;
```

```
    border-left-color: #5B4625;
    border-right-color: #C9B089;
    border-bottom-color: #C9B089;
}
```

As Figure 8-14 shows, this gives the links an embossed look.

Figure 8-14. Adding harmonized color borders gives the links an embossed look

11. The navigation bar looks very smart—unless you view it in IE6, that is. IE6 opens up a wide gap between each menu item, as shown in Figure 8-15.

Figure 8-15. IE6 adds spaces between the menu items.

The reason for this behavior is that each <li> tag in the underlying HTML is on a separate line, which IE6 incorrectly interprets as creating new block-level elements. One way to counter this incorrect behavior is to edit the HTML so that all <li> tags are on a single line. However, CSS offers a much simpler and more elegant solution: just set the display property of the <li> tags to inline like this:

```
#nav li {
  margin: 0;
  display: inline;
}
```

This closes up the gaps in IE6 and has no effect on other browsers.

That's all there is to it. You can check your code, if necessary, against journey_vert.html and css/journey_vert.css in the download files for this chapter.

ExplainED

The preceding exercise assumes you want to put the vertical navigation bar inside a container, such as the sidebar, which already has a declared width, and that you want it to fill the entire width of the container. If you want the navigation bar to be narrower than its containing element, add the width property to the style rule that controls the unordered list, or adjust its left and right margins. In the case of this exercise, make the changes in the #nav style block.

Creating a horizontal text-based navigation bar

The basic principles behind creating a horizontal navigation bar are the same as for a vertical one. However, you need to give the menu items a fixed width and float them left. Unfortunately, this poses problems with long menu items. If one or more items are too long to fit in the fixed width, the buttons end up different heights. There are also problems if the available width divided by the number of menu items doesn't result in a whole number.

Converting the links in journey.html into a horizontal navigation bar

The following exercise shows you how to convert the links at the top of the sidebar in journey.html into a horizontal navigation bar. Some of the items are too long, and the 940px width of the wrapper <div> doesn't divide evenly by six. So, the exercise proposes possible ways around these issues. Use as your starting point journey.html as it was at the end of the last exercise in Chapter 7. Alternatively, use journey_26.html and css/journey_26.css in the download files for this chapter.

1. Save your HTML file as journey_horiz.html and the style sheet as css/journey_horiz.css. Make sure the renamed style sheet is linked to the new file. The <link> tag in the <head> of the page should look like this:

```
<link href="css/journey_horiz.css" rel="stylesheet" type="text/css" />
```

2. Convert the series of paragraphs that contain the navigation links at the top of the sidebar into an unordered list, and give the list the ID nav.

3. Cut the unordered list to your clipboard, and paste it between the header and sidebar <div> tags. The HTML code should look like this:

```
<div id="header">
  <h1>Journey to the Edge</h1>
</div>
<ul id="nav">
  <li><a href="#">Home</a></li>
  <li><a href="#">How to get there</a></li>
  <li><a href="#">Where to stay</a></li>
  <li><a href="#">What to see</a></li>
  <li><a href="#">Plants &amp; animal life</a></li>
  <li><a href="#">Climate</a></li>
</ul>
<div id="sidebar">
```

If you check the page in a browser now, it should look like Figure 8-16. The links are now above both the sidebar and main content, and they're no longer styled the same color as they were in the sidebar.

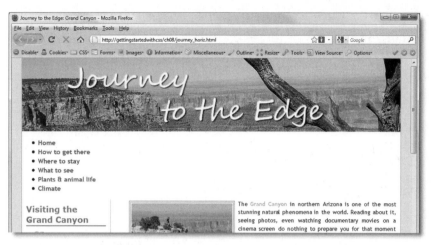

Figure 8-16. The links have been moved to an unordered list just below the header banner.

4. The conversion process starts the same way as for the vertical navigation bar. Remove the bullets from the list by setting `list-style-type` to `none`, and remove all margins and padding. Add the following style block at the bottom of the style sheet:

```
/* Horizontal navigation bar */
#nav {
  list-style-type: none;
  margin: 0;
  padding: 0;
}
```

5. Now, remove the margins from the `<li>` tags. Also, give them a fixed width, and float them left. Unfortunately, 940 ÷ 6 = 156.66. Rounding this up to 157px will result in a menu that is 2px too wide, forcing the final item onto a new line. Rounding it down to 156px will leave a 4px gap at the end. You might think that adding a background color to the #nav style rule will hide the gap, but all the `<li>` elements are floated, so the `<ul>` element has no height, and the background color won't be visible unless you add a height.

There are several ways you could solve this dilemma. The one I have chosen is to make the menu items even wider: 165px. I'll then create a special rule for the *Home* link, which can be much narrower. First, create the rule that affects all `<li>` tags inside the list:

```
#nav li {
  margin: 0;
  width: 165px;
  float: left;
}
```

6. In the HTML, add the ID, home, to the `<li>` tag that encloses the *Home* link:

`<li id="home"><a href="#">Home</a></li>`

7. Create the following style rule for the home ID:

```
#home {
  width: 115px;
}
```

8. Save the HTML page and style sheet, and test journey_horiz.html in a browser. It should look like Figure 8-17. It's a mess; the #home style rule hasn't worked.

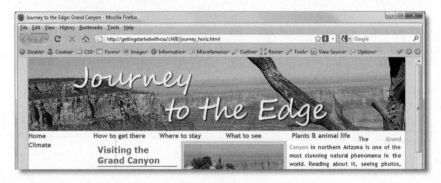

Figure 8-17. The style rule controlling the width of the Home link is ignored.

Although the rule you inserted in step 7 is below the one inserted in step 6, it has been ignored by the browser. If you read the final section of Chapter 7, you should know why. Specificity, that's why.

Rather than using a different selector to ensure this rule is given precedence, let's use the keyword, !important, which is a convenient way to enforce a specific rule and is supported by all browsers. You add this just before the semicolon of the property definition like this:

```
#home {
  width: 115px !important;
}
```

ExplainED

Using the easy method of calculation, the specificity score of #home is 100, whereas the score for #nav li is 101. So, it doesn't matter which order these style rules are in, #nav li will always win. There are several ways to solve this problem.

The first solution is to change the selector from #home to li#home, without a space between li and #home. This is not a descendant selector, but a way of saying "apply this rule to the <li> tag that has the ID, home." When using classes or ID selectors, it's normal to leave the type selector out, but you can be very specific by appending the class or ID selector in this way. The specificity of li#home now adds up to 101, so it is of equal weight to #nav li and takes precedence because it comes lower in the cascade.

Another way of handling this is to use the descendant selector, #nav #home. This has a specificity score of 200, so takes precedence over #nav li regardless of the order they appear in the style sheet.

There should be no space between the exclamation mark and important, but browsers normally accept a space.

AdvancED

Resist the temptation to use !important everywhere. It cannot be applied to a whole style block, but needs to be added to each property/value pair that you want to prioritize. If you find yourself resorting frequently to !important, it's a sign that you probably need to brush up your knowledge of the cascade, selectors, and specificity.

9. That fixes the width problem. To convert the links to look like embossed buttons, you need to apply the same rules as for a vertical navigation bar like this:

```
#nav a {
  display: block;
  padding: 0.5em 10px 0.5em 20px;
  border-top: #C9B089 2px solid;
  border-left: #C9B089 2px solid;
  border-right: #5B4625 2px solid;
  border-bottom: #5B4625 2px solid;
```

```
}
#nav a:link, #nav a:visited {
   color: #FFF;
   background-color: #AA8346;
}
#nav a:hover, #nav a:active {
   background-color: #CDB187;
   border-top: #5B4625 2px solid;
   border-left: #5B4625 2px solid;
   border-right: #C9B089 2px solid;
   border-bottom: #C9B089 2px solid;
}
```

I explained these rules in the preceding exercise, so I won't go over the details again.

ExplainED

One thing that might have slipped your notice is that I didn't make any allowance for the padding and borders around the menu items when calculating the widths for the <li> elements. This is because the padding and borders are applied to the links, and not to the <li> elements themselves. The links have no fixed width, so they just expand and contract to fill the available space inside each list item. When working with fixed-width elements, always try to take advantage of the automatic resizing of elements inside them, rather than struggling with complex calculations.

10. If you save the style sheet, and test journey_horiz.html in a browser, you'll see there are two problems, as shown in Figure 8-18.

Figure 8-18. The hover styles and long items need fixing.

11. When you mouse over one of the links, it's picking up the text-decoration property that styles all links, except in the sidebar. You need to set the value to none like this:

```
#nav a:hover, #nav a:active {
  background-color: #CDB187;
  border-top: #5B4625 2px solid;
  border-left: #5B4625 2px solid;
  border-right: #C9B089 2px solid;
  border-bottom: #C9B089 2px solid;
  text-decoration: none;
}
```

12. Dealing with menu items that are too long is trickier. Rather than doing complex calculations to equalize the height of long and short items, the most practical approach is to shorten the text as I have done in Figure 8-19.

Figure 8-19. Shorter menu items allow visitors to increase the text size several times without affecting the layout.

13. If you look closely at Figure 8-19, you'll see that the gap between the navigation bar and the first paragraph in the main content has closed up. This isn't because the p:first-child pseudo-class you added in Chapter 7 no longer works; it does. This is another effect of floating elements.

All the <li> elements in the navigation bar are floated left. As a result, the <ul> item no longer has any height, because floated elements are removed from the normal flow of the document. Matters are complicated by the fact that the sidebar is also floated, but the <div> that holds the main content isn't. To understand what's going on, you need to examine the page by selecting the ⟨div⟩ in Firebug or Safari 4's *Web Inspector* panel, as shown in Figure 8-20.

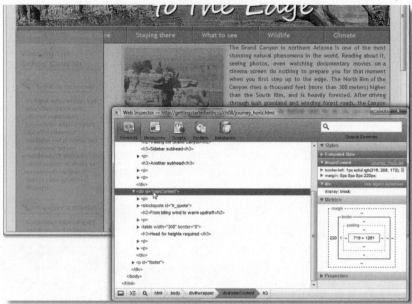

Figure 8-20. The Web Inspector panel in Safari 4 shows what's happened to the margin at the top of the main content.

When elements are floated, subsequent elements move up to fill the available space. The ⟨li⟩ elements fill the width of the wrapper, and the next floated element, the sidebar, tucks in underneath. However, the 10px margin at the top of the first paragraph in the main content interacts with the previous nonfloated element, the ⟨ul⟩ tag. The margin is there, but it's hidden underneath the floated menu items, as shown by the highlighting in Firebug or the Safari 4 *Web Inspector* panel. Unfortunately, the *Developer Tools* panels in IE8 and Opera 10 don't display the issue as clearly as either of the other two analysis tools.

14. To restore the gap at the top of the main content, you need to add a height to the ⟨ul⟩ element. After some trial and error, I found 2.5em to be a suitable amount. Add the height to the #nav style block like this:

```
#nav {
  list-style-type: none;
```

```
    margin: 0;
    padding: 0;
    height: 2.5em;
}
```

15. One final thing: change the margin on the top of the first paragraph to padding by amending the p:first-child style rule like this:

```
#mainContent p:first-child {
    padding-top: 10px;
}
```

The gap at the top of the main content is now restored. You can check your code, if necessary, against journey_horiz.html and css/journey_horiz.css in the download files for this chapter.

ExplainED

Phew! If you found the explanation about the margin at the top of the first paragraph tough going, don't worry. Even with my experience, it took me quite a while to understand exactly what was happening. Fortunately, tools like Firebug and the Web Inspector *panel in Safari 4 make it a lot easier to visualize the interaction of style rules. The important thing to remember is that you need to give the unordered list a height when you create a horizontal navigation bar like this. The height should be applied to the <ul> tag and not to the <li> elements or links. This is because the <li> elements are floated, in effect leaving the <ul> without a height.*

Using CSS sprites in a navigation bar

One of the problems with traditional rollover images for navigation bars is that they rely on JavaScript being enabled in the browser. You also need to use JavaScript to preload the rollover images to avoid a delay in their being displayed when the mouse passes over a link. However, you can now create a similar effect with CSS background images. This has the advantage that no JavaScript is required. Also the text of the link is in the HTML, rather than in an image. Best of all, you don't need to preload the rollover images, because you can use a technique known as a CSS sprite.

A **CSS sprite** is a single file that contains multiple images, only one of which is displayed at any given time. This technique takes advantage of the fact that background images are displayed only behind an element's content and padding, plus the ability to define precisely the position of a background image in CSS. You can achieve very sophisticated effects with sprites, but for the purposes of this chapter, I'm going to use a simple example just to demonstrate the basics of the technique.

LinkED

Visit www.smashingmagazine.com/2009/04/27/the-mystery-of-css-sprites-techniques-tools-and-tutorials/ *for inspiration on what you can do with CSS sprites.*

The images folder of the download files contains a file called sprite.png. Figure 8-21 shows how I created the file in Adobe Fireworks. It's two identical copies of a tab with a cut-off top right corner against a transparent background. The only difference is in the color of the highlighted ball on the left. In the top version, it's red. In the bottom one, it's green. The individual tabs are 220px × 80px, and the top-left corner of the second tab is exactly 90px from the top of sprite.png. Normally, only the top 40px or so of the tab will be visible. The tabs have been deliberately made bigger so that more of the background will be revealed if the text is enlarged in the browser.

Figure 8-21. The CSS sprite contains two images in the same file.

Building a tabbed menu with CSS sprites

This exercise shows how to build a simple tabbed navigation bar with CSS sprites. It uses sprite.png in the images folder and sprite_start.html in the download files for this chapter. If you just want to study the finished code, it's in sprite_finished.html.

1. Open sprite_start.html, and save it as sprite.html. The file contains a heading, an unordered list with four dummy links, and a couple of filler paragraphs (see Figure 8-22).

Figure 8-22. The unordered list of links before it is transformed into a navigation bar with CSS sprites

2. The unordered list already has the ID nav, so you can prepare it for conversion into a navigation bar in the same way as in the previous two exercises by removing the bullets and setting margins and padding to zero like this:

```
#nav {
  list-style-type: none;
  margin: 0;
  padding: 0;
}
```

Since this is a single-page exercise, I suggest that you embed the style rules in the <head> of the document along with the basic rules that I have already created.

3. Because all the list items are going to be floated, the unordered list needs a height. After some experimentation, I decided to set the height property of the #nav style block value to 2.3em. The tabs have a border all around them, but the bottom border will be hidden, so add it to this style rule. To give it more emphasis, I have made it 3px wide.

```
#nav {
  list-style-type: none;
  margin: 0;
  padding: 0;
  height: 2.3em;
  border-bottom: #5B4625 3px solid;
}
```

307

4. You want each list item to be the same width as the tab that will be displayed as its background image (220px). The height needs to be the same as in the #nav style rule. Also remove all margins from the list items and float them to the left with the following style rule:

```
#nav li {
  width: 220px;
  height: 2.3em;
  margin: 0;
  float: left;
}
```

5. The default background image is applied to the list item. You don't want the image to repeat, and you want to display it from the top left corner. Amend the #nav li style rule like this:

```
#nav li {
  width: 220px;
  height: 2.3em;
  margin: 0;
  float: left;
  background-image: url(../images/sprite.png);
  background-repeat: no-repeat;
  background-position: top left;
}
```

6. If you look at the page now, the tabs are there, but the links are in the wrong place and need to be styled so they look more in harmony with the tabs. Add the following rule to style the links:

```
#nav a {
  display: block;
  text-decoration: none;
  font-family: "Arial Black", Gadget, sans-serif;
  font-size: 18px;
  font-weight: bold;
  padding: 5px 5px 6px 35px;
  color: #900;
}
```

There's nothing here that you haven't seen before. The display property is set to block to make the whole tab clickable. It's also essential for moving the text into position using padding. Most important of all, the links need to be converted to block-level elements in order for the rollover image to display in full. Links are normally inline elements, so the rollover background would appear only behind the link text, rather than filling the whole <li> element.

The color of the text is made to match the red ball on the left of the tab.

7. The next stage is to define what happens when the mouse passes over a link. You want to use the same sprite.png as the background image, but this time, instead of showing the top left corner, you want to show the tab that's 90px further down. Add the following rule:

```
#nav a:hover {
  background-image: url(../images/sprite.png);
  background-repeat: no-repeat;
  background-position: 0 -90px;
  color: #060;
}
```

The background-position property is set to 0 -90px. When two lengths are specified like this, the first one represents the horizontal position, and the second represents the vertical position. Both values are measured from the top left of the image, so -90px moves the image up 90 pixels, revealing the second tab on the sprite. (Refer to Chapter 5 if you need to refresh your memory about the positioning of background images.)

The :hover pseudo-class also changes the color of the text to match the green ball on the second tab.

8. Save the page, and test it in a browser. The rollover images should work like traditional JavaScript rollovers—only without the JavaScript (see Figure 8-23).

Figure 8-23. Using the background-position property makes rollover images easy.

You can check your code, if necessary, with sprite_finished.html in the download files for this chapter.

After that exploration of ways to use unordered lists as navigation bars, I want to finish this chapter by discussing briefly a common problem concerning numbered lists. This will lead into a more advanced discussion of generating numbered sequences.

How do I continue a numbered list after a break?

Let's say you have a numbered list followed by a paragraph or two of text, and you want to resume the numbered sequence. As sequence_01.html in the download files for this chapter and Figure 8-24 demonstrate, starting a new ordered list after a break resets the counter to 1.

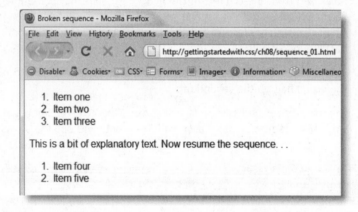

Figure 8-24. Ordered lists always start at 1.

There needs to be a way to resume the sequence. There are, in fact, two ways of doing it: one involves using HTML; the other uses CSS.

If you have studied HTML, you probably know there's a very simple answer to this problem: add the start attribute to the opening <ol> tag of the resumed list, and set its value to the first number like this:

```
<ol start="4">
  <li>Item four</li>
  <li>Item five</li>
</ol>
```

This fixes the problem, as you can see in Figure 8-25 (the code is in sequence_02.html).

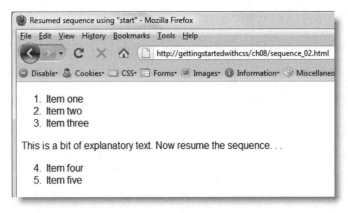

Figure 8-25. Problem solved

This is such a simple and easy solution that you might be surprised to find out that the start attribute is deprecated in HTML 4.01 and XHTML 1.0. If you use it, your code won't validate against a Strict DOCTYPE. Most of the features deprecated by the W3C were scheduled for removal from future versions of the standard, usually because CSS was considered the better way of doing the same thing.

You *can* use CSS to resume the numbering sequence, but I wouldn't recommend it—not if you want to retain your sanity. The CSS method is very powerful, but it's also quite complex. For the sake of completeness, the next section describes how it works; but even the W3C has changed its mind about the fate of the start attribute and given it a reprieve in the draft version of HTML5. If you're curious as to how to do it with CSS, the answer is in the section titled "Using generated content with numbered lists" toward the end of this chapter.

Using CSS to generate numbered sequences

The advanced techniques described in this section are supported by most modern browsers but fail completely in IE6 and IE7. Feel free to skip the rest of this chapter unless you need to generate sophisticated number sequences that cannot be handled by the start attribute.

The numbers displayed by ordered lists aren't part of the HTML markup. They're generated automatically by the browser. So, if you add or remove an item in the middle of a list, all subsequent numbers are regenerated. CSS also has the concept of generated content, which can be used to alter the numbering sequence not only of ordered lists, but of any HTML element. Table 8-3 lists the properties that control numbering.

Table 8-3. Generated Content Numbering Properties

Property	Initial Value	Inherited	Description
content	normal	No	Generates content to be displayed by the :before and :after pseudo-elements.
counter-increment	none	No	Works in conjunction with counter-reset to determine by how much a counter is incremented each time. A negative number can be used to create a back-counting sequence.
counter-reset	none	No	Defines one or more counters for use with counter-increment. By default, counters are initialized at 0. Other values can be specified by declaring a number after the counter name.

Of these three properties, content is the only one that can be used on its own. It is responsible for defining the content displayed by the :before and :after pseudo-elements. It can be used to generate several different types of content, but the easiest way to understand both the content property and the pseudo-elements is with a simple text example.

Adding content with :before and :after

As their names suggest, the :before and :after pseudo-elements add something before or after the element with which they are associated. So, for example, p:before creates a pseudo-element selector that applies to all paragraphs and adds generated content before each paragraph.

The file content_01.html in the download files for this chapter contains two paragraphs of filler text like this:

```
<p>This is the first paragraph. Blah, blah, blah. . .</p>
<p>The second paragraph isn't very interesting, either.</p>
```

In addition to a few basic rules to style the text, I have added the following two style rules:

```
p:before {
  content: 'Start of paragraph: ';
  font-weight: bold;
  color: #060;
}
p:after {
  content: ' End';
  font-weight: bold;
  color: #F00;
}
```

The value of the content property defines what the browser should insert in each pseudo-element. In this example, I have used ordinary text surrounded in quotes (it doesn't matter whether you use single or double). Because the generated content is placed immediately before or after the HTML content, I have added a space at the end of the :before text and a space at the beginning of the :after text. If you test content_01.html in a browser that supports generated content (not IE6 or IE7), you should see the text added in bold green at the start and bold red at the end of each paragraph, as shown in Figure 8-26.

Figure 8-26. The :before and :after pseudo-elements automatically add generated content to selected elements.

Admittedly, this is a rather meaningless example, but it helps explain how generated content is added to elements on a web page. As you'll see shortly, text can be combined with automatically generated numbers in a much more meaningful way.

Adding images with pseudo-elements

The content property can also handle images. You define which image to display by passing the image file path to url() in exactly the same way as for background-image and list-style-image.

In content_02.html, the p:before and p:after pseudo-elements have been changed like this:

```
p:before {
  content: url(../images/green_dot.png);
}
p:after {
  content: url(../images/red_dot.png);
}
```

This automatically adds images of a green dot at the beginning and a red dot at the end of each paragraph, as shown in Figure 8-27.

Figure 8-27. Images can also be used as automatically generated content.

As with list-style-image, there is no way to alter the position of the image, so you need to design your images carefully if you want to use this technique.

Generating content from an HTML attribute

The content property can also inspect HTML tags, search for an attribute, and use the text value of the attribute. If the attribute doesn't exist, the browser simply ignores it. To access the attribute, you insert the attribute name (without quotes) between the parentheses of attr().

In the download files for this chapter, content_03.html has two paragraphs, the second of which contains the title attribute in its opening tag like this:

```
<p>Ut labore et dolore magna aliqua. . .</p>
<p title="Second paragraph">Consectetur adipisicing elit. . .</p>
```

In the styles, the p:before pseudo-class is defined like this:

```
p:before {
  content: attr(title);
  display: block;
  font-weight: bold;
}
```

As you can see in Figure 8-28, this displays the value of the title attribute as a block-level element in bold text.

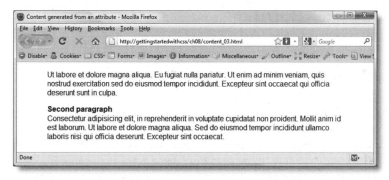

Figure 8-28. Content can be automatically extracted from an HTML attribute.

Using the content property to generate numbered sequences

It's when you start working with numbered sequences that the content property really comes into its own. Moreover, you can combine different types of content in the same declaration, so you can display an image, text, and an automatically generated number all together. However, let's take things one step at a time, because the way generated numbers work can be confusing to start with.

Before you can use a numbered sequence, you need to initialize the sequence by creating a counter and setting its value with counter-reset. You can call the counter anything you like, except the keywords, none, inherit, or initial.

The HTML code in content_04.html in the download files for this chapter contains the titles of the first three chapters of this book, all styled as <h2> headings. I have also added some <h3> headings with the titles of some subsections I would have *liked* to have written. The code looks like this:

```
<h1>Getting StartED with CSS</h1>
<h2>What is CSS and Why Should I Learn It?</h2>
<h3>Because David says so</h3>
<h3>Because it's cool</h3>
<h2>How Can I Improve the Look of Text and Links?</h2>
<h3>Read the chapter, dude</h3>
<h2>How Can I Improve the Layout of my Web Pages?</h2>
```

In order to generate a sequence to number the chapters, you need to create a counter and give it a name—chapter sounds as good as anything. So far, so good, but where do you initialize it? Because the only <h2> headings in the page are chapter titles, the most logical place is in the style block for <body> like this:

```
body {
  color: #000;
  background-color: #FFF;
  font-family: Arial, Helvetica, sans-serif;
  counter-reset: chapter;
}
```

It doesn't matter where you initialize the counter, as long as it's before you first use it. By default, counter-reset initializes the sequence at 0, but the first number displayed is 1. So, if you want the first number to be different, you need to set the value to one less than the number you want. For example, if you want the first number to be 4, you define counter-reset like this:

```
counter-reset: chapter 3; /* first number will be 4 */
```

To display the number, you need to use both the counter-increment and content properties with the :before or :after pseudo-element. Using counter-increment is easy; its value is the name of the counter you want to increment. So this is how you increment the number sequence for the chapter headings in the <h2> elements:

```
h2:before {
    counter-increment: chapter;
}
```

By default, `counter-increment` adds 1 to the number each time. If you want to use greater steps, or go in reverse, add the number after the counter name like this:

```
counter-increment: chapter 2;   /* increases in steps of 2 */
counter-increment: chapter -1; /* decreases one at a time */
```

To display the number, pass the name of the counter to the `content` property's `counter()` function like this:

```
h2:before {
    counter-increment: chapter;
    content: counter(chapter);
}
```

As I said earlier, the `content` property can display a mixture of generated content. The style rule, as it stands, will display the number immediately before the text, with no space. So, to make the generated content look more readable, the code in `content_04.html` has been amended like this:

```
h2:before {
    counter-increment: chapter;
    content: 'Chapter ' counter(chapter) ': ';
}
```

In other words, I have preceded the counter by *Chapter* followed by a space, and followed it with a colon, also followed by a space. You can see the result in Figure 8-29.

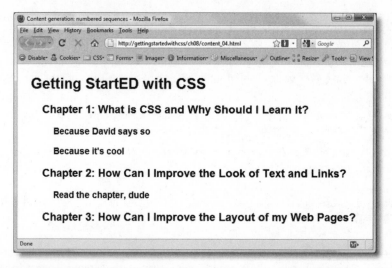

Figure 8-29. The chapter numbers and surrounding text are generated automatically.

But what about the subheadings in the <h3> tags? If you initialize the counter for them in the same way as for the <h2> headings, the subheading for Chapter 2 will have the wrong number. The answer is that you need to reset the sequence for the subheadings each time there's a new chapter—in other words, in a style rule for the <h2> headings.

In content_05.html, I have added the following style rules to generate the content for the subheadings, naming the counter subhead:

```
h2:before {
  counter-increment: chapter;
  content: 'Chapter ' counter(chapter) ': ';
}
h2 {
  margin-left: 25px;
  counter-reset: subhead;
}
h3:before {
  counter-increment: subhead;
  content: counter(chapter) '.' counter(subhead) ' ';
}
```

The h2 style block initializes the second counter, subhead, and resets its value to 0 each time an <h2> heading is displayed. The subhead counter is displayed in front of each <h3> heading by the h3:before pseudo-element, which increments its value. The content property uses the counter() function twice:

first to display the value of the chapter counter, and then to display the value of subhead. The two values are separated by a period and followed by a space. This produces the output shown in Figure 8-30.

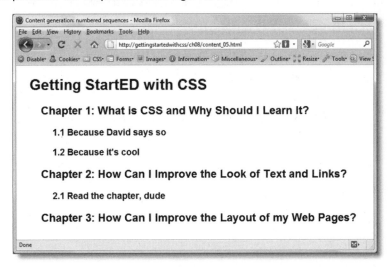

Figure 8-30. Resetting the second counter makes it possible to produce section numbering.

By default, the counter() function displays the number as 1, 2, 3, and so on. However, you can change the style of the number by using any of the values accepted by list-style-type (see Figure 8-2 at the beginning of this chapter). To do so, add a comma after the counter name, followed by the list-style-type value like this:

```
h3:before {
  counter-increment: subhead;
  content: counter(chapter) '.' counter(subhead, lower-alpha) ' ';
}
```

This displays the subhead counter as a lowercase letter of the alphabet, as shown in Figure 8-31 (the code is in content_06.html).

If you want to go the whole hog, you can add an image to the generated content like this (the code is in content_07.html):

```
h2:before {
  counter-increment:chapter;
  content: url(../images/green_dot.png) ' Chapter ' counter(chapter) ⏎
': ';
}
```

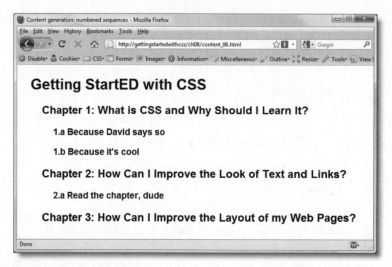

Figure 8-31. Generated number sequences can use any of the styles supported by list-style-type.

This produces the output shown in Figure 8-32.

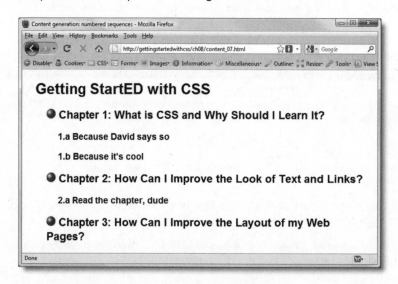

Figure 8-32. Generated content can be a combination of images, text, and automatically incremented number sequences.

It's important to note that all these examples have used ordinary HTML tags, and not numbered lists. CSS generated content extends HTML in a far more sophisticated way than can be achieved with lists. That's not to say you can't use the same techniques with numbered lists, but it does require a little adaptation.

Using generated content with numbered lists

Numbered lists automatically generate their own numbers. So, if you want to use the content, counter-reset, and counter-increment properties with a numbered list, you need to suppress the default numbers by setting the list-style-type property to none.

Earlier in this chapter, I showed how to use the HTML start attribute to resume a numbered sequence from one ordered list to another. To achieve the same effect with CSS involves a lot more work. You need to do the following:

1. Initialize a counter for numbered lists.

2. Set the list-style-type for numbered lists to none.

3. Create an li:before pseudo element to increment and display the generated numbers.

4. Reset the counter for the resumed list.

The file content_08.html produces exactly the same result as sequence_02.html. However instead of using start="4" in the opening `<ol>` tag of the second ordered list, it adds the ID, more. It then uses the following style rules to achieve the renumbering:

```
body {
  color: #000;
  background-color: #FFF;
  font-family: Arial, Helvetica, sans-serif;
  counter-reset: continue;
}
ol {
  list-style-type: none;
}
li:before {
  counter-increment: continue;
  content: counter(continue) '. ';
}
#more {
  counter-reset: continue 3;
}
```

For this type of situation, using the HTML `start` attribute wins hands down. However, CSS-generated content offers a very neat solution for numbering nested lists.

Generating subsection numbers with nested lists

By default, ordered lists start renumbering at 1 when nested at a deeper level inside another list, and they resume the sequence when moving back out to the higher level. To make the numbering of nested lists easier to follow, you can use different values for `list-style-type`, as shown in `lists_04.html` and Figure 8-4 earlier in this chapter. However, with CSS-generated content, you can automatically create subsection numbers like those shown in Figure 8-33.

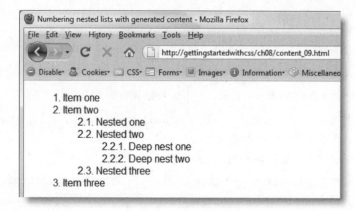

Figure 8-33. Subsection numbers can be automatically generated with CSS.

The CSS for this is incredibly simple. It consists of the following two rules (the code is in `content_09.html`):

```
ol {
  list-style-type: none;
  counter-reset: nested;
}
li:before {
  counter-increment: nested;
  content: counters(nested, '.') '. ';
}
```

The first rule suppresses the normal list numbers, and resets a counter called `nested`. The `counter-reset` property is used on the `ol` style rule in order to reset the sequence each time a more deeply nested list is encountered.

The second rule uses the li:before pseudo-element to increment the nested counter with each new list item. It also uses the counters() function of the content property to generate the subsection numbers. This is not a misprint. All previous examples have used the counter() function, which keeps track of the counter only in its current scope (or level of nesting). However, the counters() function keeps track of the counters at higher levels of nesting and takes as its second argument the text that you want to display between each number. So, the period in quotes inside the counters() function puts a dot between each number. The period and space after the counters() function adds the final dot and a space before the list item.

The counters() function takes an optional third argument, which is one of the list-style-type values. The same style is applied to all nesting levels. You cannot specify different values for list-style-type at each level.

Chapter review

This has been a packed chapter. The CSS style rules for lists are easy to use, but in combination with the display property, they open up a wide range of possibilities for creating attractive navigation bars. This chapter has shown just a few examples of what can be achieved. The possibilities are even greater when JavaScript is used to control nested lists as flyout submenus.

The last section of the chapter explored the advanced, but fascinating, concept of generated content. It's an area that most designers have ignored, because of lack of support in Internet Explorer. However, IE8 supports all aspects of generated content, so this is a feature that is likely to attract more attention as the market share of IE6 and IE7 continues to decline. Don't worry if you found the section about generated content difficult to follow. It *is* an advanced subject and definitely not something you'll need every day, but it does demonstrate just how powerful CSS can be.

In the next chapter, we'll take a look at how to style tables in CSS. This is another area where the arrival of IE8 is likely to make a difference, because it finally supports all aspects of the CSS2.1 specification.

Chapter 9

How Do I Style Tables?

Tables seem to be the most divisive of all HTML elements—you either love 'em or hate 'em. For years, they were the only way to build a grid structure to lay out web pages. But tables work in a unique way. The height of each row is determined by the tallest object in the row, and the width of each column is determined by the widest object in the column. Just when you think you have everything nicely aligned, you add something slightly bigger in a table cell, and the whole table structure shifts.

Thankfully, tables are no longer necessary—or indeed recommended—for page layout. Normally, they should be used only for the display of data that needs to be presented in a grid format—timetables, price lists, sports results, and so on. That's the focus of this chapter: styling tables that contain data.

In this chapter, you'll learn about the following:

- Styling borders around tables and individual cells
- Moving the position of the table caption
- Suppressing the display of empty cells
- Adjusting the space between table cells and inside them
- Preventing columns from exceeding a fixed width
- Styling table columns

Most of this chapter is descriptive, but there are numerous examples in the download files demonstrating the effect of different style rules. The chapter concludes with an exercise that puts all the information to practical use styling a table of weather data.

Before diving into the details of styling tables with CSS, it's important to understand the basic structure of tables and how browsers lay out the various components.

Understanding the anatomy of a table

Assuming you're not a complete beginner at web design who happens to have opened this page at random, you should be familiar with the structure of an HTML table. The first section covers very basic knowledge, so you might want to skim through it very quickly. However, I also describe the role of less frequently used table elements—including `<colgroup>` and `<tbody>`—that play an important role in styling tables with CSS.

Basic table structure

In an HTML table, everything is wrapped in a pair of `<table>` tags; each row is contained in `<tr>` tags; and individual cells are created using `<td>` tags. The following code produces the table shown in Figure 9-1 (the code is in `table_01.html` in the download files for this chapter):

```
<table width="200" border="1" cellpadding="5">
  <tr>
    <td>Row one - cell 1</td>
    <td>Cell 2</td>
  </tr>
  <tr>
    <td>Row two - cell 1</td>
    <td>Cell 2</td>
  </tr>
</table>
```

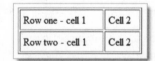

Figure 9-1. A simple table

Notice that the opening `<table>` tag has the `border` attribute set to 1. This puts a 1px border around the whole table and each individual cell, producing the effect of a raised double border around each table element. The other attribute in the opening tag, `cellpadding`, is set to 5, adding 5px of padding around the content of each cell.

If you increase the value of `border` to 10, you get the result shown in Figure 9-2 (the code is in `table_02.html`):

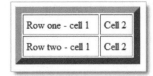

Figure 9-2. HTML draws the wider border only around the table.

The border around the table is increased, but the border around the table cells remains unchanged.

Changing the value of `cellpadding` adds the same amount of space around each side of the content in each cell. All cells are treated exactly the same, and there is no way to add different amounts of padding to each side of the content. With `cellpadding`, it's a case of "one size fits all." However, as you'll see later, CSS gives you control not only over padding on each side but also over the amount used in individual table cells.

The other main control that HTML offers over tables is the `cellspacing` attribute, which controls the amount of space between each table cell. Like `cellpadding`, the same value is applied around all sides of every cell. If you set `cellspacing` to 0, the space between cells is eliminated. However, each cell and the table still retain their own borders. Consequently, even when `border` is set to 1, the actual border is 2px (see Figure 9-3 and `table_03.html`).

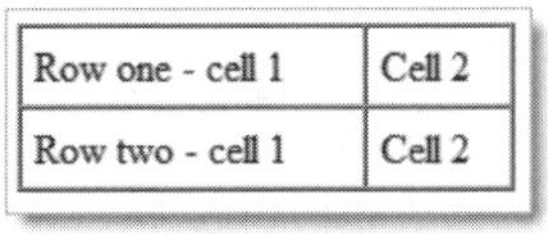

Row one - cell 1	Cell 2
Row two - cell 1	Cell 2

Figure 9-3. Setting cellspacing to 0 eliminates the space between cells.

In addition to `<td>` tags, you can use `<th>` tags to indicate that a cell should be regarded as a row or column heading. The code for the table in `table_04.html` looks like this:

```
<table width="200" border="1" cellpadding="5" cellspacing="0">
  <tr>
    <th>Header 1</th>
    <th>Header 2</th>
  </tr>
  <tr>
    <td>Cell 1</td>
    <td>Cell 2</td>
  </tr>
</table>
```

327

By default, browsers display text in <th> tags centered and in a bold font, as shown in Figure 9-4.

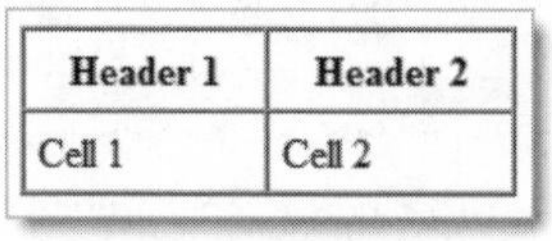

Header 1	Header 2
Cell 1	Cell 2

Figure 9-4. Text in header cells is normally bold and centered.

Using HTML tags to define sections of a table

Because tables have been so widely used for layout, many web developers are unaware that tables have several other tags, all of which are optional but which can enhance the look of a table used for data.

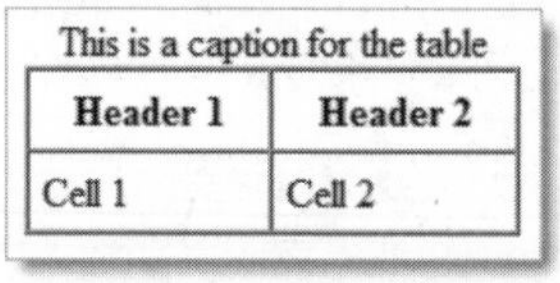

The <caption> tag displays a caption for the table. By default, it's displayed above the table (see Figure 9-5), but the tag itself must come immediately after the opening <table> tag like this (the code is in table_05.html):

```
<table width="200" border="1" cellpadding="5" cellspacing="0">
  <caption>This is a caption for the table</caption>
  <tr>
```

This is a caption for the table

Header 1	Header 2
Cell 1	Cell 2

Figure 9-5. Table captions are normally displayed above the table.

Between the caption and the first table row, you can add several tags to define columns and special header and footer rows.

Defining table columns

The ability to define table columns in HTML appears to be one of the Web's best-kept secrets, probably because columns are formed automatically by adding cells to table rows. However, if you take the trouble to define columns, you can use CSS to apply borders, backgrounds, and width to them. You should also be able to use CSS to control the visibility of columns, but at the time of this writing, IE8 is the only browser that does this correctly.

To define table columns, add one or more <colgroup> tags immediately after the table caption. If the table doesn't have a caption, the <colgroup> tags come immediately after the opening <table> tag. As the name suggests, a

`<colgroup>` tag creates a column group. The `<colgroup>` tag optionally takes an attribute called span, which specifies the number of columns in the group. So, let's say you have a five-column table, and you use the first column for labels and the remaining columns for data, you could define the column groups like this:

```
<colgroup span="1" class="labelcol" />
<colgroup span="4" class="datacol" />
```

Alternatively, if you want to apply different styles to columns within a group, you can list individual columns by creating `<col>` tags inside a pair of `<colgroup>` tags like this:

```
<colgroup>
  <col class="labelcol" />
  <col class="oddcol" />
  <col class="evencol" />
  <col class="oddcol" />
  <col class="evencol" />
</colgroup>
```

The `<col>` tag also accepts the span attribute, so you can apply the same class to multiple columns like this:

```
<colgroup>
  <col class="labelcol" />
  <col span="3" class="datacol" />
  <col class="lastcol" />
</colgroup>
```

Obviously, the number of columns in the table must equal the number of columns specified in the `<colgroup>` and `<col>` tags.

ExplainED

Although few web designers seem to use `<colgroup>` and `<col>` tags, they have been around for a long time and are supported by all current browsers. In fact, Internet Explorer has supported them since version 4 was released way back in 1997. So, you can use `<colgroup>` and `<col>` tags to style table columns in all browsers—yes, even IE6—as you'll see in the exercise at the end of this chapter.

Defining table header and footer rows

Immediately after the column definitions, you can define table header and footer rows. The table header comes first and consists of one or more table rows enclosed in a pair of <thead> tags. The table footer comes immediately after the table header and consists of one or more table rows inside a pair of <tfoot> tags.

The principal advantage of using <thead> and <tfoot> is that browsers should add the header and footer rows at the top and bottom of each page when printing a long table. Although it seems counterintuitive, the <tfoot> section must come before the main body of the table. You'll see how this works in the next section.

Grouping table rows into sections

If you want to divide your table into horizontal sections, you can wrap one or more rows in pairs of <tbody> tags. For example, a company results table might be divided into sections for each quarter using <tbody> tags. Together with header and footer sections, the code looks like this (the code is in table_sections.html in the download files):

```
<table>
  <thead>
    <tr>
      <th>Period</th>
      <th>Results</th>
      <th>Amount</th>
    </tr>
  </thead>
  <tfoot>
    <tr>
      <th>Period</th>
      <th>Results</th>
      <th>Amount</th>
    </tr>
  </tfoot>
  <tbody id="q1">
    <tr>
      <td>Q1</td>
      <td>Sales</td>
      <td>$4.5m</td>
    </tr>
    <tr>
      <td> </td>
      <td>Expenditure</td>
      <td>$4.1m</td>
```

```
      </tr>
    </tbody>
    <tbody id="q2">
      <tr>
        <td>Q2</td>
        <td>Sales</td>
        <td>$4.9m</td>
      </tr>
      <tr>
        <td> </td>
        <td>Expenditure</td>
        <td>$4.7m</td>
      </tr>
    </tbody>
</table>
```

Without any styling, the <tbody> tags don't make any difference to the way the table is displayed, but they perform a similar function to <div> tags by dividing the table into sections that can be styled independently. The screenshot on the left of Figure 9-6 shows the table with some simple styles added. Note how the <tfoot> section is displayed at the bottom of the table, even though it comes before either of the <tbody> sections. This is *not* the result of the CSS styles. It's the way the HTML works. You can verify this by turning off all the styles in the browser (in Firefox, select *View* ➤ *Page Style* ➤ *No Style*). The <tfoot> section is still at the bottom of the table, as shown in the screenshot on the right of Figure 9-6.

Period	Results	Amount
Q1	Sales	$4.5m
	Expenditure	$4.1m
Q2	Sales	$4.9m
	Expenditure	$4.7m
Period	Results	Amount

Period	Results	Amount
Q1	Sales	$4.5m
	Expenditure	$4.1m
Q2	Sales	$4.9m
	Expenditure	$4.7m
Period	Results	Amount

Figure 9-6. The position of the table footer remains the same even when CSS is disabled (right).

How browsers lay out tables

That excursion into the lesser known table tags was necessary for two reasons: as a prelude to the exercise at the end of the chapter, and more importantly, to help you understand how browsers lay out tables and the effect this has on the rendering of CSS. Browsers assemble tables in six stages, as follows:

1. Table

2. Column groups

3. Individual columns

4. Row groups

5. Individual rows

6. Individual cells

To see how styles are applied on top of each other in this six-stage process, load table_06.html into a browser. All browsers, including IE6, implement the same process, so you should see the same results as in Figure 9-7 whichever browser you use.

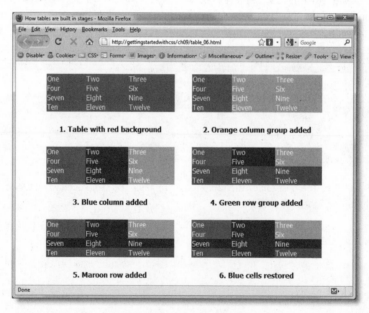

Figure 9-7. Browsers build tables in stages, starting with the whole table, followed by columns, rows, and cells.

The basic structure of all six tables in table_06.html looks like this (the same structure is used for many of the subsequent examples in this chapter):

```
<table width="300">
  <colgroup span="1" />
  <colgroup>
    <col />
    <col />
  </colgroup>
  <caption>Description of table</caption>
  <tbody>
    <tr>
      <td>One</td>
      <td>Two</td>
      <td>Three</td>
    </tr>
    <tr>
      <td>Four</td>
      <td>Five</td>
      <td>Six</td>
    </tr>
  </tbody>
  <tbody>
    <tr>
      <td>Seven</td>
      <td>Eight</td>
      <td>Nine</td>
    </tr>
    <tr>
      <td>Ten</td>
      <td>Eleven</td>
      <td>Twelve</td>
    </tr>
  </tbody>
</table>
```

All six tables have a red background color. The first table has no other styles, but in each successive table, a class has been added to one of the table elements in the same order as the stages browsers use to build a table. So, table 2 applies an orange background to the second column group, and table 3 applies a blue background to one column within that group. Because of the way browsers apply styles, the orange background is painted over the red background, and the blue background is painted over the orange.

In table 4, the green background applied to the second row group overwrites the color of all columns in the bottom two rows. Table 5 shows how a style applied to an individual row takes precedence over the row group.

Finally, in table 6, a class is applied to table cells 8 and 11 to restore the blue background to the center column.

AdvancED

If you keep this six-stage process in mind, it will help you understand why a background or style is being applied in a particular way—or more often, why a style isn't working as expected. Even IE6 works this way, so you can use this approach with confidence.

Styling tables with CSS

Styling the content that you put into table cells works exactly like everything you have studied in previous chapters, but the CSS2.1 specification also has five properties dedicated to controlling the structure of tables. These are listed in Table 9-1. Also listed are three properties you have already met—overflow, text-align, and vertical-align—which are frequently used with tables.

Table 9-1. CSS Table Properties

Property	Initial Value	Inherited	Description
border-collapse	separate	Yes	Controls the way borders are handled. By default, the table and each cell have independent borders. Borders are merged by setting the value of this property to collapse.
border-spacing	0	Yes	Controls the spacing between table cells in a similar way to the HTML cellspacing attribute. Horizontal and vertical spacing can be controlled independently.
caption-side	top	Yes	Determines whether the table caption is displayed above or below the table.

Property	Initial Value	Inherited	Description
empty-cells	show	Yes	If set to hide, turns off the display of borders and backgrounds associated with empty table cells. If all cells in a row are empty, the entire row is removed from the display when border-collapse is set to collapse.
overflow	visible	No	Controls what happens to content that is too big to fit into a table cell.
table-layout	auto	No	Determines whether a table automatically expands to accommodate oversized content. If set to fixed, the width of each column is set in the column definitions or the first row.
text-align	See description	Yes	Controls the horizontal alignment of content in table cells. In languages that are written from left to right, the default value is left.
vertical-align	middle	No	Controls the vertical alignment of content in table cells.

The following sections describe how to use each of these properties.

Using CSS for table borders

The big difference between using CSS and the HTML border attribute to create table borders is the much finer control offered by CSS. As explained at the beginning of this chapter, the HTML border attribute adds borders to the table itself and to the cells it contains. With CSS, you can control each border independently, using the same border properties described in Chapter 5.

The first implication of this is that applying a border to a table with CSS applies it only to the table, and not to the table cells. It also means that you can use any of the border styles supported by CSS2.1. The `table` style block in `table_07.html` defines the border like this:

```
border: #000 double 10px;
```

This produces the result shown in Figure 9-8.

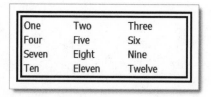

Figure 9-8. With CSS, you can use any border style for a table; the cells are not affected.

In fact, you don't need to declare a border or use the same style on every side, as you can see in Figure 9-9.

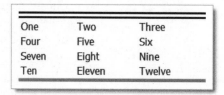

Figure 9-9. Tables can have different style borders or none at all on each side.

The table in Figure 9-9 uses the following style rules (the code is in `table_08.html`):

```
border-top: #000 double 10px;
border-bottom: #999 solid 5px;
```

Adding borders to table cells

Because adding a table border with CSS has no effect on the table cells, you need to create a separate style for the cells. This also gives you the freedom to choose a different color and/or style for the cell borders. The style rules in `table_09.html` add a 1px solid red border to all table cells like this:

```
td {
  border: #F00 solid 1px;
}
```

As you can see in Figure 9-10, the border around each cell is separate from the table border, and there is a small gap between each cell.

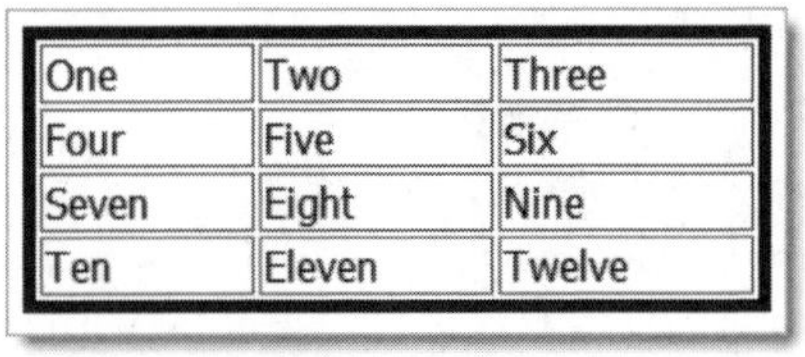

One	Two	Three
Four	Five	Six
Seven	Eight	Nine
Ten	Eleven	Twelve

Figure 9-10. By default, there is a space between each cell border.

As you will see later in this chapter, this separation of borders can be used to good effect. However, in most cases, you will want to eliminate it by using the CSS equivalent of `cellspacing`. Doing so also opens up the possibility of creating borders on columns and rows.

How do I stop border widths from being doubled?

By default, browsers insert a gap of about 2px between table cells. The normal way to eliminate this gap in HTML is to set the table's `cellspacing` attribute to 0. You can still use `cellspacing` with CSS, but it has a potentially undesirable effect. To demonstrate what happens, `table_10.html` sets `cellspacing` to 0 and adds a 5px red border to each table cell with the following style rule:

```
td {
  border: #F00 solid 5px;
}
```

Setting `cellspacing` to 0 removes the gap between the cells but leaves the separate borders intact. As a result, you end up with borders twice as thick as you probably intended.

To avoid this problem, use the CSS `border-collapse` property, and set its value to `collapse`.

In `table_11.html`, I have removed `cellspacing="0"` from the opening `<table>` tag and added `border-collapse` to the `table` style block like this:

```
table {
  margin: 20px auto;
  border: #000 solid 5px;
  border-collapse: collapse;
}
```

Figure 9-11 shows the difference between `cellspacing` and `border-collapse`. The screenshot on the left shows `table_10.html` with `cellspacing` set to 0; the borders are doubled to 10px. The screenshot on the right shows table_11.html, which uses border-collapse; the borders are merged to produce a 5px border all round.

One	Two	Three
Four	Five	Six
Seven	Eight	Nine
Ten	Eleven	Twelve

One	Two	Three
Four	Five	Six
Seven	Eight	Nine
Ten	Eleven	Twelve

Figure 9-11. Even with cellspacing set to 0, the borders are doubled (left), whereas border-collapse (right) produces the desired size.

Using border-collapse has another effect that you might not notice immediately in Figure 9-11, because this book is printed in glorious black and white. The black border around the table has disappeared, and has been replaced by the 5px red border of the outer cells.

ExplainED

The order-collapse *property follows strict rules to decide how to merge adjacent borders. Most of the time, you don't need to worry about the details, because the basic principle is that only the wider border is displayed. It's when both borders are the same width that the rules come into play. Both have the same style, so it boils down to a question of deciding which color should prevail. As explained earlier in this chapter, browsers lay out tables in six steps. The cells are laid out last, so that's the color used.*

If you make the cell borders narrower than the table border, only the table border shows. Try it out for yourself in table_11.html. Change the style rules for the table cells to give them a 1px border like this (if you're feeling lazy, you can use table_12.html instead):

```
td {
  border:#F00 solid 1px;
}
```

The 5px black border around the table is restored, and the cells have a 1px red border between them. However, there is no red border sandwiched between the outer cells and table border. The outer edge of the outer cell borders has merged with the table border, as shown in Figure 9-12.

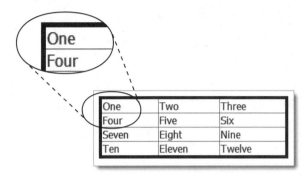

Figure 9-12. The table border is wider, so it hides the outer borders of adjacent cells.

LinkED

See www.w3.org/TR/CSS21/tables.html#border-conflict-resolution *for the full rules governing how borders are merged.*

The border-collapse property accepts just two values, namely:

- collapse: This merges adjacent borders, as just demonstrated.
- separate: This is the default setting, which leaves a small gap between table cells. To create a gap larger than the default, you need to use another property: border-spacing, which is described shortly.

When used with cell borders, border-collapse is supported by IE6, so you can safely use this technique on any table. All other modern browsers, including IE8, offer full support for border-collapse, allowing you to set borders on columns and rows.

ExplainED

Don't confuse `border-collapse` *with the HTML* `rowspan` *and* `colspan` *attributes that merge table cells. The* `border-collapse` *property affects only the way borders are drawn around table elements. To merge table cells, use the* `rowspan` *and* `colspan` *attributes in the normal way in your HTML markup.*

Adding borders to columns and rows

As long as `border-collapse` is set to `collapse`, you can define borders for table columns and rows. There are three tables in `table_13.html`. The following style rule creates a `1px` red border on the columns in `table1`, on the table rows in `table2`, and on the table row groups (`<tbody>`) in `table3`:

```
#table1 col, #table1 colgroup, #table2 tr, #table3 tbody {
  border: #F00 solid 1px;
}
```

The results are shown in Figure 9-13.

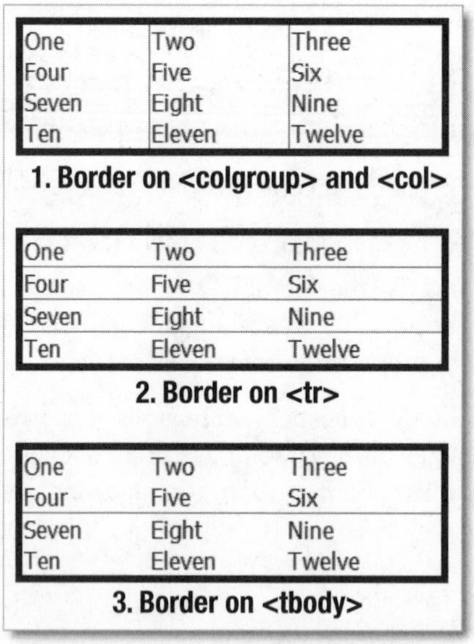

One Two Three
Four Five Six
Seven Eight Nine
Ten Eleven Twelve
1. Border on <colgroup> and <col>
One Two Three
Four Five Six
Seven Eight Nine
Ten Eleven Twelve
2. Border on <tr>
One Two Three
Four Five Six
Seven Eight Nine
Ten Eleven Twelve
3. Border on <tbody>

Figure 9-13. With border-collapse set to collapse, you can add borders to columns and rows.

Applying other styles to columns

As you have just seen, you can style columns if the border-collapse property of the table is set to collapse. Columns are unusual in that they accept only four styles, namely:

- background
- border
- width
- visibility

The only legal value for visibility is collapse. When visibility is set to collapse, the browser should hide the column and reduce the width of the table by the column's width. However, at the time of this writing, IE8 is the only browser that handles this correctly (see the notes after the exercise at the end of this chapter).

What's the CSS equivalent of cellspacing?

Although setting border-collapse to collapse removes the gap between table cells, the CSS equivalent of cellspacing is a different property called border-spacing. These two properties are mutually exclusive. If you want to control the spacing between cells, border-collapse must be set to separate or omitted altogether (it's the default way of displaying tables).

ExplainED

When you think about it for a moment, it makes sense that you can't use border-collapse *at the same time as* border-spacing. *You can't add space between cells and merge their borders at the same time.*

If you set border-spacing *to* 0, *you get the same effect as shown in the screenshot on the left of Figure 9-11. The spacing between the cells is eliminated, but the borders don't merge.*

Unlike cellspacing, which adds the same amount of space around all sides of each cell, border-spacing lets you specify different values for horizontal and vertical spacing. If you supply one value, it applies to both axes. However, if you supply two values, the first is applied to horizontal spacing, and the second to vertical spacing.

The table style rule in table_14.html looks like this:

```
table {
  margin: 20px auto;
  border: #000 solid 5px;
  border-spacing: 10px 20px;
}
```

In most browsers, this produces the result shown in Figure 9-14. The exceptions are IE6 and IE7, which don't support border-spacing at all. Also, Safari 4.0 and Chrome 2.0 incorrectly add extra vertical spacing between the two <tbody> sections.

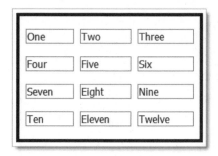

Figure 9-14. With border-spacing, you can add different amounts of vertical and horizontal space between cells.

Now you know how CSS deals with cellspacing, what about cellpadding?

What's the CSS equivalent of cellpadding?

Er, there isn't one. . .

Well, actually there is: it's the padding property you have been using since Chapter 6. Unlike cellpadding, this gives you complete control over the amount of padding in every table cell, and you can have different amounts of padding on each side of the content. You can create a single rule that applies to all cells in the table, or separate rules using classes or ID selectors. However, it's important to remember that table rows are always as high as the tallest cell; and columns normally expand to accommodate the widest cell. I say "normally" because CSS lets you control column width, as you'll see shortly.

To demonstrate how padding works in table cells, the td style rule in table_15.html applies a different amount of padding to each side like this:

padding: 2px 0 15px 20px;

However, the middle cell in the third row uses the following ID selector:

```
#eight {
  padding: 20px;
}
```

This adds 18px more padding to the top of the cell and 5px more at the bottom. As Figure 9-15 shows, this increases the height of the entire row. The extra height also affects the top padding in the cells on either side but does not apply the same value as in the center cell.

343

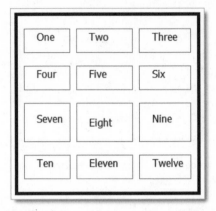

Figure 9-15. Different amounts of padding can be added to each side of a cell.

ExplainED

Controlling the height of table elements continues to be the holy grail of many web developers. The simple fact of the matter is that it can't be done, at least not in a standards-compliant browser. Heights are always calculated automatically and are controlled by the tallest element in a table row.

Controlling the position of the table caption

To add a caption to a table, you place the caption text in a pair of <caption> tags immediately after the opening <table> tag. By default, the caption appears above the table, but you can move it underneath the table by setting the caption-side property to bottom. Since the caption is an integral part of the table, you can define the caption-side property in the style rule for the table or in a separate rule for the caption itself.

According to the CSS2.1 specification, there are only two possible values for caption-side, namely:

- bottom: Put the caption under the table.
- top: Put the caption above the table. This is the default value.

In CSS2, there were two other values: left and right. However, Firefox was the only browser to offer support, so they were removed from the official specification.

344

Support for `caption-side` was added to Internet Explorer in IE8. It's not supported in IE6 or IE7.

Since the caption is part of the table, it inherits its text color and width from the table. You can style a caption like any other text element, giving it a color and font properties of its own. Most browsers support giving a caption a margin to distance it from the table. However, Safari and Chrome ignore margins on captions, so the only reliable method is to use padding.

There are examples of `caption-side` in `table_06.html` and `table_13.html` (see Figures 9-6 and 9-13).

Handling empty cells

The `empty-cells` property is supported by all browsers currently in widespread use, except IE6 and IE7. It accepts the following values:

- `hide`: Prevent the display of an empty cell's borders and backgrounds.
- `show`: Draw borders and backgrounds on every cell, even if it contains no content. This is the default setting.

An empty cell is defined as a cell that contains absolutely nothing or one that has the `visibility` property set to `hidden`. However, setting the `visibility` property of a cell to `hidden` also prevents the display of its borders and background, even when the `empty-cells` property is set to `show`.

ExplainED

Many HTML editors, such as Dreamweaver, automatically insert the HTML entity for a nonbreaking space ( ) into empty table cells. CSS regards this as content, even though nothing appears in the cell when viewed in a browser. For a cell to be treated as empty it must not contain anything other than new lines and whitespace between the opening and closing <td> or <th> tags.

The `empty-cells` property is inherited, so you can apply it to the whole table. However, if you want to affect only a certain part of a table, you can apply it to table row groups, table rows, or individual cells.

Figure 9-16 and `table_16.html` show how the `empty-cells` property works. In all four tables, the second row contains only empty cells, while the `visibility` property of the middle cell in the third row has been set to `hidden`.

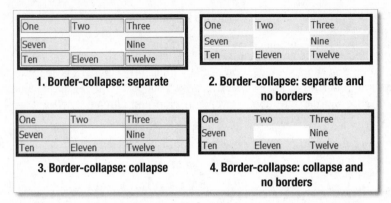

Figure 9-16. The use of cell borders affects the way browsers treat empty cells.

Although browsers should hide a complete row of empty cells, at the time of this writing, all browsers that support the empty-cells property leave a small gap for the empty row, except when border-collapse is set to collapse and the cells have no borders (see the bottom-right table in Figure 9-16).

Figure 9-17 shows a practical example of using empty-cells and border-spacing to display the color keywords supported by CSS. Only 17 keywords are officially supported, so it's necessary to hide the last three cells of the bottom row—a trivial task with empty-cells set to hide. You can examine the code in color_names.html in the download files for this chapter.

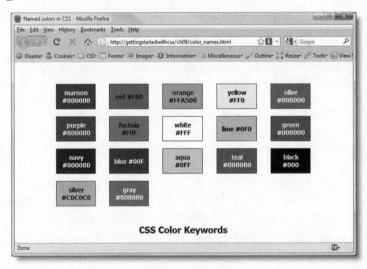

Figure 9-17. Imaginative use of a table and CSS styles produce a clean-looking chart.

How can I control the width of my table?

At times, I get the feeling that whoever drew up the HTML specification for tables must have had a cruel sense of humor. HTML allows you to specify the width attribute on tables, columns, and individual table cells. At the beginning, it seems to work, but as soon as you insert oversized content, the browser obligingly makes room and ignores the specified width. It makes herding cats seem like child's play.

CSS rides to the rescue with the table-layout property, which is supported by all current browsers, including IE6. The property accepts the following values:

- auto: This is the default way tables behave, expanding columns and the overall table width to accommodate the widest element in each column.

- fixed: The width of each column is fixed by the width attribute specified in its <col> tag. If no width is specified there, the width is taken from the size of each column in the first table row.

The table-layout property is not inherited, so you can also use the inherit keyword for nested tables. However, nested tables are rarely used when displaying data.

To demonstrate how table-layout works, the download files for this chapter contain a series of four pages that display two oversized images in a 300-pixel-wide table. The basic HTML structure in each page looks like this:

```
<table>
  <colgroup>
    <col width="25%" />
    <col width="75%" />
  </colgroup>
  <tr>
    <td width="50%">Angel's Window</td>
    <td width="50%"><img src="../images/angels_window.jpg"
      width="350" height="249" alt="Angel's window" /></td>
  </tr>
  <tr>
    <td>Kaibab National Forest</td>
    <td><img src="../images/forest_grassland.jpg" width="325"
      height="208" alt="Kaibab National Forest" /></td>
  </tr>
</table>
```

The first page, table-layout_01.html, uses the default value for table-layout, auto. The style rules in the page look like this:

```
table {
  table-layout: auto;
  border: solid #000 5px;
  border-spacing: 0;
  width: 300px;
}
td {
  padding: 5px;
}
```

As you can see in Figure 9-18, the table ignores all the width specifications and expands to accommodate the content. The table ends up about 425px wide, and the border is drawn around the outside edge.

Figure 9-18. By default, tables ignore declared widths and adjust to fit the content.

Figure 9-19 shows what happens when you change the value of table-layout to fixed (the code is in table-layout_02.html). The table is drawn to the correct width (300px), and the two columns are correctly proportioned (25%:75%), as specified in the <col> tags. The 50% widths in the <td> tags are ignored—as they should be, because only the first declared widths are valid with a fixed table layout. What might come as a surprise is that the oversized content spills out of the table.

Figure 9-19. With a fixed layout, the table widths are honored, but oversized content spills out.

To prevent the overspill, you need to add the overflow property. If you set overflow to hidden, you can add it either to the table style block or to the td one. This cuts off any oversized content, as shown on the left of Figure 9-20 and in table-layout_03.html. In theory, to generate a scrollbar for oversized content, add the overflow property to the td style block and set its value to auto, as in table-layout_04.html. However, at the time of this writing, the only browser that produces the result shown on the right in Figure 9-20 is IE8. Some browsers let the content spill out in the same way as in Figure 9-19, while others put both horizontal and vertical scrollbars on the images.

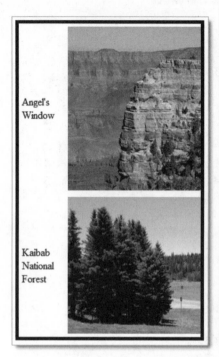

Figure 9-20. You can hide the overflow (left) or add scrollbars to make it accessible (right).

How do I create scrolling table cells that work in all browsers?

If you test table-layout_04.html in a variety of browsers, you'll soon discover that setting the value of overflow to auto usually doesn't have the desired effect on table cells. Even in IE8, it affects only content that is too wide. Setting a height on a table cell or table row is meaningless if the content is too big to fit. So, what's the secret of creating a scrollable table cell?

The answer is to use a <div> inside the cell, give it a fixed width (and height, if desired), and set the overflow property of the <div> to auto. In other words, it's the content of the table cell that needs to be scrollable, rather than the table cell itself.

ExplainED

Tables don't conform to the CSS box model: the border is always added inside the table, and not outside. When table-layout *is set to the default* auto *or omitted, this doesn't really matter, because the table automatically expands to accommodate the content. However, it makes a big difference when* table-layout *is set to* fixed*. The overall width of a 300px wide table with a 5px border all round remains 300px, and not 310px. This affects the calculation of the size of the* <div> *required for a scrolling table cell.*

The images in table-layout_05.html have each been wrapped in a <div>, to which the following class has been assigned:

```
.scrollable {
  width: 203px;
  overflow: auto;
}
```

The width of the <div> was calculated by deducting 30px from the overall width of 300px and multiplying the remainder by 75%. The 30px consists of the left and right borders (5px each) and the 5px padding on each side of each table cell. If you test table-layout_05.html in a range of browsers, you'll see that it works reliably, even in IE6 and IE7. The only problem with the older versions of Internet Explorer is that they spawn both vertical and horizontal scrollbars. Everyone else gets just horizontal scrollbars.

How do I control the position of content in table cells?

The CSS equivalents of the HTML align and valign attributes are properties that you first met in Chapter 2. To control the horizontal position of content in a table cell, use text-align. Vertical alignment is controlled by the vertical-align property.

When used with table cells, the text-align property takes the same values as with text, namely: left, center, right, and justify. The values work exactly the same way, so no further explanation is necessary.

The `vertical-align` property has many values, but only the following four work with tables:

- `top`: Align the content with the top of the cell.
- `middle`: Center the content vertically within the cell. This is the default value.
- `bottom`: Align the bottom of the content with the bottom of the cell.
- `baseline`: Align the first line of content with the baseline of the tallest similarly aligned content in the same row.

The meaning of `baseline` should become clear from Figure 9-21 (the code is in `table_17.html`). The fourth and fifth columns both have `vertical-align` set to `baseline`. Since the text in the fifth column is taller, the baseline of the first line of text in the fourth column is aligned with the baseline of the first line of text in the fifth column. The `baseline` value affects only the first line of content in a cell, and is determined independently for each row.

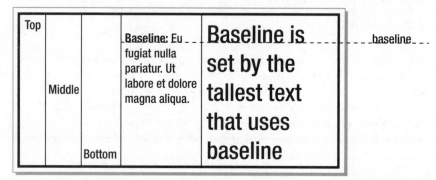

Figure 9-21. Table cells can be vertically aligned at the top, middle, bottom, and baseline of the current row.

That covers the theoretical side of styling tables with CSS. To end this chapter, let's put that knowledge to practical use by styling a data table.

Styling a weather chart

This exercise uses most of the CSS table properties described in this chapter to convert an uninspiring weather chart into something much more attractive. The start and finish versions are in the download files.

1. Copy `weather_start.html` from the download files for this chapter to your work folder, and rename it as `weather.html`.

2. Load `weather.html` into a browser to assess the task ahead. The page should look like Figure 9-22. It's a monthly summary of the average weather in London and South East England, and as drab as the weather itself.

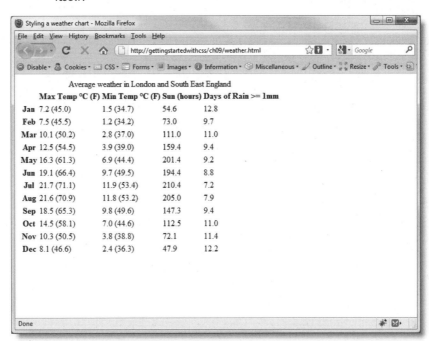

Figure 9-22. This unstyled table of weather data is desperately in need of a touch of style.

3. Let's start the transformation by giving the table a width and center it. Also give it a 1px border, a smart font, and move the caption to the bottom of the table. Create the following style block in the <head> of the page:

```
<style type="text/css">
table {
  width: 600px;
  margin: 0 auto;
  border: #002F2F 1px solid;
  font-family: Tahoma, Geneva, sans-serif;
  caption-side: bottom;
}
</style>
```

4. Next, smarten up the caption by creating a new style rule immediately after the one you added in the previous step:

```
caption {
  font-size: 18px;
  font-weight: bold;
  font-variant: small-caps;
  padding: 10px;
}
```

I have added 10px of padding all around the caption to move it away from the bottom edge of the table. I chose padding because Safari and Chrome ignore margins on captions.

5. With data tables, it's usual to center the data in each column by setting the text-align property to center. However, the numbers in each column are of varying lengths, so centering gives them a ragged appearance. Instead, I'm going to align the columns to the right, and use padding to reposition the figures. Add the following style rule to the page:

```
td {
  text-align: right;
  padding: 3px 30px 3px 3px;
  border-bottom: 1px solid #002F2F;
}
```

This adds 3px of padding to all sides of each table cell, except the right, which gets 30px. I have also added a 1px border to the bottom of each cell.

6. Save weather.html, and check it in a browser. It should look similar to Figure 9-23.

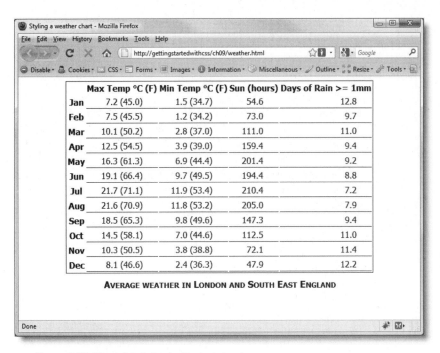

Figure 9-23. The table is beginning to take shape.

There are several points to note:

- There are gaps between the columns in the bottom borders. There's also a double border at the bottom. This can be fixed by setting border-collapse to collapse.

- There are no borders under the headings in the top row or under the months. This is because they use <th> tags, rather than <td>. If you wanted to add borders, you would need to create a group selector for both tags (td, th). However, on this occasion, I don't want a border, because I'm going to style the headings differently. Choosing different tags not only makes more structural sense; it makes styling easier.

- The columns are of varying widths. You can fix that by using the table-layout property.

7. Amend the table style block like this:

```
table {
  width: 600px;
  margin: 0 auto;
```

355

```
  border: #002F2F 1px solid;
  font-family: Tahoma, Geneva, sans-serif;
  caption-side: bottom;
  border-collapse: collapse;
  table-layout: fixed;
}
```

8. Although you could set the size of the columns by adding the `width` property to the `<th>` tags in the first row, defining the columns with `<colgroup>` and `<col>` tags opens up the possibility of styling the columns with a background color. So, add the following column definitions at the top of the table between the `<caption>` and the first table row:

```
<caption>Average weather in London and South East England</caption>
<colgroup>
  <col class="labelcol" />
  <col class="oddcol" />
  <col class="evencol" />
  <col class="oddcol" />
  <col class="evencol" />
</colgroup>
<tr>
```

This defines the five columns, assigning a class to each one. The first one will be used to style the month labels, and the others will set alternating background colors for odd and even columns.

9. To identify the table row that contains the top row of headings, you need to assign it a class. Amend the opening tag of the first table row like this:

```
</colgroup>
<tr class="headrow">
  <th> </th>
```

I used a class rather than an ID in case you want to put more than one table on the same page.

10. Now, create the three classes for the columns by adding the following style rules to the `<head>` of the page:

```
.labelcol {
  background-color: #046380;
}
.oddcol {
  background-color: #E6E2AF;
  width: 23%;
}
.evencol {
```

```
  background-color: #EFECCA;
  width: 23%;
}
```

This adds a deep teal background color to the label column, and two shades of beige to the other columns. The `oddcol` and `evencol` classes also set the width of the columns to `23%`. This leaves 8% for the `labelcol` class. However, there's no need to add a width for the first column, because the browser will work it out automatically.

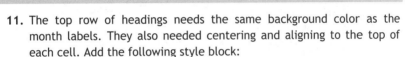

I'm not being lazy by not defining the width as 8%. Rounding errors with percentage values make it unwise to specify widths that add up to exactly 100%. I have mentioned this before, but it's worth repeating, because it's such an easy trap to fall into. The fact that the numbers all add up makes it difficult to identify the problem if your design doesn't work as expected.

11. The top row of headings needs the same background color as the month labels. They also needed centering and aligning to the top of each cell. Add the following style block:

```
.headrow th {
  background-color: #046380;
  text-align: center;
  vertical-align: top;
  font-variant: small-caps;
}
```

This uses a descendant selector, so the styles affect only the `<th>` cells in the row with the `headrow` class. The other `<th>` cells in the month of column labels are not affected.

12. To complete the styling of the `<th>` tags, add the following style rule:

```
th {
  color: #EFECCA;
  padding: 3px 10px;
  text-align: right;
}
```

This sets the text color of all `<th>` tags to the same light beige as the background of the `evencol` class. It also sets the padding for all headings. But what about that `text-align`? This affects only the `<th>`

357

tags in the month labels, because the .headrow th descendant selector created in the previous step has higher specificity. So, the headings in the top row remain centered, while the remaining <th> tags are aligned right.

13. Save the page, and view it in a browser. The uninspiring table you started with should now look much smarter, as shown in Figure 9-24.

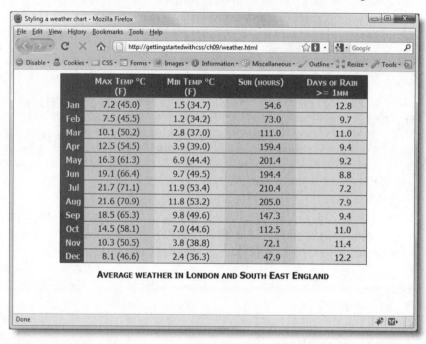

Figure 9-24. The table now looks much more visually attractive.

14. To make the table more attractive and user friendly, let's highlight each row as the cursor passes over it. The :hover pseudo-class can be applied to any element, not just a link. Well, as you might expect, IE6 won't play ball, but it has been perfectly well behaved in styling this table up to now, so I'm not going to worry about it. Add the following styles:

```
tr:hover {
  background-color: #FFF;
}
tr:hover th {
  background-color: #008080;
}
```

The first of these rules sets the background color to white on the whole row, while the second rule affects only the <th> cell of the current row, setting its background color to teal.

15. Save the page, and test it again in any modern browser. As you move your cursor over the table, the current row should be highlighted, as shown in Figure 9-25.

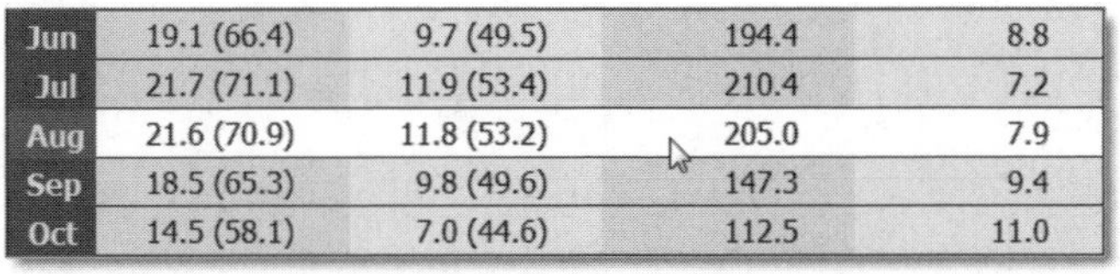

Jun	19.1 (66.4)	9.7 (49.5)	194.4	8.8
Jul	21.7 (71.1)	11.9 (53.4)	210.4	7.2
Aug	21.6 (70.9)	11.8 (53.2)	205.0	7.9
Sep	18.5 (65.3)	9.8 (49.6)	147.3	9.4
Oct	14.5 (58.1)	7.0 (44.6)	112.5	11.0

Figure 9-25. The :hover pseudo-class highlights the table row when the cursor passes over it.

IE6 supports :hover only on links. Since highlighting the current row is merely an enhancement, you can ignore IE6. The table remains perfectly usable without the highlighting.

16. There's just one minor problem: the top row of <th> tags is also highlighted when the cursor passes over it. You can fix this by grouping a new descendant selector with the .headrow th style rule like this:

```
.headrow th, .headrow:hover th {
  background-color: #046380;
  text-align: center;
  vertical-align: top;
  font-variant: small-caps;
}
```

This makes sure the same style rules are always applied to the <th> tags in the top row.

You can check your code, if necessary, against weather_finish.html in the download files for this chapter.

As you can see in Figure 9-24, the padding on the right of the <td> cells centers the minimum and maximum temperature columns, but the data in the sun and rain columns is further to the right. One way of dealing with this would be to make the last two columns narrower. You could also increase the right padding in these two columns. However, remember that you can apply only four properties to columns: background, border, width, and visibility. So, the only way to change the padding on the columns would be to apply a class to each individual cell. My personal feeling is that centering the data is less important than aligning the decimal points. However, the choice is yours.

ExplainED

The new selector added in the final step of the preceding exercise applies the :hover pseudo-class to the headrow *class, and not to the descendant* th *selector. This is because the style rules in step 14 apply the highlighting not just to the cell the cursor is currently over, but to the whole table row. Only one cell is affected if you apply :hover to the* th *selector like this:* .headrow th:hover.

It might seem strange combining a class with a pseudo-class like this. However, it should be easier to understand if you prefix the headrow *class with the table row selector like this:* tr.headrow:hover th. *This applies to* <th> *tags in a table row styled with the* headrow *class when the cursor is over the row.*

One final test that you might like to make with this table is to set the visibility of some columns to collapse. According to the CSS2.1 specification, browsers should hide the affected columns and reduce the overall width of the table by the same amount. In weather_col_visibility.html, the evencol class has been amended like this:

```
.evencol {
  background-color: #EFECCA;
  width: 23%;
  visibility: collapse;
}
```

At the time of this writing, IE8 is the only major browser that gets it right, as shown in Figure 9-26.

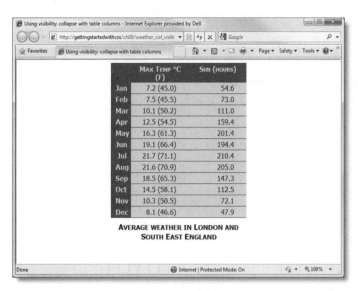

Figure 9-26. IE8 correctly hides columns when visibility is set to collapse.

Firefox 3.5 manages to hide the columns but fails to reduce the width of the table, leaving the borders, as shown in Figure 9-27.

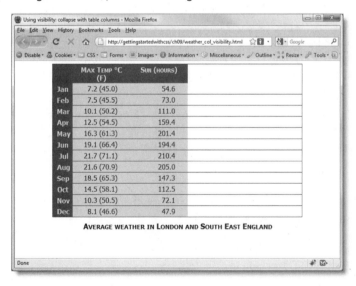

Figure 9-27. Firefox 3.5 hides the columns but doesn't reduce the width of the table.

Safari 4.0, Opera 10, and Chrome 2.0 fail to hide the collapsed columns and display the page exactly the same as Figure 9-24.

Chapter review

CSS offers many advantages when it comes to styling tables. The `border-collapse` and `border-spacing` properties are a great improvement on `cellspacing`, not only giving you control over the horizontal and vertical spacing between table cells but also improving the look of adjacent borders. Although there isn't a direct equivalent of `cellpadding`, table cells handle padding in the same way as the CSS box model, giving you the freedom to adjust it independently on each side of a cell and even use different settings in selected cells. Other advantages include the freedom to style all of a table's internal and external borders independently using any of the border styles supported by CSS2.1, and to hide empty cells.

By using advanced HTML elements, such as `<colgroup>`, `<col>`, and `<tbody>`, you can style tables efficiently without the need to apply classes to individual cells. Setting `table-layout` to `fixed` also gives you precise control over the width of columns. However, it's important to remember that tables do not conform to the CSS box model: borders and padding are not added to the overall width of a table, so this needs to be taken into account when calculating how wide each column should be when using a fixed table layout. Although IE8 handles the `overflow` property on table cells successfully, in order to create a scrollable table cell you need to use a fixed-width `<div>` inside table cells and apply the overflow property to the `<div>` for cross-browser compatibility.

What's disappointing about CSS support for tables is the fact that columns support only four properties: `background`, `border`, `width`, and `visibility`. It would make life a lot easier if all properties could be applied to columns. However, tables are a low priority for the W3C, so such support is unlikely in the near future.

In the next chapter, I'll delve into the mysteries of CSS positioning. In the early days of CSS, many developers thought it was the answer to all their problems and would replace tables for layout. That enthusiasm quickly evaporated once they realized that positioning often creates more problems than it solves. The next chapter will try to help you avoid those problems.

Chapter 10

How Do I Position Elements Precisely on the Page?

If you have just picked up this book and come straight to this chapter to learn how to position elements on a page, I urge you to stop right now. Go back and learn first about margins, padding, and floats. They're the really useful tools for CSS layout. This chapter is devoted to CSS positioning (sometimes referred to as CSS-P) using the `position` property. The basic concept is fairly simple—it allows you to specify the position of an element with great precision. It's such an attractive proposition that many beginners are seduced by the idea and use it to build complex layouts, only to discover that things aren't quite as straightforward as they originally seemed.

CSS positioning became all the rage because it was one aspect of CSS that most browsers handled predictably almost from the start. Its popularity was boosted by Dreamweaver, which made it possible to draw positioned elements on a page, reposition, and resize them in much the same way as in a desktop publishing program. Unfortunately, designs built this way have a tendency to fall apart when text size is increased or positioned elements are mixed with nonpositioned ones. Centering content is also more difficult.

Don't let these issues put you off. Understanding CSS positioning is an important part of your CSS toolbox, and it allows you to create sophisticated effects, such as text disappearing behind a static image as you scroll the page, and elements that overlap one another.

In this chapter, you'll learn how to do the following:

- Fix the position of a navigation menu so that it stays onscreen all the time
- Position elements accurately against a background image
- Overlap elements and change their stacking order
- Crop an image nondestructively

Before diving into the details, it's important to understand the different types of positioning defined in CSS.

How does CSS positioning work?

Normally, browsers display HTML elements in the same order as they appear in a page's underlying markup, using margins, padding, and the float property to adjust the position of each element in relation to its neighbors. Although the float property takes the floated element out of the normal flow of the document, its position is still controlled by where it appears in the markup. The floated element moves to one side or the other, and the immediately following elements move up to fill the vacated space. You can't arbitrarily float an image alongside text that's in a completely different part of the page.

CSS positioning takes a different approach by allowing you to remove an element from the flow of the document and place it wherever you want on the page. Before you get too excited by this prospect, there's a catch—and a pretty serious one at that. Once an element has been removed from the flow, it ceases to interact with other elements on the page. So, you can't use CSS positioning to move an image to a different part of the page and then flow the text in that part of the page around it. Positioning is best used sparingly for special effects.

Another feature of CSS positioning is that it introduces a third dimension. Unfortunately, this doesn't mean that you can create 3D effects with CSS, but you can make elements overlap and control the order in which they appear on top of each other. This can be useful when you want an image to overlap text, appear in a margin, or overlap a border, something that's impossible with a background image. You can also overlap images without needing to create a composite image in a graphics program. Table 10-1 lists the CSS properties that make all this possible.

Table 10-1. Properties Used for CSS Positioning

Property	Initial Value	Inherited	Description
position	static	No	Controls how an element is positioned. When the value of this property is set to absolute or fixed, the element is removed completely from the normal flow of the document. When set to relative, the element is moved relative to its position in the normal flow, but a space is left where it would normally have been. The default value, static, means the element remains in the normal flow and is *not* positioned.
bottom	auto	No	Specifies the offset of the bottom margin edge of a positioned element from the bottom of its containing block. A positive value moves the positioned element up; a negative value moves it down.
left	auto	No	Specifies the offset of the left margin edge of a positioned element from the left of its containing block. A positive value moves the positioned element to the right; a negative value moves it to the left.
right	auto	No	Specifies the offset of the right margin edge of a positioned element from the right of its containing block. A positive value moves the positioned element to the left; a negative value moves it to the right.
top	auto	No	Specifies the offset of the top margin edge of a positioned element from the top of its containing block. A positive value moves the positioned element down; a negative value moves it up.
z-index	auto	No	Specifies an integer to indicate the stacking level of a positioned element. Elements with a higher z-index number can overlap other elements in the same stacking context.
clip	auto	No	Defines the area of an absolutely positioned element that remains visible. Performs a similar function to the crop tool in a graphical editor, but in a nondestructive way.

To use any of the properties in Table 10-1, the style rule must include the position property, which determines how the element is to be treated.

Understanding the different types of positioning

The position property requires one of the following values:

- absolute: Remove the element, including any child elements, completely from the flow of the document, and position it at the offsets defined in the same style rule. If the element is nested inside another positioned element, the offsets are calculated with reference to the positioned parent. Otherwise, the offsets are calculated with reference to the page.

- fixed: This works similar to absolute, but the offsets are always calculated with reference to the browser viewport.

- relative: Move the element relative to its normal position in the document flow, but without affecting the position of other elements.

- static: Leave the element in the normal document flow.

The position property is not inherited, so you can use the inherit keyword if you want a child element to inherit the same type of positioning as its parent.

Most of the time, you can forget about static. This is the default way that browsers display HTML. The only time you might need it is if you want to override another style rule to make an element act like normal HTML. For example, in a print style sheet that inherits styles from a screen style sheet, it's normal to reset position to static for positioned elements to ensure they print out correctly (print style sheets are covered in Chapter 12).

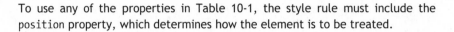

For an element to be considered positioned, its position *property must be set to* absolute, fixed, *or* relative. *An element that has its* position *property set to* static *is not considered to be positioned.*

The best way to understand how the different types of positioning work is to see them in action. The following sections describe each type of positioning in more detail, together with examples.

Fixing elements inside the browser window

Most discussions of CSS positioning begin with absolute positioning. However, I'm going to start with fixed positioning, mainly because it's easier to understand.

How do I keep my navigation onscreen all the time?

In the late 1990s, frames became a very popular way to build website. As you probably know, frames let you display multiple web pages simultaneously in the same browser window. One of the great attractions of doing so is the ability to keep a navigation menu on the page all the time, even when you scroll through the main content. However, frames have fallen out of favor for a number of reasons, including problems of accessibility, the inability to bookmark pages, and the fact that flyout menus cannot be displayed outside their containing frame.

CSS fixed positioning simulates frames, while avoiding most of the associated problems. Although fixed positioning presents problems of its own, what has really held back its widespread use is lack of support in IE6. Now that IE6 is no longer the dominant browser, fixed positioning is likely to find its way increasingly into website design. With a little planning, you can also ensure designs that use fixed positioning look acceptable in IE6.

When you add the `position` property to an element's style rules and set it to `fixed`, the browser floats the element on an independent layer in front of the static content. The `top`, `right`, `bottom`, and `left` offsets tell the browser where to position the floating layer in relation to the browser window. Any offset that isn't explicitly declared is set to `auto`. What this means is that, if you don't set a `right` or `left` offset, the element remains in the same position horizontally as it would be normally. How this works in practice is best seen through an example. So, roll up your sleeves and start experimenting with CSS positioning.

Creating a fixed header and menu

This exercise adapts the page used as a case study in earlier chapters, and makes the banner heading and horizontal navigation menu remain onscreen while the rest of the page is scrolled. The page and style sheet are in the download files for this chapter.

1. Open `journey_fixed_start.html` in the download files for this chapter, and save it in your work files as `journey_fixed.html`.

2. Open `journey_fixed_start.css` in the `css` subfolder of the download files for this chapter, and save it in your work files as `journey_fixed.css`.

3. Change the `<link>` in the `<head>` of `journey_fixed.html` so it points to the style sheet you have just saved. It should look like this:

```
<link href="css/journey_fixed.css" rel="stylesheet" type="text/css" />
```

4. Load `journey_fixed.html` into a browser, and check that the page displays correctly. It should look like Figure 10-1.

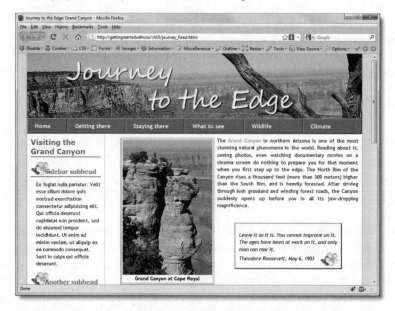

Figure 10-1. The banner heading and navigation menu are ideal candidates for fixed positioning.

If the images fail to appear, check that the path names are correct. Everything should look fine as long as your work files are at the same level in the site as the `ch10` folder.

5. Converting the banner heading and the navigation menu to fixed-position elements is simple. The first stage is to add the `position` property to their style rules, and set the value to `fixed`. Change the

#header style block like this (it's around line 19 of journey_fixed.css):

```
#header {
  height: 176px;
  background-image: url(../../images/journey_header.jpg);
  background-repeat: no-repeat;
  position: fixed;
}
```

6. Do the same to the #nav style block (it's much further down, around line 174):

```
#nav {
  list-style-type: none;
  margin: 0;
  padding: 0;
  height: 2.5em;
  position: fixed;
}
```

7. Save the style sheet, and reload journey_fixed.html in the browser. Don't panic if the top of the page looks like Figure 10-2. That's how it should be.

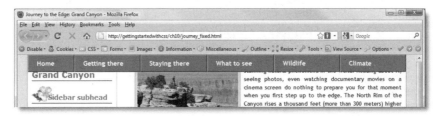

Figure 10-2. The banner heading has disappeared, and the top of the sidebar and main content is hidden behind the menu.

ExplainED

The screenshot in Figure 10-2 was taken in a browser window 1024px wide. If the window size is narrower, the last item(s) in the navigation menu will drop below the first row. The reason is explained in "Understanding the limitations of fixed positioning" later in this chapter. If possible, view the page at 1024px or wider for the time being.

As I explained earlier, absolutely positioned and fixed elements are removed from the normal flow of the document and have no interaction with nonpositioned elements. The banner heading has disappeared because it's a background image, and the <div> has no width. Consequently, the <div> collapses to nothing. The top of the sidebar and main content have disappeared behind the navigation menu because the menu now floats on an independent layer above the nonpositioned content.

8. To ensure the banner heading is displayed, you need to give the #header style block the same width as the wrapper <div>. Change the #header style block like this:

```
#header {
  height: 176px;
  width: 940px;
  background-image: url(../../images/journey_header.jpg);
  background-repeat: no-repeat;
  position: fixed;
}
```

This brings the banner heading back into view, but you need to adjust the top offset of the navigation menu so that it is positioned below the header. The header image is 176px high, so that's the offset you need. Amend the #nav style block like this:

```
#nav {
  list-style-type: none;
  margin: 0;
  padding: 0;
  height: 2.5em;
  position: fixed;
  top: 176px;
}
```

The header and navigation menu are now in the right positions, but the nonpositioned content is still hidden.

9. You need to push the remaining content down the page, so that it's visible. As you should know from earlier chapters, you move block-level elements by adjusting their margins and/or padding. So, which should you use? Padding is the safer choice; but to understand why, try adding a top margin to the #mainContent style block like this:

```
#mainContent {
  border-left: #D8D0AC solid 1px;
  margin: 215px 0 0 220px;
}
```

10. Save the style sheet, and reload the page in a browser. It should now look like Figure 10-3.

Figure 10-3. Adding a top margin to the nonpositioned content affects the position of the header.

ExplainED

What has happened is that the top margin on the main content has pushed the nonpositioned content down by the desired amount, but as you learned in earlier chapters, adjacent vertical margins collapse. Because both the header and the navigation menu use fixed positioning, they have been removed from the normal flow of the document, leaving nothing between the main content and the wrapper. So, both the wrapper and the main content are moved down by 215px. Margins are transparent, so the background color of the body shows through.

But why has the header moved? Surely it's meant to be in a fixed position? It is, but no offsets have been defined in the #header style block. When no offset is specified, the element appears where it normally would. Earlier, it appeared at the top of the page because it's the first item in the wrapper, and there was no gap between the wrapper and the top of the page. However, now that the wrapper has been pushed down 215px, the header goes too.

371

11. To make sure the header stays where you want it at the top of the page, add a `top` offset to the `#header` style block, and set its value to 0 like this:

```
#header {
  height: 176px;
  width: 940px;
  background-image: url(../../images/journey_header.jpg);
  background-repeat: no-repeat;
  position: fixed;
  top: 0;
}
```

This fixes the problem. However, browsers can be unpredictable in the way they display things, particularly when measured in ems. The height of the header image is 176px, but the navigation menu is 2.5em. Because ems are proportional to the font size, the 215px added to the top margin of the main content in step 9 is only a guesstimate of how far it needs to be moved down. If it turns out to be too much, you'll see a strip of the olive background between the bottom of the navigation menu and the top of the main content. However, padding preserves backgrounds, so it's safer to use padding when moving content that you want to appear alongside a fixed position element.

12. Change the top margin in the `#mainContent` style block to 0, and add 215px of top padding like this:

```
#mainContent {
  border-left: #D8D0AC solid 1px;
  margin: 0 0 0 220px;
  padding-top: 215px;
}
```

13. You need to add the same amount of padding to the top of the sidebar, too. It wasn't necessary when you used a top margin on the main content, because the whole wrapper moved down; but padding leaves the wrapper at the top of the page. Amend the `#sidebar` rule like this:

```
#sidebar {
  width: 219px;
  float: left;
  padding-top: 215px;
}
```

14. Save the style sheet, and reload the page in a browser. It should now look the same as it did at the beginning of this exercise. However, you'll notice a big difference when you scroll the main content. As

long as you're not using IE6, the header and navigation menu should stay put while the rest of the page scrolls, as shown in Figure 10-4.

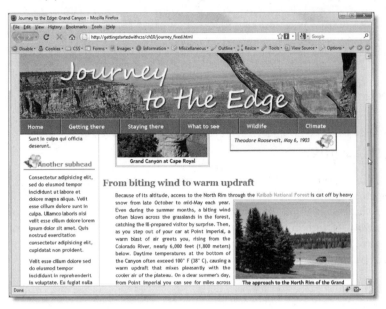

Figure 10-4. The header banner and navigation menu now remain onscreen while the rest of the page scrolls.

You can check your code, if necessary, with journey_fixed_finished.html and css/journey_fixed_finished.css in the download files for this chapter.

AdvancED

IE6 doesn't support fixed positioning, but it does support absolute positioning, which is described shortly. To ensure your pages display correctly in IE6, create separate style rules in an Internet Explorer conditional comment to override any fixed position styles, and set them to absolute. *The elements will be displayed correctly but scroll with the rest of the page. Elements intended to be displayed at the bottom of the browser window will normally be displayed at the bottom of the page.*

Hopefully, that hands-on experience has shown you how easy it is to create a page heading and navigation bar that remain onscreen while the rest of the page is being scrolled. If you found the explanation of the padding and margin difficult to understand, review the explanations in Chapters 6 through 8. Getting your head around the complexities of collapsing margins takes some time, but it's crucial to working successfully with CSS.

Fixed positioning is relatively easy to implement, and one of its advantages over frames is that flyout menus don't disappear behind another page. However, fixed positioning is not without its drawbacks. So, before you start using it in all your pages, you need to assess how well it will work.

Understanding the limitations of fixed positioning

The most serious limitation of CSS positioning is also one of its greatest strengths: positioned elements exist on independent layers in front of nonpositioned content. That's why the main content in the page you have just been working with in the previous exercise scrolls up behind the header image and navigation menu. However, try resizing the browser window. At 800 × 600, the page looks like Figure 10-5.

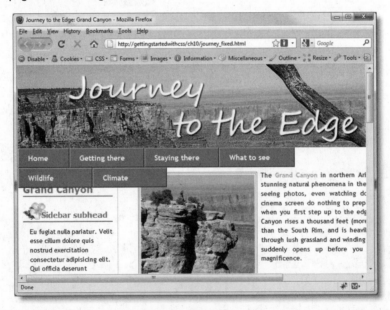

Figure 10-5. The navigation menu breaks up when the browser window is made smaller.

If you try the same with journey_fixed_start.html, you'll see that the navigation menu doesn't break up. This is because the menu is inside the wrapper <div>, which is 940px wide. The width of the <div> forces the browser to generate a horizontal scrollbar, leaving sufficient room for the navigation menu to display. However, once you give the navigation menu a fixed position, it's no longer inside the wrapper <div>, so the floated elements in the menu are forced down the page.

ExplainED

Using CSS positioning doesn't affect the underlying HTML markup. The actual HTML tags for the navigation bar remain inside the wrapper <div>, but the browser treats them as though they are completely separate.

So, what happens if you give the #nav style block a fixed width like this?

```
#nav {
  list-style-type: none;
  margin: 0;
  padding: 0;
  height: 2.5em;
  position: fixed;
  top: 176px;
  width: 940px;
}
```

You can see for yourself by testing journey_fixed_width.html. As Figure 10-6 shows, the fixed position elements remain in their fixed position, even when you move the horizontal scrollbar as far right as possible. The final menu item remains totally inaccessible until you widen the browser window. *Fixed really does mean fixed.*

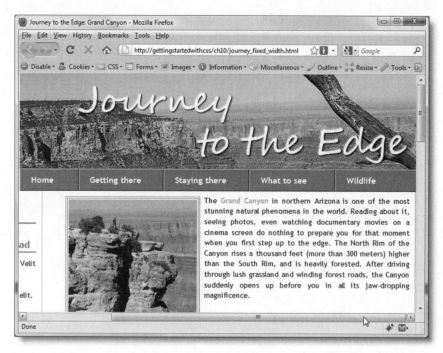

Figure 10-6. The fixed items do not move in the browser window, even when you scroll to the right.

The same problem arises if you put a vertical menu—or, indeed, any other content—in a fixed position. If the item is too tall for a visitor's browser, vertical scrolling will do nothing to reveal the hidden material. The situation is compounded if the visitor increases the text size. The bigger the text, the more of it is hidden.

Another important consideration is the amount of screen real estate being taken up by fixed elements. As you can see in Figure 10-6, the fixed elements take up the top 40% of the browser window. Even at 1024 × 768 (see Figure 10-4), the header and navigation menu hog a lot of space. For a website to be deployed on the Web, it might be better to use a less chunky navigation bar, place it above the banner image, and make only the navigation bar fixed. Alternatively, you could put a vertical navigation bar in the sidebar, and make it fixed. Either way, you would still need to ensure the navigation remains accessible in a small browser window.

To fix an element at the bottom of the browser window, set the bottom offset to 0. Nonpositioned content will scroll behind it in exactly the same way as in the preceding exercise. However, you need to ensure there's sufficient padding on the bottom of the nonpositioned content for all of it to scroll into view.

The key is to test, test, and test again. Cool effects, such as fixed navigation bars, are great, but they're no good if they impede access to your site's content.

Using relative positioning to nudge elements

Relative positioning moves an element and leaves a hole where it would normally have been, without affecting any nonpositioned elements. Figure 10-7 illustrates the basic principle.

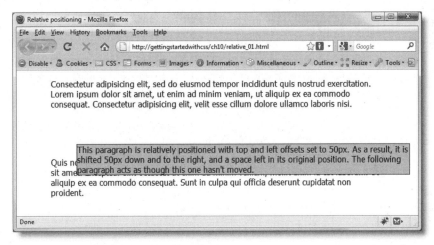

Figure 10-7. Relative positioning moves an element without affecting the position of surrounding elements.

The code for the page shown in Figure 10-7 is in relative_01.html in the download files for this chapter. The second paragraph has an ID called rel, and is styled using the following rules:

```
#rel {
  border: 1px #000 solid;
  background-color: #CCC;
  position: relative;
  left: 50px;
  top: 50px;
}
```

This example is deliberately impractical to demonstrate the potential hazards of using relative positioning. A more practical use is where you want to put something else in the place vacated by the relatively positioned element. You also need to make sure that other nonpositioned elements aren't unintentionally overlapped.

If you completed the previous exercise, change the value of position in the #nav style block from fixed to relative like this:

```
#nav {
  list-style-type: none;
  margin: 0;
  padding: 0;
  height: 2.5em;
  position: relative;
  top: 176px;
}
```

Save the style sheet, and load the page into a browser. Alternatively, use journey_relative.html in the download files. When you load the page, it should look identical to Figure 10-1. The top offset of 176px positions the navigation menu that distance from the top of the page and leaves a space for the banner heading to be displayed. The difference between fixed and relative becomes apparent only when you start to scroll the page. As you can see in Figure 10-8, the navigation menu is no longer in a fixed position, and it starts moving up in tandem with the main content. However, the menu scrolls in front of the banner heading, while the content goes behind. You'll see how to change the stacking order of positioned elements with the z-index property later in this chapter.

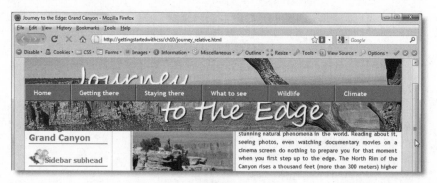

Figure 10-8. By making the navigation menu relatively positioned, it scrolls with the rest of the content.

Although this demonstrates a possible way to use relative positioning, it's still not very practical. If I wanted to scroll the navigation menu with the rest of the content, there's no need to make it a positioned element at all. Instead of adding 215px of padding to the top of the sidebar and main content, all that is necessary is to add 176px of padding (the height of the banner heading) to the top of the unordered list.

So, what's the point of relative positioning?

Using relative positioning to create a containing block

Strange though it may sound, one of the most common uses of relative positioning is to leave the element exactly where it was in the first place. To understand the logic behind this, you need to understand what positioned elements regard as their **containing block**. With nonpositioned elements, the containing block controls the element's width and inherited styles and is a tag's immediate block-level parent. With CSS positioning, however, the containing block controls the position of the element, using the top, right, bottom, and left offsets, and is determined by the type of positioning used, as follows:

- absolute: The containing block *must* be another positioned element. If no such element exists, the page itself is considered the containing block.

- fixed: The containing block is always the browser window. So, a fixed-position element with a bottom offset of 0 sits at the bottom of the browser window and stays there regardless of how big or small the window is.

- relative: The offsets of a relatively positioned element are calculated in relation to the element's position in the normal flow of the document.

The reason for making an element relatively positioned without moving it is to provide the context for absolute positioning. When you do this, the offsets for the absolutely positioned element are calculated from the edges of the relatively positioned element, rather than from the whole page.

So, without further ado, let's take a look at absolute positioning.

Moving elements precisely with absolute positioning

There are two important differences between absolute positioning and fixed positioning, namely:

- The offsets in fixed positioning are always calculated with reference to the browser window. With absolute positioning, the offsets are calculated with reference to the element's containing block, as described in the preceding section.

- With fixed positioning, the element never moves. An absolutely positioned element scrolls with the rest of the page. Its position is fixed only in relation to its containing block.

Let's start with a simple example. In the download files for this chapter, absolute_01.html contains a single <div> styled with the following rules:

```
#absolute1 {
  position: absolute;
  left: 75px;
  top: 100px;
  height: 150px;
  width: 300px;
  padding: 20px;
  background-color: orange;
  font-weight: bold;
}
```

The left property is set to 75px, and top is set to 100px. Since the <div> is not nested inside another positioned element, its containing block is the page itself, so the top left corner is positioned 75px from the left side of the page, and 100px from the top. This position remains constant, regardless of the size of the browser window, as shown in Figure 10-9.

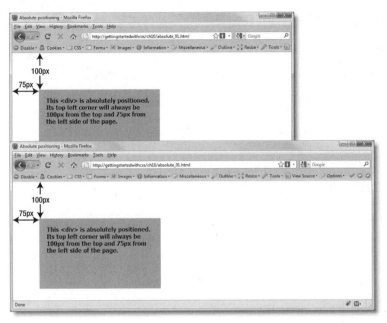

Figure 10-9. An absolutely positioned element stays where you put it, regardless of the size of the browser window.

While that seems fairly unremarkable, look what happens when the left offset is replaced by a right offset like this (the code is in absolute_02.html):

```
#absolute1 {
  position: absolute;
  right: 75px;
  top: 100px;
  height: 150px;
  width: 300px;
  padding: 20px;
  background-color: orange;
  font-weight: bold;
}
```

As Figure 10-10 shows, the absolutely positioned <div> remains 75px from the right edge of the browser window, regardless of the window's size.

381

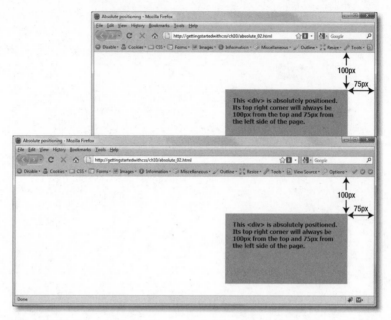

Figure 10-10. You can also anchor an absolutely positioned element to the right of the page.

The offset takes into account any border applied to the absolutely positioned element. In absolute_03.html, I have added a 10px border to the <div> like this:

```
#absolute1 {
  position: absolute;
  right: 75px;
  top: 100px;
  height: 150px;
  width: 300px;
  padding: 20px;
  background-color: orange;
  font-weight: bold;
  border: #000 solid 10px;
}
```

As Figure 10-11 shows, the content of the <div> moves down and to the left, placing the outer edge of the border at the top right corner.

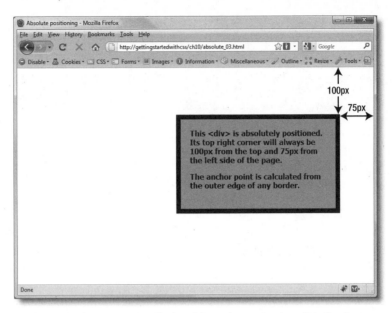

Figure 10-11. The position is calculated from the outer edge of the border.

If you add a margin to the absolutely positioned element, the anchor point is calculated from the outer edge of the margin. However, since the margins of absolutely positioned elements don't interact with other elements, there is little point in doing so. What's more, margins are transparent, so it makes more sense to adjust the offsets, rather than try to combine an offset with a margin.

Viewed in isolation like this, an absolutely positioned element seems quite useful. It's when you start mixing absolutely positioned elements with ordinary content that the fun—or misery—starts.

Why do absolutely positioned elements move?

It should be clear from the preceding discussion that absolutely positioned elements don't move. As Figures 10-9 and 10-10 show, the absolutely positioned <div> remains at the offsets defined in the style rule, no matter how much you resize the browser window. The only time an absolutely positioned element moves is when the page is scrolled. Even then, the position remains fixed in relation to the containing block.

In spite of this, many people are convinced that absolutely positioned elements move when the browser window is resized. Figure 10-12 illustrates the problem.

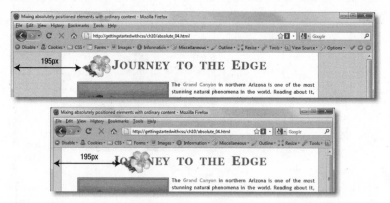

Figure 10-12. When the browser window is resized, the absolutely positioned image stays put and overlaps the heading.

The file absolute_04.html is a copy of journey.html as it looked at the end of Chapter 6. Instead of inserting the flower as a background image to the page's main heading, I have put it in a <div> just before the closing </body> tag like this:

```
<p id="footer"><span class="reversed">Design: Getting StartED with
CSS</span></p>
</div>
<div id="flower"><img src="../images/flower1.png" width="80"
height="61" alt="Flower" /></div>
</body>
```

In the style sheet, I used absolute positioning to move the flower up to the top of page like this:

```
#flower {
  position: absolute;
  top: 8px;
  left: 195px;
}
```

When viewed at 1024 × 768, the flower is positioned perfectly, as shown in the top screenshot in Figure 10-12. However, if you resize the browser to 800 × 600, the ordinary content repositions itself, but the flower stays exactly where I put it, 195px from the left side of the browser. As a result, it overlaps the heading, creating the false impression that it has moved. It hasn't. It's the rest of the page that has moved.

How do I center a page *and* use absolute positioning?

This is where the concept of the absolutely positioned element's containing block comes into play. By using relative positioning on a parent element, the offsets of the absolutely positioned element are calculated with reference to the containing block, rather than the whole page.

In absolute_05.html, I have moved the <div> that contains the flower inside the wrapper <div> like this:

```
<p id="footer"><span class="reversed">Design: Getting StartED with
CSS</span></p>
<div id="flower"><img src="../images/flower1.png" width="80"
height="61" alt="Flower" /></div>
</div>
</body>
```

In the style sheet, css/absolute_05.css, I have added the position property to the #wrapper style rule and set its value to relative like this:

```
#wrapper {
  width: 720px;
  margin: 0 auto;
  background-color: #FFF;
  background-image: url(../../images/grand_canyon.jpg);
  background-repeat: no-repeat;
  background-position: bottom;
  border-left: 2px solid #D8D0AC;
  border-right: 2px solid #D8D0AC;
  position: relative;
}
```

The flower <div> is still absolutely positioned, but the left offset is now measured from the left side of the wrapper <div> and not from the left side of the page. The #flower style rule has been changed to this:

```
#flower {
  position: absolute;
  top: 8px;
  left: 55px;
}
```

As Figure 10-13 shows, changing the containing block results in the flower staying in the desired position, regardless of the size of the browser window.

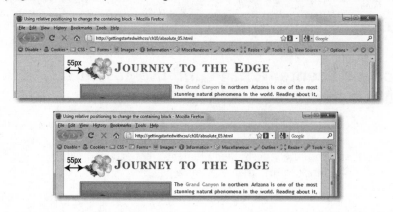

Figure 10-13. The flower is now absolutely positioned relative to the wrapper <div>.

Nesting an absolutely positioned element inside a <div> like this, and making the outer <div> relatively positioned with no offsets, is a useful technique. However, you still need to be careful about overlapping elements. Because the flower is absolutely positioned in absolute_05.html, the start of the heading will disappear underneath the image if the text is enlarged in the browser. You also get an overlap with a background image, but the text remains on top, so should still be readable.

You can also nest absolutely positioned elements inside one another.

What happens if I nest absolutely positioned elements?

Not surprisingly, when you nest absolutely positioned elements, the parent element becomes the nested element's containing block. However, that doesn't necessarily mean that the nested element remains inside its parent.

The containing block is simply the reference point from which the offsets are calculated.

The code in absolute_06.html contains one <div> nested inside another like this:

```
<div id="absolute1">
  Content of absolute1
  <div id="nested">
  Content of nested
  </div>
</div>
```

The style rules look like this:

```
#absolute1, #nested {
  position: absolute;
  width: 300px;
  padding: 20px;
  font-weight: bold;
  border: #000 solid 10px;
}
#absolute1 {
  right: 75px;
  top: 100px;
  height: 150px;
  background-color: orange;
}
#nested {
  top: -100px;
  left: -450px;
  height: 85px;
  background-color: teal;
}
```

Notice that #nested has negative values for the top and left offsets. These move the nested <div> up 100px and left 450px from the top left of its containing block. When viewed in a browser, the page looks like Figure 10-14.

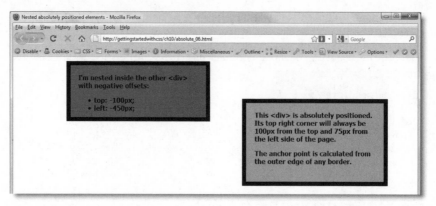

Figure 10-14. Even though the smaller <div> is nested inside the larger one, absolute positioning displays it outside.

However, take a closer look at the measurements. The larger <div> is 100px from the top of the page. The smaller <div> has a negative top offset of 100px, but there's a gap between its border and the top of the page. What's going on? You might think it's because browsers add a 10px margin on web pages; but that's not the cause. Absolutely positioned elements are not affected by the margins of other nonpositioned elements.

The answer is that the offset from a containing block is measured from the edge of the padding, and not from the outer edge of the border. If you remove the border from both elements in absolute_06.html, the smaller <div> is flush with the top of the page.

Look what happens if you view absolute_06.html at 800 × 600. As you can see in Figure 10-15, the smaller <div> disappears beyond the left edge of the browser. What's more, the browser doesn't generate a horizontal scrollbar, so there's no way anyone can see the rest of the content of the <div> without making the browser window larger. As with fixed positioning, you need to test everything carefully when using absolute positioning.

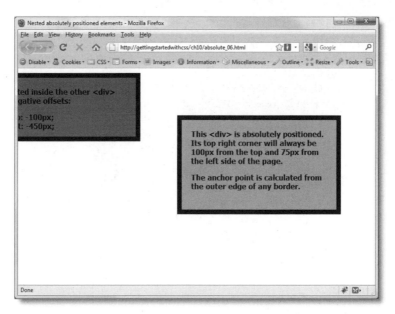

Figure 10-15. With absolute positioning, content might be cut off on a small monitor.

AdvancED

Having content disappear off screen is not necessarily a bad thing. You can use absolute positioning with a large negative top offset to hide elements. In Chapter 7, I showed you how to use a negative left margin to hide the text content of the <h1> heading from visual browsers. An alternative would be to make it absolutely positioned and set the top *offset to a similarly large negative value.*

How do I control which element is on top when they overlap?

One of the advantages of absolute positioning is that elements can be made to overlap each other. Of course, it's an advantage only if that's what you intend. As you saw in Figure 10-12, overlapping can be a major headache if you're not careful.

389

Figure 10-16 shows a simple example of images overlapping each other using absolute positioning.

Figure 10-16. Absolutely positioned elements overlap each other in the same order as they appear in the code.

The code for this screenshot is in absolute_07.html. The HTML looks like this:

```
<div id="images">
  <img src="../images/flower1.png" alt="Flower" width="80" height="61"
    id="flower1" />
  <img src="../images/angels_window.jpg" alt="Angel's Window"
    width="350" height="249" id="angel" />
  <img src="../images/flower1.png" alt="Flower" width="80" height="61"
    id="flower2" />
</div>
```

The style rules look like this:

```
#images {
  position: relative;
  width: 350px;
  margin: 40px auto;
}
#images img{
  position: absolute;
}
#flower1 {
  left: -30px;
  top: -30px;
}
#angel {
  top: 0;
```

```
    left: 0;
}
#flower2 {
  right: -30px;
  top: 220px;
}
```

The <div> is relatively positioned to provide a containing block for the three images, all of which are absolutely positioned by the descendant selector #images img. The main image has its top and left offsets set to 0, which places it at the top left of the <div>. The top and left offsets of flower1 are set to -30px. This moves the image upward and to the left of the containing block. The right and top offsets of flower2 are set to -30px and 220px respectively. This moves the second flower 30px to the right and 220px down from the top of its containing block.

The flowers have been positioned so they overlap the main image. As you can see in Figure 10-16, the first flower is behind, and the second one is in front. The browser has displayed each image in the same order as it appears in the HTML code, placing each image in front of its predecessor where they overlap.

ExplainED

Since the main image hasn't been moved, you might wonder why I have made it absolutely positioned. It's because nonpositioned content always appears behind absolutely positioned elements. If the main image is not absolutely positioned, both flowers appear in front of it.

One way to change how the images overlap is to change their order in the underlying HTML. In absolute_08.html, I have moved the <img> tag for angels_window.jpg below the two flowers like this:

```
<div id="images">
  <img src="../images/flower1.png" alt="Flower" width="80" height="61"
    id="flower1" />
  <img src="../images/flower1.png" alt="Flower" width="80" height="61"
    id="flower2" />
  <img src="../images/angels_window.jpg" alt="Angel's Window"
    width="350" height="249" id="angel" />
</div>
```

391

As a result, the main image is rendered last by the browser, and appears in front of the flowers, as shown in Figure 10-17.

Figure 10-17. The order of the underlying HTML changes the way in which the images overlap.

However, it's much more convenient to change how elements overlap with CSS, using the z-index property. This controls the stacking order of overlapping elements. Higher numbers appear in front of lower ones.

The stacking order of the images has been changed in absolute_09.html by adding the z-index property to each image's style rules like this:

```
#flower1 {
  left: -30px;
  top: -30px;
  z-index: 3;
}
#angel {
  top: 0;
  left: 0;
  z-index: 2;
}
#flower2 {
  right: -30px;
  top: 220px;
  z-index: 1;
}
```

As you can see in Figure 10-18, the first flower now appears in front of the main image, and the second one is tucked behind.

Figure 10-18. The stacking order of the images has been changed by using z-index.

AdvancED

Each containing block sets its own stacking context for z-index. If you find that giving a higher z-index to a positioned element still leaves it stacked behind one with a lower z-index, check the z-index of the element's containing block. It must be higher than the z-index of the other element's containing block.

What are the drawbacks of using absolute positioning?

Many designers, particularly those from a print background, initially regard absolute positioning as the answer to their prayers, because it lets you specify precisely where you want elements to appear on a page. It certainly does, but a major problem with absolute positioning is the way positioned elements float above nonpositioned content without any interaction between them, as shown in Figure 10-19 (the code is in `absolute_10.html`).

393

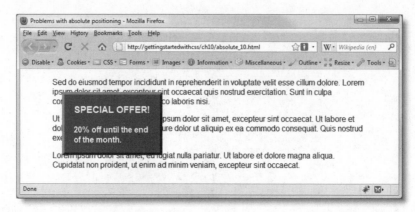

Figure 10-19. Nonpositioned content cannot flow around an absolutely positioned element.

Admittedly, this is a trivial example, but the problem is far from trivial. Once you start using absolutely positioned elements for page layout, everything needs to be absolutely positioned. Even if you manage to get a page to look the way you want by using absolute positioning for every element, you need to remember that users can change the size of text in their browsers. If they use the zoom feature that resizes everything proportionately, your design will probably hold together. However, you cannot rely on everyone using that setting. If the browser is set to resize text only, the text in absolutely positioned elements at the top of the page will begin to overflow the text in elements lower down.

You also need to take into consideration that the content of each page in a website tends to be of different lengths. Unless you are creating something like a photo gallery, where all content is of a fixed size, you would need to create a separate style sheet for each page, losing one of the principal benefits of CSS. Even if you're prepared to do that, it still doesn't solve the problem of text being enlarged.

This doesn't mean that absolute positioning is useless—far from it.

Absolute positioning comes into its own when used to position elements where you know they won't come into conflict with other content. As you'll see in the next chapter, you can use absolute positioning for sidebars instead of floating them. You make room for the sidebars in the same way by adding a wide margin to the content you want to appear alongside. However, you need to be sure that the content in the sidebar will always be shorter than the nonpositioned content alongside. Otherwise, you end up with the same problem as with the fixed position menu earlier in this chapter (see Figure 10-6 and "Understanding the limitations of fixed positioning").

Positioning elements against a background image

Perhaps the best use of absolute positioning is to superimpose HTML elements accurately on top of a background image, as shown in the following exercise.

Adding a search field in a precise position

The following exercise adds an HTML form to the page used in the exercise at the beginning of this chapter. The form is nested inside the banner heading, which uses fixed positioning. The form is then moved into position inside the heading with absolute positioning. Because it's nested inside a fixed position element, the search form remains onscreen when the rest of the page is scrolled. If you completed the previous exercise, continue working with the same files. Alternatively, use journey_absolute_start.html and css/journey_absolute_start.css in the download files for this chapter.

1. If you are using journey_absolute_start.html and its associated style sheet, copy them to your work folder, and rename them journey_absolute.html and css/journey_absolute.css respectively. Make sure that the renamed style sheet is linked to the renamed file like this:

```
<link href="css/journey_absolute.css" rel="stylesheet"
type="text/css" />
```

2. Test the page in a browser to make sure it displays correctly. It should look like Figure 10-1 at the beginning of this chapter.

3. In the HTML code, add a search form inside the header <div> like this:

```
<div id="header">
  <h1>Journey to the Edge</h1>
  <form id="search" method="get" action="">
    <input type="text" name="searchterm" id="searchterm" />
    <input type="submit" name="find" id="find" value="Search" />
  </form>
</div>
```

This is a simple HTML search form with a text field and submit button. The form won't do anything, because the action attribute is empty. The purpose of this exercise is to position the form with CSS, not to create a search system.

4. Save the page, and view it in a browser. The search form should be on top of the banner heading on the left of the page, as shown in Figure 10-20.

Figure 10-20. The form obscures part of the text in the banner heading.

The banner heading is a background image, so the form is displayed in front of it. The form has been pushed away from the top of the page because the <h1> heading still occupies the vertical space, even though it has been pushed off screen by a large negative margin. Otherwise, the form is as far left and as high up as it can go.

Because the form is nested inside a fixed position element, it stays put when the main content of the page is scrolled. However, its current position is unsatisfactory, so you need to move it with absolute positioning.

5. The heading <div> is positioned, so it acts as the form's containing block. Consequently, the bottom offset relates to the <div>, and not to the page or browser window. Try repositioning the search form by adding the following style block at the bottom of the style sheet:

```
/* Search form */
#search {
  position: absolute;
  left: 20px;
  bottom: 20px;
}
```

6. Save the style sheet, and reload the page in the browser. The search form should now be positioned 20px from the bottom left corner of the banner heading, as shown in Figure 10-21.

Figure 10-21. The search form has been repositioned relative to its containing block.

7. That's a lot better than before, but I think the best position for the search form is between the two branches of the tree. Change the offsets like this:

```
#search {
  position: absolute;
  top: 10px;
  right: 50px;
}
```

This repositions the search form 10px from the top of the banner heading and 50px from its right side.

8. To make the submit button blend better with the design, add the following to the style sheet:

```
#find {
  background-color: #AA8346;
  color: #FFF;
  font-weight: bold;
  border-top: #C9B089 2px solid;
  border-left: #C9B089 2px solid;
  border-right: #5B4625 2px solid;
  border-bottom: #5B4625 2px solid;
}
```

The submit button has the ID find, so this styles it with the same colors as the navigation menu.

9. Save the style sheet, and reload the page in a browser. The search form should have been repositioned and styled as shown in Figure 10-22.

Figure 10-22. The search form now blends in well with the rest of the design.

You can check your code, if necessary, against journey_absolute_finish.html and css/journey_absolute_finish.css in the download files for this chapter.

ExplainED

The submit button in the search form will remain unstyled in older versions of Safari. Prior to version 4.0, Safari did not support the styling of form elements.

Hopefully, this has shown you a practical use of absolute positioning. It's rarely, if ever, suited for use in laying out a complete page. But it's extremely useful in positioning small elements accurately within a containing block, which must also have its position property set to absolute, fixed, or relative.

An important thing to realize about this example is why the search form remains onscreen when the page is scrolled. It's *not* because the form is absolutely positioned, but because its containing block used fixed positioning. The terminology is potentially confusing, so it's worth repeating the difference.

- When position is set to absolute, the element is positioned relative to its containing block or, in the absence of a containing block, the page. An absolutely positioned element scrolls with the rest of the page. The only exception is when the containing block is fixed.

- When position is set to fixed, the containing block is the browser viewport. Elements that use fixed positioning never scroll, but they always retain the same offsets from the edge of the browser window whenever the viewport is resized.

To demonstrate the difference between the two, I have changed the value of the position property from fixed to absolute in the #header and #nav style blocks in the style sheet for journey_all_absolute.html in the download files for this chapter. When you load the page into a browser, it should look the same as Figure 10-22. However, when you scroll the page, everything moves together. This is because the containing block for the header and the navigation menu is no longer the browser viewport, but the wrapper <div>, which is relatively positioned. The absolute positioning fixes each element precisely within the wrapper, but the wrapper itself is scrollable.

LinkED

You can combine absolute positioning with the display *property set to* none *to create disjointed rollover effects. For examples of how to do this, visit* http://meyerweb.com/eric/css/edge/popups/demo.html. *Roll over the dummy menu on the left of the page to see the effect with text. Eric Meyer also demonstrates how to do it with images at* http://meyerweb.com/eric/css/edge/popups/demo2.html.

Cropping an image nondestructively with CSS

The clip property is similar to a mask or cropping tool in that it creates a window through which part of an element is displayed. The best way to understand it is to compare Figures 10-23 and 10-24. Figure 10-23 shows a photo of the Strip in Las Vegas with just the Statue of Liberty highlighted. Figure 10-24 shows the same image, lasvegas.jpg, displayed in clipping.html. If you check the download files, you'll see that lasvegas.jpg hasn't been cropped. It's the same image as in the scaling image exercise in Chapter 6. The clip property simply masks the sections of the image dimmed in Figure 10-23.

Figure 10-23. The clip property lets you select a rectangular area to be displayed while the rest is hidden.

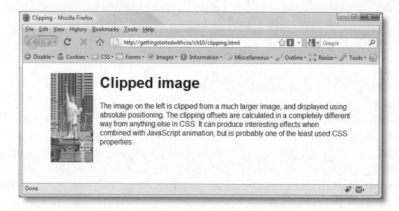

Figure 10-24. Only the selected area of the image is displayed, even though it hasn't been physically cropped.

The `clip` property works *only* with absolutely positioned elements, and the only shape you can use is a rectangle. You define the area that you want displayed by supplying four offsets in clockwise order starting from the top like this:

```
clip: rect(top, right, bottom, left);
```

However, *all the offsets are calculated from the top-left corner* of the element you want to mask, and each must be defined as a length. You cannot use percentages.

The top edge of the highlighted section is 146px from the top of lasvegas.jpg; the right side is 140px from the left; the bottom is 336px from the top; and the left side is 45px from the left. So, to clip the image, this is the style rule I created:

```
#clipped_image {
  position: absolute;
  clip: rect(146px, 140px, 336px, 45px);
}
```

Just to make life even more difficult, the clipped element doesn't move—it is, after all, absolutely positioned. So, in clipped.html, the Statue of Liberty was 146px too far down the page and 45px too far right. To compensate for that, I needed to use negative top and left offsets like this:

```
#clipped_image {
  position: absolute;
  clip: rect(146px, 140px, 336px, 45px);
  top: -146px;
  left: -45px;
}
```

Oh yes, another snafu—IE6 and IE7 won't play ball if you separate the offsets with commas, which is the correct way of doing things. Fortunately, other browsers accept leaving the commas out like this:

```
  clip: rect(146px 140px 336px 45px);
```

With all these problems, it's small wonder that clip is one of the least used CSS properties. However, it can be combined with JavaScript to create animated effects, revealing and concealing images.

LinkED

For an example of how to combine the clip *property with a JavaScript animated effect, see* www.overset.com/2008/08/07/jquery-css-clip-animation-plugin/.

Chapter review

CSS positioning gives you control over the placement of an element by setting the position property and specifying how far the sides should be offset from the element's containing block by using the top, right, bottom, and left properties. It's rarely, if ever, suitable for laying out complete pages but is very useful in controlling the location of page elements, such as search forms or navigation menus.

Fixed positioning, which is supported by all current browsers except IE6, uses the browser window as its containing block. Once an element is fixed, it remains in the same position in the browser window, even when the rest of the page is scrolled. In this sense, fixed positioning is similar to frames and is useful for keeping navigation menus on the page at all times. A major drawback of fixed positioning is that elements are cut off if they're too wide or too tall to fit into the browser window. The only way to access their content is to increase the size of the browser window, something that visitors to the site might not realize or be able to do.

Absolute positioning uses as its containing block the closest element higher up the page's HTML structure that has its position property set to absolute, fixed, or relative. If no such element exists, the containing block is the page itself. Relative positioning, on the other hand, simply moves elements relative to their normal position in the flow of the document, leaving a space where the element would normally have been. Used in this way, relative positioning is of limited value. However, it plays a very important role when used with no offsets, creating the containing block for absolutely positioned elements.

The most important aspect of CSS positioning is that it removes elements from the normal flow of the document, and floats them on independent layers in front of nonpositioned content. You can change the stacking order of positioned elements by setting the z-index property; elements with a higher z-index appear in front of those with a lower one. Because positioned elements float in front of nonpositioned ones, you should normally use them in places where they won't obscure other content or to position elements precisely against a background image.

The clip property is arguably the least useful part of the CSS positioning toolkit. It masks an absolutely positioned element, displaying only one rectangular section.

You have now studied all visual properties in the CSS2.1 specification, apart from a small number of rarely used ones, which are covered in Chapter 12. So, in the next chapter, I'll provide an overview of CSS page layout strategies.

Chapter 11

Are There Any Guidelines for Basic Page Layout?

Designing a web page that works well in all the main browsers requires a combination of inspiration and technical knowhow. It's impossible in a book of this nature to cover every type of page layout, but there are some basic principles that should help guide you. Once you have mastered the technical details of margins, borders, padding, and CSS positioning, you can begin to let your creative juices flow. But until you master that technical knowledge, page layout will remain an exercise in frustration.

The purpose of most websites is to provide information of some sort. It might be purely visual, as in a photo gallery, or it could be entertainment, as in a game or music site, but it's information all the same. For visitors to be able to find the information they want, it needs to be laid out in a logical way. That's why most websites use some sort of grid pattern for layout. In the early days of the Web, tables provided the basic grid structure. Now, with CSS, the grid is formed through the use of blocks, floats, and positioning.

The most commonly used grid structures for websites consist of one, two, or three columns. Within a wide column, you might also find mini-columns, but the basic techniques remain the same. So, in this chapter, I'll discuss the various ways you can create multicolumn layouts. Most of the time, I'll use floats and margins to control the layout, but I'll also show how you can use absolute positioning for sidebars.

And at the end of the chapter, I'll take a peek into the future using the table-related values of the display property, which make ordinary HTML elements act like table elements—table layout without tables. It's a useful technique, but unfortunately not ready for prime time, because it's not supported by IE6 or IE7.

In this chapter, you'll learn about the following:

- What factors to take into account before embarking on a design
- How to build one-, two-, and three-column layouts
- How to make backgrounds fill uneven columns
- Eliminating the double-margin bug in IE6
- Creating subcolumns

Let's start with the basic decisions that affect which layout to choose.

ExplainED

If you come from a traditional print background, you might think of columns as being of equal width with text flowing from one column to the next. That's not the way that web pages are normally designed. Neither HTML nor CSS2.1 supports continuous columns, and even if they did, reading from one column to the next would be difficult because of the landscape orientation of most computer screens. Columns used for web page layout tend to be self-contained, with one wide column for the main content, and one or more narrower columns for subsidiary material.

Getting the basics right

Before you start laying out a website, you need to consider a few basic questions, such as the target audience, the optimal width, and whether to use a fixed width or go for a more flexible design.

Who is the target audience?

The target audience makes a big difference to the appropriate design and layout. This is not simply a question of aesthetics, such as bright colors for children or sober colors for a law firm. A site aimed at children will need text that's clear and easy to read. Sections of text should be short, with plenty of space around them. The site will also need lots of images or illustrations.

A site for elderly people, on the other hand, can have larger blocks of text. But older people are likely to have less than perfect eyesight, so there's a strong chance they'll increase the text size. You need to make sure your design won't fall apart if that happens.

Whoever your audience is, you need to remember that scanning long lines of text is tiring, and it's easy to lose your place. Text areas need to be a comfortable width for reading.

What size browser window should I design for?

This is a perennial question in online forums. Desktop and laptop monitors are getting bigger, so you can usually count on more horizontal space than in the days when 640 × 480 was the norm. At the time of this writing, the market share of monitors with a resolution of 1024 × 768 or higher was estimated to be 80 percent.

LinkED

Visit http://marketshare.hitslink.com/report.aspx?qprid=17 *for the most recent statistics on monitor resolutions.*

Monitor resolution isn't necessarily an accurate guide to how your website will be viewed. People with large monitors don't always maximize their browsers. And the trend isn't always for bigger and bigger monitors. Many people now use netbooks, which tend to have small screens but often with high resolution. Small screen + high resolution = small text. Increasing numbers are also viewing the Web on mobile devices like the iPhone and BlackBerry.

AdvancED

Mobile device browsers usually have considerably fewer features than those designed for desktops. To learn more about designing web pages for mobile devices, see AdvancED CSS *by Joseph R. Lewis and Meitar Moscovitz (friends of ED, ISBN: 978-1-4302-1932-3).*

Nevertheless, the vast majority of people still use desktops or laptops. Table 11-1 lists the approximate usable width of most browsers when displayed full screen at a range of common monitor resolutions. The figures take into account the need to leave space for a vertical scrollbar.

Table 11-1. Usable Width of Browsers at Various Common Resolutions

	800×600	1024×768	1280×800	1280×1024	1440×900	1680×1050
Market share (July 2009)	3.8%	32%	20%	11.8%	9%	5.8%
Usable width in pixels	762	990	1245	1245	1404	1645

To allow for differences in browsers, it's a good idea to deduct a few pixels. If you're going for a fixed-width design, 960–980px now seems the optimal size. This fits comfortably in any monitor with a resolution of 1024 × 768 or larger.

What type of layout is best—fixed or flexible?

There's no simple answer to this question. In the early days of the Web, everyone had small monitors, so it didn't matter that everything stretched the full width of the page. The problem was trying to cram everything into such a small space. As monitors started to get bigger, some designers took advantage by using percentages for widths, letting their pages occupy as much of the screen as available; but when screens got bigger still, many opted for fixed-width designs. Unfortunately, a design that looked brilliant when 800 × 600 was the most common monitor resolution often looks rather lost in today's larger monitors.

The main types of layout can be categorized as follows:

- **Fixed-width:** This is the most comfortable type of layout to work with, and generally looks best when centered in a page. When working with a fixed-width layout, it's important to plan ahead with regard to the size of page elements. Although images don't need to be a fixed size, you need to make sure your layout is wide enough to accommodate the largest image you're likely to use. Alternatively, you need to resize the images to fit your design. To prevent fixed-width layouts from looking lost on a large monitor, it's a good idea to use different backgrounds for the body and center section to focus the visitor's attention on the main content. Figures 11-1 and 11-2 show the case study on a 24-inch monitor. In Figure 11-1, the background color of the body has been turned off. Admittedly, the page looks swamped in both screenshots, but the contrasting backgrounds in Figure 11-2 help draw the eye to the center of the page.

Figure 11-1. The vast expanse of white makes the attention wander on a large monitor

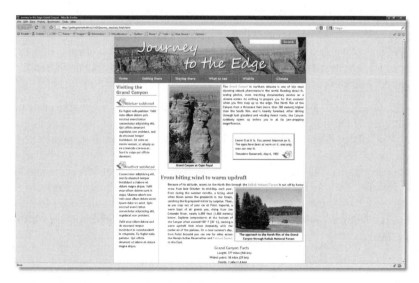

Figure 11-2. The contrast in colors helps focus attention on content in the center of the page.

- **Liquid:** Dimensions in a liquid layout are specified as percentages, allowing the content to behave in a fluid way, expanding and contracting as the browser window is resized. The principal disadvantage is that, on a large monitor, lines of text stretch too wide to be read easily. Equally, on a small monitor, everything risks being scrunched up. You can overcome these problems to some extent by setting the max-width and min-width properties. However, this makes it difficult to center content. Moreover, IE6 ignores maximum and minimum widths, although you can simulate them with CSS expressions, as described in Chapter 6.

- **Elastic:** Dimensions in an elastic layout are set using ems. This has the advantage of keeping everything in proportion with the text size, thereby overcoming the problem of lines of text becoming too long—unless the text is greatly resized, that is. The downside is that the page gets wider as the text is increased in size, potentially spawning a horizontal scrollbar when it exceeds the width of the browser.

- **Hybrid:** You can compromise by combining one or more fixed-width sidebars with a liquid or elastic main content area. This has the advantage that the sidebars remain a constant size. Use the min-width property on the main content area to prevent it from being squeezed on a small monitor. It is probably also a good idea to use the max-width property as well, to avoid impractical widths on bigger monitors.

As the preceding descriptions indicate, there is no perfect solution. The key to successful layout is to test, test, and test again, preferably in a range of browsers at different monitor resolutions.

You'll notice that I have focused exclusively on width. As a general principle, don't specify the height of web page elements unless they are fixed, such as an image or video. Even if visitors never resize your text, the amount of text on each page is likely to vary. The default value of the height and width properties is auto, so they automatically expand and contract to accommodate the content. Visitors to websites are accustomed to scrolling up and down a page, so let the height adjust itself. Horizontal scrolling tends to be less well tolerated by users, hence the emphasis on deciding how to control the width of your pages.

AdvancED

If you have a large monitor, you can simulate the experience that a visitor would get at a lower resolution by resizing the browser window. IE8 has a built-in resizing feature. Press F12 or select Tools ➤ Developer Tools *to launch the* Developer Tools *window. In the new window, select* Tools ➤ Resize, *and choose one of the preset sizes. It's rather counterintuitive, but this resizes the main browser window, not the* Developer Tools *window. You can also define custom sizes.*

For Firefox, use the Resize *button on the Web Developer Toolbar by Chris Pederick. You can get the toolbar as a free plugin from* https://addons.mozilla.org/en-US/firefox/addon/60.

The most common layouts for web pages consist of a header, the main page navigation, the main content, and a footer section. The header and footer typically stretch the full width of the active section of the page, while the remaining content is displayed in one, two, or three columns. Of course, that's not the only way a page can be constructed, but the purpose of this chapter is to offer a few basic structures. Once you have mastered them, you can strike out in more adventurous directions on your own.

Creating a single-column layout

There's very little to say about creating a single-column layout. All the HTML elements are displayed in the order they appear in the underlying code, so the only real considerations with regard to the basic layout are the width of the column, and whether you want it centered. To restrict the width, wrap everything between the <body> tags in a <div>, give the <div> an ID, and create a style rule using an ID selector. To center the content, give the <div> a width, and set the left and right margins to auto.

The download files for this chapter contain the following three examples of a single-column layout:

- **Fixed-width**: onecol_fixed.html sets the width of the column to 760px.
- **Elastic**: onecol_elastic sets the width to 47.5em.

- **Liquid**: `onecol_liquid.html` sets the left and right margins to 12% and uses `max-width` to prevent the column from exceeding 760px in most modern browsers. An Internet Explorer conditional comment overrides these settings for IE6 and uses a fixed width instead.

When loaded into a browser sized 800 × 600, the first two files look like Figure 11-3. This is because `47.5em` is equivalent to `760px` when the browser's default text size (16px) is used (760 ÷ 16 = 47.5).

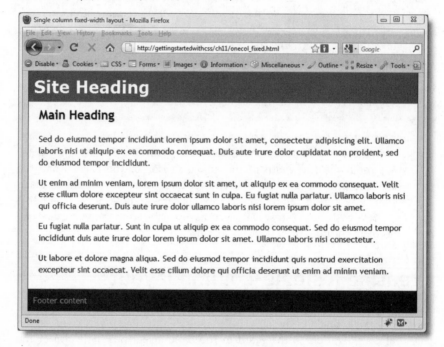

Figure 11-3. A simple single-column layout with header, main content, and footer

The style rule that controls the width of the column and centers it looks like this in `onecol_fixed.html`:

```
#wrapper {
  width: 760px;
  margin: 0 auto;
  background-color: #FFF;
  border-left: #252017 solid 1px;
  border-right: #252017 solid 1px;
}
```

In onecol_elastic.html, it looks like this:

```
#wrapper {
  width: 47.5em;
  margin: 0 auto;
  background-color: #FFF;
  border-left: #252017 solid 1px;
  border-right: #252017 solid 1px;
}
```

The only difference in the way the pages are displayed is when you increase the size of the text in the browser. In the fixed-width version, the text is reflowed to fit inside the column, whereas in the elastic version, the text isn't reflowed, and the page generates a horizontal scrollbar.

The liquid layout in onecol_liquid.html doesn't specify a width for the column but uses the left and right margins to control its width and position. However, to prevent the text from becoming unreadable when the browser window is opened very wide, the max-width property is set to 760px like this:

```
#wrapper {
  margin: 0 12%;
  max-width: 760px;
  background-color: #FFF;
  border-left: #252017 solid 1px;
  border-right: #252017 solid 1px;
}
```

Why choose 12% as the width for the left and right columns? I based this on the most common monitor resolution being 1024 × 768. As Table 11-1 shows, this gives a usable width of approximately 990px. A 12% margin on either side results in the column being about 752px wide. So, all three pages look almost identical at 1024 × 768. However, at 800 × 600, the 12% margin squeezes the central column, considerably reducing the text area, as shown in Figure 11-4. With text, this isn't serious, but it could cause problems with images.

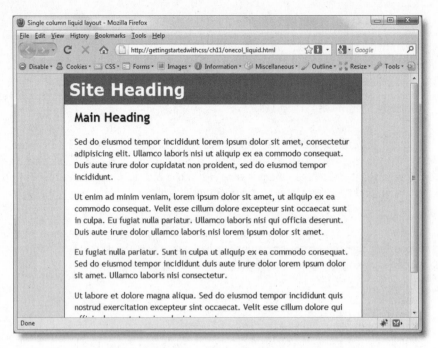

Figure 11-4. Using a liquid layout squeezes the column when the browser window is reduced in width.

Because IE6 and older versions of Internet Explorer don't understand max-width, I have added the following IE conditional comment after the main style rules:

```
<!--[if lte IE 6]>
<style type="text/css">
#wrapper {
  width: 760px;
  margin: 0 auto;
}
</style>
<![endif]-->
```

Only IE6 and earlier versions of Internet Explorer will see this style rule, which overrides both the margin and width properties, making the page behave the same as the fixed-width version.

ExplainED

I could have used a CSS expression in the same way as in Chapter 6. However, as I explained there, IE6 gives precedence to the margins when the browser window is narrower than the minimum width. Using a conditional comment to make the page a fixed width in IE6 is much simpler and easier to maintain.

Keeping a liquid display centered

The problem with setting the max-width property on the <div> that centers the column is that the percentage margins cease to work once the browser window exceeds a certain width. In the case of onecol_liquid.html, the tipping point is 1000px. At this width, 12% equates to 120px, so two margins of this size plus the 760px column fit the browser window exactly. Once the window is made any wider, you need a bigger margin on both sides to keep the column centered. What happens is that the browser applies the left margin of 12%, and ignores the right margin, as you can see in Figure 11-5, which shows onecol_liquid.html displayed in a browser at 1440 × 900.

Figure 11-5. The browser can't center a a liquid layout on a large monitor if you restrict the containing <div> with max-width.

ExplainED

If you're wondering how I arrived at 170px as 12%, I got the answer from Firebug. This measurement implies that the usable space in Firefox 3.5 is 1417px when the browser is displayed at 1440 × 900, 13px more than the figure given in Table 11-1. The discrepancy is explained in part by the fact that Firefox leaves no room for a vertical scrollbar if one isn't needed.

The other thing to bear in mind is that browsers need to round percentages up or down to the nearest whole pixel. Rounding errors make working with percentages difficult, so you should never create a layout where the percentages add up to exactly 100. Always leave about 2% leeway to account for such errors. Also remember that borders measured in pixels are added to your percentages, again potentially throwing out your calculations. Since there is a 1px border on either side of the column, its overall width is actually 762px, not 760px. In this case, the extra two pixels don't affect the layout, so I chose to ignore them. But, even a single pixel can destroy a layout that relies on floats.

In order to keep a liquid layout centered, remove any restriction on the width of the <div> that centers the column, and control the width of individual text areas inside the column instead. You can find an example of this approach in onecol_liquid_enhanced.html in the download files for this chapter. The style rule that centers the column looks like this:

```
#wrapper {
  margin: 0 12%;
  background-color: #FFF;
  border-left: #252017 solid 1px;
  border-right: #252017 solid 1px;
}
```

Control of the text area is handled by the following style rule:

```
#mainContent {
  padding: 10px 20px;
  max-width: 720px;
  margin: 0 auto;
}
```

In browsers that understand the max-width property, the main content area is never greater than 720px wide, and it remains centered within the column. The maximum width has been reduced from 760px to 720px because of the 20px padding on the left and right sides. Figure 11-6 shows how this looks in a browser at the following sizes: 800 × 600, 1024 × 768, 1280 × 800, and 1440 × 900.

Figure 11-6. The main column and text remain centered, but the margins on either side of the text increase in size.

As you can see from Figure 11-6, the main problem with this approach is the increasingly wide margins on either side of the text inside the column. However, by adding a separate background to the main content, you might turn this into a positive, rather than a negative feature.

Creating a two-column layout

When it comes to using two columns, you are faced with considerably more choices than a single-column layout. For a start, you have to decide how the columns are to be used. Normally, one column is much wider than the other and contains the most important content. The narrower column often contains the site navigation followed by subsidiary material. Depending on what you plan to put in the narrower column, or sidebar, you need to decide whether it goes on the left or the right. Fortunately, as you saw in Chapter 7, there's no need to change the underlying HTML structure to switch the sidebar from one side of the page to the other. It's easily done with CSS.

The technique used for a two-column layout in Chapter 7 was to float the sidebar to one side and put a wide margin on the wider column to make room for the sidebar. For this technique to work, the sidebar *must* come before the main content in the HTML markup. So, for a simple two-column layout that floats the sidebar, the underlying order of the HTML looks like this:

1. Header

2. Sidebar

3. Main content

4. Footer

The disadvantage is that your sidebar, which usually contains subsidiary information, precedes the main content of the page. Some people argue that this is bad for search engine optimization. In any event, it certainly affects people with visual disabilities, who are using a screen reader to access your site. Another problem with two-column layout is getting the background on both columns to be the same height.

Fortunately, there are ways of getting around all of these problems. However, to start with, I'll briefly outline the basic technique you used in Chapter 7, which involves putting the sidebar content first in the HTML markup.

Putting the sidebar first and floating it to one side

The basic technique for creating a two-column layout with a header and footer is to divide the page into four sections using <div> tags, and then wrap the whole page in an outer <div>, which is used to control the overall width and center the layout. In skeleton form, the HTML markup looks like this:

```
<body>
<div id="wrapper">
  <div id="header">
    Header content
  </div>
  <div id="sidebar">
    Sidebar content
  </div>
  <div id="mainContent">
    Main content
```

```
    </div>
    <div id="footer">
      Footer content
    </div>
  </div>
</body>
```

To display the sidebar on the left, float the sidebar to the left, and set a wide left margin on the <div> that contains the main content. The purpose of the wide margin is to prevent the main content from filling the full width of the outer <div> when the sidebar comes to an end. The basic style rules for a fixed-width two-column layout look like this:

```
#wrapper {
  width: 760px;
  margin: 0 auto;
}
#sidebar {
  width: 220px;
  padding: 10px;
  float: left;
}
#mainContent {
  margin-left: 240px;
}
```

To display the sidebar on the right, change the value of float to right, and switch the margin in the #mainContent style block to the opposite side like this:

```
#wrapper {
  width: 760px;
  margin: 0 auto;
}
#sidebar {
  width: 220px;
  padding: 10px;
  float: right;
}
#mainContent {
  margin-right: 240px;
}
```

In the download files for this chapter, left2col_basic.html uses these basic style rules, plus some extra properties to give each section of the page a different background color. As you can see in Figure 11-7, the background of the sidebar stretches only as far as the content.

417

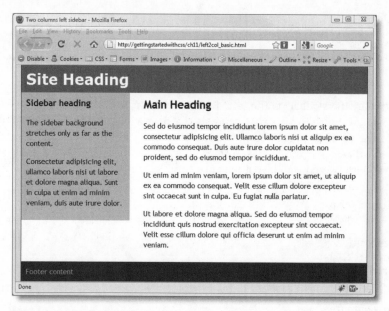

Figure 11-7. Getting columns of even height presents a challenge.

Some designers try to trick the browser into stretching the background color of the sidebar by adding empty paragraphs. This is not only tedious; it frequently doesn't work, because the user might resize the text in the page, throwing out your calculations of the number of extra lines needed.

If you're going to cheat, you might as well do it elegantly with faux columns (*faux* is French for "false").

LinkED

The faux column technique was popularized by Dan Cederholm in the following article: www.alistapart.com/articles/fauxcolumns/. *Dan is also the author of* Web Standards Solutions: The Markup and Style Handbook, Special Edition *published by friends of ED (ISBN: 978-1-4302-1920-0).*

Using a background image to simulate equal columns

The problem with a floated sidebar is that you have no idea how long it will be. However, you can use CSS to tile background images vertically by setting the background-repeat property to repeat-y. So, the simple trick is to create a background image the same width as the sidebar, and apply it as the background of its *parent* element.

In left2col_basic.html, the overall width of the sidebar is 240px (220px, plus 10px on either side). So, I created an image 240px wide and 20px high, using the same background color as the sidebar. To give it an extra lift, I added a bevel effect on the right. I then used my graphics editor to flip the image horizontally to put the bevel on the left, as shown in Figure 11-8. This gave me two images that can be used to simulate a column for a left sidebar or one on the right.

Figure 11-8. Two background images—one for a left sidebar, and the other for a right sidebar

Because the background image needs to be applied to the parent element, I amended the #wrapper style block in left2col.html like this:

```
#wrapper {
  width: 760px;
  margin: 0 auto;
  background-color: #FFF;
  background-image: url(../images/sidebar_left.jpg);
  background-repeat: repeat-y;
  border-left: #252017 solid 1px;
  border-right: #252017 solid 1px;
}
```

This tiles sidebar_left.jpg vertically down the left side of the outer <div>, producing the effect of a column that stretches the full height of the sidebar, as shown in Figure 11-9.

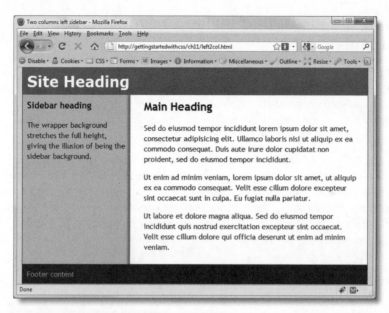

Figure 11-9. Tiling a background image vertically on the parent element creates the illusion of a full-height column.

ExplainED

As explained in Chapter 5, background images are placed by default at the top-left of an element. So, setting the background-repeat *property to* repeat-y, *tiles the image nicely down the left of the wrapper* <div>*. This works fine because the header and footer have backgrounds of their own, so they conceal the faux column. If the header and footer didn't have their own backgrounds, you would need to wrap the sidebar and main content in a separate* <div> *and apply the background image to that.*

Moving the sidebar and its faux column to the right simply involves changing the background image and controlling its position by setting background-position to right like this:

```
#wrapper {
  width: 760px;
  margin: 0 auto;
  background-color: #FFF;
  background-image: url(../images/sidebar_right.jpg);
  background-position: right;
```

```
    background-repeat: repeat-y;
    border-left: #252017 solid 1px;
    border-right: #252017 solid 1px;
}
```

Of course, you also need to switch the value of float to right in the #sidebar style block and change the wide margin in the #mainContent block from margin-left to margin-right. This switches the sidebar and its faux column to the right, as shown in Figure 11-10, without the need for any changes to the HTML. You can examine the full CSS code in right2col.html in the download files.

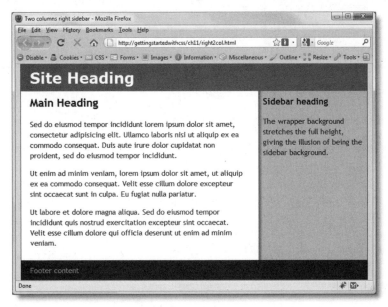

Figure 11-10. It's just as easy to create a faux column on the right of the page.

What happens if the sidebar is longer?

Most of the time, the sidebar is likely to be shorter than the main content. However, when elements are floated, all subsequent content moves up to fill the vacated space. Consequently, if the main content is shorter than the sidebar, the footer also moves up, and the sidebar protrudes beneath it, as shown in Figure 11-11 (the code is in left2col_longsidebar.html).

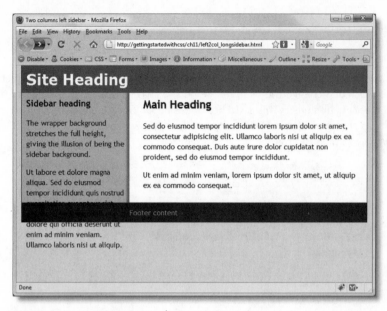

Figure 11-11. The design falls apart if the sidebar is longer than the main content.

The solution is simple: just add the `clear` property to the `#footer` style block like this:

```
#footer {
  background-color: #252017;
  color: #DB9924;
  padding: 10px;
  clear: both;
}
```

This ensures that the footer remains beneath both columns, as shown in Figure 11-12 (the code is in `left2col_clear.html`).

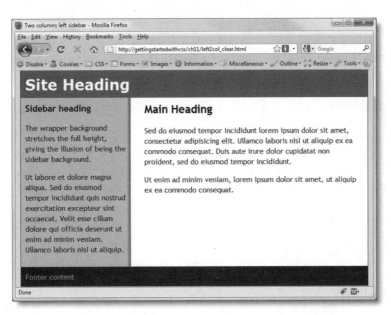

Figure 11-12. The clear property moves the footer back into position.

Adding a "skip to main content" link for screen readers

Blind and partially sighted people frequently access the Web using screen readers, assistive technology that reads the content of a web page aloud. Listening to the same content, such as a navigation menu, over and over again becomes tedious, making your site less user-friendly to disabled people. So, it's a good idea to create a "skip to main content" link to allow them to get to the meat of the page.

Creating the link is very simple. Assuming that your main content is in a <div> with an ID, you just link to the <div> by prefixing the ID with a hash sign like this:

```
<a href="#mainContent">Skip to main content</a>
```

The link should go after the page heading, but before the navigation menu. The Royal National Institute of Blind People (RNIB) in the United Kingdom recommends leaving the skip link visible, but if this destroys your design, you can hide it using absolute positioning. In left2col_skiplink.html, the skip link has been added at the top of the sidebar and has been given an ID like this:

```
<div id="sidebar">
```

423

```
<a href="#mainContent" id="skiplink">Skip to main content</a>
<h3>Sidebar heading</h3>
```

The link is hidden using the following style block:

```
#skiplink {
  position:absolute;
  top: -200px;
}
```

The negative top position moves the link above the top of the page, so it's hidden from visual browsers but remains accessible to screen readers. It's also a good idea to provide another link at the top of the main content for screen readers to skip back to the main navigation. You can hide it in the same way, using absolute positioning.

LinkED

For information and advice on how to make your website accessible, visit the RNIB Web Access Centre at www.rnib.org.uk/xpedio/groups/public/documents/code/public_rnib008789.hcsp. *The advice covers all types of disability, not just sight problems.*

In the United States, websites developed or purchased by federal agencies must be compliant with Section 508 accessibility guidelines. Jim Thatcher, one of the authors of Web Accessibility: Web Standards and Regulatory Compliance *(friends of ED, ISBN: 978-1-59059-638-8), has created an online tutorial for Section 508 compliance at* http://jimthatcher.com/webcourse1.htm.

Even if you're not obliged to be compliant with Section 508 or legislation in your own country, making your sites accessible to people with disabilities is a good idea. Most of the time, it's not difficult, particularly if you design your sites to be accessible from the outset.

Putting the main content first

If you have a lot of material in your sidebar, or are paranoid that search engines will penalize you if your main content doesn't come first, there are a number of ways to create a two-column layout with the HTML in the following order:

```
<body>
<div id="wrapper">
```

```
<div id="header">
   Header content
</div>
<div id="mainContent">
   Main content
</div>
<div id="sidebar">
   Sidebar content
</div>
<div id="footer">
   Footer content
</div>
</div>
</body>
```

The most obvious solution is to float the <div> that contains the main content.

Floating the main content

When you float the main content, the roles are reversed. A floated element must have a defined width, so you apply the width to the main content and a wide margin to the sidebar. Otherwise, everything else is exactly the same as floating the sidebar.

In left2col_mainfloat.html, the main style rules are as follows:

```
#sidebar {
  margin-right: 520px;
  padding: 10px;
}
#mainContent {
  width: 480px;
  padding: 10px 20px;
  float: right;
}
```

This puts a wide right margin on the sidebar, making room for the main content to float to the right. The margin is calculated by subtracting the width of the sidebar from the width of the wrapper <div>. It's also equivalent to the width of the main content <div>, plus the padding on either side of the <div>.

To put the sidebar on the right, just reverse the side of the margin and float like this (the code is in right2col_mainfloat.html):

```
#sidebar {
  margin-left: 520px;
  padding: 10px;
}
#mainContent {
  width: 480px;
```

425

```
  padding: 10px 20px;
  float: left;
}
```

Using absolute positioning for the sidebar

Instead of floating either the main content or the sidebar, you can use absolute positioning to move the sidebar alongside the main content. The technique is very similar to floating the sidebar. You put a wide margin on one side of the main content to make room for the sidebar and then move it into place. To ensure that the sidebar moves with the rest of the layout when the browser window is resized, you need to establish a containing block for it by setting the position property of the wrapper <div> to relative.

The relevant style rules in left2col_absolute.html look like this:

```
#wrapper {
  width: 760px;
  margin: 0 auto;
  background-color: #FFF;
  background-image: url(../images/sidebar_left.jpg);
  background-repeat: repeat-y;
  border-left: #252017 solid 1px;
  border-right: #252017 solid 1px;
  position: relative;
}
#sidebar {
  position: absolute;
  top: 63px;
  width: 220px;
  padding:10px;
}
#mainContent {
  margin-left: 240px;
  padding: 10px 20px;
}
```

To position the sidebar on the right, you need one extra property: the left offset for the sidebar. The following styles are used in right2col_absolute.html:

```
#wrapper {
  width: 760px;
  margin: 0 auto;
  background-color: #FFF;
  background-image: url(../images/sidebar_right.jpg);
  background-position: right;
  background-repeat: repeat-y;
  border-left: #252017 solid 1px;
  border-right: #252017 solid 1px;
```

```
  position: relative;
}
#sidebar {
  position: absolute;
  top: 63px;
  left: 520px;
  width: 220px;
  padding: 10px;
}
#mainContent {
  margin-right: 240px;
  padding: 10px 20px;
}
```

This technique works very well when the sidebar content is shorter than the main content. However, there is no way of controlling the sidebar's overspill if the main content is shorter. As Figure 11-13 shows, the extra content goes over the footer and continues down the page (the code is in `left2col_absolute_long.html`).

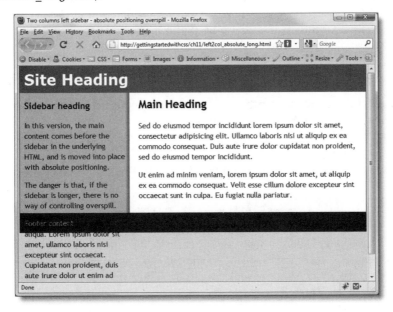

Figure 11-13. Absolute positioning is suitable only when the sidebar will always be shorter than the main content.

ExplainED

If you compare this with Figure 11-11, you'll see an important difference between floating the sidebar and using absolute positioning. When the sidebar was floated in left2col_longsidebar.html, *the footer content was pushed to the right. In other words, the footer interacted with the floated element. However, when you use absolute positioning, there is no interaction.*

In Figure 11-13, the sidebar overspill lies on top of the footer. Even though the clear *property has been declared in the* #footer *style block in* left2col_absolute_long.html, *it has no effect. The* clear *property works only with floats, not with absolutely positioned elements.*

This is a major drawback of using absolute positioning for a sidebar. However, it's worth considering if you know the sidebar content will always be shorter than the main content. It can also be useful if you want to align the sidebar content with a background image.

Using a negative margin to float the sidebar into position

Yet another way of moving the sidebar into position when it comes after the main content in the HTML markup involves floating both columns in the same direction, and then adjusting their relative positions by applying a negative margin to the sidebar. The concept is a little difficult to understand just by looking at the code, so the following exercise takes you through the process step by step.

Using a negative margin for a left sidebar

The download files for this chapter contain a file called left_negative_start.html, which you can copy to your work files to follow this exercise. If you just want to study the finished code, it's in left_negative_finish.html.

1. Save left_negative_start.html in your work folder as left_negative.html, and load it into a browser. It should look like Figure 11-14. The page contains only basic styling, and the sidebar content appears after the main content.

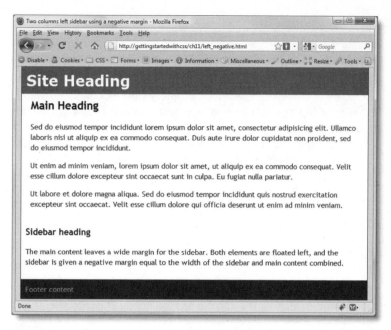

Figure 11-14. The sidebar content comes after the main content before styling.

2. Add the background image to create the faux column for the sidebar by amending the #wrapper style block like this:

```
#wrapper {
  width: 760px;
  margin: 0 auto;
  background-color: #FFF;
  border-left: #252017 solid 1px;
  border-right: #252017 solid 1px;
  background-image: url(../images/sidebar_left.jpg);
  background-repeat: repeat-y;
}
```

If necessary, adjust the file path to sidebar_left.jpg to match your site setup. This tiles the background image down the left side of the wrapper <div> to simulate a full-height column.

3. Both the sidebar and the main content need to be given a width and floated left. The faux column is 240px wide, so that's how wide the sidebar should be. However, the #sidebar style block has already applied 10px of padding all around, so the width property needs to be set to 220px. Amend the style block like this:

```
#sidebar {
```

```
  padding: 10px;
  width: 220px;
  float: left;
}
```

4. The width of the wrapper is 760px, so that leaves 520px for the main content. However, the #mainContent style block has already applied 10px of top and bottom padding, and 20px of padding on the left and right. As a result the width property needs to be set to 480px (520px – 20px – 20px = 480px). You also need to give the <div> a 240px left margin to make room for the sidebar and float the <div> to the left. Change the #mainContent style block as follows:

```
#mainContent {
  padding: 10px 20px;
  width: 480px;
  margin-left: 240px;
  float: left;
}
```

5. Save the page, and view it in a browser. It should now look like Figure 11-15.

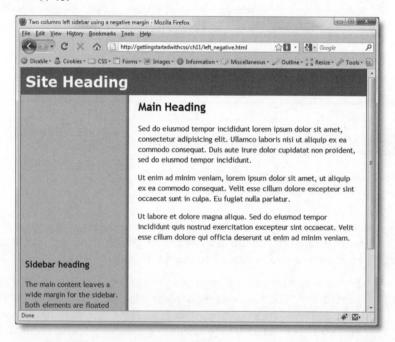

Figure 11-15. The trick of a negative margin is to get the sidebar to move up into the space created for it.

6. The large left margin leaves room for the sidebar, but it can't occupy that space because it comes after the main content in the HTML markup. However, CSS lets you use negative values for margins. To see how negative margins affect a float, try a little experiment by amending the #sidebar style block like this:

```
#sidebar {
  padding: 10px;
  width:2 20px;
  float: left;
  margin-left: -50px;
}
```

The result is shown in Figure 11-16.

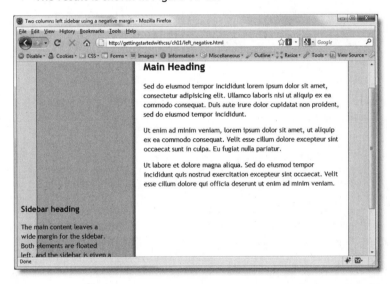

Figure 11-16. Adding a small negative left margin to the sidebar moves it to the left and out of the wrapper <div>.

7. That's probably not surprising. But what happens if the negative margin is the same size as the width of the sidebar? Change the value of the negative margin like this:

```
#sidebar {
  padding: 10px;
  width: 220px;
  float: left;
  margin-left: -240px;
}
```

Figure 11-17 shows the result.

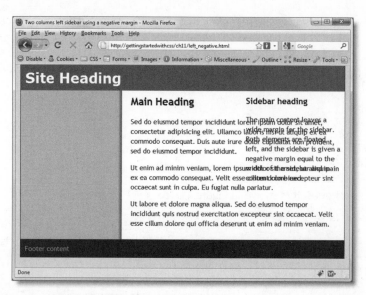

Figure 11-17. Applying a negative left margin the same size as the width of the sidebar allows it to float over the main content.

ExplainED

You're probably wondering why the sidebar has moved to the right after applying a negative left margin. It's because both the main content and the sidebar are floated left in that order. If there were sufficient space for both of them, they would be alongside each other, with the sidebar on the right. Adding the 240px positive left margin to the main content `<div>` resulted in all horizontal space being taken up inside the wrapper, forcing the sidebar down below the main content, as shown in Figure 11-15.

Applying a negative left margin of -50px to the sidebar didn't create sufficient space for it to move back up to the same level as the main content. So, the sidebar simply moved further left (see Figure 11-16). However, making the negative margin as wide as the sidebar created enough space for the sidebar to move back up to the same level as the main content. The fact that they now overlap is irrelevant. The bigger the negative margin, the further left the sidebar will go. The plan is to move it far enough so that it sits in the empty space to the left of the main content.

8. To maneuver the sidebar into place, you need to move it further to the left by the same width as the main content <div>—in other words, 520px including padding. In fact, the negative margin needs to be the same as the overall widths of the sidebar and main content combined: 760px. Amend the #sidebar style block as follows, and the sidebar moves exactly into place:

```
#sidebar {
  padding: 10px;
  width: 220px;
  float: left;
  margin-left: -760px;
}
```

9. There's just one fly in the ointment. Yes, you've guessed it—IE6. This technique triggers the **IE double-margin bug**. When you add a margin to an element and float it to the same side, IE6 doubles the margin. In addition, IE6 has problems with the clear property in the #footer style block. The result is the mess you see in Figure 11-18.

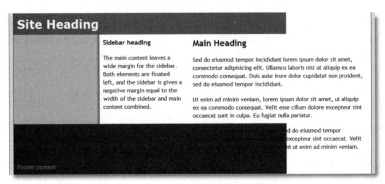

Figure 11-18. The double-margin bug and problems with the footer destroy the layout in IE6.

Fortunately, both problems are fixed simply—and in ways that don't cause problems in other browsers.

10. To get rid of the double-margin bug, all that's necessary is to set the display property to inline on the element that has a margin on the same side as it has been floated. Amend #mainContent style block like this:

```
#mainContent {
  padding: 10px 20px;
  width: 480px;
  margin-left: 240px;
```

```
  float: left;
  display: inline;
}
```

   11. To solve the problem with the footer, add an empty <div> above the
       footer, with an inline style like this:

```
<div style="clear:both"></div>
<div id="footer">Footer content</div>
```

> Because the <div> is empty, it adds no height, but the inline style
> makes sure that IE6 clears the floats correctly. You could use a class
> or ID selector instead of the inline style, but using an inline style is a
> quick and simple fix for this problem.
>
> You can check your code, if necessary, against left_negative_
> finish.html in the download files for this chapter.

If you want to use this technique to locate the sidebar on the right, you still
float both the main content and the sidebar to the left. However, you give the
main content a positive right margin and the sidebar a negative left one. The
size of both margins should be the same—in other words, the width of the
sidebar. You can study the code in right_negative.html in the download files.
The relevant style rules look like this:

```
#sidebar {
  width:220px;
  padding:10px;
  float: left;
  margin-left: -240px;
}
#mainContent {
  padding:10px 20px;
  width:480px;
  float: left;
  margin-right: 240px;
  display:inline;
}
```

How do I make a more flexible two-column layout?

All the two-column examples so far have used a fixed width for the outer
wrapper. But what if you want a liquid or elastic design? The underlying
principles are the same. All you need to do is to replace the pixel
measurements with percentages or ems. However, there is a problem: the faux
column technique used in the preceding examples won't work with a variable-
width sidebar, because the background image is tiled vertically in the wrapper

<div>. The image that creates the illusion of a column remains the same size regardless of the width of the sidebar.

If you're happy for the sidebar to remain a fixed width, you can create a hybrid two-column layout by allowing the <div> that contains the main content to expand and contract when the browser window is resized. In left2col_hybrid.html, the #wrapper style block uses the min-width and max-width properties for a more flexible two-column layout like this:

```
#wrapper {
  min-width: 760px;
  max-width: 980px;
  margin: 0 auto;
  background-color: #FFF;
  background-image: url(../images/sidebar_left.jpg);
  background-repeat: repeat-y;
  border-left: #252017 solid 1px;
  border-right: #252017 solid 1px;
}
```

If you want a genuinely liquid two-column layout based on percentage widths, you need to use a technique developed by web standards activist Zoe Gillenwater (http://zomigi.com/). It involves creating a background image at least 2000 pixels wide. The technique relies on the way the background-position property handles percentage values. As explained in Chapter 5, percentages are calculated not only in relation to the background but also in relation to the image itself. So, if you set the horizontal position of a background image to 25%, the point at 25% of the image's width is placed at 25% of the way across the element's background. So, if you want to create a liquid layout that has a sidebar occupying 25% of the horizontal width, you need to create a background image for both columns like sidebar_liquid.jpg in the download files for this chapter. This image is 2000px × 10px. The left side acts as the sidebar background and is 500 pixels wide. The rest is white and acts as the background to the main content.

Because backgrounds are visible only within the element to which they are applied, and not through the element's border or margins, any excess is hidden from view. For example, if the overall width of the element containing the two columns is 800px wide, the 25% point of the background image is displayed at 200px from the left, and the remaining 300 pixels on the left are hidden from view. But if the element is expanded to 1200 pixels, the 25% point is displayed at 300px, revealing 100 pixels of the image that was previously hidden. This is shown diagrammatically in Figure 11-19. When the element is 800 pixels wide, everything outside the solid box is hidden, but when the element is expanded

435

to 1200 pixels, the parts of the background image within the dotted lines are revealed.

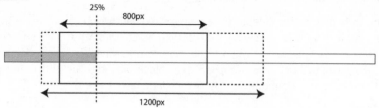

Figure 11-19. Using an extra wide background image makes it possible to create faux columns for a liquid layout

You can see this technique in action in left2col_liquid.html in the download files. The style rules that control the outer wrapper and the two columns look like this:

```
#wrapper {
  margin: 0 10%;
  background-color: #FFF;
  background-image: url(../images/sidebar_liquid.jpg);
  background-position: 25% 0;
  background-repeat: repeat-y;
  border-left: #252017 solid 1px;
  border-right: #252017 solid 1px;
}
#sidebar {
  width: 21%;
  float: left;
  padding: 2%;
}
#mainContent {
  margin-left: 25%;
  padding: 10px 20px;
}
```

The width of the sidebar is 21%, but the 2% padding on either side makes 25% overall. The main content column is kept in position by its 25% left margin.

LinkED

This technique is described in detail by Zoe Gillenwater in "Creating Liquid Faux Columns" at www.communitymx.com/content/article.cfm?cid=afc58. *Zoe's article also describes how to apply a similar technique to a three-column layout.*

Creating a three-column layout

Once you understand how to create a two-column layout, there isn't a great deal of difference in creating three or more columns. Most of the work is done with floating and margins. You can also use absolute positioning for the outside columns if you constrain the center one with margins on both sides. When using absolute positioning for the column on the right, use the right offset instead of the left one. Another technique is to wrap two elements within an outer <div> and float them into position. You can then treat the outer <div> as a single element, and if necessary, float it, too.

Let's take a look at some of the options.

Creating faux columns for a three-column layout

In CSS2.1, you can apply only one background image to an element. So, to create faux columns for a three-column layout, you cannot add different background images for each column. Creating faux columns for a fixed-width layout is the simplest option.

Using a single image for a fixed-width layout

If you have a fixed-width layout, the answer is simple: create a single image that acts as the background for all three columns. In threecol_fixed.html (see Figure 11-20), the background to the three columns is created by sidebar_both.jpg, which is 960px × 20px. The sidebar backgrounds are 220px wide, separated by 520px of white background.

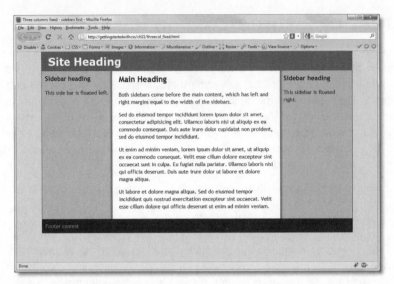

Figure 11-20. A single image creates the backgrounds for all three columns in a fixed-width layout.

As in the two-column layouts, the background image is tiled vertically down the wrapper <div>. The style rules that control the three-column fixed-width layout in threecol_fixed.html look like this:

```
#wrapper {
  width: 960px;
  margin: 0 auto;
  background-color: #FFF;
  background-image: url(../images/sidebar_both.jpg);
  background-position: center;
  background-repeat: repeat-y;
  border-left: #252017 solid 1px;
  border-right: #252017 solid 1px;
}
#sidebar1, #sidebar2 {
  width: 200px;
  padding: 10px;
}
#sidebar1 {
  float: left;
}
#sidebar2 {
  float: right;
}
#mainContent {
  margin: 0 220px;
```

```
  padding: 10px 20px;
}
```

Using multiple images for a hybrid layout

Creating a hybrid three-column layout, in which the sidebars have a fixed width, but the center column is liquid, involves adding an extra wrapper <div>. The <div> serves no other purpose than to provide an element to which the second background image can be applied. The basic HTML structure of threecol_hybrid.html looks like this:

```
<body>
<div id="wrapper">
  <div id="innerwrapper">
    <div id="header">
      Heading content
    </div>
    <div id="sidebar1">
      Left sidebar content
    </div>
    <div id="sidebar2">
      Right sidebar content
    </div>
    <div id="mainContent">
      Main content
    </div>
    <div id="footer">
      Footer content
    </div>
  </div>
</div>
</body>
```

The style rules that control the two wrappers look like this:

```
#wrapper {
  margin: 0 10%;
  background-color: #FFF;
  background-image: url(../images/sidebar_left.jpg);
  background-repeat: repeat-y;
  border-left: #252017 solid 1px;
  border-right: #252017 solid 1px;
}
#innerwrapper {
  width: 100%;
  background-image: url(../images/sidebar_right.jpg);
  background-position: right;
  background-repeat: repeat-y;
}
```

439

The outer <div> has no fixed width, but the inner one is set to 100%. Since it's nested inside the outer one, both are always the same width. The background image for the right sidebar is then applied to the inner <div> in the same way as before.

AdvancED

To create faux columns for a fully liquid three-column layout, follow the instructions in Zoe Gillenwater's article that I referred to earlier in this chapter: www.communitymx.com/content/article.cfm?cid=afc58.

Both threecol_fixed.html and threecol_hybrid.html put the sidebar content before the main content in the HTML markup. What if you want to put the main content first?

Putting the main content first in a three-column layout

You can either use the negative margin technique described earlier in the chapter or create a column container to float two columns together. Both techniques work best with fixed-width layouts. The following exercises take you through each technique step by step.

Using a negative margin for the left sidebar

To follow this exercise, use threecol_negative_start.html in the download files for this chapter. If you just want to study the finished code, it's in threecol_negative_finished.html.

1. Copy threecol_negative_start.html to your work folder, and save it as threecol_negative.html. If you test it in a browser, it should look like Figure 11-21.

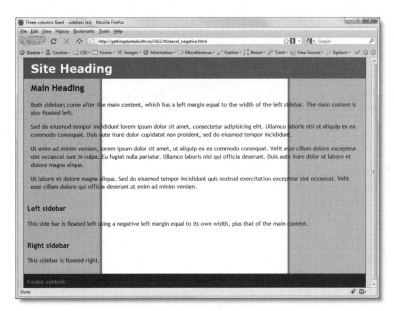

Figure 11-21. To start with, the content for both sidebars is after the main content.

2. The sidebar backgrounds in sidebar_both.jpg are 220px wide. The existing style rule adds 10px of padding to the sidebars, so you need to set the width property to 200px. Also create style rules to float the sidebars in opposite directions like this:

```
#sidebar1, #sidebar2 {
  padding: 10px;
  width: 200px;
}
#sidebar1 {
  float: left;
}
#sidebar2 {
  float: right;
}
```

3. The overall width of the wrapper is 960px, leaving 520px for the main content. However, the main content has 20px on either side, so its width property needs to be set to 480px. Also float the main content to the left. Amend the #mainContent style block like this:

```
#mainContent {
  padding: 10px 20px;
  width: 480px;
  float: left;
}
```

4. If you save and test the page now, it should look like Figure 11-22.

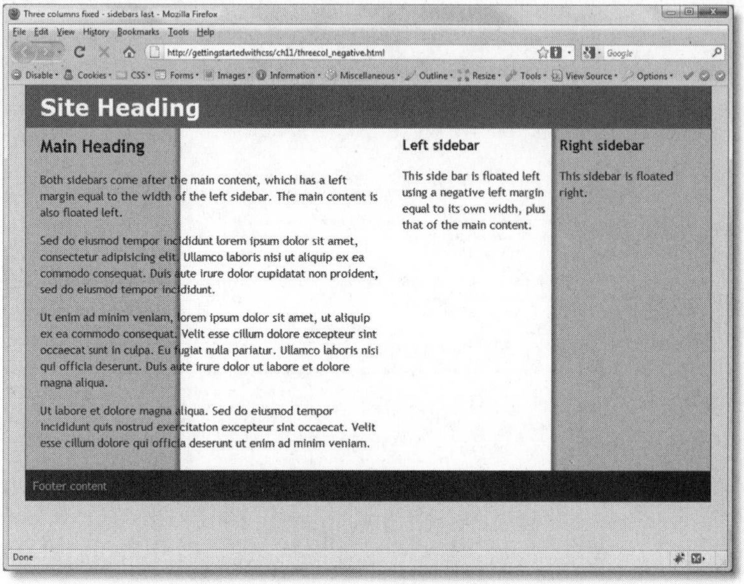

Figure 11-22. The main content and left side bar are in the wrong places.

5. Apply a left margin to the main content to make room for the sidebar like this:

```
#mainContent {
    padding: 10px 20px;
    width: 480px;
    float: left;
    margin-left: 220px;
}
```

6. To move the left sidebar into place, give it a negative left margin equal to its own width plus that of the main content. Don't forget that you need to add any padding and borders in the calculation. There are no borders on either element in this case, so the calculation is 200px + 10px + 10px + 480px + 20px + 20px = 740px. Amend the #sidebar1 style block like this:

```
#sidebar1 {
    float: left;
    margin-left: -740px;
}
```

7. Save the page, and test it in a browser. All columns should now be in the right place. You need to make just two small amendments to prevent the layout from falling apart in IE6. The main content <div> has a margin on the same side as it is floated, so you need to set its display property to inline to prevent the IE6 double-margin bug like this:

```
#mainContent {
  padding: 10px 20px;
  width: 480px;
  float: left;
  margin-left: 220px;
  display: inline;
}
```

8. Also, to constrain the footer in IE6, add an empty <div> just above the footer with an inline style to clear the floats:

```
<div style="clear:both"></div>
<div id="footer">Footer content</div>
```

You can compare your code, if necessary, with threecol_negative_finish.html in the download files for this chapter.

Another technique for creating a three-column layout is to wrap two of the columns in a container <div>, give the container a width, and float the columns inside it. You can then treat the container as a single element, and float it to one side, as shown in the following exercise.

Using a column container

To follow this exercise, use threecol_wrapfloat_start.html in the download files for this chapter. If you just want to look at the finished code, it's in threecol_wrapfloat_finish.html.

1. Copy threecol_wrapfloat_start.html to your work folder, and save it as threecol_wrapfloat.html. If you load the file into a browser, it should look similar to Figure 11-21. The only significant difference is that I have already assigned widths to the main content and sidebars to save time. Both sidebars come after the main content in the HTML markup.

2. Wrap the main content and left sidebar in a <div>, and assign it the ID, inner, like this (the line with three dots indicates HTML code omitted for reasons of space):

```
<div id="inner">
  <div id="mainContent">
```

443

```
   . . .
   <p>This side bar is floated left inside the inner wrapper.</p>
   </div>
</div>
```

3. Create a style rule for the new <div>. It needs to be the same width as its content. The main content <div> is 480px, plus 20px padding on either side (520px), and the left sidebar is 200px, plus 10px of padding on either side (220px), making a total of 740px. Also float the new <div> left. The style block should look like this:

```
#inner {
  width: 740px;
  float: left;
}
```

4. Float the main content and left sidebar in opposite directions inside the new <div>:

```
#sidebar1 {
  float: left;
}
#mainContent {
  width: 480px;
  padding: 10px 20px;
  float: right;
}
```

5. Float the second sidebar right by creating the following style rule:

```
#sidebar2 {
  float: right;
}
```

6. Keep IE6 happy by adding an empty <div> with an inline style just before the footer to clear the floats like this:

```
<div style="clear:both"></div>
<div id="footer">Footer content</div>
```

That's all there is to it. You can check your code, if necessary, against threecol_wrapfloat._finish.html in the download files for this chapter.

Creating subcolumns

Creating a column container, as in the preceding exercise, is a convenient way to add further columns to your layout. Figure 11-23 shows a highlighted two-column subsection embedded in the center column.

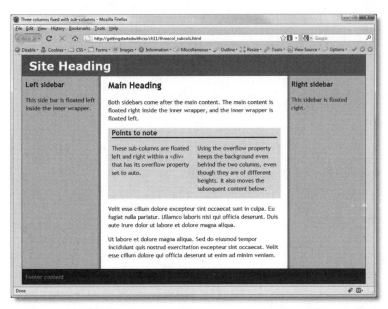

Figure 11-23. Using a combination of floats and the overflow property, it's easy to create columns within columns.

The highlighted section in the center column in Figure 11-23 is created by floating two elements in opposite directions inside a <div>, which has its overflow property set to auto. As explained in Chapter 6, you can use this technique to maintain a background behind floated elements.

You can examine the full code in threecol_subcols.html, but the basic HTML markup for the highlighted section looks like this:

```
<div id="subcol_wrapper">
  <h3>Points to note</h3>
  <div id="subcol1">
    <p>These sub-columns are floated. . .</p>
  </div>
  <div id="subcol2">
    <p>Using the overflow property. . .</p>
  </div>
</div>
```

The following styles control the highlighted section and subcolumns:

```
#subcol_wrapper {
  background-color: #EAE5CE;
  overflow: auto;
}
```

445

```
#subcol1 {
  width: 220px;
  padding:0 10px;
  float: left;
}
#subcol2 {
  width: 220px;
  padding: 0 10px;
  float: right;
}
```

Unfortunately, IE6 doesn't respect the overflow property, so you need to add the following IE conditional comment after the main styles:

```
<!--[if lte IE 6]>
<style type="text/css">
#subcol_wrapper {
  zoom: 1;
}
</style>
<![endif]-->
```

This proprietary property fixes the problem in IE6. Since it's in an IE conditional comment, it's ignored by other browsers and the W3C validator.

AdvancED

I have used ID selectors for the highlighted section and subcolumns, but you could use classes instead if you want to have several sections like this on a page.

Table-related display—the future of layout?

HTML tables were the mainstay of web page layout for a long time. In fact, many people still haven't made the transition to CSS layouts. So, does this section suggest we're about to come full circle? The answer's a mixture of no and maybe.

The table-related display that I'm referring to are the values of the display property listed in Table 11-2.

Table 11-2. Table-Related Values of the Display Property

Table	inline-table	table-caption
table-header-group	table-footer-group	table-column-group
table-column	table-row-group	table-row
table-cell		

As you have seen in previous chapters, you can use the `display` property to change the way browsers treat elements, for example, turning inline elements into block-level ones and vice versa. The implication of the list of values in Table 11-2 is that you can get a paragraph, `<div>`, or indeed any element to act like a table cell. You can also get elements to act like table rows. The great advantage of this is that the height of all the cells in a table row is automatically the same as the tallest element. So, if you can get elements to act like table cells, you solve at a stroke the problem of equal height columns, without the need for faux columns.

The good news is that you can—all modern browsers support these table-related values. The bad news is that the term "modern browser" doesn't include IE6 or IE7. At the time of this writing, IE6 and IE7 account for roughly 40 percent of all browsers in current use, so this isn't yet a realistic method of layout.

In all modern browsers, including IE8, `threecol_table.html` looks the same as the other three-column layouts described in this chapter (see Figure 11-20). However, when viewed in IE6 or IE7, the columns are not rendered, and you get the result shown in Figure 11-24 (the screenshot was taken in IE7 compatibility mode in IE8).

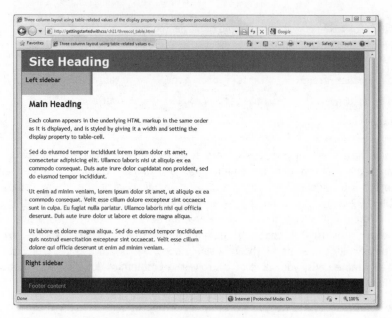

Figure 11-24. IE6 and IE7 ignore the table-related values of the display property, displaying each <div> as a separate block.

Although these table-related values force elements to act like parts of a table, you don't need to create the same type of structure as an HTML table. So, to create a three-column layout that looks the same as Figure 11-10, all that's necessary is to put the columns in the same order as you want them to appear and set their display property to table-cell. There's no need for a table element or for a table row. The CSS specification says that browsers should create "anonymous" table elements if they are missing.

The HTML markup in threecol_table.html looks like this:

```
<body>
<div id="wrapper">
  <div id="header">
    Header content
  </div>
  <div id="sidebar1">
    Left sidebar
  </div>
  <div id="mainContent">
    Main content
  </div>
  <div id="sidebar2">
    Right sidebar
```

```
    </div>
  <div id="footer">
    Footer content
  </div>
</div>
</body>
```

The style rules for the three columns look like this:

```
#sidebar1, #sidebar2 {
  width: 180px;
  padding: 10px;
  display: table-cell;
  background-repeat: repeat-y;
}
#sidebar1 {
  background-image: url(../images/sidebar_left.jpg);
  background-position: right;
}
#sidebar2 {
  background-image: url(../images/sidebar_right.jpg);
  background-position: left;
}
#mainContent {
  padding: 10px 20px;
  display: table-cell;
  width: 520px;
}
```

Simply setting the `display` property of each `<div>` to `table-cell` is all that it takes! Because the header and footer are block-level elements, the browser automatically assumes that the three elements in between are to be treated as a single-row table. There is no need to create artificial elements to simulate the table or table row.

After seeing this simple example, you're probably hoping for the instant demise of IE6 and IE7, so that you can dispense with all the floats and faux columns. It certainly works well for a basic column layout, but things begin to get more complicated once you attempt anything more ambitious. As with HTML tables, you can nest a CSS table inside an element that has its `display` property set to `table-cell`. However, there is no equivalent of the HTML `rowspan` and `colspan` attributes.

Another drawback is that using the table-related values restricts the properties you can apply to an element. For example, you can't apply margins or padding to an element that simulates a table row; you can apply padding, but not margins, to an element that simulates a table cell; and so on.

449

Figure 11-25 shows threecol_table_subcols.html, which contains a highlighted section with subcolumns similar to the one in Figure 11-23. The highlighted section is a <div> with its display property set to table. Each column inside the highlighted section is a <div> with its display property set to table-cell. However, the lack of equivalent for the colspan attribute presented problems for creating the top row. To get it to span across the whole section, I eventually wrapped the <h3> heading in a <div> with its display property set to table-header-group. Although this worked, adding a bottom border to the heading resulted in it going only halfway across the row, because the browser automatically created an anonymous empty cell alongside. To get the border, I applied it to the <div> simulating the table row, but it goes all the way across, rather than having the elegant 10px margin on either side that you can see in Figure 11-25.

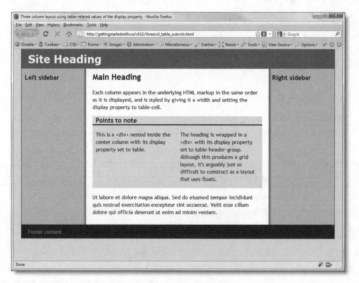

Figure 11-25. You can use the table-related display values to nest a table-like structure inside a table cell.

I'm sure designers will come up with attractive and inventive uses of the table-related values of the display property, but I think the ecstatic welcome that some people have given to them finally being supported in IE8 is premature. Using these techniques will become a practical reality only when IE6 and IE7 finally disappear from the scene. Then they will become another useful tool in the web designer's toolbox, but they're not a magic wand that solves all the problems of CSS layout.

Chapter review

This has been a long chapter, with a lot of information to absorb, yet it has merely scratched the surface of page layout with CSS. All the layouts covered here have a distinctly boxy look, but don't let that put you off. The purpose has been to provide a series of techniques to create a solid framework upon which to build your designs. What you put in the one-, two-, or three-column layouts is up to you. Once you have the columns, you can put other elements inside them, and position them using margins and padding, without the need to worry about nesting tables or the effect of one element on the rest of a row or column.

In the next, and final, chapter, I'll show you how to create a style sheet that controls how your web pages look when printed out. I'll also tidy up a few loose ends by describing a handful of lesser-used CSS2.1 properties that didn't fit conveniently into earlier chapters.

Chapter 12

How Do I Create Styles for Printing?

Web designers put a lot of effort into creating pages that look great onscreen but rarely give a thought to what they look like when printed out. How often have you bought something online and wanted to print out the invoice? Instead of a professional-looking document, you get all the website navigation down the side, leaving not enough room for the figures that indicate how much you paid. If you're lucky, they come out on a second sheet. It's not at all necessary. CSS gives you considerable control over the way your web pages print out. There's no need to create a separate page for printing. It can all be done with a style sheet.

In this chapter, I'll show you how to create a print style sheet and use some of the special properties for printed output. After that, I'll take a look at the remaining three CSS2.1 visual properties that have not been covered elsewhere in the book: cursor, outline, and quotes.

In this chapter, you'll learn about the following:

- What considerations should go into planning a print style sheet
- How to set the margins for a printed page
- How to avoid page breaks at inconvenient points
- Using the content property to display the URL of links
- Changing the look of the cursor
- Improving accessibility with outlines
- Automatically generating curly quotes and nesting them in correct sequence

Let's start by looking at the main differences between using CSS for viewing web pages onscreen and printing.

What's different about print CSS?

In many respects, creating a style sheet for printing is no different from the type of style sheet discussed so far. Margins and padding work the same way. So do things like font definitions and line height. However, the crucial difference is that printing is a static medium. The width of a printed page is fixed, but you have no idea what size paper will be used, so the content of a wide onscreen layout is likely to be truncated.

By default, most browsers don't print background colors and images. This can have disastrous consequences if your web page uses a light color on a dark background: you risk having text that's virtually illegible when printed. The only exception appears to be white text on black. Most browsers automatically reverse the colors and print the text in black. Another consideration is that links cannot be followed, and the URL is hidden unless you use the URL as the link text.

Other things that need to be taken into consideration are fonts and font sizes. Most typographical experts recommend serif fonts for print and sans-serif fonts for web pages. The thinking behind this is that serifs (the hooks on the ends of letters) often don't display clearly on a computer screen, particularly at small font sizes. It's also widely believed that serifs make it easier to read text on a printed page. However, there appears to be little scientific evidence for this— which is, perhaps, a good thing since friends of ED books are printed in sans-serif fonts!

LinkED

For a succinct analysis of the evidence regarding the relative legibility of sans-serif and serif fonts, see www.alexpoole.info/academic/literaturereview.html.

Users can increase the font size in a browser but not on a printed page. So, it's important to make sure all your text prints at a size that is comfortable for the average person to read.

Perhaps the biggest consideration with a print style sheet is deciding which parts of your web page are unnecessary. Before insisting that everything is necessary and in the right place, think again. Do you really want your navigation menu printed out? What about the search form? Neither is going to be any use on the printed page, so they're good candidates for exclusion by setting their display property to none. You also need to exclude parts of the page that consist solely of background images, because they won't normally be printed out and will leave unsightly gaps in the page. If an image is important, and you want it included in printouts, it should be embedded in the HTML with the <img> tag. It's only background images that printers ignore.

ExplainED

Printing out background colors and images is controlled by the browser, and it's up to the individual user to decide whether to turn on the option to print them. By default, most browsers turn off this option to speed up printing and avoid wasting ink. There is no way to override the user's setting with CSS or any other web technology.

While I'm on the subject of restrictions, let's look at what else you can't do with a print style sheet.

What print style sheets cannot do

Print style sheets can do a lot of things, but several potentially useful features are not supported, namely:

- You cannot specify the size of the printed page.
- You cannot change the orientation of the page.
- As mentioned in the previous section, you have no control over the printing of background colors and images.

Controlling the size and orientation of the page were originally part of CSS2, but browsers were unable to implement these two features, so they were dropped from CSS2.1. The size property, which is not part of CSS2.1, was intended to have controlled these features. You might see references to it in older books or online tutorials. Changing the orientation to landscape would be particularly useful when information needs to spread across the page. Unfortunately, Opera is the only major browser that supports the size property. So don't waste time trying to fathom why it doesn't work.

LinkED

The size *property has been moved to the Paged Media module of CSS3. When eventually implemented by browsers, it will allow you to specify both the size and orientation of the page. For details of what's proposed, see* www.w3.org/TR/css3-page/#page-size-prop.

Setting page margins with the @page rule and pseudo-classes

Although you can't yet set the size of the printed page, you can—and should—set the page's margins. You do this with the @page rule. The @page rule accepts only the margin shorthand property or the individual margin properties, such as margin-left. Moreover, you cannot use em or ex as units of measurement with the @page rule.

Technically speaking, you can use pixels to specify the margins of the printed page, but it's not a good idea. When creating a print style sheet, you're no longer working in a fluid medium, so you should use the absolute units of measurement listed in Table 12-1.

Table 12-1. Absolute Units of Measurement for Use in Print Style Sheets

Unit	Description
in	Inch (2.54 centimeters)
cm	Centimeter (0.394 in)
mm	Millimeter (0.039 in)
pt	Point, a typographical unit equivalent to 1/72 of an inch (0.353 mm)
pc	Pica, a typographical unit equivalent to 12 points (4.233 mm).

So, to add a one-inch margin all around a page (the same as a default document in Microsoft Word), put the following rule in your print style sheet:

```
@page {
  margin: 1in;
}
```

The following does the same using metric measurements:

```
@page {
  margin: 2.54cm;
}
```

Or, if you come from a traditional print background, you might prefer this:

```
@page {
  margin: 6pc;
}
```

As with styles that are rendered in a browser, there must be no space between the number and the unit of measurement.

In addition to absolute units of measurement, you can also use percentages. Percentage values for the left and right margins are relative to the width of the printed page; those for the top and bottom margins are relative to the page's height.

The @page rule supports three pseudo-classes, namely:

- :left
- :right
- :first

As their names suggest, the :left and :right pseudo-classes define the margins for multiple pages as if they were bound in a book. So, odd numbered pages use the margins defined for the :right pseudo-class, and even numbered pages use those defined for the :left pseudo-class. The :first pseudo-class defines the margins for the first page. For the sake of clarity, the page numbers refer to the number of pages printed out by a single web page. A web page is a single, continuous entity, but when printed out, it often covers several pages of print.

So, for example, if you expect pages to be printed out double-sided and want to leave a wider margin for binding, you could use the following rules:

```
@page {
  margin: 2cm;
}
@page :left {
  margin-right: 3cm;
}
@page :right {
  margin-left: 3cm;
}
```

AdvancED

At the time of this writing, IE8 and Opera are the only mainstream browsers that support setting page margins with the @page rule. In fact, Opera has supported all aspects of print CSS since version 6. Other browsers default to a margin of approximately 1 inch (2.54 cm) all around the page.

IE8 and Opera disagree on how to handle the :left and :right pseudo-classes In languages that are written from right to left, such as Arabic, Hebrew, and Urdu. Opera gets it wrong by treating odd numbered pages as being on the right, whereas in right-to-left languages, they are normally on the left.

Controlling where to break content between pages

It can be infuriating when printing out a web page to discover that a heading is printed at the bottom of a page, and all the information relating to that heading is on the next page without anything to identify it. To avoid such situations, CSS provides the five properties listed in Table 12-2.

Table 12-2. Page Properties used for Print Style Sheets

Property	Initial Value	Inherited	Description
page-break-after	auto	No	Lets you specify how to handle page breaks after a particular element. For example, you can tell the browser to start a new page immediately after a table.
page-break-before	auto	No	Lets you specify whether a new page should be started before a particular element.
page-break-inside	auto	No	Lets you specify whether a new page can be started in the middle of an element.

Property	Initial Value	Inherited	Description
orphans	2	Yes	Specifies the minimum number of lines of an element that must be displayed at the bottom of the page. If fewer lines would be displayed, the whole item is moved to the next page.
widows	2	Yes	Specifies the minimum number of lines of an element that must be displayed at the top of a page. If fewer lines would be displayed, the whole item is moved from the previous page.

The `page-break-after` and `page-break-before` properties accept one of the following values:

- `auto`: Leave it up to the browser to decide where to put the page break. This is the default.

- `always`: Force a page break before or after the specified element.

- `avoid`: Avoid a page break, if possible.

- `left`: Force one or two page breaks before or after the specified element, so the next page is formatted as a left page.

- `right`: Force one or two page breaks before or after the specified element, so the next page is formatted as a right page.

- `inherit`: These properties are not inherited by default, so this value can be used to force the element to take the same value as its parent.

The `page-break-inside` property accepts only `auto`, `avoid`, or `inherit`.

The `orphans` and `widows` properties should be familiar to anyone with a print background. It's generally considered bad practice in printing to leave only a single line of a paragraph at the top or bottom of a page. By default, browsers are expected to print at least two lines of a block-level element before and after a page break. So if, for example, a three-line paragraph appears at the bottom of a page, but there is room for only two lines, the whole paragraph will be moved to the next page. You can use these properties to change the minimum number of lines that should be kept together. It goes without saying, the value should be a positive integer; negative numbers and decimals would make no sense. The bigger the number you use, the more uneven your printed pages are likely to look. For example, if you set both orphans and widows to 4, the whole of any paragraph with fewer than eight lines will be moved to the next page if there isn't sufficient room for it at the bottom of the current page.

AdvancED

Normally, you would use the same value for orphans and widows; but if you do want different values, the easy way to remember which is which is that orphans are the little ones at the bottom, and widows are the lonely ones at the top.

The five properties in Table 12-2 apply to block-level elements, but the CSS2.1 specification says that browsers are free to apply them to other elements, such as table rows. Unfortunately, like the @page rule, this aspect of CSS2.1 is still poorly supported by browsers. At the time of this writing, only IE8 and Opera implement any of the properties listed in Table 12-2.

ExplainED

Setting page breaks in a print style sheet should be regarded as indicating a desirable outcome, rather than something that can be relied up. You have no way of predicting the size of paper that will be used. Also, there might be conflicting demands of where the page should be broken. It's left up to the browser to decide what is possible in any given set of circumstances.

Displaying the URL of links

There's better news about a really useful feature for print CSS. Most websites use ordinary text to link to other pages and external websites; the URL is buried in the HTML code. Unfortunately, the URL is lost when the page is printed out. However, all current browsers except IE6 and IE7 support generated content. As explained in Chapter 8, the content property in combination with the :after pseudo-element can display the value of an HTML attribute. This means you can extract the URL of a link from its href attribute, and print it out after the link.

460

The basic rule for printing out the URL in parentheses after a link looks like this:

```
a:after {
  content: " (" attr(href) ") ";
}
```

This adds a space after the link text, followed by an opening parenthesis. The attr() function extracts the value of the href attribute, and displays it followed by a closing parenthesis and space.

There's one small problem with this in that it displays all URLs. Assuming that you don't use fully qualified URLs for internal links, you can display only external URLs with an advanced selector like this:

```
a[href^="http://"]:after {
  content: " (" attr(href) ") ";
}
```

This adds the URL after a link only if the href attribute begins with http://. If you want to include the URLs for secure pages that begin with https://, use the following:

```
a[href^="http"]:after {
  content: " (" attr(href) ") ";
}
```

What if you want to display the URLs for your internal links, too? Internal links don't normally use a full URL, so using a:after on its own isn't really suitable. However, as long as you make all your internal links relative to the site root, the content property can handle the situation beautifully with the following advanced selector:

```
a[href^="/"]:after {
  content: " (http://www.example.com" attr(href) ") ";
}
```

This adds http://www.example.com in front of the site-root-relative link, automatically producing the full URL when the page is printed out.

461

ExplainED

Most HTML editors create internal links relative to the current document. In fact, all the links in the download files for this book are document-relative. You can identify them because they begin with a file or folder name, or a pair of dots. However, you can also create internal links that are relative to the site root. This type of link always begins with a forward slash like this: `href="/images/lasvegas.jpg"`*. You must use this type of link to display the URLs of internal links with the* `content` *property.*

The advanced selector used in this technique is part of the proposals for CSS3, but it is already supported by all modern browsers (but not IE6). The selector tells the browser to look for links with an `href` *attribute that begins with the character(s) inside the quotes. So, the first example looks for links where the* `href` *attribute begins with* `http://`*, the second one looks for links that begin with* `http` *(so it gets both* `http` *and* `https`*), and the third one for links that begin with a leading forward slash. This and other advanced selectors are described in this book's appendix. Although IE7 supports the selector used here, it doesn't support generated content.*

Creating styles for printing

There are two basic approaches you can take to creating special style rules for printing. One is to start from scratch with a completely separate set of print style rules. The other approach is to use the CSS cascade to override specific rules.

Neither approach is inherently better than the other. Which you choose depends on the nature of the site and the amount of changes that are necessary for the printed version. For example, a site that predominantly consists of text might need only a few changes, so using the cascade to override the choice of fonts and color is all you need. On the other hand, a site that uses a lot of background images, floats, and positioned elements is probably much easier to handle by creating a dedicated print style sheet from scratch.

Using the media attribute to specify where styles are applied

The optional media attribute (see Table 1-2 in Chapter 1) tells the browser the types of devices to which you want to apply specific rules or style sheets. The values supported by CSS2.1 are all, braille, embossed, handheld, print, projection, screen, speech, tty, and tv.

For a small amount of changes, you can use the @media rule with one or more of these values to specify how to handle the same styles for different devices. The advantage of the @media rule is that both screen and print rules can be defined in the same style sheet like this:

```
@media screen {
  body {
    font-family: Arial, Helvetica, sans-serif;
    color: #C00;
    background-color: #CCC;
  }
}
@media print {
  body {
    font-family: "Palatino Linotype", "Book Antiqua", Palatino, serif;
    color: #000;
    background-color: #FFF;
  }
}
```

This sets different fonts and colors for display onscreen and in printouts and is an efficient solution for a basic site. However, mixing styles like this is likely to become confusing on a more sophisticated site.

For more extensive changes, it's better to split your style rules into separate external style sheets for onscreen and print display. If you omit the media attribute from the <link> tag or @import when linking a style sheet, the styles apply to *all* devices, including printers. However, once you include any of the media values (except all), the browser applies those styles only to the specified devices. For example, the following <link> tag applies the styles in basic.css only when the page is viewed on a computer screen:

```
<link href="css/basic.css" rel="stylesheet" type="text/css" ↵
media="screen" />
```

Similarly, this @import rule also hides the styles from all devices except computer screens:

```
<style type="text/css">
@import url("css/basic.css") screen;
</style>
```

When attaching an external print style sheet, you must set the media attribute to print like this:

```
<link href="css/print.css" rel="stylesheet" type="text/css" ↵
media="print" />
```

If you prefer to use @import, attach the style sheet like this:

```
<style type="text/css">
@import url("css/print.css") print;
</style>
```

Using the cascade for print styles

If you want to make a relatively small number of changes to the way a page is styled when printed out, you can apply your styles to all media devices and then use a specialized style sheet to override selected styles for printing. Because of the way the cascade works, the print style sheet must be attached *after* the main style sheet. Otherwise, the main style sheet will take precedence, and your print styles will be ignored. Omit the media attribute from the main style sheet, but specify it for the print one like this:

```
<link href="css/main.css" rel="stylesheet" type="text/css" />
<link href="css/print.css" rel="stylesheet" type="text/css" ↵
media="print" />
```

With @import, attach the style sheets like this:

```
<style type="text/css">
@import url("css/main.css");
@import url("css/print.css") print;
</style>
```

The disadvantage with this approach is that it can be difficult to keep track of which rules you are overriding in the print style sheet. There's also a danger that you might add a new style to the main style sheet and not realize that it affects the way the page is printed. To avoid these problems, create completely independent style sheets.

Attaching independent style sheets

By specifying the `media` attribute for each style sheet, you ensure that the styles are applied only by the targeted devices. This allows you to create a completely independent print style sheet. Attach the style sheets like this:

```
<link href="css/main.css" rel="stylesheet" type="text/css" ↵
media="screen" />
<link href="css/print.css" rel="stylesheet" type="text/css" ↵
media="print" />
```

With @import, attach the style sheets like this:

```
<style type="text/css">
@import url("css/main.css") screen;
@import url("css/print.css") print;
</style>
```

This gives you a completely blank canvas on which to create your print styles.

To learn more about using CSS for handheld devices, see AdvancED CSS by Joseph R. Lewis and Meitar Moscovitz (friends of ED, ISBN: 978-1-4302-1932-3).

So much for all the theory, let's create a print style sheet for journey_horiz.html, the case study page from the earlier part of this book as it looked at the end of Chapter 8.

Creating a print style sheet

This exercise takes you through the basic process of creating and testing a print style sheet. The HTML page and main style sheet are in the download files for this chapter.

1. Copy journey_print_start.html and css/journey_horiz.css from the ch12 folder to your working folder, and save the HTML file as journey_print.html.

2. Test the page in a browser. It should look like Figure 12-1.

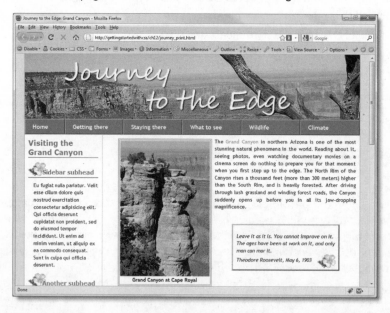

Figure 12-1. The case study from earlier in the book as it looks in a browser.

If the images or styles don't display correctly, check the file paths.

3. Select your browser's *Print Preview* option. Most browsers have the option to shrink the web page to fit. Reset that option to display the print preview at *100%*, its normal size. In Firefox 3.5, it looks like Figure 12-2.

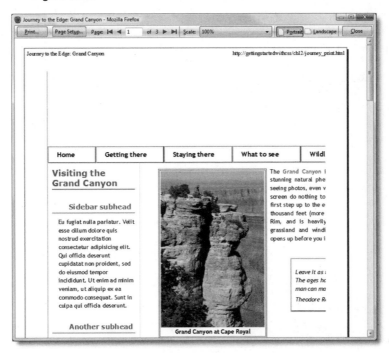

Figure 12-2. The onscreen styles are not suitable for printing the page.

As you can see, the background images and colors are not rendered. More important, the right side of the page is cut off. To get the full width of the page to display, I needed to change the *Scale* option in Firefox to *70%*. This means that the text and images will be proportionately smaller. Printers normally convert pixels to points, so the 14px text would be converted to approximately 9.5pt—OK for someone with good eyesight but not ideal.

4. Close *Print Preview*, and open journey_print.html. Amend the <link> tag that attaches the style sheet to include the media attribute for screen like this:

```
<link href="css/journey_horiz.css" rel="stylesheet" type="text/css" ↵
media="screen" />
```

5. Save `journey_print.html`, and reload it in the browser. It should look exactly the same as before. Select the browser's *Print Preview* again. This time, the page should look completely unstyled, as shown in Figure 12-3.

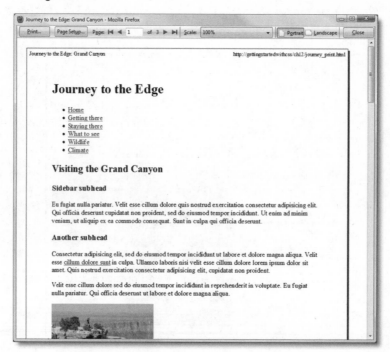

Figure 12-3. Setting the media attribute to screen prevents the styles from being applied to the printout.

If you don't have the time to create a dedicated print style sheet, this is an effective way of ensuring that everything in your page is printed out. However, it looks rather bland, particularly with the text not being wrapped around the images. So, let's get to work on creating the print style sheet.

6. The simplest way to create a print style sheet is to copy the existing style sheet and work your way through the rules, eliminating those you don't need and amending those that need to be handled differently.

Make a copy of `css/journey_horiz.css`, and save it in the `css` folder as `journey_print.css`.

7. Attach the new style sheet to journey_print.html, and set the media attribute to print like this:

```
<link href="css/journey_horiz.css" rel="stylesheet" type="text/css" ↵
media="screen" />
<link href="css/journey_print.css" rel="stylesheet" type="text/css" ↵
media="print" />
```

ExplainED

Because you have set the media attribute in both `<link>` tags, it doesn't matter which order they are in, but it's common practice to put the print style sheet last.

8. The first thing you need to do for the print style sheet is to set the page margins. Even though not all browsers support setting margins with the @page rule, it's a good idea to include it in your print style sheet. Browsers that support it will create the correct margins, and the rule will be in place when other browsers finally catch up with the standard.

    Open journey_print.css, and add the following code at the top of the page:

```
/* Print styles */
@page {
  margin: 1in;
}
```

I have used inches as the measurement, since most readers are likely to be in the United States. If you prefer metric, change 1in to 2.54cm or the size of your choice.

9. It's a reasonable assumption that most people will print on white paper, so the background color of the page needs to be changed. You might also want to change the fonts. The margin and padding properties are no longer needed in the body style block, because they're handled by the @page rule. Amend the body style block like this:

```
body {
  background-color: #FFF;
  color: #000;
```

```
    font-family: "Minion Pro", Garamond, "Times New Roman", Times, serif;
}
```

10. The #wrapper, #header, #sidebar, and #mainContent style blocks provide structure and decorative elements for the onscreen version but are not needed for printing. Delete them.

11. The only part of the #footer style block that you need is the text-align property. Delete the margin and text-indent properties. Also delete the .reversed style block. That completes the page infrastructure section of the style sheet.

12. In the headings section, you can get rid of the rule that hides the <h1> heading, as well as the one that puts 10px of padding on top of the first paragraph in the main content <div>.

    You don't want page breaks immediately after any headings, so add the page-break-after property, adjust the margins, and change the fonts. The headings section should now look like this:

```
/* Headings */
h1, h2, h3, h4, h5, h6 {
  font-family: "Myriad Pro", "Gill Sans", "Lucida Sans", Verdana, ↵
    Geneva, sans-serif;
  margin: 6pt 0;
  page-break-after: avoid;
}
h1 + p, h2 + p, h3 + p, #mainContent p:first-child {
  text-indent: 0;
}
```

13. Next come the styles for the main text. The onscreen version uses 14px for the size of the font in the paragraphs and table. Most browsers and printers will convert this to 14pt, which is rather large for a printout. So, change this to 12pt. Also adjust the text-indent property to use a print measure. I have chosen 2pc, which is one-third of an inch (0.85cm). Also reduce the vertical distance between lines, and adjust the margins on the paragraphs. Change the rules for paragraphs and tables like this:

```
/* Main text */
p, table {
  font-size: 12pt;
}
p {
  text-align: justify;
  text-indent: 2pc;
  line-height: 1.2;
  margin: 0 0 3pt 0;
}
```

14. In the printed version, it's a good idea to underline links. And in case people are printing in color, there's no need to distinguish between links that have and have not been visited. Replace the existing link styles with the following:

```
a[href^="http://"]:after {
  content: " (" attr(href) ") ";
}
a:link, a:visited {
  color: #00C;
}
```

15. The styles for the Roosevelt quote are mainly decorative. None of the background elements will be printed out, so you can slim the style blocks to the bare bones like this:

```
#tr_quote {
  margin: 2pc 2.5pc 1pc auto;
  width: 40%;
}
blockquote p {
  font-style: italic;
  text-indent: 0;
}
```

As explained in Chapter 4, setting the margins of an element alongside a floated element presents considerable problems. With the onscreen version, it was possible to calculate the correct margins for the quote. However, with a print style sheet you have no idea what size of paper will be used. So, I have set the width of the quote to 40%, and used picas (1 pica equals 12 points) for the margins. After some experimentation, 2.5pc seemed to work well for the right margin. This offsets it about 0.4in (1cm) from the right edge. The left margin is set to auto.

AdvancED

I have used points and picas for margins and padding, because they make it easy to calculate sizes in proportion to the 12pt main text. A quick rule of thumb is that 1 pixel is equivalent to 1 point, and 12 pixels are equal to 1 pica.

If you don't feel comfortable with traditional print measurements, use inches, centimeters, or millimeters instead. However, you should always specify the size of fonts in points or picas unless you know the exact metric size.

16. The remaining style rules in this section apply to the table and caption. You don't want the table to be broken when printing, so add the `page-break-inside` property. Also change the size of the caption font to 14pt. This section of rules should now look like this:

```
table {
  margin: 0 auto;
  page-break-inside: avoid;
}
caption {
  font-size: 14pt;
  font-weight: bold;
  text-transform: capitalize;
}
th {
  font-weight: normal;
  text-align: right;
}
```

17. You don't need to make many changes to the image alignment rules apart from changing the pixel values to points. Also remove the padding and border from the images, and set a rule to prevent them from being split over a page break. The image alignment section should be amended like this:

```
/* Image alignment */
.floatleft {
  float: left;
  margin: 3pt 8pt 3pt 0;
}
.floatright {
  float: right;
  margin: 3pt 0 3pt 8pt;
```

```
}
.imgcentered {
  margin: 3pt auto;
  display: block;
}
.floatleft, .floatright, .imgcentered {
  font-weight: bold;
  text-align: center;
}
.floatleft img, .floatright img {
  display: block;
  page-break-inside: avoid;
}
```

18. Delete all the sidebar and navigation styles and prevent the navigation menu from being displayed like this:

```
/* Horizontal navigation bar */
#nav {
  display: none;
}
```

19. Save the style sheet, reload the page in a browser, and test *Print Preview*. Then try *Print Preview* in at least one other browser. This is one area where modern browsers still display considerable inconsistency. Compare Figures 12-4 and 12-5, which show the first page as rendered in Firefox 3.5 and IE8 respectively.

Journey to the Edge

Visiting the Grand Canyon

Sidebar subhead

Eu fugiat nulla pariatur. Velit esse cillum dolore quis nostrud exercitation consectetur adipisicing elit. Qui officia deserunt cupidatat non proident, sed do eiusmod tempor incididunt. Ut enim ad minim veniam, ut aliquip ex ea commodo consequat. Sunt in culpa qui officia deserunt.

Another subhead

Consectetur adipisicing elit, sed do eiusmod tempor incididunt ut labore et dolore magna aliqua. Velit esse cillum dolore sunt in culpa. Ullamco laboris nisi velit esse cillum dolore lorem ipsum dolor sit amet. Quis nostrud exercitation consectetur adipisicing elit, cupidatat non proident.

Velit esse cillum dolore sed do eiusmod tempor incididunt in reprehenderit in voluptate. Eu fugiat nulla pariatur. Qui officia deserunt ut labore et dolore magna aliqua.

The Grand Canyon (http://www.nps.gov/grca/index.htm) in northern Arizona is one of the most stunning natural phenomena in the world. Reading about it, seeing photos, even watching documentary movies on a cinema screen do nothing to prepare you for that moment when you first step up to the edge. The North Rim of the Canyon rises a thousand feet (more than 300 meters) higher than the South Rim, and is heavily forested. After driving through lush grassland and winding forest roads, the Canyon suddenly opens up before you in all its jaw-dropping magnificence.

Leave it as it is. You cannot improve on it. The ages have been at work on it, and only man can mar it.
Theodore Roosevelt, May 6, 1903

Grand Canyon at Cape Royal

From biting wind to warm updraft

Because of its altitude, access to the North Rim through the Kaibab National Forest (http://www.fs.fed.us/r3/kai/recreation/trails/index.shtml) is cut off by heavy snow from late October to mid-May each year. Even during the summer months, a biting wind often blows across the grasslands in the forest, catching the ill-prepared visitor by surprise. Then, as you step out of your car at Point Imperial, a warm blast of air greets you, rising from the Colorado River, nearly 6,000 feet (1,800 meters) below. Daytime temperatures at the bottom of the Canyon often exceed 100° F (38° C), causing a warm updraft that mixes pleasantly with the cooler air of the plateau. On a clear summer's day, from Point Imperial you can see for miles across the Navajo Indian Reservation and Painted Desert

The approach to the North Rim of the Grand Canyon through Kaibab National Forest

Figure 12-4. The print styles as rendered by Firefox 3.5

Journey to the Edge

Visiting the Grand Canyon

Sidebar subhead

Eu fugiat nulla pariatur. Velit esse cillum dolore quis nostrud exercitation consectetur adipisicing elit. Qui officia deserunt cupidatat non proident, sed do eiusmod tempor incididunt. Ut enim ad minim veniam, ut aliquip ex ea commodo consequat. Sunt in culpa qui officia deserunt.

Another subhead

Consectetur adipisicing elit, sed do eiusmod tempor incididunt ut labore et dolore magna aliqua. Velit esse cillum dolore sunt in culpa. Ullamco laboris nisi velit esse cillum dolore lorem ipsum dolor sit amet. Quis nostrud exercitation consectetur adipisicing elit, cupidatat non proident.

Velit esse cillum dolore sed do eiusmod tempor incididunt in reprehenderit in voluptate. Eu fugiat nulla pariatur. Qui officia deserunt ut labore et dolore magna aliqua.

Grand Canyon at Cape Royal

The Grand Canyon (http://www.nps.gov/grca/index.htm) in northern Arizona is one of the most stunning natural phenomena in the world. Reading about it, seeing photos, even watching documentary movies on a cinema screen do nothing to prepare you for that moment when you first step up to the edge. The North Rim of the Canyon rises a thousand feet (more than 300 meters) higher than the South Rim, and is heavily forested. After driving through lush grassland and winding forest roads, the Canyon suddenly opens up before you in all its jaw-dropping magnificence.

Leave it as it is. You cannot improve on it. The ages have been at work on it, and only man can mar it.
Theodore Roosevelt, May 6, 1903

From biting wind to warm updraft

Because of its altitude, access to the North Rim through the Kaibab National Forest (http://www.fs.fed.us/r3/kai/recreation/trails/index.shtml) is cut off by heavy snow from late October to mid-May each year. Even during the summer months, a biting wind often blows across the grasslands in the forest, catching the ill-prepared visitor by surprise. Then, as you step out of your car at Point Imperial, a warm blast of air greets you, rising from the Colorado River, nearly 6,000 feet (1,800 meters) below. Daytime temperatures at the

Figure 12-5. IE8 handles the same page differently.

20. One thing noticeable about the way Firefox 3.5 handles the print styles is that the heading after the Roosevelt quote doesn't clear the floated image. So, add the `clear` property to the rule that styles the headings like this:

```
h1, h2, h3, h4, h5, h6 {
  font-family: "Myriad Pro", "Gill Sans", "Lucida Sans", Verdana, ⏎
  Geneva, sans-serif;
  margin: 6pt 0;
  page-break-after: avoid;
  clear: both;
}
```

21. The other problem is that there is no clear delineation between the sidebar and the main content. You can rectify this by adding a border and margin to the bottom of the sidebar like this:

```
/* Sidebar styles */
#sidebar {
  border-bottom: 2pt solid;
  margin-bottom: 0.25in;
}
```

22. If you save the style sheet and test the page again, you'll see that all browsers handle the border and margin at the bottom of the sidebar nicely, but Firefox 3.5 cuts the second image in two, as shown in Figure 12-6.

Figure 12-6. Firefox 3.5 ignores the rule about page breaks, and slices the image in two.

Compare your style sheet, if necessary, with css/journey_print.css in the download files for this chapter.

ExplainED

I tested the same print styles in several browsers, and each one produced significantly different results. This is both ironic and frustrating, because print is a fixed medium, where sizes and layout should be predictable for a specific paper size. The discrepancies are partly due to incomplete support for print styles in some browsers, but they also reflect the fact that browsers have been designed for a flexible medium. They are not desktop publishing programs.

> *When designing a print style sheet, you need to accept that different browsers and paper sizes will result in highly unpredictable results. For the foreseeable future, at least, it's best to go for simple styles.*

In spite of the inconsistencies, creating a print style sheet for your pages is worthwhile. The results in Figures 12-4 and 12-5 are a considerable improvement on Figures 12-2 and 12-3. If nothing else, it's a good idea to get rid of unnecessary elements, such as navigation bars and advertising, to provide a clean printout.

To round out this chapter, I want to take a brief look at a handful of CSS2.1 properties that haven't been covered elsewhere in this book.

The ones that got away—UI properties and quotes

This book has covered all the visual and paged properties defined in CSS2.1 with the exception of the user interface (UI) properties and quotes. The following sections fill that final gap in your knowledge of CSS.

Table 12-3 lists the properties that affect the UI. One controls the look of the cursor; the rest are related to outlines, which are similar to borders but normally used to aid accessibility by indicating that an element has focus. The quotes property lets you specify which types of quotation marks to use in certain locations.

Table 12-3. UI Properties in CSS2.1

Property	Initial Value	Inherited	Description
cursor	auto	Yes	Changes the shape of the cursor from the browser default
outline-color	invert	No	Controls the color of an outline
outline-style	none	No	Controls the style of an outline
outline-width	medium	No	Controls the width of an outline
outline	See individual properties	No	Shorthand property that combines the individual outline properties into a single declaration

Changing the cursor

The cursor property accepts any of the values listed in Table 12-4.

Table 12-4. Values Accepted by the Cursor Property

Value	Description
auto	Use the browser default cursor for the current context.
crosshair	Display two thin intersecting lines.
default	Use the browser default, regardless of context. Usually an arrow.
help	Display a symbol indicating help is available. Usually a question mark.
move	Indicate that something is to be moved.
pointer	Indicate a link. Usually a hand.
progress	Indicate that something is happening, but that the user can still interact with the program.
e-resize, ne-resize, nw-resize, n-resize, se-resize, sw-resize, s-resize, w-resize	Indicate the direction in which the current object can be resized.
text	Indicate that text can be selected. Usually an I-beam.
wait	Indicate that the user must wait.

The shape displayed by each value in Table 12-4 is dependent on the browser and operating system. Figure 12-7 shows how each value is rendered in Firefox 3.5 on Windows Vista.

Figure 12-7. The different types of cursor rendered by Firefox 3.5 in Windows Vista

You can also create your own cursor and apply it using url() in the same way as a background image. The cursor property is similar to font-family in that it accepts a comma-separated list of values to be used in order of precedence. So, if the browser or operating system can't handle the first value, it tries each one in turn. You should always end the list with one of the keywords in Table 12-4 as a fallback like this:

```
cursor: url(assets/mycursor.ani), url(assets/mycursor.cur), progress;
```

LinkED

Static cursors use a .cur *file name extension. Animated ones use* .ani. *For more information, visit* www.evotech.net/blog/2007/04/controlling-cursors-with-css-and-creating-cur-files/.

AdvancED

An imaginative, custom-built cursor could be just the thing that gives your website that extra wow factor. It could also confuse a lot of people if its purpose isn't obvious to visitors. Most people are creatures of habit, and expect their cursor to look, well . . . like a cursor. Don't sacrifice your site's usability merely for the sake of looking different.

Adding an outline

"What's an outline?" you may well ask. Well, an outline is like a border, except it's different in the following ways:

- Outlines are not part of the CSS box model, so they do not take up horizontal or vertical space, but are drawn on top of other styles.

- An outline can be added in addition to a border and normally goes outside it (see Figure 12-8 and outline_plus_border.html in the download files).

- Each side of an outline is the same as all the others. Sides cannot be styled independently.

- The outline of an inline element surrounds the whole element, even when the element wraps onto another line. It doesn't break like a border (see Figure 12-9 and outline_inline.html in the download files).

This <div> has a 5px solid green border and a 2px dashed outline.

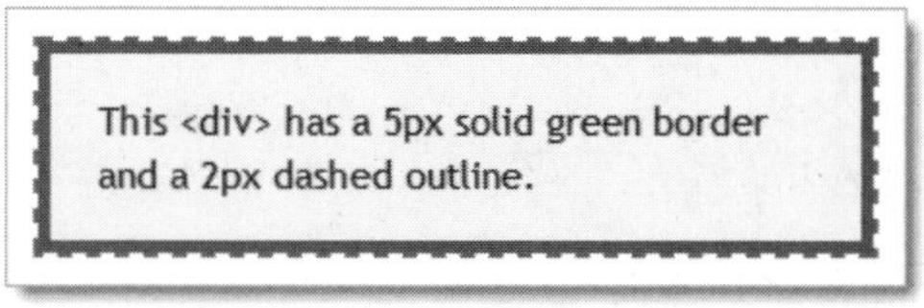

Figure 12-8. An element can have both a border and an outline.

All browsers don't handle the outlines of inline elements the same way. Most browsers draw an irregular line surrounding the element, as shown in the screenshot on the left of Figure 12-9. However, Firefox 3.5 draws separate boxes around each line, as shown in the screenshot on the right. However, all browsers treat borders on inline elements in the same way, breaking the border at the end of each line.

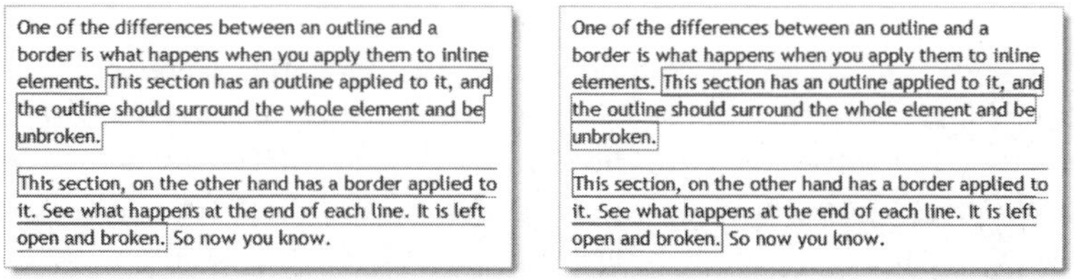

One of the differences between an outline and a border is what happens when you apply them to inline elements. This section has an outline applied to it, and the outline should surround the whole element and be unbroken.

This section, on the other hand has a border applied to it. See what happens at the end of each line. It is left open and broken. So now you know.

One of the differences between an outline and a border is what happens when you apply them to inline elements. This section has an outline applied to it, and the outline should surround the whole element and be unbroken.

This section, on the other hand has a border applied to it. See what happens at the end of each line. It is left open and broken. So now you know.

Figure 12-9. Most browsers draw an outline as an irregular box around inline elements, but Firefox 3.5 (right) draws a separate box on each line.

As you can see from Figure 12-9, neither borders nor outlines are very attractive on inline elements. Although they look the same as the equivalent style of border on a block-level element, they are less versatile. Even the fact that an outline doesn't add to the width or height of an elements can be a disadvantage, because a wide outline overlaps adjacent elements.

So, you might still be wondering why CSS has the outline property. The answer, quite simply, is that outlines are normally used to improve accessibility. If you load outline_form.html into a JavaScript-enabled browser, the focus goes immediately to the *Name* field in the form, and the element is surrounded with a 4px double, red outline, as shown in Figure 12-10.

Figure 12-10. The outline indicates which form field has focus.

Even if JavaScript is disabled in the browser, the red outline appears as soon as you click inside the text field. Press tab to move to the next field (or click inside), and the outline shifts to the new field to indicate it has focus. The key point about using the outline property is that it doesn't affect the box model, so the form isn't redrawn each time you move the focus to a new field. The style rule that adds the outline looks like this:

```
input:focus, textarea:focus, select:focus {
  outline: #F00 double 4px;
}
```

Change the outline property to border like this:

```
input:focus, textarea:focus, select:focus {
  border: #F00 double 4px;
}
```

Save the page, and reload it in a browser. As you tab through each field, you should be able to see the labels and fields shifting slightly as the border is removed from one field and redrawn on the next. Using outline to provide this accessibility feature avoids this unsightly movement.

You use the outline properties in a similar way to the equivalent border ones, which were described in Chapter 5. However, outlines are always the same on all four sides, so the individual properties—outline-color, outline-style, and outline-width—each take only one value.

The outline-color property takes any color value or the keyword invert, which is also its default value. The purpose of invert is to ensure that the outline remains visible regardless of the background color. You can test how different browsers treat invert by loading outline_invert.html into them. The page has a black background with an <h1> heading in a light brown. The heading has a 20px solid outline with outline-color set to invert. Figure 12-11 shows the result in IE8.

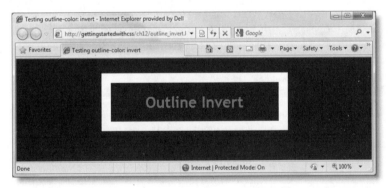

Figure 12-11. IE8 uses a white outline to distinguish it from the black background.

IE8 and Opera 9 both render the outline in white. Safari 4 and Chrome 2 use the same color as the heading. Firefox 3.5, however, fails miserably by rendering black on black.

The outline-style property accepts the same keywords as border-style, with the exception of hidden, namely: dashed, dotted, double, groove, inset, none, outset, ridge, and solid.

The outline-width property is self-explanatory.

The outline shorthand property allows you to specify the color, style, and width in a single declaration. If you omit any value, it takes the initial value listed in Table 12-3.

Removing a default outline without destroying accessibility

Designers often ask how to get rid of the dotted lines that appear around links. They hate them, because they destroy the harmony of their designs. You can get rid of them, but before rushing to find the solution, pause to think why browsers put them there.

ExplainED

The dotted outline that browsers put around links is known as a focus rectangle. It's put there for the benefit of people who can't use a mouse, usually as a result of disability. Typically, such people navigate web pages using their keyboard. Pressing the tab key moves from one link or form field to the next. The dotted outline serves as an important visual clue, telling the user "You are here." Pressing Enter/Return follows the link or submits the form. If you remove the dotted outline without compensating for it by adding a visual clue to the current focus, your website becomes inaccessible to keyboard surfers.

Design isn't simply about what something looks like. It's also about usability, and in many countries, building a website that discriminates against disabled people is against the law. So, don't just zap the dotted outline. Use your design skills and knowledge of CSS to come up with a good alternative.

The focus rectangle is normally generated by the browser's default styles, which use the outline property to add a dotted line around the element that currently has focus. Getting rid of the dotted outline is simply a matter of setting the outline property to none like this:

```
a {
  outline: none;
}
```

However, depending on your design, a better solution might be to change the color of the outline with the outline-color property. You can do this by adding a style rule that uses the **:focus pseudo-class**. Like the :link, :visited, :hover, and :active pseudo-classes that you learned about in Chapter 2, the :focus pseudo-class styles an element in response to it receiving the current focus in the browser. So, to change the color of a link when it has focus, you can create a style rule like this:

```
a:focus {
  outline-color: #008080;
}
```

Choose a color that stands out sufficiently but still blends in with your design.

If you still don't like the focus rectangle, an alternative visual clue is to use the same style as the :hover pseudo-class. All it involves is adding the :focus pseudo-class to the selector like this:

```
a:hover, a:active, a:focus {
  color: #8E2800;
  text-decoration: underline overline;
}
```

A little extra attention to detail ensures your site remains accessible.

Curly quotes, anyone?

I started my writing career hammering out scripts on a typewriter long before the days of word processors and "smart quotes." So, straight quotes on websites don't particularly offend my sensibilities. Other people are driven to distraction by what they regard as a typographical abomination.

If you're willing to do a bit of work—and accept the fact that not all browsers yet support it—the quotes property can automatically generate the right sort of quotation marks for you. Not only that, it's smart enough to nest quotes correctly, so you can follow the American typographic convention of double quotes first, followed by single quotes for nested quotations, or the British convention of single quotes first, followed by double ones. In fact, you can choose any characters you like for your quotation marks.

485

The quotes property works in conjunction with the content property and the :before and :after pseudo-elements that you learned about in Chapter 8. It takes as its value one or more pairs of quotes (or hexadecimal codes that represent quotation marks), each of which must be enclosed in quotes. If that sounds confusing, all should become clear in a moment.

To generate curly quotes or other types of quotation marks, use the hexadecimal codes listed in Table 12-5.

Table 12-5. Hexadecimal Codes for Generating Quotation Marks

Hexadecimal code	Mark	Description
\2018	'	Left single quotation mark
\2019	'	Right single quotation mark
\201C	"	Left double quotation mark
\201D	"	Right double quotation mark
\201E	„	Double low-9 quotation mark
\00AB	«	Left double-angle quotation mark
\00BB	»	Right double-angle quotation mark

You define the sequence of quotes in the quotes property. Each pair specifies the type of opening and closing quotes you want. So, this is how you specify using double quotes with a class called quoted:

```
.quoted {
  quotes: '\201C' '\201D';
}
```

However, it's quite common to nest quotes inside a quoted passage, so it's a good idea to specify the type of nested quotes you want to use. To do so, just add a second pair. The following definition uses double quotes for outer pairs, and single quotes for nested pairs:

```
.quoted {
  quotes: '\201C' '\201D' '\2018' '\2019';
}
```

In the event that quotes are nested deeper, and you haven't defined more than two pairs, the styles alternate.

After defining the type of quotes you want, you use the `content` property with the `:before` and `:after` pseudo-elements to generate the quotes using the following values:

- open-quote: Use the correct opening quote for the current level of nesting.

- close-quote: Use the correct closing quote for the current level of nesting.

- no-open-quote: Suppress the opening quote, but move to the next level of nesting.

- no-close-quote: Suppress the closing quote, but move to the next level of nesting.

Although it sounds complicated, it's quite simple once you have seen it in action. So, sound a fanfare for the final exercise in this book.

Generating quotes automatically

This exercise demonstrates how to use the `quotes` property to generate curly quotes in the correct sequence with nested quotes. The download files for this chapter contain a file with some dummy text to work with.

1. Copy `quotes_start.html` from the `ch12` folder to your work files, and save it as `quotes.html`.

2. Inspect the HTML markup inside the wrapper `<div>`. It consists of four paragraphs. The middle two are wrapped in a `<blockquote>` like this:

```
<blockquote>
  <p>Alice replied eagerly, for she was always ready to talk about
her pet: <q>Dinah's our cat. And she's such a capital one for catching
mice you can't think! And oh, I wish you could see her after the birds!
Why, she'll eat a little bird as soon as look at it!</q></p>
  <p>This speech caused a remarkable sensation among the party. Some
of the birds hurried off at once: one old Magpie began wrapping itself
```

up very carefully, remarking, **<q>**I really must be getting home; the night-air doesn't suit my throat!**</q>** and a Canary called out in a trembling voice to its children, **<q>**Come away, my dears! It's high time you were all in bed!**</q>** On various pretexts they all moved off, and Alice was soon left alone.</p>
</blockquote>

The markup uses the <q> tag, which is greatly underused—and probably unknown to most web developers. It's for an inline quote, and browsers are meant to wrap the contents of the tag in quotes. Internet Explorer always ignored this tag, but it's now supported in IE8, so it might eventually find its way into wider use.

3. Load quotes.html in to Firefox, IE8, and Opera to see how they handle the <q> tag. Figure 12-12 shows the first paragraph inside the <blockquote> as rendered by each browser.

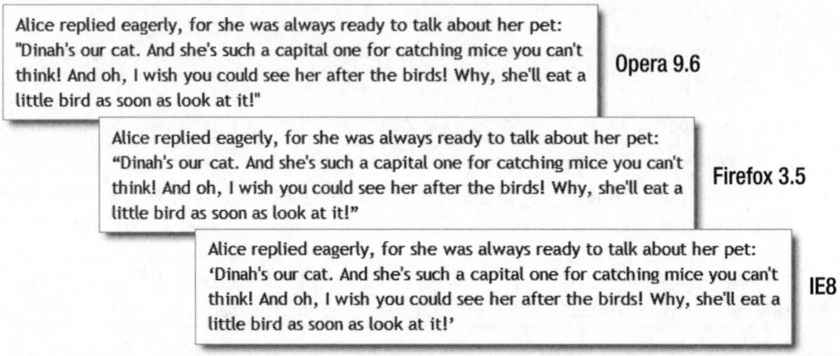

Figure 12-12. The three browsers all render quotes for the <q> tag, but use different styles.

Opera 9.6 surrounds the content of the <q> tags in double quotes, but they're straight. Firefox 3.5 also uses double quotes, but adds a touch of style by making them curly. IE8 is also stylish, but it opts for single quotes.

4. Let's bring a bit of order into this chaos by using the quotes property. Add the following style rules to the <head> of the page:

```
q {
  quotes: '\201C' '\201D';
}
q:before {
  content: open-quote;
}
q:after {
```

```
content: close-quote;
}
```

This uses a type selector to specify double curly quotes for the `<q>` tag. The `:before` and `:after` pseudo-elements set the `content` property to `open-quote` and `close-quote` respectively.

5. Save the page, and test it again in each browser. This time, they all display double curly quotes. That's much smarter. However, you can generate quotes on any element, not just convert the existing quotes on `<q>` tags.

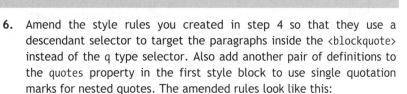

Opera 9.6 seems to get confused with the way it handles quotes if you simply click the reload button. Click inside the address bar, and press Enter if the quotes look wrong. The other browsers are not affected.

6. Amend the style rules you created in step 4 so that they use a descendant selector to target the paragraphs inside the `<blockquote>` instead of the q type selector. Also add another pair of definitions to the `quotes` property in the first style block to use single quotation marks for nested quotes. The amended rules look like this:

```
blockquote p {
  quotes: '\201C' '\201D' '\2018' '\2019';
}
blockquote p:before {
  content: open-quote;
}
blockquote p:after {
  content: close-quote;
}
```

7. Save and test the page again. The paragraphs outside the `<blockquote>` are not affected, but those inside should be opened and closed with double quotes. This time, the nested quotes should be enclosed in single quotes, as shown in Figure 12-13.

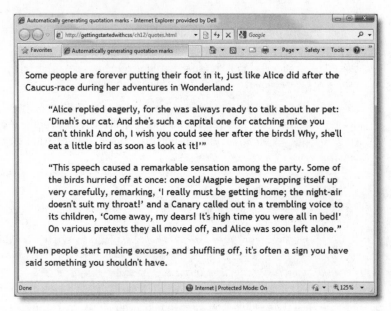

Figure 12-13. The outer and inner quotes are now being generated dynamically.

8. This looks good, but when a quotation continues over more than paragraph, the closing quotes should be omitted from each paragraph until you reach the end of the quotation. Change the :after pseudo-element like this to remove the closing quotes:

```
blockquote p:after {
  content: no-close-quote;
}
```

9. The problem with this is that it suppresses the closing quotes on every paragraph. So you need to create a new class to apply to the final paragraph. Add this new style rule:

```
blockquote p.last:after {
  content: close-quote;
}
```

This tells the browser to apply the closing quote after any paragraph the last class inside a <blockquote>.

10. Add the last class to the class definition in the opening <p> tag of the final paragraph like this:

```
<p class="last">This speech caused. . .
```

11. Save the page, and test it again. The closing double quotes from the first paragraph should have been suppressed, but the opening quotes of the following paragraph and the nested quotes still use the correct sequence of quotes, as shown in Figure 12-14.

Figure 12-14. The correct sequence of opening and closing quotes is preserved when the quotation spans several paragraphs.

Check your code, if necessary, against `quotes_finish.html` in the download files for this chapter.

The formatting of a `<blockquote>` usually gives a visual clue that you are quoting something, so it doesn't matter if some browsers don't yet support the `quotes` property. They simply ignore the style rules for the generated quotes, while browsers that do understand them display your quotations as intended.

In this exercise, I have used the `blockquote p` descendant selector with the `:before` and `:after` pseudo-elements to generate the quotes. However, you can use the `quotes` property with any element. For example, you could create a class called `quoted`, and apply it to any paragraph or to selected text with a `<span>`.

AdvancED

To get the result I wanted in all browsers that currently support the quotes property, I used a class to identify the final paragraph in the <blockquote>. However, the CSS3 proposals include a :last-child pseudo-class that avoids the need to add a class in the HTML markup. Firefox and Opera already support this pseudo-class, but IE8 doesn't. So, for the foreseeable future, an ordinary class is needed.

Chapter review

So, here we are at the end of what I hope has been an enjoyable and instructive journey through CSS2.1. Over the past 12 chapters, I have covered all the visual and paged media (printing) properties in the CSS2.1 specification. Admittedly, some of them are not as useful as the others, but knowing of their existence might just solve a tricky problem that you encounter in future.

What I have tried to do is to give you a solid understanding of the basics of CSS without relying on hacks or concentrating on the oddities of older browsers. If you know how CSS is meant to work, and how it's rendered in modern, standards-compliant browsers, you can style your websites with confidence. The mistake that many people have made in the past is to test their pages only in IE6, on the assumption that they should design for the most prevalent browser. However, pages designed specifically for IE6 not only break in Firefox and Safari, but also in IE8. At the time this book went to press, IE8, Firefox, Safari, Opera, and other standards-compliant browsers already represented more than 50 percent of the market share, and that will continue to grow. CSS has finally come of age.

Of course, it's essential to check how your pages look in older versions of Internet Explorer. If there's a serious problem, you can usually fix it with rules hidden from other browsers in an IE conditional comment. If the difference is relatively minor, you can probably ignore it. Solving problems for older browsers won't necessarily always be easy, but your deeper knowledge of CSS should make it easier to understand the solutions that others have developed.

LinkED

You'll find a lot of helpful articles on Internet Explorer problems and other CSS issues on www.positioniseverything.net *run by "Big John" Gallant.*

Another excellent resource is http://css-discuss.incutio.com/. *It not only has a lot of articles about CSS bugs but is also the home of the css-discuss mailing list administered by two leading experts on the subject, Eric Meyer and John Allsopp.*

The appendix that follows contains a handy reference for all CSS2.1 properties, as well as a full list of selectors, including those in the CSS3 proposal that are already supported in IE7, IE8, Firefox, Safari, and Opera.

Appendix

CSS Properties and Selectors

The following pages list all visual and paged media (printing) properties and selectors in the CSS2.1 specification, together with a brief description and a list of accepted values. Currently, IE8 is the only browser that supports the CSS2.1 specification in its entirety. However, the most recent versions of Firefox, Safari, Opera, and Chrome support the specification with only a few minor exceptions. Of browsers in widespread current use, IE6 and IE7 are the most likely to cause problems. The descriptions indicate the main difficulties you are likely to encounter with specific properties. However, this section is intended only as a quick reference, so it does not claim to be exhaustive.

Recent versions of browsers, including IE7 and IE8, already support some selectors in the proposed CSS3 specification, so I have included those with the most widespread support.

This appendix covers the following topics:

- Specifying values for colors, sizes, and URLs
- All CSS2.1 properties for onscreen display and printing, grouped by type
- All CSS2.1 selectors
- Widely supported CSS3 selectors

Specifying property values

Most CSS properties use predefined keywords, which are listed individually for each property. However colors, sizes, and URLs have their own syntax.

Specifying color values

Colors can be specified using hexadecimal notation, RGB (red, green, blue) values, or one of the 17 keywords listed in Table A-1.

Table A-1. Color keywords in CSS2.1

Keyword	Hexadecimal equivalent	Keyword	Hexadecimal equivalent
aqua	#0FF	olive	#808000
black	#000	orange	#FFA500
blue	#00F	purple	#800080
fuchsia	#F0F	red	#F00
gray	#808080	silver	#C0C0C0
green	#008000	teal	#008080
lime	#0F0	white	#FFF
maroon	#800000	yellow	#FF0
navy	#000080		

When using hexadecimal notation, remember the following:

- The color value must begin with a hash sign (#).
- You can use the full six-digit version or the three-digit shorthand (see Chapter 2 for an explanation of hexadecimal shorthand values).
- Do not mix up the letter *O* with 0 (zero) or lowercase *L* with 1. The only letters permitted in a hexadecimal value are A–F.
- The letters A–F in the hexadecimal value are case-insensitive. It doesn't matter whether you use uppercase or lowercase.

To specify colors using RGB values, enter the red, green, and blue values as a comma-separated list between the parentheses of rgb(). The values can be numbers in the range of 0–255 or percentages from 0% to 100%.

For example, red can be specified in any of the following ways:

- red
- #FF0000
- #f00
- rgb(255, 0, 0)
- rgb(100%, 0%, 0%)

Specifying sizes

The CSS2.1 specification uses the term "length" to describe a value that uses a unit of measurement. The only units permitted are those listed in Table A-2.

Table A-2. CSS units of measurement for length (size)

Type	Unit	Description
Relative units		
	em	The height of the current font (with a 16px font, 1em = 16px; with a 24px font, 1em = 24px)
	ex	Half an em in most browsers
	px	Pixel
Absolute units		
	in	Inch (2.54 centimeters)
	cm	Centimeter (0.394 in)
	mm	Millimeter (0.039 in)
	pt	Point (1/72 of an inch or 0.353 mm)
	pc	Pica (12 points or 4.233 mm)

For onscreen measurements, use em or px. Absolute units should be used only for print style sheets.

Most sizes can also be specified as a percentage. This normally refers to a percentage of the size of the parent element or containing block.

When a zero value is used, the unit of measurement or percentage is optional: 0px and 0 are both equally valid.

When using a unit of measurement or percentage, there must be no space between the number and unit or percentage sign. For example, 1px and 10% are correct; 1 px and 10 % will not work.

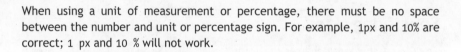

Always use whole numbers with px. All other units of measurement can be used with decimal fractions. For values smaller than 1, the leading 0 of the decimal fraction is optional (0.5 and .5 are both OK).

When using percentages to specify sizes, never use values that add up to exactly 100%. This is because the browser needs to convert the percentage values to pixels, which must be whole numbers. Use 98% to allow for rounding errors.

Specifying URLs

Properties such as `background-image` and `list-style-image` require the URL of the file you want to use. To specify the location of a file, enter its file path between the parentheses of `url()`. You can use either an absolute file path or a relative one. The file path can be optionally enclosed in single or double quotes. Whitespace between the parentheses and the file path is also permitted.

The following examples are all valid:

```
url(../../images/grand_canyon.jpg)
url(   /images/grand_canyon.jpg   )
url('http://www.example.com/images/grand_canyon.jpg')
url(   '../../images/grand_canyon.jpg'   )
url("/images/grand_canyon.jpg")
url(   "../../images/grand_canyon.jpg"   )
```

If using a relative file path, the location should be relative to the style sheet.

CSS2.1 Properties

Each CSS2.1 property is listed according to its function, as follows:

- Background
- Border

- Box model, including properties related to width, height, margins, and padding
- Display and visibility
- Floating
- Generated content
- Lists
- Positioning
- Printing
- Tables
- User interface (cursor and outline)

In addition to a brief description, each property lists the values it accepts. All properties accept the keyword inherit. Refer to the preceding sections for the correct way to specify colors, sizes, and URLs.

ExplainED

The default value for each property is shown. When this is listed as none, *it refers to the keyword* none. *It does not mean the property has no default.*

Background properties

These properties control the background color and images of individual HTML elements. Backgrounds apply only to the content and padding. They do not stretch into the margins of an element. If no background is specified, the background of the parent element shows through. See Chapter 5 for a detailed description.

background-attachment

Accepted values: scroll, fixed

Default: scroll

Inherited: No

Determines whether a background image scrolls in relation to the rest of the document or remains in a fixed position within the browser viewport. Not supported by IE6.

background-color

Accepted values: A color value or the keyword transparent

Default: transparent

Inherited: No

Determines the color of an element's background. If a background image is also specified, the image appears in front of the color.

background-image

Accepted values: A URL or the keyword none

Default: none

Inherited: No

Only one background image can be applied to an element. By default, background images are tiled (repeated) both horizontally and vertically so they fill the entire background area. If the image is larger than the element's content and padding, it is positioned at the top left of the padding, and cut off at the bottom and right edges. By default, background images scroll together with the element.

Use background-attachment to control scrolling, background-position to change the position of the image, and background-repeat to control tiling.

background-position

Accepted values: Percentages, values with units of measurement, or keywords (see description)

Default: 0% 0%

Inherited: No

This enables you to control the position of a background image both horizontally and vertically. In addition to inherit, the keywords left, center, and right control the horizontal position; top, center, and bottom control the vertical position. The property accepts one or two values, and applies them as follows:

- If you use only one value, the other value is automatically set to center or 50%.
- If you use two values, and *both* are keywords, they can be in either order.

- If you use two values, and at least one of them is *not* a keyword, the first value controls the horizontal position, and the second controls the vertical position.

Percentages are calculated not only in relation to the background, but also in relation to the image itself. So, 50% aligns the center of the background image with the center of the element.

background-repeat

Accepted values: repeat, repeat-x, repeat-y, no-repeat

Default: repeat

Inherited: No

The keywords control the tiling of a background image as follows:

- repeat: Tiles the image horizontally and vertically to fill the entire background area.
- repeat-x: Tiles the image across the horizontal axis.
- repeat-y: Tiles the image along the vertical axis.
- no-repeat: Prevents the image from tiling.

The keywords repeat-x and repeat-y fill the horizontal and vertical axes respectively in both directions. For example, if you set background-position to center and background-repeat to repeat-x, the background image fills the entire horizontal axis. However, its starting point is the center of the element, rather than the top left.

background

Default: see individual properties

Inherited: No

Shorthand property. Allows you to specify all background properties in a single declaration. Accepts the same values as the individual properties. Values can be listed in any order with the exception of those controlling the position of a background image. They follow the same rules as background-position.

Border properties

These properties control the color, style, and width of an element's borders. Each side can be styled independently. Because there are so many options, the border properties have a large number of shorthand versions. For a border to display, you must specify at least the border-style property, or its equivalent in one of the shorthand properties. See Chapter 5 for a detailed description.

border-color

Accepted values: One, two, three, or four color values or the keyword transparent

Default: The color of the text in the current element

Inherited: No

Shorthand property that lets you specify the color of all four borders in a single declaration. Accepts a space-separated list of one, two, three, or four values, which are applied as follows:

- **One value**: Applies equally to all four sides.
- **Two values**: The first one applies to the top and bottom, and the second one to the left and right.
- **Three values**: The first one applies to the top, the second one to the left and right, and the third one to the bottom.
- **Four values**: The values are applied in clockwise order starting from the top.

border-style

Accepted values: Up to four of the following keywords: dashed, dotted, double, groove, hidden, inset, none, outset, ridge, solid

Default: none

Inherited: No

Shorthand property that lets you specify the style of all four borders in a single declaration. Accepts a space-separated list of one, two, three, or four values. See border-color for an explanation of how the values are applied. The hidden keyword applies only to table borders.

border-top, border-right, border-bottom, border-left

Default: See individual properties

Inherited: No

Shorthand properties that let you specify the color, style, and width of the selected border in a single declaration. The values can be specified in any order. If color and width are omitted, a medium border using the same color as the current element's text is used. For the border to display, a style must be specified.

border-top-color, border-right-color, border-bottom-color, border-left-color

Accepted values: A color value or the keyword transparent

Default: The color of the text in the current element

Inherited: No

Individual property that specifies the color of the selected border.

border-top-style, border-right-style, border-bottom-style, border-left-style

Accepted values: dashed, dotted, double, groove, hidden, inset, none, outset, ridge, solid

Default: none

Inherited: No

Individual property that specifies the style of the selected border. The hidden keyword applies only to table borders.

border-top-width, border-right-width, border-bottom-width, border-left-width

Accepted values: A percentage or size with a unit of measurement

Default: medium

Inherited: No

Individual property that sets the width of the selected border. Border width is added to the overall width of an element. Negative values are not permitted.

border-width

Accepted values: Percentages or values with a unit of measurement

Default: medium

Inherited: No

Shorthand property that specifies the width of all four borders in a single declaration. Accepts a space-separated list of one, two, three, or four values. See border-color for an explanation of how the values are applied.

border

Default: See individual properties

Inherited: No

Shorthand property that lets you set the color, style, and width of all four borders in a single declaration. All sides must have the same values, which can be in any order. For the borders to display, you must specify at least one of the styles accepted by border-style.

To style borders individually, use the individual border properties or the border-color, border-style, and border-width shorthand properties.

Box model properties

These properties control the height and width of elements, as well as the vertical and horizontal space around them. Although the default value for margin-related properties is 0, browsers often add a value of their own. Vertical margins of adjacent elements collapse or overlap, so that only the largest value is applied. Horizontal margins never collapse, nor does vertical or horizontal padding. See Chapter 6 for a detailed description of the CSS box model. Margins are covered in Chapter 3.

height

Accepted values: A percentage, size using a unit of measurement, or the keyword auto

Default: auto

Inherited: No

Specifies the height of an element's content. Padding and borders are added outside this value, and increase the element's overall height. The height property cannot be applied to inline text, table columns, or column groups. Although 0 is valid, negative values are not permitted.

margin-right, margin-left, margin-top, margin-bottom

Accepted values: A percentage, size using a unit of measurement, or the keyword auto

Default: 0

Inherited: No

Specifies the size of the margin on the selected side. Cannot be used on table cells, rows, or columns. If the element does not have a declared width, auto is treated as 0. A negative value can be used to reduce the margin and move the element closer to its neighbor(s).

margin

Accepted values: Up to four values, consisting of percentages, sizes with a unit of measurement, or the keyword auto

Default: 0

Inherited: No

Shorthand property that lets you specify margins for all four sides in a single declaration. Accepts a space-separated list of one, two, three, or four values, which are applied as follows:

- **One value**: Applies equally to all four sides.
- **Two values**: The first one applies to the top and bottom, and the second one to the left and right.
- **Three values**: The first one applies to the top, the second one to the left and right, and the third one to the bottom.
- **Four values**: The values are applied in clockwise order starting from the top.

Negative values are permitted.

max-height

Accepted values: A percentage, size with a unit of measurement, or the keyword none

Default: none

Inherited: No

Specifies the maximum height of an element. Cannot be applied to inline text, table columns, or column groups. Negative values are not permitted. Not supported by IE6.

max-width

Accepted values: A percentage, size with a unit of measurement, or the keyword none

Default: none

Inherited: No

Specifies the maximum width of an element. Cannot be applied to inline text, table columns, or column groups. Negative values are not permitted. Not supported by IE6.

min-height

Accepted values: A percentage, or size with a unit of measurement

Default: 0

Inherited: No

Specifies the minimum height of an element. Cannot be applied to inline text, table columns, or column groups. Negative values are not permitted. Not supported by IE6.

min-width

Accepted values: A percentage, or size with a unit of measurement

Default: 0

Inherited: No

Specifies the minimum width of an element. Cannot be applied to inline text, table columns, or column groups. Negative values are not permitted. Not supported by IE6.

padding-top, padding-right, padding-bottom, padding-left

Accepted values: A percentage, or size with a unit of measurement

Default: 0

Inherited: No

Specifies the amount of padding to be added to the content's width or height on the selected side. Background color and/or image show through padding. Padding can be added to table cells and captions, but not to other table elements. Negative values are not permitted.

padding

Accepted values: Up to four values, consisting of percentages, or sizes with a unit of measurement

Default: 0

Inherited: No

Shorthand property that allows you to specify padding for all four sides in a single declaration. Refer to margin for details of how the values are applied.

width

Accepted values: A percentage, size using a unit of measurement, or the keyword auto

Default: auto

Inherited: No

Specifies the width of an element. Padding and borders are added to this value, increasing the element's overall width. Cannot be applied to inline text, table columns, or column groups. Although 0 is valid, negative values are not permitted.

Display and visibility properties

These properties change the way elements are displayed. See Chapter 8 for the main description of how they work. The table-related display properties are discussed in Chapter 11 (see also Chapter 9 for detailed coverage of CSS and tables).

display

Accepted values: inline, block, list-item, run-in, inline-block, table, inline-table, table-row-group, table-header-group, table-footer-group, table-row, table-column-group, table-column, table-cell, table-caption, none

Default: inline

Inherited: No

Changes the default display of an element, e.g., turns an inline element into a block-level one and vice versa.

The only values fully supported by all browsers in current widespread use are block, inline, and none. Most browesers support inline-block, but IE6 and IE7 support inline-block only when applied to elements that are normally displayed inline.

IE8 and Opera are the only mainstream browsers that support run-in correctly.

The table-related values are not supported by IE6 and IE7. All other browsers in widespread use support them, but with some minor inconsistencies in Safari 3.

overflow

Accepted values: visible, hidden, scroll, auto

Default: visible

Inherited: No

Controls the display of content that is too big to fit into a fixed-size container in the following ways:

- visible: Content is permitted to spill out of its container, but the container's background and borders are not resized.
- hidden: Excess content is hidden and cannot be accessed by the user.
- scroll: Vertical and horizontal scrollbars are added to the container, even if there is no overspill.
- auto: Scrollbars are added to the container only if the content is too big to fit.

Setting overflow to hidden or auto can also be used to extend the background of an element to clear any floated elements nested inside, as described in Chapter 6.

visibility

Accepted values: visible, hidden, collapse

Default: visible

Inherited: Yes

Controls the visibility of an element, but does not remove it from the flow of the document. Used mainly in conjunction with JavaScript dynamic effects.

If visibility is set to hidden, the browser leaves a space where the element would normally have been. To remove an element entirely from the page layout, use display and set its value to none.

The collapse value is used only with table columns. When the visibility of a table column is set to collapse, the browser should hide it, and reduce the width of the table by the same width. At the time of this writing, IE8 is the only browser that supports this correctly.

Float properties

There are just two properties connected with floating, the process whereby an element is moved to the left or right, and all subsequent content moves up to fill the horizontal space alongside. Typical uses are flowing text around images (see Chapter 4), creating sidebars (see Chapter 7), and creating a horizontal row of elements that would normally sit one on top of the other, such as converting an unordered list into a navigation bar (see Chapter 8). The float property is also used extensively in page layout, as described in Chapter 11.

clear

Accepted values: none, left, right, both

Default: none

Inherited: No

Prevents an element from moving up alongside a previously floated element. The property's value determines whether this applies to all floated elements (both) or to those floated to a particular side.

float

Accepted values: left, right, none

Default: none

Inherited: No

Moves an element to the specified side, and allows following elements to move up to fill the horizontal space vacated alongside it. When applied to inline elements, such as images, the inline element is treated as a block.

Generated content properties

These properties automatically generate content in conjunction with the :before and :after pseudo-elements. They are used mainly to generate sequences of numbers or letters, and quotation marks. See Chapters 8 and 12

509

for a detailed description of how to use these properties. Not supported by IE6 or IE7.

content

Accepted values: The keywords normal or none, or a combination of any of the following: text in quotes, a URL value, a counter value, attr(), open-quote, close-quote, no-open-quote, no-close-quote

Default: normal

Inherited: No

Defines the content the browser should insert in the :before and :after pseudo-elements. The keywords normal and none suppress the generation of the pseudo-element.

The attr() function extracts the value of an HTML attribute as text.

The open-quote, close-quote, no-open-quote, and no-close-quote keywords specify how to display quotation marks defined by the quotes property.

counter-increment, counter-reset

These properties control the numbering of sequences displayed by a counter value defined in the content property. See "Using CSS to generate numbered sequences" in Chapter 8.

quotes

Defines pairs of quotation marks to be used as opening and closing quotes by the content property. See "Curly quotes, anyone?" in Chapter 12. Currently supported only by IE8, Firefox (since v1.8), and Opera (since v6).

List properties

These properties control the appearance of unordered (bulleted) and ordered (numbered) lists, giving control over the position and type of symbol displayed alongside each item. See Chapter 8 for a detailed description.

list-style-image

Accepted values: A URL value or the keyword none

Default: none

Inherited: Yes

Specifies an image to be used as the symbol alongside each list item. It is recommended to specify a fallback symbol with list-style-type in case the image is not available.

list-style-position

Accepted values: inside, outside

Default: outside

Inherited: Yes

Specifies whether the symbol should be displayed in the margin alongside each list item, or whether it should be indented in the first line.

list-style-type

Accepted values: disc, circle, square, decimal, decimal-leading-zero, lower-roman, upper-roman, lower-greek, lower-latin, upper-latin, armenian, georgian, lower-alpha, upper-alpha, none

Default: disc

Inherited: Yes

Specifies the symbol that appears alongside each list item. Use none to suppress the symbol.

The only values that work with unordered lists (<ul>) are disc, circle, and square. The remaining values are for ordered lists (<ol>).

The following values are *not* supported by IE6 or IE7: decimal-leading-zero, georgian, lower-greek, lower-latin, upper-latin.

list-style

Default: See individual properties

Inherited: Yes

Shorthand property that lets you specify the individual properties in a single declaration. The values can appear in any order. If a value is omitted, the default for the individual property is used.

Positioning properties

These properties permit elements to be removed from the normal flow of the document and positioned as though floating on separate layers in front of other content. CSS positioning is an advanced subject, covered in detail in Chapter 10.

bottom, left, right, top

Accepted values: A percentage, size with a unit of measurement, or the keyword auto

Default: auto

Inherited: No

Offsets that determine the position of the element in relation to the sides of its containing block. They apply only to elements that are positioned using absolute, fixed, or relative positioning.

The containing block of a fixed-position element is the browser viewport. For other positioned elements, it is the element's first ancestor that has the position property set to absolute, fixed, or relative. In the absence of such an element, the document becomes the containing block.

The keyword auto sets the offset to the position the element would have had in the normal flow of the document.

clip

Accepted values: rect(), auto

Default: auto

Inherited: No

Defines the area of an absolutely positioned element that remains visible. Performs a similar function to the crop tool in a graphical editor, but in a non-destructive way. The area to be displayed is defined by entering four sizes with a unit of measurement between the parentheses of rect(). The values passed to rect() should be offsets measured from the top-left corner of the absolutely positioned element that you want to clip, and should be in clockwise order starting from the top.

According to the specification, the values passed to rect() should be separated by commas. However, this is not supported by IE6 and IE7. Fortunately, other browsers support leaving out the commas.

position

Accepted values: absolute, fixed, relative, static

Default: static

Inherited: No

Defines how an element should be positioned. The default value, static, displays the element in the normal way. Because the position property is not inherited by default, the only time you need to specify its value as static is if you need to override an existing value. For example, when creating a print style sheet that inherits styles from another style sheet, it's a good idea to set position to static for absolutely-, fixed-, and relatively-positioned elements to make sure they print out correctly.

The other values have the following effects:

- absolute: Removes the element, including any child elements, completely from the flow of the document, and positions it at the offsets defined in the same style rule. If the element is nested inside another positioned element, the offsets are calculated with reference to the positioned parent. Otherwise, the offsets are calculated with reference to the page.

- fixed: Similar to absolute, but the offsets are always calculated with reference to the browser viewport.

- relative: Moves the element relative to its normal position in the document flow, but without affecting the position of other elements.

z-index

Accepted values: An integer (whole number) or the keyword auto

Default: auto

Inherited: No

Sets the stacking order of absolutely-, fixed-, and relatively-positioned elements. When such elements overlap, those with a higher z-index value appear in front of those with a lower one. If no z-index is specified, positioned elements are stacked in the same order as they appear in the underlying HTML, with those appearing first at the bottom of the stack.

Each containing block sets its own stacking context. When positioned elements from different stacking contexts overlap, the z-index of the containing block determines which appears on top. This can lead to a situation where an element with a z-index of 2 will appear in front of one with a z-index of 2000, if the z-index of the first element's containing block is higher than the z-index of the second element's containing block.

Print properties

These properties control page breaks when the media value is set to print. See Chapter 12 for a detailed description. At the time of this writing, IE8 and Opera are the only browsers that support these properties.

orphans

Accepted values: An integer (whole number)

Default: 2

Inherited: Yes

Specifies the minimum number of lines of a block-level element that should be printed at the bottom of a page. If fewer lines would be printed, the browser should force a page break, and move the whole element to the next page.

page-break-after

Accepted values: auto, always, avoid, left, right

Default: auto

Inherited: No

Specifies whether to force or avoid a page break after a particular block-level element. The left and right values refer to the :left and :right pseudo-classes defined by an @page rule, as described in Chapter 12.

page-break-before

Accepted values: auto, always, avoid, left, right

Default: auto

Inherited: No

Specifies whether to force or avoid a page break before a particular block-level element. The left and right values refer to the :left and :right pseudo-classes defined by an @page rule, as described in Chapter 12.

page-break-inside

Accepted values: avoid, auto

Default: auto

Inherited: No

Specifies whether to permit a page break inside a particular block-level element.

widows

Accepted values: An integer (whole number)

Default: 2

Inherited: Yes

Specifies the minimum number of lines of a block-level element that should be printed at the top of a page. If fewer lines would be printed, the browser should move the whole element to the current page.

Table properties

These properties control the appearance of tables. They provide a more sophisticated way to control table borders and spacing than the HTML border and cellspacing attributes. Using the padding property (see "Box model properties" earlier in this appendix) within table cells also offers much greater flexibility than the HTML cellpadding attribute. The table-layout property makes it possible to fix the width of a table, overriding the default behavior of automatically expanding the table to accommodate the widest content. See Chapter 9 for a detailed description.

border-collapse

Accepted values: collapse, separate

Default: separate

Inherited: Yes

Controls the way table and cell borders are handled. By default, the table and each cell have independent borders. Adjacent borders are merged by setting the value of this property to collapse. If the borders are of different widths, the wider one is applied. If both are the same width, the single width is used. For example, if a 2px border is adjacent to a 5px one, the resulting width is 5px; but if both borders are 2px wide, the resulting width is 2px.

border-spacing

Accepted values: One or two sizes with a unit of measurement

Default: 0

Inherited: Yes

Controls the spacing between table cells. A single value is applied to both horizontal and vertical spacing. If two values are supplied, the first one is applied to horizontal spacing, and the second to vertical spacing. Not supported by IE6 or IE7.

caption-side

Accepted values: top, bottom

Default: top

Inherited: Yes

Controls whether the table caption is placed above or below the table. Not supported by IE6 or IE7.

empty-cells

Accepted values: show, hide

Default: show

Inherited: Yes

If set to hide, turns off the display of borders and backgrounds associated with empty table cells. If all cells in a row are empty, the entire row is removed from the display when border-collapse is set to collapse. Not supported by IE6 or IE7.

table-layout

Accepted values: auto, fixed

Default: auto

Inherited: No

Determines whether a table automatically expands to accommodate oversized content. If set to fixed, the width of each column is set in the column definitions or the first row.

text-align

Accepted values: left, right, center, justify

Default: left for languages written left to right

Inherited: Yes

Although this is principally a text property, it also controls the horizontal alignment of content in table cells.

vertical-align

Accepted values: top, middle, bottom, baseline

Default: middle

Inherited: No

Controls the vertical alignment of content in table cells. See Chapter 9 for a definition of baseline as applied to tables.

Text properties

These properties are used to control the appearance of text. See Chapter 2 for a detailed description.

color

Accepted values: A color value

Default: Officially depends on user agent, but is usually black

Inherited: Yes

Sets the color of text. Borders and outlines inherit this color if not defined separately.

direction

Accepted values: ltr, rtl

Default: ltr

Inherited: Yes

Controls the display of text according to whether it should be read left to right (ltr) or right to left (rtl). If direction is set to rtl on the page body, the vertical scrollbar moves to the left side of the browser window. Setting direction to rtl with a language normally read from left to right, such as English, does *not* reverse the order of characters in the text.

font-family

Accepted values: A comma-separated list of font names

Default: Depends on user agent

Inherited: Yes

Sets the font used for text. Browsers use the fonts available on the user's computer, so a selection of fonts should be specified in order of preference. Font names that include spaces should be enclosed in quotes. The final value in the list should be one of the following keywords indicating the type of font to be used if none of the others is available: serif, sans-serif, monospace, cursive, fantasy.

font-size

Accepted values: A percentage, size with a unit of measurement, or one of the following keywords: xx-small, x-small, small, medium, large, x-large, xx-large, larger, smaller

Default: medium

Inherited: Yes

Sets the size of the font. See Table 2-4 in Chapter 2 for definition of the keywords.

font-style

Accepted values: normal, italic, oblique

Default: normal

Inherited: Yes

Changes the font between italic and regular text. If the font has an oblique version, it is used when this property is set to oblique. Otherwise, the text is italicized.

font-variant

Accepted values: normal, small-caps

Default: normal

Inherited: Yes

Setting this property to small-caps displays the text as small capitals. If the font does not support them, the text is rendered in uppercase.

font-weight

Accepted values: normal, bold, bolder, lighter, 100, 200, 300, 400, 500, 600, 700, 800, 900

Default: normal

Inherited: Yes

Displays the text in a bold or regular font. The comparative and numerical keywords are of little practical value. Use normal or bold.

font

Default: See individual properties

Inherited: Yes

Shorthand property that permits you to combine into a single declaration the values for font-style, font-variant, font-weight, font-size, line-height, and font-family. Difficult to use.

The first three values are optional, and can be in any order. The remaining values must be in the order listed, but line-height is optional. If both font-size and line-height are specified, they must be separated by a forward slash.

When using the font shorthand property, values for font-size and font-family are mandatory. A common mistake is to use font as a synonym for font-family. Browsers ignore the entire rule if font-size is omitted.

letter-spacing

Accepted values: A size with a unit of measurement, or the keyword normal

Default: normal

Inherited: Yes

Increases the horizontal spacing between characters—the equivalent of tracking in typography. Decreases horizontal spacing if used with a negative value.

line-height

Accepted values: A positive number, percentage, size with a unit of measurement, or the keyword normal

Default: normal

Inherited: Yes

Increases or decreases the vertical spacing between lines of text—the equivalent of leading in typography. Decimal fractions, and values less than 1 are permitted, but not negative values. The most reliable way of specifying line-height is with a number, such as 1.4, which ensures that the vertical space remains proportional to the current font.

text-align

Accepted values: left, right, center, justify

Default: left for languages written left to right

Inherited: Yes

Controls the horizontal alignment of text.

text-decoration

Accepted values: The keyword none, or any combination of underline, overline, line-through, blink

Default: none

Inherited: No

Underlines, overlines, and strikes through text. Setting the value to blink causes the text to flash on and off continuously. These four effects can be applied in any combination by specifying the values as a space-separated list. Setting the value to none removes all effects.

text-indent

Accepted values: A percentage, or a size with a unit of measurement

Default: 0

Inherited: Yes

Indents the first line in a block of text by the specified amount. Cannot be used to indent the whole block of text (use margin and/or padding for this purpose).

text-transform

Accepted values: capitalize, uppercase, lowercase, none

Default: none

Inherited: Yes

Converts text to uppercase, lowercase, or initial capitals. Setting the value to none renders the text in the original letter case.

unicode-bidi

Accepted values: normal, embed, bidi-override

Default: normal

Inherited: No

Controls how text is displayed when left-to-right and right-to-left languages are displayed in the same document, e.g., English and Arabic or Hebrew. See www.w3.org/TR/CSS21/visuren.html#propdef-unicode-bidi for details.

vertical-align

Accepted values: A percentage, size with a unit of measurement, or one of the following keywords: baseline, sub, super, top, text-top, middle, bottom, text-bottom

Default: baseline

Inherited: No

Controls the vertical alignment of text, images, and other inline content. It *cannot* be used to control block-level elements, except inside a table cell or when the element's display property has been set to one of the table-related values or inline-block. See Chapter 2 for a description of the values.

white-space

Accepted values: normal, pre, nowrap, pre-wrap, pre-line

Default: normal

Inherited: Yes

Controls the treatment of spaces in the underlying HTML code. The keywords have the following effect:

- pre: Preserves spaces and new lines in a similar way to the HTML <pre> tag, but without changing the font.
- nowrap: Prevents text from wrapping

- `pre-wrap`: Preserves spaces and new lines, but wraps the text at the right boundary of the page or containing element

- `pre-line`: Closes up sequences of whitespace as in normal text, but honors new lines.

word-spacing

Accepted values: A size with a unit of measurement, or the keyword `normal`

Default: `normal`

Inherited: Yes

Increases or decreases the width of spaces in text.

User interface properties

These properties affect the display of the cursor and outlines. An outline is similar to a border in that it surrounds an element. However, outlines do not add to the overall width or height of an element, and all four sides must be the same color, style and width. The main purpose of outlines is to improve accessibility through a visual indication of the element that currently has focus. Neither IE6 nor IE7 supports outlines. See Chapter 12 for details.

cursor

Accepted values: A comma-separated list of URL values, or one of the following keywords: `auto`, `crosshair`, `default`, `help`, `pointer`, `move`, `progress`, `text`, `wait`, `e-resize`, `ne-resize`, `nw-resize`, `n-resize`, `se-resize`, `sw-resize`, `s-resize`, `w-resize`

Default: `auto`

Inherited: Yes

Changes the appearance of the cursor. The shape depends on the individual browser. The difference between `auto` and `default` is that `auto` leaves the choice of cursor up to the browser dependent on context, whereas `default` forces the browser to display the default cursor (usually an arrow) regardless of context.

Prior to IE6, Internet Explorer used the non-standard value `hand` instead of `pointer` to display the hand-shaped cursor normally used for links. Although all versions of Internet Explorer still support `hand`, you should now use `pointer`.

outline-color

Accepted values: A color value or the keyword invert

Default: invert

Inherited: No

Sets the color of all four sides of an outline. The invert keyword instructs the browser to choose a color that ensures the outline remains visible against the background. Firefox 3.5 does not support invert.

outline-style

Accepted values: dashed, dotted, double, groove, inset, none, outset, ridge, solid

Default: none

Inherited: No

Sets the style for all four sides of an outline.

outline-width

Accepted values: A percentage, or size with a unit of measurement

Default: medium

Inherited: No

Sets the width for all four sides of an outline.

outline

Default: See individual properties

Inherited: No

Shorthand property that allows you to set the color, style, and width of an outline in a single declaration.

Selectors

Choosing the right selector is the key to working successfully with CSS. Many browsers now support at least part of the much wider range of selectors proposed for CSS3. The following sections list separately all selectors in the

CSS2.1 specification, plus the more advanced selectors from the CSS3 proposal that already have wide support.

CSS2.1 selectors

Most browsers currently in widespread use support the full range of CSS2.1 selectors. The exceptions are IE6 and IE7, which have problems with some pseudo-classes and pseudo-elements. In addition, IE6 does not support child selectors, adjacent sibling selectors, or any of the attribute selectors.

Universal selector

The universal selector is an asterisk (*). It matches any element.

Type selectors

A type selector redefines the default style of an HTML tag. It consists of the name of the tag, without the angle brackets. For example, h1 redefines the default style of <h1> tags.

Because they affect HTML tags, type selectors are sometimes called "tag selectors."

Class selectors

A class lets you apply styles to any HTML element, regardless of which tag it uses. Properties inherited by default are also applied to the element's children. The class name can be anything of your choice, as long as it follows these rules:

- It cannot contain any spaces.
- The only punctuation characters permitted are the hyphen (-) and underscore (_).
- The name cannot begin with a number, or a hyphen immediately followed by a number.

You create a class selector by prefixing the class name with a period (dot). For example, this creates a class called warning:

```
.warning {
  font-weight: bold;
  color: #F00;
}
```

The class is applied by adding the adding the class name with the `class` attribute to the opening tags of the elements you want to style like this:

```
<h1 class="warning">A bold, red heading</h1>
<p class="warning">Please fill in the missing items.</p>
```

You can apply more than one class to the same element by assigning a space-separated list of values to the `class` attribute like this:

```
<h1 class="warning reallyBig">A really big, bold, red heading</h1>
```

This applies the style rules in both the `warning` and `reallyBig` classes to the same element. For example, if the `reallyBig` class assigns a `font-size` of `72px`, the heading in the preceding example will be bold, red, and `72px`. However, the font-size of the paragraph in the earlier example will be unaffected, because it uses only the `warning` class.

AdvancED

Because class selectors can be applied to any element, it's common practice to use the selector on its own. In the preceding examples, the selector has been left as `.warning`, *so it could be applied to both a heading and a paragraph. However, if you want a class selector to apply to only one type of element, you can prefix it with another selector, e.g.,* `p.warning` *applies the styles only to paragraphs that use the* `warning` *class. There should be no space surrounding the period (dot).*

Adding a space between the first selector and the dot of a class selector creates a descendant selector (described later). So, instead of applying to a paragraph that uses the `warning` *class,* `p .warning` *targets elements that use the* `warning` *class and are also nested inside a paragraph, e.g., a* `<span>` *or* `<em>` *tag that uses the* `warning` *class.*

To create a selector that targets a subset of classes, join two or more class selectors together in the style sheet without any spaces like this:

```
warning.reallyBig {
  color: orange;
}
```

This targets only elements that have `class="warning reallyBig"` in their opening tags. The heading in the previous example will now be in a bold `72px` font, but colored orange. However, elements that use only one of the classes will be unaffected.

525

ExplainED

Support for more than one class on an element is unreliable in IE6.

Pseudo-classes

A pseudo-class does not require the class attribute in the element's opening tag. Instead, it applies styles to an element automatically when it meets certain conditions, such as its position in the HTML hierarchy, or the cursor passing over a link. The CSS2.1 specification defines following pseudo-classes:

- :first-child: Styles an element that is the first child of its parent. For example, li:first-child applies a style to the first list item in an ordered or unordered list. It also applies the same style to the first item in each nested list, because it will be the first child of the nested parent. However p:first-child would apply only to the first paragraph in a page or <div> if nothing else precedes it. If it is preceded by a heading, it is no longer the first child of its parent, so the style would not apply. Not supported by IE6.

- :link: Styles unvisited links.

- :visited: Styles visited links.

- :hover: Styles an element when the cursor is hovering over it. IE6 supports this only on links. Other browsers in widespread use support it on all elements.

- :active: Styles an element at the moment it is being clicked. IE6 and IE7 support this only on links.

- :focus: Styles an element if it has the current focus. Not supported by IE6 or IE7.

- :lang(): Styles an element based on its language (if identified in the HTML markup). See www.w3.org/TR/CSS21/selector.html#lang for details.

When used with links, the pseudo-classes should be used in the same order as presented here. Otherwise, they will fail to work.

There are also three pseudo-classes for print styles: :left, :right, and :first. They are currently supported only by IE8 and Opera. See "Setting page margins with the @page rule and pseudo-classes" in Chapter 12 for a detailed description.

Pseudo-elements

Like a pseudo-class, a pseudo-element is not identified as such by HTML markup. It is used to apply styles to content based on its position in the HTML hierarchy. The CSS2.1 specification defines the following pseudo-elements:

- :first-letter: Styles the first letter of an element, e.g., p:first-letter defines a style for the first letter of every paragraph.

- :first-line: Styles the first line of an element, e.g., p:first-line defines a style for the first line of every paragraph. The length of the line is determined by where the browser wraps the text onto the next line.

- :before: Used in conjunction with the content property, this adds generated content before an element. See Chapters 8 and 12 for a detailed description. Not supported by IE6 or IE7.

- :after: Same as :before, but adds generated content after an element. Not supported by IE6 or IE7.

ID selectors

An ID selector applies styles to an element in the same way as a class. The main difference between an ID selector and a class is that an ID can be used only once on each page, whereas a class can be used many times. Properties inherited by default are also applied to the element's children, so this is a powerful way to style whole sections of a page by wrapping the section in a <div>, assigning it a unique identity through the id attribute in the opening tag, and creating an ID selector.

The naming rules are the same as for a class, namely:

- It cannot contain any spaces.

- The only punctuation characters permitted are the hyphen (-) and underscore (_).

- The name cannot begin with a number, or a hyphen immediately followed by a number.

To create an ID selector, prefix the ID name with a hash sign (#). For example, the following style rule applies to an element with the ID container:

```
#container {
  width: 960px;
  margin: 0 auto;
}
```

Some developers prefix the ID selector with the element's type selector, e.g., div#container. However, this is normally unnecessary, because an ID should be unique within the page, so the ID selector should be sufficient to identify where the style is to be applied.

AdvancED

JavaScript dynamic effects, such as flyout menus, make extensive use of IDs, so ID selectors are frequently a convenient way of adding styles to specific page elements without the need to add extra HTML markup.

Descendant selectors

A descendant selector matches any element that is a descendant of another. To create a descendant selector, separate the two selectors by a space, putting the ancestor first. For example, the following rule is applied to all paragraphs inside a <blockquote> element:

```
blockquote p {
  font-style: italic;
}
```

The preceding example uses two type selectors, but you can create a descendant selector from any other types of selectors. For example, the following descendant selector targets unvisited links that are descendants of an element with the ID sidebar:

```
#sidebar a:link {
  color: #008080;
}
```

The descendant can be at any level of the HTML hierarchy, as long as it is in the same branch of the family tree.

Child selectors

A child selector matches an element that is a child of another—in other words, it must be at the next level of the HTML hierarchy, and no deeper. Take the following example:

```
<blockquote>
  <p>To be, or <em>not</em> to be. . .</p>
</blockquote>
```

In this example, the <em> tag is a child of <p>, but not of <blockquote>. The <em> tag is a descendant of the <blockquote> tag, but not one of its children.

To create a child selector, add a greater than sign (>) after the parent selector, and follow it with the selector for the child element. For example, the following child selector targets all paragraphs that are direct children of a <blockquote> element:

```
blockquote > p {
    font-style: italic;
}
```

ExplainED

When elements are nested only one level deep, it is marginally more efficient to use a child selector, because the browser doesn't need to check any further down the hierarchy. The reason I have avoided using child selectors throughout this book is because they're not supported by IE6.

Until IE6 disappears from the scene, it is more practical to use descendant selectors.

The space on either side of the greater than sign is optional, but is normally included for readability. However, the following is equally valid:

```
blockquote>p {
    font-style: italic;
}
```

To target the <em> tag in this example, you can chain child selectors like this:

```
blockquote > p > em {
    font-style: normal;
}
```

Adjacent sibling selectors

An adjacent sibling selector matches an element immediately preceded by a sibling of the specified type. To create an adjacent sibling selector, add a plus sign (+) between the two selectors like this:

```
h1 + p {
    text-indent: 0;
    font-weight: bold;
}
```

529

This targets a paragraph that immediately follows an <h1> heading. Both elements must have the same parent in the HTML hierarchy, and no other elements must come between them. Not supported by IE6.

In CSS3, this selector is called the adjacent sibling combinator. It works exactly the same way.

AdvancED

The specification does not say the spaces surrounding the plus sign are optional, but all browsers that currently support the adjacent sibling selector support it with or without spaces.

Attribute selectors

Attribute selectors target elements based on attributes defined in their opening HTML tags. CSS2.1 specifies four types of attribute selectors, none of which is supported by IE6. The attribute selectors use the following syntax, in which E represents a selector, and foo represents the name of the attribute:

- E[foo]: Matches any E element with the foo attribute set (whatever the value).

- E[foo="warning"]: Matches any E element where the foo attribute value is exactly equal to warning.

- E[foo~="warning"]: Matches any E element where the foo attribute value is a list of space-separated values, one of which is exactly equal to warning.

- E[lang|="en"]: Matches any E element where the lang attribute has a hyphen-separated list of values beginning (from the left) with en.

Several examples should help clarify how these selectors are used. The following style rule uses the universal selector in combination with an attribute selector to add a 2px blue border to every item that has a title attribute:

```
*[title] {
  border: solid 2px blue;
}
```

The following style rule selects all elements that use *only* the warning class:

```
*[class="warning"] {
  font-weight:bold;
  color:#F00;
}
```

The following rule selects all elements that use at least the warning class:

```
*[class~="warning"] {
  font-weight:bold;
  color:#F00;
}
```

ExplainED

There is an important difference between the two preceding examples. If you have a page where some elements have class="warning" *in their opening HTML tags, and others have* class="warning reallyBig", *all of them will be selected by* *[class~="warning"]. *However,* *[class="warning"] *selects only those that have* class="warning"; *it does not select elements with* class="warning reallyBig".

The equal sign on its own means "exact match." The equal sign preceded by a tilde (~=) expands the search to a space-separated list. However, the value must still be an exact match for one of the values in the list. *[class~="warn"] *does not match* class="warning". *For that, you need to use the CSS3 selector* *[class*="warn"] *described later.*

The following rule targets all paragraphs that have the lang attribute set to fr (French) or fr-ca (Canadian French):

```
p[lang|=fr] {
  font-style: italic;
}
```

Note that quotes around the value following the equal sign are optional, except when the value contains spaces.

You can also chain attribute values like this:

```
h1[class~=reallyBig][title="main heading"] {
  background-color:#00F;
}
```

This targets an <h1> heading that uses the reallyBig class, and has the title attribute set to main heading.

Grouping selectors

To avoid repetition when applying the same styles to several elements, you can group selectors as a comma-separated list. For example:

```
h1, h2, h3, h4, h5, h6 {
```

```
    color: #468966;
    font-family: Georgia, "Times New Roman", Times, serif;
    margin: 10px 0;
}
```

This has the same effect as creating six identical style rules for each level of heading.

ExplainED

Do not confuse grouping selectors with descendant selectors. The descendant selector blockquote p *targets paragraphs inside* <blockquote> *elements. Adding a comma after* blockquote (blockquote, p) *changes the meaning completely, to target both* <blockquote> *elements and paragraphs.*

Building complex selectors

Once you understand each type of selector, you can combine them in virtually endless ways to target specific elements. However, you should avoid the temptation to try to be too clever. The more complexity you introduce, the more fragile your design is likely to be. If you create a complex descendant or child selector, the style will cease to be applied if you move a key element out of the document's hierarchy. Keeping selectors simple makes for easier maintenance.

Widely-supported CSS3 selectors

Unlike the CSS2.1 specification, which is a single document covering everything, CSS3 is being created in modules, with each module concentrating on a specific area. The idea is to speed up the process, moving ahead with parts that are ready for adoption without being held back by areas that are more controversial or technically difficult. That's the theory, anyway. The CSS3 process has been glacial, but the Selectors module is one of the most advanced, and it has been embraced enthusiastically by some browsers even before its official approval.

CSS3 supports all the selectors in CSS2.1, and adds a large number of more advanced ones. Since IE7, Internet Explorer has adopted a small subset of the CSS3 selectors, which means that at the time of this writing, they are now supported by about 70 percent of all browsers in current use. So, you might like to experiment with some of the new selectors to offer an enhanced experience to visitors whose browsers recognize them.

LinkED

I have included only those CSS3 selectors supported by a wide range of modern browsers in widespread use, including IE7 and IE8. They are not supported by IE6. For a full list and description of the CSS3 Selectors module, visit www.w3.org/TR/css3-selectors/.

Matching an attribute that begins with a value

The syntax for this selector is E[foo^="bar"]. It matches any E element where the value of the foo attribute begins with bar.

A particularly useful example of this is using the following selector to target links to external sites (assuming you don't use fully qualified URLs for internal links):

```
a[href^="http://"]
```

Matching an attribute that contains a substring

The syntax for this selector is E[foo*="bar"]. It matches any E element where the value of the foo attribute contains the substring bar.

The following selector matches all images that contain "Paris" in the alternate text:

```
img[alt*="Paris"]
```

Matching an attribute that ends with a value

The syntax for this selector is E[foo$="bar"]. It matches any E element where the value of the foo attribute ends with bar.

You could use the following selector to apply a special style to all links to PDF files:

```
a[href$=".pdf"]
```

General sibling combinator

The general sibling combinator matches elements that are preceded by another element at the same level of the HTML hierarchy. You create it by adding a tilde (~) between two selectors.

Understanding how this selector works is relatively straightforward, but it requires a little thought in practice. The following rule changes the color of the text in paragraphs that follow an <h1> heading:

```
h1 ~ p {
   color: red;
}
```

However, this rule affects *all* paragraphs that are siblings of the <h1> heading. So, paragraphs after an <h2> heading will also be affected as long as there is an <h1> heading at the same level of the family tree. To style paragraphs differently after each type of heading, you need separate rules like this:

```
h1 ~ p {
   color: red;
}
h2 ~ p {
   color: blue;
}
h3 ~ p {
   color: green;
}
```

Index